More Than Shelter

More Than Shelter

ACTIVISM AND COMMUNITY IN
SAN FRANCISCO PUBLIC HOUSING

Amy L. Howard

A Quadrant Book

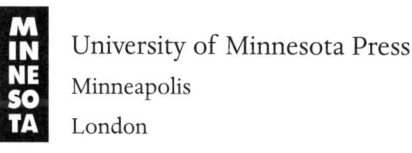

University of Minnesota Press
Minneapolis
London

QUADRANT

Quadrant, a joint initiative of the University of Minnesota Press and the Institute for Advanced Study at the University of Minnesota, provides support for interdisciplinary scholarship within a new, more collaborative model of research and publication.

http://quadrant.umn.edu.

Sponsored by the Quadrant Design, Architecture, and Culture group (advisory board: John Archer, Ritu Bhatt, Marilyn DeLong, and Katherine Solomonson) and by the University of Minnesota's College of Design.

Quadrant is generously funded by the Andrew W. Mellon Foundation.

Copyright 2014 by the Regents of the University of Minnesota

All rights reserved. No part of this publication may be reproduced, stored in a retrieval system, or transmitted, in any form or by any means, electronic, mechanical, photocopying, recording, or otherwise, without the prior written permission of the publisher.

Published by the University of Minnesota Press
111 Third Avenue South, Suite 290
Minneapolis, MN 55401-2520
http://www.upress.umn.edu

Library of Congress Cataloging-in-Publication Data
Howard, Amy Lynne, 1971–
  More than shelter : activism and community in San Francisco public housing / Amy L. Howard.
  Includes bibliographical references and index.
  ISBN 978-0-8166-6581-5 (hc : alk. paper)
  ISBN 978-0-8166-6582-2 (pb : alk. paper)
  1. Public housing—California—San Francisco.   2. Housing Authority of the City and County of San Francisco.   I. Title.
  HD7288.78.U52S264 2014
  363.5'850979461—dc23
                                                                    2013028370

Printed in the United States of America on acid-free paper

The University of Minnesota is an equal-opportunity educator and employer.

21 20 19 18 17 16 15 14   10 9 8 7 6 5 4 3 2 1

*For my loving parents, Donna and David Howard,
and my daily joy, Rob and Meseret*

Contents

ABBREVIATIONS   ix

INTRODUCTION   xi

1. "To Provide Decent, Safe, and Sanitary Housing"
   San Francisco's Housing Authority   1

2. The Contested Mission of Valencia Gardens   45

3. "Peace and Prosperity Dwell among Virtuous Neighbors"
   Chinatown's Public Housing   97

4. "The Best Project in Town"
   North Beach Place   147

   Conclusion
   Looking Back, Moving Forward   195

ACKNOWLEDGMENTS   207

NOTES   211

INDEX   297

Abbreviations

BART	Bay Area Rapid Transit
CCHC	Chinese Community Housing Corporation
CCU	Council for Civic Unity
Chinatown CDC	Chinatown Community Development Center
CREA	California Real Estate Association
EOC	Economic Opportunity Council
FAP	Federal Art Project
FEPC	Fair Employment Practices Commission
FWA	Federal Works Agency
HEW	Department of Health, Education, and Welfare
HOPE VI	Housing Opportunities for People Everywhere VI
HPTU	Hunters Point Tenants Union
HUD	Department of Housing and Urban Development
I-Hotel	International Hotel
LIHTCs	Low-income Housing Tax Credits
MCO	Mission Coalition Organization
MOH	Mayor's Office of Housing
NAACP	National Association for the Advancement of Colored People
NBRMC	North Beach Resident Management Corporation
NBTA	North Beach Place Tenants Association
NTO	National Tenants Association
PHA	Public Housing Administration
PHTA	Public Housing Tenants Association
PYRIA	Ping Yuen Residents Improvement Association
QHWRA	Quality Housing and Work Responsibility Act
RMC	Resident Management Corporation
SFAIA	San Francisco Branch of the American Institute of Architects

Abbreviations

SFHA	San Francisco Housing Authority
SFRA	San Francisco Redevelopment Agency
SRO	single-room occupancy
TB	tuberculosis
Tel-Hi	Telegraph Hill Neighborhood Association
USHA	United States Housing Authority

Introduction

ON A SUNNY DAY IN MAY 2009, I SAT INSIDE A COZY LIVING ROOM in the Valencia Gardens public housing development in San Francisco's Mission District and reconnected with a tenant I had first met years earlier. Much had changed in Anita Ortiz's life and in the built environment of Valencia Gardens since our first meeting: after serving in a prominent leadership role in the tenants' association for many years before Valencia Gardens was redeveloped with federal HOPE VI (Housing Opportunities for People Everywhere) funds, Anita had fought to return to the new development after it reopened in 2006. Many of her previous neighbors did not return, and the "old VG community," along with the sixty-one-year-old buildings, had been dismantled and replaced by modern apartments and new neighbors. Anita struggled to find her place in the new Valencia Gardens while holding fast to the ideal that community means "working together with everyone to restore the neighborhood" with "all neighbors coming together."[1] Not long after she moved back in, Anita's husband passed away. Her grief was evident, and I felt sheepish sitting down to hear her views on the redeveloped Valencia Gardens. My privilege as a white, middle-class academic was mediated only by my awareness of it and my sense that our conversation might in some ways be mutually beneficial. Anita wanted to be heard and over the years had demonstrated excitement that her experiences were of interest to people outside her community. Tenants' stories, including Anita's, were a critical component in helping me understand community formation and the ways residents experienced locally implemented federal policy in San Francisco public housing.

Like millions of other people and many of the tenants I met, Anita Ortiz was happy to call San Francisco home. With its blend of natural beauty from the ocean and the bay, its rolling hills and impressive architecture, its unique neighborhoods and diverse population, San Francisco is a city beloved by residents and tourists alike. Its political

Introduction

and social reputation as "liberal" enhances or detracts from the city's reputation depending on whom you talk to. Taken together, the richness of the cityscape, its appeal to tourists, and the city's status as a "progressive" locale provides a compelling foundation for an examination of the history of public housing. In the midst of the nation's current economic turmoil and the dismantling of the traditional public housing program, investigating the history and persistence of the federally supported program that aims to provide affordable housing for low-income Americans takes on new urgency. Understanding the federal government's public housing policies, the variation of local implementation in cities and even in particular neighborhoods, and the specific experiences and actions of tenants deepen in turn—and in critical ways—our understanding of the intersections among housing, race, ethnicity, activism, and community formation.

More Than Shelter focuses on the concept of community as both an ideological construct—as deployed by the San Francisco Housing Authority (SFHA) through its practices and policies—and a complex, contingent process whereby tenants formed relationships as part of a shared identity. Under this dual approach, public housing in San Francisco becomes a site for reexamining segregation, integration, inclusion, exclusion, and racially and ethnically diverse living environments in the West during the second half of the twentieth century. Focusing on three developments—Valencia Gardens, Ping Yuen, and North Beach Place—I investigate the ways tenants created communities that mattered to them out of rented, federally subsidized public housing units, and I analyze the various modes of activism they used to sustain and strengthen those communities.

The history of the Valencia Gardens, Ping Yuen, and North Beach Place communities demonstrates a range of activist strategies used by tenants to create change. Low-income Americans are often written off in terms of their civic participation: in the United States, voting is privileged as the ultimate exercise in civic duty, and voting rates among this population tend to be lower than average. A more capacious definition of civic responsibility and action challenges this view. Numerous tenants at these public housing projects responded to federal policies and local implementation and practices with different forms of activism. Through what I call "affective activism" at Valencia Gardens

Introduction

(that is, activism focused on intentional relationships and community building to fortify residents in the face of shared challenges), coalition building across sectors at Ping Yuen, and cross-racial and cross-ethnic mobilization efforts at North Beach Place, public housing tenants in San Francisco engaged in wide-ranging activist practices to improve their public housing developments. Understanding the conditions that fostered tenant activism, as well as the nuances of the tenants' activist strategies, in turn furthers our understanding of civic engagement and the politicization and empowerment of low-income tenants that occurred through living in public housing.[2] Through their efforts, tenants' civic engagement shaped both the public housing program and tenants themselves.

Ultimately, the persistence of public housing in San Francisco—particularly in the increasingly sought-after tourist and gentrifying neighborhoods of the Mission District, Chinatown, and North Beach—and redevelopment efforts in the twenty-first century raise important questions, cautions, and possibilities regarding the supply, design, location, and investment in affordable housing in the United States. As public housing is refashioned into mixed-income neighborhoods through public–private partnerships, the push to deconcentrate poverty must include more than simply a nod to the relationships, social ties, and activist connections that low-income tenants have forged in public housing. Finding ways not only to honor but also to incorporate and strengthen these vital networks in redeveloped public housing is essential to building vibrant communities. Understanding the challenges faced by tenants in this study and their strategies for change over time provides some insights that might allow for the creation of the "decent home and suitable living environment" in future public housing that was promised in the Housing Act of 1949.

In the last twenty years, scholars have produced a wealth of important studies on public housing in the United States.[3] These texts have explored federal policies, local implementation, large-scale failures, and occasional successes and have provided rich local studies of public housing in Chicago; Baltimore; Boston; Philadelphia; St. Louis; New York; Atlanta; Detroit; Washington, DC; Los Angeles; and elsewhere. From expert policy analysis, to rigorous histories of the New York City, Chicago, and Boston Housing Authorities, to microstudies

Introduction

that include the importance of architectural design and the architects themselves, public housing has received much-deserved attention. Over the past decade, scholars Rhonda Y. Williams, Roberta M. Feldman, Susan Stall, Sudhir Venkatesh, Lawrence Vale, John Baranski, and others have increasingly focused on tenants' roles in shaping public housing, advocating for improved policies and practices, and demanding a better living environment for themselves and others.[4]

More Than Shelter builds on this work by expanding the analysis of public housing to the West, an underrepresented region in the literature. It also seeks to further our understanding of the role of community, activism, and leadership in public housing developments in the context of particular neighborhoods. Unlike the midwestern and eastern high-rise projects populated primarily by African Americans that many scholars and the media have focused on, public housing in San Francisco has been architecturally and demographically diverse. Valencia Gardens, Ping Yuen, and North Beach Place are unique among the public housing projects studied so far because of their location in mixed-use urban areas that over time came to attract locals and tourists. The influence of race and racial politics on public housing in Boston, Chicago, Philadelphia, Baltimore, Detroit, and New York City is generally well understood; the narrative of black occupancy and white opposition is also well established. But the ways in which the racial and ethnic diversity of the West shaped public housing in the second half of the twentieth century has not yet been explored in depth. In contrast to the large-scale residential segregation cemented in many cities across the United States in the twentieth century, San Francisco's Valencia Gardens and North Beach Place offer rare sites of interracial, cross-cultural residential living. Ping Yuen in Chinatown, intentionally segregated first as a Chinese American project and later as an Asian American development, also puts pressure on the prevailing black–white binary in public housing history.[5] Valencia Gardens, Ping Yuen, and North Beach Place push the boundaries of our scholarly and popular understanding of the public housing program and how it worked in a particular place over time.

More Than Shelter probes the intersection between the institutional history and implementation of public housing and the lived experience of tenants. By combining the oftentimes disparate approaches of institutional and social history with an attention to public policy,

Introduction

urban design, and spatial politics, I use an interdisciplinary approach to examine the complex intersections among plans, policies, practices, and lived experience in San Francisco public housing over seven decades. Oral histories, newspaper articles, San Francisco Housing Authority Commission meeting minutes, San Francisco Housing Authority annual reports, maps, architectural plans, photographs, letters, participant observation, interviews, and other archival materials inform this interdisciplinary microstudy of three public housing communities.

The imperfections of oral history methodology for fully understanding the past are evident here. Memories fade and change. Life histories are narrated to emphasize a particular point of view. Identity and power dynamics can shape the interview process, as I experienced through my research.[6] Nonetheless, this method gave me insights I would not have gleaned from archival materials alone. The conversations and interactions I had with public housing tenants, such as Anita Ortiz, helped form my arguments; they have also deepened and broadened the book's investigation of community formation, civic engagement and activism, and leadership. Ultimately, the oral histories surfaced the buried stories and daily interactions that demonstrated the complex webs of trust and the importance of relationships within these public housing communities.

As San Francisco embraces the aim of redeveloping all its public housing, based in part on the federal HOPE VI model, understanding the history of public housing in some of the city's most beloved neighborhoods is particularly relevant. Public housing is intermingled with the broad currents of social and economic change within neighborhoods, the city, and the region; to understand the complexities of these currents in public housing in San Francisco, this study explores tenants' relationships with each other, with the built environment of the project, with the neighborhood, and with the state. *More Than Shelter* further analyzes the leadership successes and failures of SFHA administrators and tenants within the context of the challenges cities faced in the twentieth century. Such history offers important lessons for shaping successful public housing and affordable housing programs in the twenty-first century.

Chapter 1 traces the tumultuous institutional history of the San Francisco Housing Authority from its inception in 1938 to its attempts to improve its reputation and credibility in the 1990s, with particular

Introduction

attention both to the SFHA's push to impose a specific vision of community onto public housing and to its repeated leadership failures. Steeped in the language and ideology of white, middle-class moral superiority and enacted through racial and ethnic segregation and other regulations restricting tenant organizing, the agency's notion of community clashed with San Francisco's image as an inclusive, welcoming city. The SFHA became increasingly corrupt during the late 1960s and 1970s and by the mid-1980s was one of the country's most troubled housing authorities. Tenants across the city suffered as a result. In recent years, the SFHA has tried to regain the respect of the city and the federal government by redeveloping troubled projects through the HOPE VI program, with indeterminate results, as I discuss in chapters 2 and 4. The legacy of the SFHA's failed leadership, management, and racist practices continues to reverberate even as the city works on a major overhaul of the public housing program.

Chapters 2, 3, and 4 present case studies to examine the ways in which tenants reacted to federal housing policies, to local implementation of these policies, and to the SFHA's definition of, and actions in, their communities. These chapters highlight the perspectives of tenants and tease out how they defined and created communities. They describe the modes of activism tenants employed to protect themselves and their neighbors, and they show which strategies succeeded and which failed over time. The tenants' varied experiences living in public housing challenge the stereotypes of who lives in public housing, what it is like living there, and why residents stay. The residents who shared their stories continually voiced their frustration with being stigmatized for living in the "projects." My aim is to unsettle these generalizations about "what kind of people" live in public housing while also acknowledging the hardships faced, and at times perpetuated, by public housing tenants themselves. These narratives create a framework for analyzing different definitions of community and the functions of activist strategies in federally subsidized housing. They also illuminate the varied and changing views of home and community that exist among tenants—as well as between tenants and neighbors living near public housing. These differing and at times contested definitions have had a critical impact on the image and reality of public housing.

Introduction

Chapter 2 examines the Valencia Gardens project in the Mission District. Built by the SFHA in 1943 despite an outcry from district residents, the project has remained a contested space for six decades. Over the years, tenants have endured crime sprees and the scorn of district neighbors and the city as their project morphed from what the SFHA viewed as a "model" community into what outsiders saw as an anti-public space—a dangerous and stigmatized place they wanted to avoid. Residents living in the project, however, formed relationships and came together to construct a community much different than what the SFHA envisioned. Born out of a need for relationships and assistance and, ironically, nurtured by the stigma separating tenants from the neighborhood, this community has aided and encouraged many tenants over the years. By creating bonds through the tenants' association and informal networks, many residents in this racially diverse project have seized psychological ownership of their public housing apartments and used "affective activism" to improve Valencia Gardens.[7]

Chapter 3 explores the history of the Ping Yuen project in Chinatown. Ping Yuen primarily housed Chinese immigrants and Chinese Americans, mirroring the surrounding neighborhood. This project complicates the historiography on race and public housing, which has focused mainly on the segregation of black tenants. Ping Yuen remained segregated for most of the twentieth century, and neither tenants nor the SFHA pushed for integration there. Welcomed by the district and praised locally, nationally, and internationally, the post–World War II Ping Yuen housing project demonstrates the importance of community ties between project residents and the surrounding community as well as the impact of cross-sector coalition building. By forming an active tenants' association, Ping Yuen residents, many of whom were immigrants from China, challenged the SFHA through petitions and rent strikes to create a safer project. Forming strong ties within the project and a robust coalition between the tenants' association and district social service organizations, Ping Yuen residents have worked to improve their homes and the greater Chinatown community. The cooperation between social service agencies and these tenants provides a successful example of the possibilities for sustaining livable public housing environments through cross-sector alliances. These strong ties, yielding decades of social service support, along

Introduction

with the consistent, strong leadership and activism of the tenants' association, contributed to the health of the Ping Yuen community over time. Unfortunately, popular discourse about the project has tended to attribute this success to the ethnicity of the residents—a tendency that both perpetuates the "model minority" stereotype and overlooks the importance of all of the factors that worked together to provide a strong foundation for Ping Yuen public housing over the years. Although it is perhaps easy to view Ping Yuen's success simply through the model minority lens, it is this complex set of factors, I argue, that provided a strong foundation for Ping Yuen public housing over the years.

North Beach Place, the case study in chapter 4, raises questions about the politics of development and redevelopment and examines the difficulties of community formation in a multiracial and multiethnic housing project. The history of North Beach Place demonstrates the importance of understanding the impact of regional racial and ethnic patterns and attitudes on public housing. As a result of a 1952 lawsuit brought against the SFHA by African American applicants, North Beach Place became the first racially integrated public housing complex in the city. These activists' efforts contributed to the civil rights movement in meaningful ways. Decades later, tenants crossed racial and ethnic lines to fight against the forces of redevelopment and the specter of being forced out of a thriving neighborhood. Located on prime real estate in one of San Francisco's most popular tourist districts, North Beach Place unsettles the image of public housing through its look and location, and it challenges assumptions about the way gentrification operates. Through a multiracial and multiethnic alliance, tenants successfully maintained the number of public housing units at North Beach Place in the shadow of gentrification and economic development efforts in the area.

Taken together, the histories of Valencia Gardens, Ping Yuen, and North Beach Place demonstrate that for many tenants, public housing has served as more than shelter. Through the formation of communities within public housing and the use of a range of activist strategies, residents have found ways to cope with the shared and individual problems in their respective projects. They have also collectively organized for change. The communities studied here resist—and

Introduction

in some ways disrupt—the declension model of public housing that shows public housing in steady decline since the 1950s. *More Than Shelter* demonstrates how groups of low-income residents refashioned federal housing, rebuked stigmas, and fought for a modicum of control to create homes for themselves and their families. Although problems with other tenants, with district neighbors, and with the state did plague residents over the years, many came together and deployed a variety of activist strategies to improve public housing for themselves and their neighbors. Living in convenient locations in San Francisco even as increasing numbers of low-income families left the city in search of cheaper rents, tenants living at Valencia Gardens, Ping Yuen, and North Beach Place prior to HOPE VI redevelopment endured in important but understudied ways.

A brief conclusion examines San Francisco's bold vision for public housing redevelopment in the twenty-first century. Eschewing decades of leadership and management failures within the SFHA, and recognizing the limits of federal assistance available to transform distressed public housing, the city has embarked on an ambitious plan to create vibrant, healthy communities where long-neglected public housing developments now stand. Echoes of tenants' activism reverberate in the vision, mission, and aims of the HOPE SF program, as the city works to revitalize public housing amid an affordable housing shortage and to resuscitate its public housing legacy. Examining this new program through the lens of the past demonstrates the possibilities for public housing in the twenty-first century.

ONE

"To Provide Decent, Safe, and Sanitary Housing"
San Francisco's Housing Authority

"The City That Knows How"

Visitors to the 1939–1940 Golden Gate International Exposition in San Francisco could marvel at the breadth of architectural design, the displays highlighting a range of cultures from Japan to Colombia tied to the theme "The Pageant of the Pacific," and spectacular programming such as Billy Rose's Aquacade. Celebrating the opening of the newly constructed Golden Gate Bridge and San Francisco–Oakland Bridge, the Expo stimulated the Depression-era economy by providing work for artists, architects, construction workers, and others.[1] Inside the San Francisco building, visitors could further glimpse the city's modernization efforts and the federal government's support for subsidized housing in the San Francisco Housing Authority (SFHA) exhibit on public housing.

The SFHA's display demonstrated the new agency's and the federal government's early ideal of molding citizens and strengthening democracy through public housing.[2] Opened in 1938, the San Francisco Housing Authority had not yet completed any developments but instead displayed models of public housing slated for construction alongside photographs showing devastating slum conditions across the city. An SFHA representative was on site to answer questions. Several times throughout the day, the agency screened the film *Housing in Our Time* by the United States Housing Authority (USHA).[3] The film captured the "story of what our dynamic democracy is doing to house its citizens," and the SFHA distributed it to clubs and churches for screenings after the Exposition ended.

The film reflects the SFHA's larger strategy of marketing public housing as a public good during its first two decades. As the camera pans

"To Provide Decent, Safe, and Sanitary Housing"

across run-down row houses followed by images of the U.S. Capitol and Supreme Court buildings, an authoritative male voice exclaims: "The story of homes and how people live is the story of the foundation on which a nation is built. The United States is the most prosperous nation in modern times. It promises to every citizen equal rights to enjoy life, liberty, and the pursuit of happiness." The film goes on to follow a white Jacksonville, Florida, family of four living in "slum" conditions. By the end of the film, the family has moved into a clean, modern walk-up public housing apartment with amenities that include a refrigerator, electric stove, and a bathroom with a toilet and sink. The closing line of the film reminds viewers of the critical link between constructing public housing and upholding the tenets of democracy: "Every dedication in the United States of low-rent public housing is a rededication to our democracy and to the principle that all men are created equal."[4] Quality housing for all will, the film suggests, strengthen the nation.

Promoting the new public housing program was an important step for the USHA and local housing authorities. Spurred by the nation's economic depression, the federal government intervened in the housing industry with the goals of "improving housing conditions [and] promoting economic growth in the economy as a whole," establishing what historian Gail Radford has described as a two-tier policy framework for housing. The first tier, which has become increasingly invisible as a form of government intervention, included insurance guarantees and subsidized interest rates for middle-class home buyers. The second tier, established by the Housing Act of 1937, created the public housing program, tying new construction of publicly funded, subsidized apartments for lower-income families to slum clearance and means testing for tenants.[5]

In 1938, the California legislature passed the Housing Authorities Law, enabling cities throughout the state to form local agencies to build and manage public housing.[6] San Francisco acted quickly. The eleven elected members of the Board of Supervisors, who shared power with the mayor, passed a resolution on March 28, 1938, declaring the need for a Housing Authority and asking the mayor to appoint five housing commissioners who would govern the SFHA, serving four-year terms without compensation.[7] The commissioners would name an executive director to oversee the agency and meet with them. Mayor Angelo Rossi filled the new posts with prominent leaders representing business, labor, and civic interests that formed a dominant coalition in the city:[8] Chairman Marshall Dill, an importer and former president of the San Francisco Chamber of Commerce who went on to serve as the president of the Golden Gate International Exposition in 1940; Vice Chairman Alexander Watchman, president of the San Francisco Building Trades Council and the American Federation of Labor; Alice Griffith, cofounder of the Telegraph Neighborhood House and participant in the San Francisco Housing Association; Edgar Nichol (E. N.) Ayer, an apartment house operator and director of the San Francisco Apartment House Association; and Carlton Wall, vice president and manager of the Grant Company.[9] A. D. Wilder was hired as the first executive director to manage the day-to-day operations and the budget. Once appointed, the commissioners, along with the executive director, had full control over the city's public housing program. This structure of governance and oversight, predicated on mayoral appointments, opened the door for the perception and practice of political patronage over time that undermined the oversight of San Francisco's public housing program.[10]

During the first two decades of operation, the SFHA, through its practices, policies, and publications, established the public housing program as a vehicle for promoting "good citizenship" and strengthening neighborhoods across the city. In its early years, the SFHA received national recognition for public housing design and management.[11] The agency's choices—from architectural design to tenant selection—focused on more than simply fulfilling its mission "to provide simple, safe, and sanitary housing for families of low income."[12] Rooted in environmental determinism, a circumscribed view of citizenship as compliant, rule-following, orderly, and aspiring to upward mobility, and the notion that racial and ethnic uniformity aided healthy community development, the SFHA directed resources in the early years to building and sustaining racially homogenous public housing projects shaped by white, middle-class ideals of family and community life.

Over time, a combination of internal factors, including SFHA executive directors' and commissioners' leadership, organizational structure, and policy decisions, and external factors, such as federal policies and funding levels, eroded the public housing program and quality of life for the increasingly low-income tenants moving into San Francisco public housing. Political appointees and patronage, coupled with entrenched leadership by Executive Director John Beard from 1943 to 1965, eroded trust between tenants and the SFHA and increasingly drew criticism from civil rights and housing advocates. The Supreme Court's 1954 ruling in *Banks vs. The Housing Authority of San Francisco* (see chapter 4), banning segregation in SFHA public housing, challenged the long-held policy of racial and ethnic segregation vehemently upheld by the agency. Likewise, as the federal government mandated that public housing become the purview of poorer tenants and subsequently decreased funding for the program, the SFHA abandoned its vision of molding upstanding citizens through subsidized housing.

By the 1960s, tenants once excluded because of their low income or family status (i.e., single parents) began moving into public housing as federal policies shifted. With the influx of poorer families, the SFHA moved away from the goal of helping residents become "better citizens" on their way toward homeownership and middle-class "respectability." Federal cutbacks and decreased rental receipts resulted in fewer funds for social services and maintenance. These changes, combined with the politicized organizational structure, uneven leadership, and employee scandals, eroded the SFHA's reputation with residents and the city and set a three-decade course of decline for the agency and its public housing projects.

The SFHA, once nationally praised, began to decline organizationally by the 1970s. Tenants battled crime, poor upkeep, and waves of corruption in the SFHA. The Housing Authority that had vowed to create "more than shelter" failed to manage its properties effectively.[13] A decade later, San Franciscans living in a city with some of the highest rental rates in the country had to contend with a Housing Authority rife with internal problems and at times immobilized by decreased federal funding. The agency's increasing troubles, active ignoring of race-fueled problems within public housing, and clashes with the Department of Housing and Urban Development (HUD) humiliated city leaders, angered housing activists and residents, and contributed to the deterioration of the built environment for public housing tenants.

"To Provide Decent, Safe, and Sanitary Housing"

During the 1990s, the SFHA attempted to recapture its early focus on community building and to earn citizen and city support by applying for and winning federal HOPE VI (Housing Opportunities for People Everywhere) grants to redevelop five distressed public housing projects. Touted as "public housing for tomorrow," the HOPE VI program called for combining public and private funds to create garden-style apartments integrated with neighborhoods and populated by mixed-income tenants. By excluding tenants with police records or multiple missed rent payments, and by placing low-income residents in a mixed-income environment, the program sought to reestablish federal public housing as a laboratory for modeling middle-class "standards" and "good citizenship" to low-income residents.[14] The long-term results of the program have yet to be fully realized, but the city demonstrated its confidence in the model by replicating the tenets of the federal HOPE VI program in a local initiative, HOPE SF, beginning in 2006.

As the largest landlord in a city with a perpetual housing shortage since World War II, the SFHA has played a critical role in building and managing affordable housing for low-income tenants. The agency's early paternalistic aim of shaping citizens shifted over time in response to internal and external factors that rendered the execution of high-quality design, continual maintenance, and stable management unsustainable. The SFHA faced major hurdles in addressing its legacy of patronage, politics, poor leadership, criminal activity within the agency, and racism. These elements, combined with decreased federal funding and support, created numerous challenges for the tenants who lived in San Francisco public housing.

Creating "A Way of Life": The SFHA's Early Decades, 1937–1965

During its first three decades, the San Francisco Housing Authority set out to plan, promote, and build public housing projects that would improve the neighborhood and lives of the tenants living there while replacing substandard buildings across the city. At the same time, the combination of policy choices, leadership decisions, and the organizational structure of the Housing Commission created a shaky foundation for sustainable, decent, inclusive public housing communities. Like many other housing authorities across the country, and in line with federal guidelines, the agency enacted strict requirements and screening processes for tenants to reside in the new public housing projects.[15] The agency also adopted and upheld race-based policies that would affect the public housing program for decades. Granted control over tenant selection by the federal government, the SFHA staff, like other agencies across the nation, preferred "complete," "stable" families—two parents with children and an employed father—holding fast to the belief that "the experience of living in public housing would make their children better future citizens."[16] Applicants were subject to interviews with social workers, employment verifications, credit checks, police record checks, and home visits to inspect the "inadequacy" of their living conditions and to assess the family's ability to adapt to a new environment.[17] The SFHA also required that one member of the family, "preferably the head," be a U.S. citizen.[18] Once admitted, public housing residents had to follow strict regulations dictating paint color, laundry schedules, visitor policies, yard maintenance, and income levels.[19] In 1942, the SFHA adopted a "neighborhood pattern policy" based off of federal guidelines that effectively segregated future public housing projects by race and ethnicity. Taken together, the application process and resident restrictions, along with the SFHA's management practices and policies, created restricted and exclusionary public housing in San Francisco.

The SFHA's aims of molding citizens in public housing and contributing to the wider community through subsidized housing were evident in the agency's first public housing project, Holly Courts, located in the Bernal Heights neighborhood. Widely hailed in the architectural press as the first public housing project "West of the Rockies" and praised for its "refreshing Modern design," Holly Courts opened in June 1940.[20] Notable architect Arthur Brown Jr., whose designs for the Golden Gate International Exposition and Coit Tower in San Francisco and federal offices in Washington, DC, were widely known, designed the SFHA's first public housing units.[21] The modern project consists of ten two-story blocks with separate entrances, flat roofs, and small garden plots behind or in front of each two-story row house dwelling.[22] Interior courtyards, gardens, and playgrounds provided

"To Provide Decent, Safe, and Sanitary Housing"

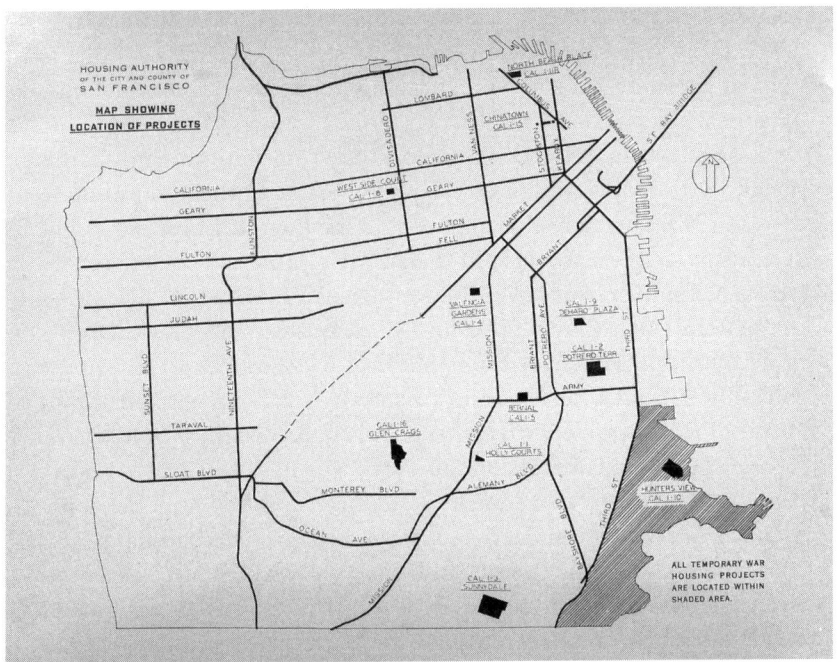

Figure 1. Map showing locations of public housing, 1943, Housing Authority of the City and County of San Francisco, *Fifth Annual Report*.

communal outdoor space for residents. The new project replaced "118 insanitary dwellings units."[23]

The design and amenities, as well as the new residents themselves, were hailed by the SFHA as valuable assets to the surrounding neighborhood. Housing Commissioner Marshall Dill described Holly Courts as "integrated into the neighborhood," with residents who "will trade in local stores, attend local churches, [and] send children to local schools."[24] Holly Courts, he claimed, would seamlessly fit into the neighborhood, with a social hall "for the use of the community" and "sand boxes, slides, swings [and] play spaces" for "all the children in the neighborhood to use." The new families moving in, Dill assured neighboring property owners, had been carefully selected by the SFHA to ensure "they believed in the wholesome values of family life" and would make "a contribution to the community."[25] Endorsing public housing as a transitional space for morally upright, industrious families en route to the middle class, the SFHA set out to create a community based on white, middle-class, culturally constructed norms of family life and behaviors.

The Housing Authority demonstrated its commitment to this specific notion of community by aiding tenants in their transition to living in federally subsidized housing. Drawing on European public housing strategies, the Housing Authority hired a "Consultant for Homemaking." In this role, Else Reisner had intimate knowledge of the new residents, having previously worked with the Tenant Selection Division researching the applicants' backgrounds to determine their eligibility. As a consultant, Reisner was charged with creating a "way of life" for residents to emulate.[26] From furnishings to child care, Reisner instructed tenants on the "best" way to live. Using a budget based on tenants' average income, Reisner furnished a model apartment for incoming tenants to tour. She also provided guidance and answered questions about furnishings and organizing apartment space. After tenants moved in, she aided them in arranging their apartments and establishing a wash schedule for shared clotheslines, and she attended to requests for towel bars, hooks, and other items. Reisner also provided training on how to use the gas stove, heater, and electric washing machines. Caring about tenants' domestic concerns and working to eliminate resident dissatisfaction, Reisner reasoned, facilitated cooperation and created a strong public housing community made up of selected tenants living according to SFHA standards.[27] Further, acknowledging the continual struggle to overcome opposition to the new public housing program, Reisner claimed, "Happy, satisfied tenants constitute the most important factor in a sound and effective public relations program."[28] As the nascent public housing program tried to grow, publicity and promotion seemed as important as building design and construction in ensuring the SFHA's future success.

The SFHA's focus on these "deserving" tenants and the importance of public housing in strengthening communities, the city, and democracy in the nation permeated the agency's publicity campaign during its first decade. Through a multimedia marketing campaign, the SFHA promoted its agenda to "provide the framework for a way of life for its tenants . . . set within the greater framework of the community and the city."²⁹ The elaborate display at the Golden Gate International Exposition in 1939–1940 was just the beginning of the SFHA's publicity efforts. The model apartment at Holly Courts was open to the public for tours that included high school and college classes in the Bay Area.³⁰ These early marketing efforts promoted public housing for its potential to mold deserving citizens—as defined by the SFHA—in support of a healthy democracy.

San Franciscans had a variety of other ways to learn about the new housing program as well: radio spots, newspaper articles, film screenings of *Housing in Our Time* and *Our City*, and public talks by the housing commissioners all promoted the public housing program amid increased skepticism.³¹ Using donated radio time, the Authority presented *The Housing Reporter*, a weekly dramatization about San Francisco's public housing program.³² Along with these radio spots, the SFHA commissioned its own film to depict "in dramatic style" the agency's methods for "solving the age-old problem of providing more than four walls and roof as a center of family life." Directed by Works Progress Administration photographer William Abbenseth, *More Than Shelter* was screened at the SFHA office, in churches, unions, and other organizations across the city. The film became a popular tool for educating citizens on "the 'whys' and 'hows' of the low-rent housing program."³³

Garnering support for the nascent public housing program meant quelling citizens' concerns about two different kinds of values: the values and morals of public housing tenants and property values. The SFHA had to contend with San Franciscans "who held fantastical ideas concerning the type of persons to be housed and the effect on private property."³⁴ The SFHA, like other housing authorities across the country, stressed the "morality" of public housing and through the 1950s turned away applicants who might present a moral or financial risk.³⁵ The marketing campaign also championed the new public housing projects for replacing blighted buildings and improving safety and sanitation in neighborhoods. These efforts, the agency argued, would lead to increased property values for neighboring landowners.

As the SFHA began completing public housing projects across the city, the agency branded itself as an integral player in building the health of the city and the nation. For its seal, the authority emphasized its commitment to both the city's past and future by selecting the

"To Provide Decent, Safe, and Sanitary Housing"

"legendary Phoenix, fabulous eagle of antiquity and patron bird of San Francisco" (the bird also adorned the city's seal). The 1946 minutes of the Housing Authority Commission explained the meaning of the oft-displayed SFHA emblem:

> Arising from the flames it commemorated the indomitable and virile city that arose again time after time from the ashes of disastrous early fires with new strength and spirit. In this seal the Phoenix symbolizes as well the building of good homes and a better city from the ashes of destroyed slums. The five stars represent the five low-rent developments constructed during the Authority's first decade after its founding in 1938. The scroll beneath carries the moving message "In love of home the love of country has its rise," by Charles Dickens, the motto of the SFHA.[36]

Through its seal and motto, the Housing Authority aligned itself with San Francisco's history of renewal after the fire and earthquake of 1906 while advocating a particular view of community and citizenship. By creating modern projects that housed selected tenants subject to numerous regulations, the SFHA pledged to improve tenants and neighborhoods. In selecting Dickens's phrase for the SFHA motto, the housing commissioners also demonstrated their belief in environmental determinism's premise that good homes produce good citizens. Public housing, seen by the SFHA as the training ground for middle-class living, would, in officials' eyes, inculcate tenants on how to behave as they worked and waited to move up and out of federally subsidized housing.

The SFHA promoted itself, in part, to secure buy-in from city residents to build more public housing in neighborhoods across the city. The agency opened Holly Courts (118 units) in 1940, Potrero Terrace (469 units) and Sunnydale (767 units) in 1941, and Valencia Gardens (246 units) and Westside Courts (136 units) in 1943. Located in the Western Addition, Westside Courts housed African Americans and "a few white families;" the other 1,600 new housing units had no black tenants.[37] Plans to build six other projects were delayed by World War II, as the country shifted its resources to the war effort.

The onslaught of military, government, and civilian workers arriving in the Bay Area exacerbated the prewar housing shortage and created a housing crisis as the population of San Francisco increased

"To Provide Decent, Safe, and Sanitary Housing"

by 90,000 between 1940 and 1942. With war workers in the region reportedly living in converted sheds and chicken shacks, and thousands of new arrivals flooding the area each month, the SFHA responded to the federal Lanham Act and local conditions by prioritizing the housing needs of military families and building temporary war housing under federal ownership.[38]

The wartime shift to temporary housing demonstrated the SFHA's emerging administrative acumen and the positive potential of collaboration across city departments and with unions and the business sector. SFHA wartime construction included 5,500 units of temporary housing for naval dockworkers and their families in southeast San Francisco. Together the SFHA and federal government leased 500 acres of land to construct Hunters Point. The SFHA successfully led infrastructure planning on the temporary units, working with city departments and trade unions to bring roads, sewers, schools, police, and firefighters to Hunters Point.[39] Along with these necessities, the SFHA also provided a library, a social hall, a gymnasium that held a variety of activities, including dances, volleyball, and boxing, and a government-funded day care center. In collaboration with the city's public health department and the U.S. Public Health Service, the SFHA also opened a health center, well baby clinic, and infirmary for war workers. Transportation to the Naval Yards was provided, as were a range of other services from barbershops to a movie theater. This "city within a city" eventually housed a population of 35,000.[40] The extent of interagency cooperation in constructing wraparound resources for tenants waned in the postwar period when the SFHA returned to its original mandate to house low-income families. Likewise, the level and amount of services provided to Hunters Point residents proved more robust than the meager amenities eked out of tight federal funding allocations for permanent public housing projects.

The most significant difference, however, between the SFHA's oversight of temporary war housing and the permanent public housing program was arguably not tied to resources or interagency and cross-sector cooperation. Rather, Hunters Point was racially integrated. Perhaps because it was temporary housing or because of the dire housing shortage, the SFHA went against its own stated policy and practice and opened Hunters Point to all civilian workers regardless of race.

"To Provide Decent, Safe, and Sanitary Housing"

By 1945, Hunters Point had grown to 20,000 residents, one-third of them black. As historian Albert Broussard has described, Hunters Point emerged as "one of the most thoroughly integrated communities in San Francisco."[41]

Despite maintaining the color line in its five permanent public housing projects, the SFHA documented and seemingly celebrated racial integration at Hunters Point. In 1944, the *Beacon*, the SFHA's newspaper for Hunters Point–area residents, hosted a photo contest. The winning photo was taken at the Navy Point Infirmary. In the photograph, Quentin Anderson, a smiling white little boy and a patient at the infirmary, sits on a bed feeding a black baby girl, Joy Knightson, with a bottle. The *San Francisco Housing News* reported that the five-month old baby had refused to eat until Quentin fed her.[42] The photo—reproduced in other SFHA publications and, according to the SFHA, in over thirty publications nationwide—captured an image of racial accord that, ironically, the SFHA was simultaneously stymieing within the permanent public housing program through its policies, Commission appointees, and politicized leadership.

The democratic ideal of public housing promoted through the SFHA's publicity campaign, including the widespread image of racial integration at Hunters Point, began to weaken under the agency's race-based policies and political gamesmanship. Even as the SFHA emphasized its aim of strengthening individuals and communities, commissioners wrestled with the explosive issue of integration in the permanent public housing program. What would it mean to integrate public housing? How much more resistance would neighbors bring to bear on site selection and land purchases if public housing "in their backyard" was integrated? Following what became a well-established pattern in housing authorities across the nation, the SFHA commissioners pledged to uphold the federal "neighborhood pattern policy" guidelines. The Housing Commission passed Resolution 287 in 1942.[43] The neighborhood pattern policy stated that "in the selection of tenants for projects of this Authority, this Authority shall act with reference to established usages, customs, and traditions of the community with a view of the preservation of public space and good order and shall insofar as possible maintain and preserve the same racial composition."[44] Put into place as San Francisco's African American population began to increase dramatically as a result of wartime in-migration, the policy served as a conservative response to the city's shifting demographics. Racial integration at Hunters Point was a wartime anomaly. The impact of the neighborhood pattern policy—which allowed Housing Authority staff to select and place public housing residents on the basis of the existing racial and ethnic composition in a neighborhood— reverberated for decades in San Francisco.

The strain of the city's shifting demographics, the housing shortage during the war, and the philosophical differences among the appointed housing commissioners led to a politically motivated shake-up in the SFHA Commission a mere five years after the organizational structure was established. In September 1938, after Wilder's short time as executive director of the SFHA, the commissioners unanimously appointed to that position local architect and urban planner Albert Evers, who had experience surveying slum areas and designing low-rent housing.[45] Evers shepherded the agency through receiving federal approval for several public housing projects and worked to develop processes and systems for the growing organization. Evers's skills, however, were overshadowed by the increasingly polarized views of Housing Commission members. Veteran commissioners Marshall Dill and Alice Griffith regarded public housing as a critical vehicle for social reform; in contrast, newer mayoral appointees E. N. Ayer, William Cordes, and Timothy Reardon were, as historian John Baranski put it, "determined to limit the authority in the areas of civil rights."[46] These tensions finally erupted in a showdown. On August 17, 1943, a special emergency meeting of the housing commissioners was called to hear the grievances of Management Division head John Beard and a few other employees who resigned in protest over Evers's creation of a new Maintenance Department. During the meeting, Commissioner Ayer limited the testimonies to two employees who spoke against Evers. After the employees spoke, he quickly proposed a motion calling for Evers's resignation. Cordes and Reardon seconded the motion, and their majority vote forced Evers out without cause. The three commissioners then appointed John Beard as acting executive director of the SFHA. Beard had started at the SFHA in the Tenant Selection Division, was then promoted to the Management Division, and had become the chief of that department. He had no training or experience

"To Provide Decent, Safe, and Sanitary Housing"

in planning or architecture. He did, however, have ample experience in "filtering out nonwhite applicants from white-only projects" from his work in the Tenant Selection Division.[47] Appalled by the "unfair practices" of their fellow commissioners, Griffith and Dill resigned in protest the day after the meeting. Despite an outpouring of support for Evers from local, state, and national organizations, his dismissal and Beard's appointment stood. Mayor Angelo Rossi filled the two vacated Commission seats with a social worker, Katherine Gray, and a labor leader, John Spalding. Both of these mayoral appointees, Baranski writes, "ensured that the SFHA leadership would not attack the city's color line."[48] The loss of the institutional knowledge shared by Dill, Griffith, and Evers, as well as their collective expertise in urban planning, housing, and architecture, left a void in SFHA leadership: the political jockeying within the organizational structure laid bare the inherent vulnerability in a system so easily shaped by patronage and politics.

Under Beard's leadership, the SFHA held fast to its segregationist policy and continued to shape and enforce the role of public housing as a place to mold compliant citizens. As newcomers continued to crowd into the city, the SFHA was only one of many players enforcing housing segregation. White private property owners, like their counterparts in the Northeast and Midwest, used restrictive covenants to confine African Americans to the Western Addition/Fillmore District and Chinese Americans to Chinatown. As the city's population continued to swell and the housing crisis deepened, the fear of racial tensions resulting in violence intensified in the wake of the deadly 1943 Detroit race riot. In response to rumors of an impending race riot at Hunters Point in November 1944, Mayor Roger Lapham created the Council on Civic Unity (CCU), a group of civil rights and housing activists charged with improving race relations with a particular focus on public housing.[49] Although the CCU's investigation showed that rumors of the alleged race riot were but "idle gossip," the committee found discontent among white residents at Hunters Point and began focusing on improving intergroup race relations.[50] The CCU's ultimate recommendation was for the SFHA to desegregate public housing and to support the creation of tenants' associations, a position they would continue to advocate after the war.

"To Provide Decent, Safe, and Sanitary Housing"

Through its choice of architectural designs for public housing and its practice of prohibiting meetings of "a political nature" in its buildings, the SFHA under John Beard successfully curtailed tenant organizing during the first decade and a half of operation.[51] As the new head of the SFHA, John Beard had no intention of changing course or sharing power with tenants in any way. In his view, tenants' organizations were "unnecessary and undesirable."[52] With an eye toward other California locales, historian John Baranski argues, Beard may have feared the conflation of racial foment and tenant organizing. He had only to look at nearby Marin City and Richmond, California, to see that tenants' organizations could mobilize for change. In Marin City, tenants' organizations had provided a platform for cross-racial dialogues and community-building among residents. African American tenants in Richmond, California, leveraged their tenants' organization, as Baranski notes, "to demand better and more public housing, end discriminatory policies, and stop evictions."[53] When their needs were not met, the tenants launched a rent strike, joining other public housing tenants nationwide who directly challenged housing authorities in the late 1940s. Despite continued pressure from the CCU and some Public Housing Administration (PHA) officials to support the creation of tenants' organizations, the SFHA consistently refused to support tenant organizing. Instead, Beard opted to handle tenants' problems individually, stating that the SFHA would "look with disfavor on any effort to organize the tenants for political reasons."[54]

Wielding sole power over tenant selection, race-based placement, and management, with no input from the tenants themselves, the SFHA reinforced housing segregation patterns in the city and quashed criticism from public housing tenants. The agency's actions increasingly came under fire. In November 1945, representatives from the National Association for the Advancement of Colored People (NAACP), the Communist Party, the CCU, and the Congress of Industrial Organizations urged the SFHA to repeal the neighborhood pattern policy.[55] The SFHA refused. Commissioner Ayer used democratic principles to justify the Housing Authority's position: As a "public body this Authority must follow the will of all the people. This has been the policy in the past and must necessarily be the policy in the

15

future."⁵⁶ Local activists continued to push for change, viewing public housing as a viable way to challenge the color line in the city's neighborhoods. In 1946, the San Francisco Urban League, the CCU, the American Veterans League, and the San Francisco Council of Churches pressured the mayor and Board of Supervisors to replace the neighborhood pattern policy with "a non-color policy of first come, first serve."⁵⁷ A citizen's survey published the same year and covering the five permanent public housing projects called on the SFHA "to revise its racial policy to permit minority groups in all public housing."⁵⁸ The mayor responded to this growing public pressure by appointing Dr. William McKinley Thomas, the first African American to serve on the Housing Commission, when a vacancy opened up in 1946.⁵⁹ The Board of Supervisors took a bolder step: in July 1946 they voted nine to one for a resolution calling for the end of segregation in San Francisco public housing. The SFHA ignored the resolution as the housing commissioners demonstrated their autonomy from local governance. While some other housing authorities made strides in integrating public housing and supporting tenants' organizations, the SFHA held fast to its policies under Beard's leadership.⁶⁰

When tens of thousands of families who had migrated to the city for war work decided to stay, San Francisco became "one of the Nation's most critical cities in the lack of housing."⁶¹ In the immediate postwar period, the Housing Authority responded by focusing attention on constructing public housing projects delayed by the war. Rising land and building costs and the exhaustion of federal funds for public housing, however, stalled construction. It was only after Congress passed the Housing Act of 1949 that the SFHA finally had the funds to move ahead with its building program.⁶² The Taft-Ellender-Wagner bill that became the Housing Act of 1949 called for 810,000 units of public housing. However, by dividing power between local housing authorities and redevelopment agencies, the legislation in many ways bowed to private developers and real estate pressures. In anticipation of the federal legislation, the San Francisco Redevelopment Agency (SFRA) was established in 1948. Governed by mayoral appointees, the semiautonomous agency with "vast independent legal, financial, and technical powers and resources" grew into a pro-business urban renewal juggernaut. The vagueness of the Housing Act language and the focus on "urban redevelopment" opened the door for

"To Provide Decent, Safe, and Sanitary Housing"

the construction of high-end apartments, parking lots, and other developments that were more lucrative and accepted than low-rent housing. In San Francisco, the SFRA used millions in federal funds over several decades to construct the controversial Yerba Buena Center and the Golden Gateway project, supporting a pro-business, pro-growth agenda that displaced thousands of low-income residents in a city where public housing demand outpaced supply.[63]

In California and San Francisco, state and local governments responded to the public housing provision of the new federal legislation in markedly different ways. The California state legislature aimed to curtail public housing construction, passing Article 34 in 1949, which required voters to approve any construction of new public housing projects. Locally, the CCU seized on the federal act and allocation of 3,000 units of public housing in San Francisco to continue to push for desegregation. Each SFHA application for federal funds had to be approved by the Board of Supervisors. Under the leadership of Director Edward Howden, the CCU convinced the board supervisor and future mayor George Christopher to add a clause forbidding segregation in public housing to the SFHA's application. The Board of Supervisors approved the application with the nondiscrimination clause.[64] Beard and the Housing Commission balked, postponing the submission of the application to the federal government. With the city's critical housing need and millions of dollars in construction, administrative, and maintenance jobs hanging in the balance, the Board of Supervisors, activists, and eventually the local press blasted the SFHA for refusing to desegregate public housing and potentially forgoing federal funding because of delays. Supervisor George decried the neighborhood pattern policy as "a policy of discrimination." The *San Francisco News* editorialized that "government agencies cannot justify discrimination against any group of citizens where public monies, provided by the citizenry as a whole, are being spent."[65] Amid growing pressure, the Housing Commission finally agreed to a compromise: in its 1,741 existing units and 1,200 deferred units, the neighborhood pattern policy would be grandfathered in while all new permanent projects would uphold a nondiscrimination policy, housing tenants "in order of application."[66]

After winning local voter approval in 1950 for construction of new public housing units, the SFHA resumed its building program across San Francisco, continuing segregationist practices as well as

"To Provide Decent, Safe, and Sanitary Housing"

efforts to stymie tenant organizing. With whites in four projects and African Americans in one, the SFHA focused on completing additional segregated developments.[67] In 1952, the SFHA opened two deferred projects: Ping Yuen in Chinatown, designated as an all-Chinese project, and North Beach Place in North Beach, opened to white tenants. During the finalization process for both developments, John Beard urged the housing commissioners to convert planned meeting spaces into additional apartment units. These spaces, he argued, were costly to maintain and duplicated Parks and Recreation facilities. As news spread about the elimination of community spaces, the San Francisco Housing and Planning Association, Youth Council, and former housing commissioner Alice Griffith fought to reclaim the community spaces by demonstrating the importance of these sites for accommodating adult and youth programs.[68] Ultimately, it would be future tenants themselves who would successfully push the Housing Commission to provide communal meeting spaces at Ping Yuen and North Beach Place.

At Ping Yuen, widely celebrated by Chinatown residents and the city, the Housing Authority's commitment to providing Chinese Americans with modern housing, and segregating them in Chinatown, drew praise. City dwellers lauded the SFHA for tearing down crowded "tenements" in the district that had San Francisco's "highest tuberculosis and death rates" and replacing them with projects that attracted tourists with their faux Chinese architectural style.[69] Containing the Chinese in Chinatown, which Ping Yuen residents themselves readily accepted, did not incite controversy, as when North Beach Place opened a few months later. African American applicants protested their exclusion from North Beach Place but not from Ping Yuen, possibly because they did not want to live in Chinatown and would not have been welcomed there.

Although San Francisco took pride in its "history as a multiracial, multiethnic city" that "proved a mixed population could coexist without deadly violence," African Americans and Chinese Americans in the post–World War II era faced systemic discrimination in housing.[70] A long history of diversity did not result in peaceable integration. It was the exclusion of African Americans from a white housing project, rather than the segregation of Chinese Americans in Chinatown, that intensified criticism about segregation in public housing. The racist system characterized by the black–white binary in the American South and challenged by the growing civil rights movement emerged as a contentious issue at North Beach Place. The NAACP sued the SFHA on behalf of three African American applicants denied admittance to North Beach Place in 1952 (see chapter 4). In 1954, the U.S. Supreme Court justices refused to hear the *Banks v. The Housing Authority of San Francisco* case, thus upholding the California Supreme Court ruling against segregation in San Francisco public housing. Despite the court ruling, the SFHA's continuing practice of segregating African Americans and Chinese Americans aroused controversy and created problems for the agency and some tenants over the next four decades.

Under Beard's leadership, and against the backdrop of the deepening Cold War, the SFHA as the city's largest landlord continued its focus on maintaining and controlling public housing.[71] Over its twelve years in operation, the SFHA had housed 173,750 tenants, generated total revenues of $28,607,000, and employed thousands of workers while supporting public and nonprofit services in public housing.[72] Asserting top-down control, Beard had the SFHA hire its own police force and conduct its own surveillance. These measures ensured the SFHA's tight control over tenants living in public housing while slight tweaks to tenant eligibility requirements continued to determine who future tenants would be. The SFHA prioritized low-income nuclear families headed by "live-in" veterans; preferred citizens; and, after 1952, enforced the federal Gwinn Amendment "requiring public housing tenants to be free of subversive ideas and associations."[73] At the same time, the agency began to expand eligibility for public housing to the elderly, receiving federal approval in 1954 to construct a housing development solely for seniors. The combination of smaller apartments, which were less expensive to build, and the public perception of the elderly as law-abiding good neighbors, made public housing for seniors an appealing option for the SFHA. The 1956 Housing Act legislated seniors as eligible tenants in government-funded housing. Over time, the SFHA responded to the need for senior housing by setting aside units equipped for elderly tenants in new public housing developments.[74]

19

"To Provide Decent, Safe, and Sanitary Housing"

In responding to San Franciscans' need for affordable housing, the SFHA continued to segregate many of its projects under Beard's leadership. The Supreme Court's 1954 decision dismantling the neighborhood pattern policy and the 1962 executive order issued by President John F. Kennedy outlawing segregation in all federal housing had little effect on the SFHA's actual operations. As the African American population of San Francisco increased after the war, the Housing Authority looked for ways to discourage black in-migration. In a May 16, 1962, letter to John C. Houlihan, the mayor of Oakland, the San Francisco housing commissioners commended the mayor for his statement on the "Freedom Train" migration and joined him in asking the "Southern States" to discontinue their push for African American migration to the west. The mayor criticized white southerners for "capitalizing on the misfortune of the Negroes for which the whites themselves are much to be blamed."[75] Houlihan also reminded them that the West did not welcome the exodus of African American migrants: "The City of Oakland and the enlightened people of the West face our own problems, and these people may become one of them. We do not send our problems off to other states."[76] Limiting the population of African Americans, the Housing Authority seemed to conclude, would perhaps lessen the problem surrounding public housing integration. At the same time that the SFHA voiced concern about the growth of the African American population in the city, it provided more public housing in Chinatown, opening the 194-unit Ping Yuen Annex in 1962. Although the agency claimed to have accepted applicants who were not Chinese, over 97 percent of the tenants were of Chinese descent. The SFHA continued to defend Ping Yuen's demographics on the grounds that tenants were happy living in a segregated project.[77]

The persistence of segregation in public housing and in the private housing market in California increasingly came under fire as fair housing and civil rights advocates worked for change. Fair housing legislation was critical to ensuring racial integration and became a key piece of civil rights reform. Statewide battles between civil rights advocates and the state and national real estate lobby raged on in the early 1960s. In response to the California Real Estate Association (CREA) planning for a statewide measure to block fair housing legislation,

"To Provide Decent, Safe, and Sanitary Housing"

W. Bryan Rumford (D-Berkeley) sponsored the California Fair Housing Bill in 1963, which would make racial discrimination in housing illegal. By the time the bill was set for a vote, it made discrimination in public housing and property of more than five units illegal. Governor Brown signed the bill into law in June 1963, but insufficient enforcement made it more of a symbolic victory.[78] Resistance from the real estate industry and segregationists persisted and included the CREA-backed ballot initiative Proposition 14, which would amend the state constitution to legalize housing discrimination.[79] The highly controversial proposal appeared on the ballot in the 1964 election: in an eight-to-seven margin, San Franciscans voted for Proposition 14, while also supporting Lyndon Johnson over Barry Goldwater for president and approving local measure H authorizing 2,500 units of new public housing in the city.[80] Governor Brown reflected on the election returns supporting Proposition 14, stating that the "majority of whites in this state just don't want Negros living in the same neighborhood with them."[81] In 1966, the California Supreme Court ruled that Proposition 14 was illegal.

President Johnson's Great Society programs—the Civil Rights Act of 1964, the Voting Rights Act, and the Immigration Act of 1965, as well as the creation of Medicare, Medicaid, Legal Aid, Head Start, and the Office of Economic Opportunity—buttressed civil rights supporters in San Francisco and elsewhere and brought much-needed antipoverty programs to the city. These programs, many promoted by neighborhood-based Economic Opportunity Councils, sought to empower low-income citizens in the social and economic improvement of their communities. The antipoverty and community action programs, as well as the creation of HUD, established to coordinate housing and redevelopment initiatives, factored into ongoing changes in San Francisco public housing over the next decade.

Although many San Franciscans had voted to maintain segregation in the private housing market, citizen pressure for the SFHA to comply with federal mandates to desegregate public housing intensified. Despite the SFHA's integration of Valencia Gardens, North Beach Place, and a number of other projects after 1954, the NAACP and the United Freedom Movement, a San Francisco offshoot of the NAACP, nonetheless criticized the agency for not breaking up segregation in all public housing across the city. Civil rights organizations focused their attention on integrating projects that had mostly white or black residents rather than attacking the homogeneity at Ping Yuen. They also condemned the Housing Authority for discriminatory hiring practices. The NAACP and the United Freedom Movement pointed to the lack of black–white integration in public housing and attacked the "racial imbalance" among Authority maintenance workers, blaming the inequity on the SFHA's practice of "hiring workers from union hiring halls which are operated in such a manner as to foreclose or discourage Negro applicants."[82] Picketing at Hunters Point and Potrero Terrace and repeatedly marching at the Housing Authority office on Turk Street with signs reading "Discrimination Must Go" and "Hire Apprentices," the NAACP vocally and publicly pressured the SFHA to change its housing and hiring practices.[83]

The combination of the protests and a 1965 ruling by the California Fair Employment Practices Commission (FEPC) that found that the SFHA "was using various devices to perpetuate the Negroes' housing and job-getting plight" forced the agency to act. Two months after the FEPC ruling, the commissioners voted to "begin negotiations with a management firm which would look into the Authority's hiring and rental policies."[84] The Housing Commission followed the recommendations of the FEPC and took steps "to improve the agency's public image" by approving a new set of hiring rules "that would give minority groups greater employment opportunities in the agency" and eliminate "references to race in rental applications."[85] The agency also created a new position, director of human relations and tenant services, "to insure that neither housing assignment nor job discrimination is practiced by Housing Authority personnel."[86]

These changes failed to quell the increasing criticism levied against the agency as a whole, and longtime Executive Director John Beard in particular. As executive director of the Housing Authority for twenty-two years, Beard had presided over the agency's entrenched segregationist policy and practices and had blocked tenant organizing in San Francisco public housing. Despite the 1954 Supreme Court ruling and Kennedy's executive order, he had continued to promote segregation in public housing.[87] Criticized by the NAACP, State Assemblyman John Burton, and the Catholic Interracial Council for failing to integrate public housing, Beard was the target for allegations of discrimination lodged against the SFHA since the 1950s.[88]

Bolstered by the civil rights movement and the emergence of antipoverty programs in the city that advocated for their active involvement, tenants began to organize and mobilize for change: removing Beard became a priority. After years of systematic repression of tenants' organizations, public housing residents drew "on the city's civic culture and history of resistance to capital and authority" to voice their concerns and work for change.[89] From attending and addressing the commissioners at meetings, to writing newsletters, to demanding better maintenance and services, tenants exercised their democratic rights, pushing against Beard and decades of attempts to silence them. Following the scathing FEPC findings outlining the SFHA's failure to administer housing and employment fairly, tenants and community allies joined together to push Beard out. At a packed Housing Commission meeting in October 1965, representatives from four tenants' associations representing thousands of tenants presented a list of grievances before sharing the microphone with Assemblyman John Burton's (D-San Francisco) assistant, who read a telegram from his boss. In the telegram, Burton endorsed the tenants' organizations, criticized the SFHA for its treatment of tenants, and blamed Beard for running "a third rate operation."[90] The dramatic changes and dynamism of the decade, coupled with intense scrutiny and criticism of his leadership, eventually led to the end of Beard's tenure. During an executive session of the Housing Commission in 1965, the commissioners voted to oust Beard. His departure from office, however, did not signal the end of the SFHA's problems.

Beyond "Hope"? Decline and Renewal, 1965–2000

The sense of possibility for change within the nation, the city, and public housing galvanized by the Great Society and civil rights movement seemed to resonate with tenants and the emerging new leadership at the SFHA. In a 1965 Housing Commission meeting, tenant representative Alma Burleigh from the newly formed North Beach Place Improvement Association described residents' optimism in their organization:

> We have initiated new and more friendly relations between all tenants, between tenants and management, and management and the commission. The tenants in this project have begun to develop a new spirit of enthusiasm and optimism concerning their homes. . . . For the first time people in public housing have begun to do something to help themselves.[91]

Tenants' hopefulness may have initially been buoyed by Mayor John Shelley's appointment of Eneas Kane as the new executive director of the SFHA in 1965. Kane viewed public housing as necessary to mitigate housing problems and believed that social support for tenants was crucial. With John Beard gone and a new leader at the helm who had the backing of like-minded commissioners, the SFHA seemed to be making a new start. Commissioner Stephen Walter asserted that Kane's "well-known sympathies for matters of civil rights" would be an immeasurable help to the SFHA.[92] Kane, now the head of 7,000 units of public housing, aimed to reorganize the agency. His efforts included cutting administrative costs, clarifying staff roles, and working with the Commission to create an SFHA staff manual on reducing discrimination and promoting integration in the city's neighborhoods.[93] In a clear departure from Beard's agenda, Kane also prioritized outreach to tenants: he requested that managers increase communication with tenants, and he welcomed "tenant councils to join with the Authority in the solution of joint problems."[94] To achieve this aim, he established a program to develop tenants' organizations and formed committees to work with specific populations, including parents, youth, and elderly tenants. Through the Human Relations Department, Kane sought to connect tenants to social services and to help tenants tap into local and federal benefits, such as Aid to Families with Dependent Children. The SFHA also facilitated voter registration, child care, and job training for some public housing tenants even as federal funding diminished.[95]

Even with a new outlook and agenda in place, the process of Kane's appointment signaled a continuation of patronage. Kane, previously the executive secretary to the mayor and a personal friend, had allegedly asked for the executive director post. Born and educated in San Francisco, Kane had worked in public relations. He had no previous experience in the housing field. The politics of the appointment process continued to undermine real organizational change.

"To Provide Decent, Safe, and Sanitary Housing"

Kane and the commissioners' aim of establishing a more collaborative relationship with tenants and improving social services proved too little, too late for the long-neglected African American public housing residents at Hunters Point. Once a highlight of the SFHA's wartime housing program, the Hunters Point District, including public and private housing, had undergone significant changes since the economic heyday of the Naval Shipyard during World War II. Decades of housing discrimination kept African Americans concentrated in Hunters Point and the Western Addition/Fillmore. Marshaling federal funds generated by the urban development and urban renewal focus of the Housing Acts of 1949 and 1954, the San Francisco Redevelopment Agency "renewed" the Western Addition/Fillmore area, a Japanese American and African American enclave since World War II. After razing stores, jazz clubs, community centers, and housing that ultimately displaced some 4,000 families during the 1960s, the SFRA went on to construct high-rise apartments and condos and later the Japanese Cultural and Trade Center.[96] Many displaced African Americans crowded into Hunters Point; discrimination kept them out of other neighborhoods.[97] By 1960, 50 percent of the Hunters Point District population was African American, up from 21 percent in 1950.[98] As the population grew, the number of jobs in the area declined; with the navy reducing its workforce and regional deindustrialization increasing, residents felt the impact of their spatial isolation from the rest of the city and the weight of overt employment discrimination.[99]

Public housing residents at Hunters Point, along with their neighbors, demanded a change. The Hunters Point Tenants Union (HPTU) wrote a letter to the SFHA with a list of twenty-two questions and threatened to start a rent strike if they did not receive answers within three weeks. On September 27, 1966, less than a week after the letter was written, a race riot broke out in the district after a white policeman shot and killed a sixteen-year-old African American who was running away from a stolen car. The National Guard was called in, and the riot ended three days later.[100]

In a show of good faith, Kane met with the HPTU executive committee to discuss the group's questions and demands two weeks later. Kane responded to the tenant leaders' key concern of deferred maintenance by assuring them that the SFHA had applied for $3.3 million in emergency funds for rehabilitation projects. After talking with members,

"To Provide Decent, Safe, and Sanitary Housing"

the HPTU decided that this was not good enough. On November 1, tenants began a rent strike to put pressure on the SFHA to improve the physical environment of Hunters Point. After learning that HUD did not grant funds to rehabilitate existing projects, the SFHA submitted a grant application to the Department of Health, Education, and Welfare (HEW) for funds to improve health and safety at Hunters Point. Tenants continued to withhold rents, with 900 residents pooling their rent monies for painting and renovations. When neither HEW nor HUD provided assistance to the SFHA, Mayor Shelley pledged $300,000 in city funds to the SFHA that then put another $150,000 in reserves toward maintenance at Hunters Point, putting an end to the strike. After the withheld rents were returned to the SFHA, Kane attended a ceremony at Hunters Point in September 1967 to kick off the much-needed renovations.[101]

conditions in p.h.

In their demands to the SFHA, tenants had also protested the scheduled eviction of an unemployed resident unable to pay his rent. In response to the tenants' protest, the SFHA changed its rent delinquency policy, dropping the late fee and sending managers to talk with tenants about a payment plan rather than immediately starting legal proceedings. Executive Director Kane, hoping to appease residents further, next issued a moratorium on evictions.[102] The new policy decreased the agency's rent rolls significantly. In 1967, the SFHA changed its policy again, reinstating evictions to get rid of "freeloaders" and promising to work out a payment plan for tenants who fell behind on rent payments because of financial hardships or illness.[103] With the rent owed by residents at the end of the moratorium totaling $175,000 and a growing deficit predicted to top $500,000 in 1967, the Housing Authority contradicted earlier policies and promises by raising rents up to $4 a month, increasing the number of tenants who could not pay their rent on time.[104] Defending the measure, Kane argued, "We must increase our income, in order to stay solvent."[105]

The agency, like many others across the country, operated with a deficit and faced increasing financial difficulties as a result of federal policy shifts and spending cuts beginning in the late 1960s. In 1969, the federal government passed the first Brooke Amendment, which capped rents in public housing at no more than 25 percent of tenant income, "thereby keeping public housing affordable to those of lowest incomes, but exacerbating the shortfall of rent receipts."[106] Under the Nixon administration, the federal government cut off the already marginal funds to housing authorities by declaring a moratorium on public housing expansion in 1973. The direct effect on the SFHA was highlighted during a Housing Commission meeting in February of that year. The secretary gloomily predicted that with "no funds available and no potential for funding . . . it is estimated that this Authority will 'go into the red' in the amount of $775,000 this year." A housing commissioner summed up the situation: "It does not bode well for the future unless there is a change in Federal policies."[107] The combination of the rental shortages stemming from the Brooke Amendment, congressional delays in delivering subsidies to make up for lower rents, and Nixon's moratorium forced the SFHA to draw on and deplete its reserves. Tenants suffered as a result.[108]

As the Housing Authority struggled to make ends meet, public housing tenants in San Francisco, like others across the country, relied on tenants' associations to lobby for their needs. Amid the national groundswell of welfare, tenant, community, student, and civil rights organizing that occurred between 1964 and 1968, public housing tenants in San Francisco began to organize themselves. The Public Housing Tenants Association (PHTA), an organization representing tenants and tenant associations in public housing across the city, formed to gain "'tenant control' of the SFHA . . . to handle 'complaints and problems' and decide 'how millions of dollars in federal funds will be used in public housing.'"[109] In April 1971, the steering committee of the newly formed organization, made up of two representatives from each of the public housing developments, pressed for more self-governance and won the SFHA's designation of the San Francisco PHTA "as the organizational representative of 26 public housing projects." The PHTA also won a significant gain with the implementation of a new Grievance Panel Procedure, which handled 223 cases its first year.[110] Previously the SFHA's Human Relations Department had dealt with tenant disputes over building maintenance, repairs, or overdue rents. Under the terms of the new Grievance Procedure, the PHTA would form a panel of tenants to conduct grievance and arbitration procedures "between the Housing Authority and residents of the 7,000 housing units it administers." The Housing Authority made an important

27

but limited move toward ceding some control to tenants. The agency maintained veto power by asserting that commissioners could review hearing decisions and intervene if they "believe[d] that the tenants have acted capriciously or beyond their authority."[111]

By the end of the year, the PHTA had challenged the Housing Authority for more power. Spurred on by the National Tenants Organization meeting held in San Francisco, the PHTA demonstrated at city hall, demanding that tenants be appointed to the SFHA commission after a decade of asking for representation. When Mayor Joseph Alioto, Shelley's successor, appointed nontenant Dr. Amancio Ergina to a vacancy, rather than following through on his promise to consider nominations submitted by the PHTA before filling the position, the PHTA threatened a rent strike. The Board of Supervisors responded by passing a formal resolution asking the mayor to "name a tenant to fill the next Housing Authority vacancy."[112] The mayor agreed. The rent strike threat quickly dissipated with the city's vocal support for tenant representation. In August 1973, the SFHA added two tenant seats: Martin Helpman and Cleo Wallace were elected by peers and appointed by the mayor to serve on the Housing Commission. The decades of SFHA suppression of tenant organizing and self-advocacy had been reversed, and the commission was strengthened by the inclusion of tenant voices.[113]

Even as tenants pushed the SFHA for more tenant representation, maintenance, and safety, they found common ground with the agency around the need for more federal funding to keep up and expand the public housing program. Responding to the Nixon administration's opposition to public housing, the SFHA and public housing tenants wrote Congress with pleas to pass the 1974 Housing and Community Development Act, which would provide more federally subsidized units for low-income families and the elderly. Along with other tenants across the country, San Francisco public housing residents "bombarded Congress with wires and letters in opposition to the demise of public housing." After the act passed in the fall of 1974, San Francisco Housing Commissioner Wallace acknowledged the critical role tenants in the city had played: "This correspondence certainly let [Congress] know in Conference as well in the Committees that the tenants of public housing were very much aware of the apparent attitude of the Administration to allow and foster the death of public housing." The commissioner went on to acknowledge "the San Francisco Housing Authority and its tenants have worked more diligently than any other group across the country in terms of that Bill."[114]

The final bill provided $150 million for new developments and an additional $150 million for a new program called Section 8 and later the Housing Choice Voucher program.[115] This program, as scholar Lawrence Vale points out, "dramatically expanded the ability of local housing authorities to administer a system of housing allowances, and also enabled tenants to go out and identify the units they wished to rent instead of being assigned to particular properties."[116] Using Section 8 vouchers, public housing tenants could apply to live in private apartments with the rent offset by government subsidies. Residents and the SFHA cheered the federal government's continuation of public housing but soon found that the demand for Section 8 vouchers in San Francisco far outweighed the supply of apartments in the tight private market. When the Housing Authority publicized vouchers in 1981, over 5,000 people, described by the press as "an unruly mob," went to the SFHA to sign up.[117] The SFHA, coming under scrutiny by the Department of Housing and Urban Development and the city, increasingly failed to meet the needs of residents living in public housing and the demand for Section 8 vouchers.

From the 1970s through the 1990s, the Housing Authority's inconsistent leadership, management, and financial problems became chronic, taking a heavy toll on the agency and, in turn, tenants. The selection of housing commissioners by various mayors drew public criticism and accusations of patronage. Even seemingly prudent appointments caused trouble for the SFHA. For instance, Mayor George Moscone's selection of Reverend Jim Jones for an appointment to the Housing Commission in 1976 seemed in line with his efforts to reach out to different constituencies in the city. He appointed Reverend Jones, leader of the People's Temple congregation "of 8,000 black and white members," and Reverend A. C. Ubalde Jr., a Filipino known for his leadership in social welfare and educational organizations.[118] Within a year of his appointment, Reverend Jones left his post and the city and moved to Jonestown, an alternative society in Guyana, South America, that he had started developing in 1974. Jones called the SFHA from South America and resigned. On November 18, 1978, following the murder of Congressman Leo Ryan and four other people by Jones's followers, Jones led 912 Jonestown residents in a mass suicide.[119] Moscone's appointment of Jones ultimately embarrassed the SFHA. Though no selection would end as tragically as Jones's, public criticism of housing authority commission posts would continue in succeeding years.

No less damaging than the appointment of Jones was the failed leadership of the persons in the SFHA executive director role. In January 1977, after twelve years as executive director of the SFHA, Eneas Kane resigned. Several months later he pleaded guilty to one count of grand theft for embezzling funds from the SFHA and was sentenced to three years of probation.[120] Walter Scott replaced Kane. During Scott's tenure, a private audit of the SFHA revealed $150,000 of unrecorded funds drawn from the agency along with excessive salaries, a lack of documentation for SFHA executive business trips totaling over $43,000, and a failure to collect thousands of dollars in unpaid rent. Mayor Moscone, responding to the audit, ordered the agency "to clean house." Scott was demoted to a deputy post and Carl Williams became executive director in 1978. The agency's problems persisted. In 1985, citing the agency's deep debt, Housing Commissioner Preston Cook recommended that the SFHA sell a few of its smaller properties to reduce the deficit. Although one commissioner agreed to sell the projects "only as a last resort," Executive Director Williams opposed the proposal. The SFHA ultimately decided to reduce its workforce, cut management salaries by 10 percent, and decrease the workload of 385 employees from forty to thirty-six hours a week, resulting in benefit cuts for these workers, who were reclassified as part-time employees. Tenants feared they would pay the price for the agency's debt when the commissioners voted to lay off seventy-two employees, including maintenance workers, a decision that threatened to compromise services to public housing tenants.[121]

Increasingly, the SFHA came under fire for its poor management and financial troubles. In 1985, HUD put the agency on its "troubled list." The agency had a monthly deficit of $170,000 and nearly $6 million in unpaid bills. Not long after HUD recognized the agency's problems, Executive Director Carl Williams, hired to replace Walter Scott, resigned. Williams left office allegedly for mishandling finances. He was described "as the fourth consecutive director to leave the agency under a cloud of controversy."[122] As media headlines exclaimed, "Housing Projects in San Francisco Reported out of Control," the SFHA scrambled to hire David Gilmore as executive director.[123] Known as a specialist in saving troubled public housing authorities, Gilmore faced the challenge of running an authority HUD claimed had "virtually lost control of entire developments." In half of the agency's buildings, drug dealers paralyzed repair and maintenance efforts, and vandalism was rampant.[124] During his time in office, Gilmore managed to reduce the authority's vacancy rate, speed up repairs and the re-rental process, improve record keeping, and pay off most of the authority's long-term debt. As a result, the SFHA moved off of HUD's troubled agency list but still received an "F" for the condition of its units and housing repairs.[125] Even as he facilitated improvements at the SFHA, Gilmore made some questionable financial decisions, including large expenditures at "trendy restaurants."[126] Consequently, Mayor Frank Jordon ousted Gilmore in 1993, a move many tenants—who viewed Gilmore "as unresponsive to their needs"—applauded.[127]

The negative reputation of the SFHA was furthered by the continuation of segregation and racial and ethnic tensions in public housing. The legacy of the neighborhood pattern policy and persistent patterns of segregation upheld by the SFHA and, at times, reinforced by tenants' choices resulted in increased tensions. SFHA policies coupled with some applicants' preferences for living near friends and family resulted in a 98 percent Asian population at Ping Yuen in the 1980s and an 80 percent African American tenancy at Hunters Point.[128] In 1983, the SFHA, in what Corrie Anders of the *San Francisco Chronicle* described as "an administrative move to cut costs rather than implement integration," passed a new occupancy policy whereby applicants had to accept the first available apartment offered to them or "they shall be removed from the waiting list and be prevented from applying for housing for one year's period of time."[129] The SFHA had previously allowed applicants to select where they wanted to live when possible, and "many turned down housing unless they could be near friends or relatives." Housing officials claimed the new policy would promote integration. They were wrong. Many applicants refused housing offered to them and went to the bottom of the waiting list in hopes that an apartment would open up in the neighborhood where they wanted to live.[130] Integration, pushed by lawmakers and policies, was not fully embraced by many prospective public housing tenants.[131]

During the late 1980s and early 1990s, the demographics at the mostly segregated projects had not changed. HUD, in a move signaling that the SFHA had not fully enforced its 1983 policy, ordered the agency to better integrate its projects by changing its policy "whereby applicants could pick where they wanted to live." A HUD audit found that African Americans were heavily concentrated in certain projects and Asian Americans in others. It was not until 1992, according to the *San Jose Mercury News*, that "applicants generally had to take whatever apartments opened up."[132] The SFHA began forcing applicants to take the first available apartments and at times steered African Americans and Asian Americans away from projects housing their own racial and ethnic groups. According to the article, if an apartment opened up in a predominantly African American project, the SFHA steered African Americans away from that project to another location with fewer black tenants; the same policy held for Asian Americans waiting to move into Ping Yuen. Following orders from HUD to increase integration, the SFHA began "steering families—many of them [Southeast Asian] immigrants—into various developments [other than Ping Yuen] based on their ethnicity and leaving whatever cultural adjustments ensued almost entirely up to them."[133] The SFHA's implementation of a "Voluntary Compliance Agreement" to appease HUD "was done without any explanation to the established residents, who saw Southeast Asians as 'intruders' and interpreted their sudden arrival as simply a displacement of needy African Americans."[134] Without interrelations officers to help ease in families or community social services in place either for new immigrant or long-term residents, the authority's haphazard integration process provoked residents' fears and frustrations.

By March 1993, a pattern of difficulties for Southeast Asian residents in African American projects had emerged. Over one hundred Vietnamese and Cambodian residents at Potrero Terrace, Sunnydale, Hunters Point, Hunters View, and Alice Griffith, enlisting the Asian Law Caucus, filed a class action suit against the SFHA for "wanton disregard" of their safety. Southeast Asian tenants complained of being "the targets of steady harassment, including rock throwing, tire sla ings, [and] more serious crimes, including beatings, home robberies, and even murder."[135] The Nguyen family blamed the SFHA for the death of their eighteen-year-old son, who was fatally shot in front of the family's Potrero Terrace unit in September 1992. Mrs. Nguyen explained to the press, "I think we were attacked because we [are] Vietnamese."[136] Gen Fujioka, the Asian Law Caucus representative for the tenants, criticized the SFHA's careless integration policy. "The Housing Authority has placed these families in dangerous, racially hostile situations with no regard for their safety. . . . You can't have integration by just dropping people into the projects without an effort to bring together communities."[137] The lack of social services, community programs, and staff to bridge cultural and language differences between new families and other tenants undermined the integration process and imperiled residents as the Housing Authority relocated only "families who suffered extreme injury."[138] The SFHA settled the suit in 1994 and agreed to a modified policy allowing applicants to refuse a housing assignment for safety reasons without losing their place on the waiting list and facilitating quick transfers for residents threatened with violence.[139]

The SFHA's altered policies did not solve the difficulties of integration that also plagued other housing authorities in the Bay Area and across the nation. In the Bay Area, Asian immigrant public housing tenants in Oakland, Richmond, and Fresno reported racial harassment in the early 1990s. Discrimination affected other groups across the United States as well. Federal marshals in Vidor, Texas, escorted four black families into public housing in early 1994 amid Ku Klux Klan protests that "blacks were being forced on the community."[140] With targets of racial animosity varying from place to place, including Latino/as in Los Angeles, Russian Americans "experiencing resentment" in Sacramento, and recent immigrants from Cambodia, Laos, and Vietnam "having the roughest time" in several cities in the United States, the practice of integrating public housing proved increasingly complex.[141]

The SFHA faced the challenge of housing a diverse tenant population and dealing with ingrained patterns of racial and ethnic segregation that had been supported by the agency for decades. In the early

1990s, SFHA tenant demographics revealed that public housing had 49 percent African American, 27 percent Asian American, and 17 percent Latino/a and white residents.[142] In 1994, ten projects predominantly housed African Americans, while Ping Yuen and Ping Yuen North mostly had Asian American tenants.[143] African American tenants railed over the attention given to Asian American victims when "the vast majority of the victims of violent crime in the city's public housing developments [were] black." Many black tenants suffering from violence in their own neighborhoods coveted the transfers and Section 8 vouchers provided to some harassed Asian American families. They resented the fact that "their complaints have not been taken as seriously—and that their requests for Section 8 vouchers have not been handled as expeditiously."[144] Whereas black families in black projects felt that SFHA officials ignored their complaints and had for decades, black families pushed into Asian American public housing developments experienced social isolation. A black tenant who the SFHA "ordered" to live at Ping Yuen in 1993 described in a stark statement her hardships communicating and making friends: "It was a very bad situation."[145]

For the Asian American families who endured racial slurs and violence throughout the 1990s in a few African American projects, the Housing Authority "had not lived up to its commitment" made in the 1994 settlement.[146] News reports of racial violence in San Francisco's housing projects further decreased the SFHA's credibility with the city, HUD, and tenants. During the late 1990s, the Alice Griffith project in Hunters Point received extensive press coverage of allegedly racially motivated attacks against Asian immigrants by African Americans. But the larger, decades-long story—the structural forces that shaped the district—was not addressed in the press coverage. The trend of disinvestment and high unemployment in the area that began in the 1950s had continued for decades, contributing to the social and economic isolation of residents in the neglected southeast Hunters Point area. The articles did not report whether the perpetrators lived in public housing. Complaining of "official indifference," six Vietnamese families shared harrowing stories with the *San Francisco Examiner*. Journalist Leslie Goldberg reported that a seventy-eight-year-old man, Ngu Vo, "got down on his knees, hands clasped as in prayer, as two

"To Provide Decent, Safe, and Sanitary Housing"

young thugs tried to rob him at gunpoint in front of his home"; that a young Vietnamese woman had a rock with glass in it thrown at her face; and that an assailant put a gun to the head of a three-year-old as he demanded money from the child's father, among other accounts.[147] These negative stories implicated the SFHA for making little progress in improving the integration process five years after HUD criticized the agency. City Supervisor Leland Yee captured San Franciscans' dismay over the problems in the projects: "It's very sad to see [this racial hatred] in a city such as San Francisco, which prides itself on diversity and tolerance for others."[148] The SFHA's failure to find solutions to the persistent problem of integrating some of its projects further damaged its own compromised public image and undermined the city's as well.

Against the background of failed integration, Mayor Jordan and the Housing Commission approved the hire of Felipe Floresca to replace Gilmore as executive director in 1994. Tenants claimed that Mayor Jordan had promised that an African American would fill the vacant post. Instead Floresca, a Filipino American who grew up in New York City public housing, took the $120,000 position with the goal of turning San Francisco's public housing complexes "into active parts of their neighborhoods rather than segregated enclaves or no zones."[149] Eleven months later, the mayor's initial endorsement had changed to criticism and Floresca, in danger of being fired, resigned.

The practice of making political appointments in the SFHA came to an abrupt halt in 1996 when Mayor Willie Brown and the Housing Commission recognized that the agency's "bureaucratic incompetence" would be overcome only with a complete overhaul and ceded control of the city's public housing portfolio to HUD.[150] According to HUD, the Housing Authority's incompetent management had "forced tenants to live in housing that was not 'decent, safe, or sanitary.'"[151] The SFHA's management errors also threatened to jeopardize tens of millions of dollars in federal grants. HUD Secretary Henry Cisneros vowed that his agency would operate the SFHA and manage the city's projects, housing 30,000 people until he determined the Housing Authority could do the job itself. The extent of the SFHA's problems emerged a few months later when a HUD report landed the SFHA on HUD's troubled list again, jeopardizing its funding eligibility.[152] Federal funds were critical for tenants living in neglected units with conditions that received another grade of "F." The federal official in charge of the report, Kevin Marchman, chastised the Housing Authority for not improving the city's projects with the $90 million in federal funds allocated to the agency between 1991 and 1996.[153] HUD finally seemed to realize the depth of the SFHA's mismanagement, which "tenants had been complaining about for years." A year into the federal takeover, however, tenants reported little improvement in their living environments. HUD officials blamed their lack of progress on the fact that the SFHA "was broke."[154]

At the end of 1997, the SFHA aimed to make a new start. The agency resumed control of its operations with seven new commissioners appointed by Mayor Willie Brown and with Ronnie Davis, the acting executive director brought in from the Cleveland Housing Authority by HUD as a consultant, at the helm. Davis quickly won the approval of tenants by promising to prioritize their needs. In 1997, Davis described his management philosophy: "I'm not here to play politics. I'm here to empower the tenants, the residents of public housing."[155] The Housing Authority, thrilled at his popularity with tenants and employees, asked Davis to stay on when it regained management over the city's projects later that year. Within three years, the SFHA praised Ronnie Davis for cleaning up San Francisco's worst projects and redeeming "the agency's tarnished image."[156] During his tenure, the SFHA moved off of HUD's troubled list, jump-started renovations, and earned a score of 95 out of 100 on HUD's review. The SFHA rewarded Davis with a new contract classifying him as a city employee (rather than as a consultant) and offering him a $188,000 annual salary plus a $12,000 signing bonus, a car, six weeks' paid vacation, and other benefits, making him one of the highest-paid officials in city government.[157]

Even as Davis raised review scores and won the approval of some tenants by visiting public housing projects and listening to tenants' complaints, he was not able to stop the spreading corruption at the Housing Authority or the investigation into allegations against him. In 1999, a federal grand jury indicted the SFHA's relocation manager, Patricia Williams, and her assistant, Yolanda Jones, along with twenty other employees on bribery charges. Capitalizing on the perpetual shortage of affordable housing in San Francisco, a city with one of the highest rental rates in the country, Williams and other employees solicited bribes as high as $25,000 from public housing residents displaced by redevelopment of their run-down projects between 1996 and 1998. In exchange, the staff placed tenants in other housing projects in the city or gave out coveted Section 8 vouchers.[158] Williams was found guilty of thirty counts of bribery and conspiracy in 2000.

According to a HUD audit that same year, corruption in the agency was not limited to midlevel employees. Federal authorities lambasted Ronnie Davis's financial practices, decrying the director's "$11 million in questionable spending at his former job in Cleveland." The report warned that Davis's role as executive director of the SFHA "continues HUD's exposure to additional loss of funds." A separate audit of the SFHA released a few days later supported HUD's concern. The audit charged the agency with squandering hundreds of thousands of dollars by "handing out contracts without proper bidding and paying excessive salaries to managers."[159] The SFHA's punishment came in December 2000, when HUD withheld $20 million in special grants for renovating public housing. An Ohio grand jury indicted Davis in March 2001, charging him "with stealing hundreds of thousands of dollars in public money during his tenure at the Cleveland Housing Authority."[160] The public failures of the SFHA continued.

Amid the corruption and scandals, the SFHA worked to improve public housing and its own reputation as landlord in the 1990s. While Davis was still at the helm, the SFHA applied for federal funds through the new HOPE VI (Housing Opportunities for People Everywhere) grant program. In applying for and administering HOPE VI funds, the SFHA returned to its early definition of and focus on "community." The HOPE VI program, according to urban design and planning scholar Lawrence Vale, was HUD's "most ambitious comprehensive redevelopment program yet undertaken."[161] HUD created the program in 1992 with the goal of improving some of the worst public housing projects in the country by redeveloping public housing into mixed-income developments and thus deconcentrating poverty.[162] HOPE VI was a competitive grant program under which Public Housing Authorities (PHAs) could apply to HUD for up to $50 million to redevelop or demolish up to 500 "severely distressed" public housing units. As stipulated by HUD, HOPE VI grantees would leverage additional public and private funds to redevelop public housing into garden-style apartments or town houses that "blended in" with the surrounding community and housed residents with mixed incomes. Local housing authorities awarded HOPE VI money were required to use 15 percent of the grant for community and supportive services "to increase opportunities for resident employment and self-sufficiency."[163]

Beyond these requirements, HUD did not stipulate a set of formal guidelines for the HOPE VI program. As a result, the initiative has been criticized for "a lack of clear standards [and] a lack of hard data on program results."[164] Because of the program's loose structure, local housing authorities have had extensive flexibility in deciding which housing projects merit HOPE VI funding, in relocating tenants, and in determining the criteria for tenant eligibility in redeveloped HOPE VI projects. By failing to require a one-for-one replacement of low-income units, the HOPE VI program has reduced the nation's supply of public housing at a time when low-income families are already facing a dramatic shortage of affordable housing in the United States.[165] Although the HOPE VI program has received much attention and praise from cities, PHAs, and some returning residents, its long-term effect on public housing and tenants remains inconclusive.[166] However, many supporters and critics agree today that deconcentrating poverty and building housing that melds architecturally with the surrounding neighborhood are positive steps in improving the public housing program.

During the 1990s, San Francisco won five HOPE VI grants totaling $118.6 million to revitalize five public housing projects.[167] Leveraging an additional $188.2 million in public and private funds, the SFHA once again set out to rehabilitate public housing and its own reputation, this time by redeveloping Hayes Valley and Plaza East in the Western Addition, Bernal Dwellings and Valencia Gardens in the Mission District, and North Beach Place in North Beach.[168] Although the SFHA applied for funds to refurbish Valencia Gardens and North Beach Place, the agency ultimately decided to demolish and rebuild all five projects, forcing thousands of tenants to relocate. Eligible tenants wanting to return to the three completed HOPE VI projects—Bernal Dwellings, Plaza East, and Hayes Valley—had to wait more than three years.

"To Provide Decent, Safe, and Sanitary Housing"

Returning residents found transformed buildings and altered communities. Hayes Valley, fully occupied by 1999, provided private open space, electronic security systems in each unit, and windows facing the street. In 2001, residents moved into the new Bernal Dwellings, reconstructed as neo-Victorian townhouses and flats with two new private streets, a child-care center, and a 3,000-square-foot business incubator facility. A few months later, Plaza East opened, demonstrating design features similar to those of the other two projects, with windows facing the street, individual front doors with sidewalks, washers and dryers in each unit, and a community room. The SFHA promised similar amenities and design features at North Beach Place and Valencia Gardens. With much fanfare, Mayor Willie Brown and the press attended the opening ceremonies for the developments, praising the SFHA for revitalizing public housing and stylistically connecting the buildings to the surrounding areas. Speaking at Bernal Dwellings, Mayor Brown assured the crowd, "No one's going to be able to tag them for living in public housing."[169] Returning resident Kimberly Coleman-Curry expressed gratitude, saying, "I feel really blessed. This is like when you win the sweepstakes, you know, when they come to your door?"[170] Lyria Decuire, moving back to Plaza East, rejoiced as well: "There's no comparison to the way it was." At the Plaza East opening, SFHA employee Juan Monsanto confirmed the agency's return to its early ideal of "community" and emphasis on the environment's ability to foster "good citizens": "We are making better homes and building up the community."[171]

For all the program's rhetoric about improving public housing by creating "communities," the HOPE VI initiative has displaced existing communities and decreased the number of affordable housing units in the United States. With over 14,000 families on the SFHA waiting list in the late 1990s, the reduction of the low-rent housing supply in San Francisco was, as scholar–activist Chester Hartman phrased it, "more than a little disturbing."[172] When the last of the five projects opened in 2006, San Francisco had redeveloped its way to a net loss of around 230 units.[173] Even though the overall loss of units was low compared with that experienced in some other cities, the SFHA worked hard to focus attention on "bedrooms rather than units." Redevelopment yielded

39

larger units—that is, more bedrooms per unit—in an effort to respond to residents' needs, and ultimately the SFHA increased the number of bedrooms available to qualified public housing applicants while decreasing units.[174] As San Francisco's vacancy rates hovered around 1 percent in 1998, with "rents skyrocketing, where even the wealthy must overbid for housing," the HOPE VI program threatened to increase the exodus of low-income families out of the city even as it improved the living environment for new and returning residents.[175]

Residents pushed out of public housing undergoing redevelopment were particularly vulnerable. The SFHA did offer relocation options for public housing tenants living in designated HOPE VI projects. Tenants could take a voucher and find housing in the private market, they could move into another public housing project, or they could make their own arrangements. Prior to making relocation plans, the SFHA alerted residents that those taking Section 8 vouchers or moving into a renovated HOPE VI project would not be allowed to return to their public housing communities. San Francisco's constricted rental market forced many residents opting for Section 8 vouchers out of the city. Private landlords turned away low-income tenants with vouchers as middle-class renters competed for apartments.[176] Critics, including a number of African American public housing tenants, accused the SFHA of swelling the black out-migration trend. According to Chester Hartman, a substantial number of former public housing families displaced by HOPE VI left the city because they could not find relocation housing locally:

> Thirty percent of the families displaced from Bernal Dwellings left the city, as did over a third of those displaced from the Hayes Valley project. And since about half of all families in San Francisco public housing are African American, such displacement has been a major factor in reducing the city's black population—San Francisco is one of the very few major U.S. cities with a declining black population—and an increasing neighborhood racial concentration as well.[177]

Hunters View residents protested black out-migration and gathered more than 190 signatures (representing three-quarters of the families in the development) to oppose the SFHA's application for HOPE VI funds to redevelop their project. Nonetheless, the SFHA submitted its fourth application for a HOPE VI grant to redevelop Hunters View in 2001. And HUD once again rejected the SFHA's application for the competitive funds.[178]

When public housing sites did receive funding for redevelopment, the ensuing relocations often deeply disrupted the lives of residents and particularly affected tenants who were eligible and eager to return to their public housing homes. Tenants with good rent histories and without criminal records had "first dibs" on the new units.[179] Delays stretched out the redevelopment process for several years at Hayes Valley, Bernal Dwellings, and Plaza East. Kimberly Coleman-Curry's enthusiasm about her new townhouse at Bernal no doubt partly came from knowing she was finally settled. For four years, Coleman-Curry and her daughter had "drifted from one apartment to the next, waiting for the city's housing authority to replace the torn-down tower and let her move back."[180]

The HOPE VI program, with its focus on providing housing for "upstanding tenants," has returned public housing to its original emphasis on "morality." Under the model, PHAs allow "deserving" tenants who have a good rent history to return to a redeveloped project where they can "learn" from higher-income neighbors who "serve as positive role models for low-income residents." Supporters of mixed-income communities argue that "proximity to higher income households is supposed to 'reduce the social pathology caused by the concentration' of poverty suffered by public housing residents."[181] In promoting the program, HUD has adopted—and the SFHA has reestablished—an emphasis on building public housing communities designed to model and "train" low-income tenants in the "appropriate" ways of living. The reliance on public–private partnerships to fund, build, and manage public housing in San Francisco has meant that low-income tenants looking to live in redeveloped HOPE VI sites are subject to HUD income limits, "background checks, credit checks, and home visits," as well as a competitive selection process by which reportedly only one of every four applicants is accepted.[182] At the beginning of the twenty-first century, it was private companies, rather than the SFHA, who were operating as property managers and thus helping make decisions about who deserved to live in public housing and who upheld residency requirements. By redesigning public housing projects to fit the look of the surrounding area, and by bringing in a new set of tenants into spaces once occupied by low-income public housing residents, HUD and the SFHA can make a claim for increasing community ties between residents and improving relationships between tenants and neighbors living near the projects.[183]

HUD and the SFHA's assumptions in promoting HOPE VI as the path to creating communities ignore the critical fact that low-income residents living in public housing projects have already formed important bonds over time. The following chapters examine community formation at three public housing projects in San Francisco: Valencia Gardens, Ping Yuen, and North Beach Place. Located in bustling urban districts with easy access to public transportation, shopping, hospitals, and parks, these public housing projects offered residents easily accessible amenities, a critical factor in resident satisfaction. The convenient locations, widely praised architectural designs, and diverse tenant populations differentiate these public housing developments from popular stereotypes and scholarly accounts of public housing as high-rise failures located in run-down center cities or in isolated outlying areas. Although these elements merit and receive attention here, both for their historical importance and as markers of the SFHA's early ideals in planning communities, tenants' interactions with each other, with the surrounding neighborhood, with social service organizations, and with the state ultimately reveal the complexities of community dynamics in public housing.

Examining these relationships demonstrates the ways tenants at Valencia Gardens, Ping Yuen, and North Beach Place have negotiated racial and ethnic differences, crime, maintenance problems, and the failings of the SFHA to support community formations within public housing. Through the formal networks of tenants' associations, as well as more informal ties, residents at these projects have navigated both similar problems related to living in San Francisco public housing and specific difficulties associated with their individual developments and neighborhoods. The culture, context, and community formation in these three projects gave rise to varying forms of tenant activism. From forming deep relationships as neighbors, friends, and at times activist allies to multicultural tenant alliances and cross-sector coalitions, tenants challenged the SFHA's policies and practices and worked

"To Provide Decent, Safe, and Sanitary Housing"

for change. These tenants defined their own communities and civic engagement strategies and in doing so redefined public housing in San Francisco. Located in the very areas pro-growth leaders and the SFHA would later describe as lucrative redevelopment zones and as key gateways to the city's tourist industry, these public housing projects and their tenants have survived, at times thrived, and in many ways reshaped the tenants who live there, the surrounding neighborhoods, and in some cases the SFHA itself.

TWO

The Contested Mission of Valencia Gardens

> One of the things I have always loved about being in here was that we care for each other. Sure you have those who don't want to fall in with anyone else. That is the way it is anywhere. Otherwise, we care about each other.
>
> —Gabrielle Fontanella, Valencia Gardens resident, 2003

ON MAY 6, 1940, MORE THAN 500 RESIDENTS AND BUSINESS owners from the Greater Mission District in San Francisco stormed the city's Board of Supervisors meeting. Exercising their "high privilege of assembly and petition," and lauded as an exemplar of engaged citizenship by the local press, the business and homeowners protested what they viewed as an assault on their neighborhood: public housing in the Mission.[1] The Housing Authority Commission's proposal to construct two public housing developments in the Greater Mission District, they argued, would deprive the area of tax revenue (because the developments were exempt) and misrepresent the neighborhood as one riddled with problems.[2] With only one public housing project completed, the two-year-old San Francisco Housing Authority faced vocal opposition.

The participants rallied around I. S. McCulloch, spokesperson for the Mission Street Property Owners and Merchants Association, as he put forth his group's demand to keep public housing out of the Mission District. The group's repeated catcalls and cheers forced the chairman to call in five police officers to maintain order.[3] Five days earlier, McCulloch and 150 supporters had attended a Housing Authority Commission hearing where they had verbally attacked the commissioners for their alleged secrecy in site selection and for "putting the stigma of 'slum area' on the Greater Mission District."[4] Fearful that the Housing Authority would overlook their concerns, opponents called on the city's Board of Supervisors to stop the housing commissioners from moving forward with their plans to construct public housing projects on the Valencia Street and Cogswell School sites. Their message was clear: public housing did not belong in their neighborhood.[5]

As residents and business owners in San Francisco's oldest neighborhood, opponents of the Valencia and Cogswell sites spoke proudly of the Mission District, evoking a rich history while appearing to ignore its growing problems. Rather than housing low-income residents, opponents argued, the site should continue to be zoned for commercial use; new businesses would positively affect the mixed-use district.[6] First as the location of Woodward Gardens, San Francisco's most popular amusement park from 1866 to 1894, and later, from 1907 to 1931, as the site of the Pacific Coast League's San Francisco Seals stadium, the five-acre plot of land on Valencia Street between Fourteenth and Fifteenth Streets sparked pleasant memories for Mission inhabitants and other residents across the city.[7]

For many Mission residents, the public housing plan posed a threat to the bonds of community and way of life that had solidified during the interwar years. Home to the first Spanish Mission settlement in 1776, the flat, sunny district was one of the few areas spared by the fires that followed the 1906 earthquake.[8] As foreign immigration slowed during World War I and again in the late 1920s, the Mission District became "chiefly an area of secondary ethnic settlement, a place to establish familial roots after immigrants had already arrived in the city."[9] Primarily a blue-collar neighborhood for European ethnic groups from Ireland, Germany, Italy, and Scandinavia, and also home to some of the city and state's political elite until the early 1930s, the district was stable during the interwar years and produced a close, localized community with its own accent, called "Mish."[10] Longtime resident Geraldine Fregoso recalled that the "neighborhood was our world.... Our church and school were only a few blocks away and nearby Mission Street offered complete shopping and entertainment.... There was an overpowering sense of continuity."[11] This sense of a strong local community buttressed the opposition as Mission neighbors squared off against supporters in the public housing debate.

By May 1940, the opposition seemed to have the upper hand. Taking the floor at the Board of Supervisors meeting, McCulloch outlined the chief arguments against public housing: decreased property values and compromised child safety. He began by warning the board

The Contested Mission of Valencia Gardens

that the construction of the two developments "would bring tremendous reduction in property values in the Mission District.... The drop has already begun.... One apartment house across the street from the Valencia site was built at the cost of $160,000 and has been bringing its owner a return of over 12 percent per year. Today we couldn't get a speculator to bid $65,000."[12] He tempered the group's economic argument with concerns about child safety. The locations, he argued, were unsafe for children. Valencia Street, long a major transportation route as the first graded street in the district, later part of the cable car line, and then as an automobile route, was no place to house children.[13] Citing statistics showing that 44 percent of all accidents involving children under twelve years of age in the city occurred in the Mission District, McCulloch questioned the logic of developing public housing for families with children in the Mission. "Why, in the name of common sense," he continued, "should we even think of exposing children to needless slaughter by placing them in a housing project between two of the most dangerous and fastest traveled vehicular arteries in the Mission District?"[14] After laying out his evidence, McCulloch reminded the board that more than 3,000 merchants, property owners, and residents near the sites had signed petitions against the developments. The proponents of public housing, he charged, cheated on their own petition, collecting some of its 2,000 signatures from minors and persons living outside the Mission District.[15] These accusations reflected the level of contention over public housing development in the area. As the turbulent meeting drew to a close, the Board of Supervisors voted 7–4 to ask the Housing Authority to "respectfully desist in plans" for the two public housing projects.[16] However, the SFHA housing commissioners had the final say.

While opponents celebrated their victory with the Board of Supervisors, proponents continued gathering support for public housing, with its promise of slum clearance and affordable housing for working families. Groups as diverse as the Bay Area Agricultural Workers, the Negro Civic Council, the League of Women Shoppers, the Congress of Industrial Organizations Council, the Women's Christian Temperance Union, Associated Jewish Charities, and others—many with an organizational scope beyond the Mission—appeared at the Housing

Commission meetings to support public housing in the district.[17] Individuals without organizational affiliation also offered encouragement. Ruth Kraucer, a resident in the Mission, challenged the economic interests of groups opposing public housing in a letter supporting Housing Commission Chairman Marshall Dill's "courage":

> While I am among the more fortunate of the Mission's residents, my frequent walks about the district bring to my attention habitations that are a fire menace and a disgrace to the so-called American standards of living. . . . That anyone for venal profit, should wish to condemn his fellow human beings to such conditions is past my understanding. Their economic arguments, all facts considered, seem to me to be points ill taken.[18]

Chairman Dill, in response to the uproar over proposed public housing sites in the Mission, called a secret emergency Housing Commission meeting on May 21, 1940, preempting the regularly scheduled bimonthly meeting that was open to the press and the public. In a 3–2 vote, the housing commissioners rejected the Board of Supervisors' request to reconsider the selection of the Valencia and Cogswell sites.[19] Marshaling evidence from the 1939 Real Property Survey showing an increase in low-income, "dilapidated," and "substandard" residential areas in the Mission District during the 1930s, and fearing the loss of federal funds for public housing development, the Housing Authority moved forward with its plans.[20] Opponents met the Commission's decision with cries of "secrecy" and "un-American activity," a protest rally, and a resolution voted on by 600 Mission business owners and residents demanding Chairman Dill's resignation.[21] Dill kept his job, and despite controversy over the sites, the SFHA rapidly moved ahead with the Valencia Street development. Construction on the Cogswell site, later developed as the Bernal Dwellings public housing project, was delayed until after the war.[22]

The history of Valencia Gardens reflects recurring national themes in public housing. Many attributes of Valencia Gardens correlate with the well-told declension narrative of public housing: contestation over the placement of public housing in the Mission, early years of relative stability and security for residents, followed by decades of decline fueled by federal funding cuts, decreased rent payments, deferred maintenance, and rising crime in the urban core. In San Francisco, leadership and management missteps within the SFHA contributed further to the challenges in public housing. A closer examination, however, offers new insights that destabilize popular perceptions of public housing by focusing on tenants' lived experiences, community formation, and activism. Teasing out the overlapping sets of relationships among tenants within Valencia Gardens (and in chapters 3 and 4, among tenants within Ping Yuen and North Beach Place), as well as between tenants and the surrounding district and between tenants and the SFHA, illuminates a range of community engagement strategies forged in particular places by particular people in response to shifting public housing policy and SFHA practices over time. These efforts, different and diffuse, amplify a wide range of low-income citizens' civic engagement and complicate perceptions of public housing in the United States.

In contrast to racially homogenous projects that sprang up across the United States and in San Francisco, by the 1950s, Valencia Gardens housed racially and ethnically diverse tenants within an increasingly Latino/a neighborhood. While institutional racism and failed integration strategies plagued the SFHA through the 1980s and 1990s, Valencia Gardens residents forged cross-racial, cross-ethnic relationships to cope with an increasingly difficult living environment. The diversity of residents in the development became an important marker of community pride as tenants faced sporadic crime waves, unruly neighbors inside and outside the development, SFHA neglect, and the scorn of many district residents. Amid the hardships of an environment that was at times hostile, and in buildings that deteriorated over time, tenants created a community separate from the surrounding neighborhood and made Valencia Gardens their home. Racial and ethnic diversity, pride in and a shared love of the public sculptures within the housing project, and a diverse set of relationships and networks all served as critical elements in community building and the basis for what I will call "affective activism." Whereas tenants at Ping Yuen and North Beach organized formal tenants associations earlier and challenged the SFHA openly in numerous ways, Valencia Gardens residents relied on a more fluid, relational approach to creating change in public housing. This affective activism—activism focused on intentional relationships and community building to fortify participants in the face of shared challenges—further separated Valencia Gardens tenants from the Mission, though the Mission itself was (ironically) starting to be viewed as a hotbed for grassroots activism in response to urban renewal and later gentrification.

By participating in community building and affective activism and seizing "psychological ownership" of their apartments, Valencia Gardens residents have redefined as home what the government has labeled as temporary housing and the city has deemed a troubled project.[23] Claiming a sense of ownership of public housing, Valencia Gardens' low-income tenants have forged a community that turns the SFHA's early ideal of public housing on its head and demonstrates that affective activism is a form of civic engagement that can effect change both individually and institutionally. Through everyday acts of community building, some residents worked to improve the quality of life for themselves and others in their development and, in the process, created their own circumscribed community in the pre–HOPE VI Valencia Gardens.

Dignity by Design

When Valencia Gardens opened in 1943, the New York Museum of Modern Art praised the design as "outstanding among urban housing schemes for its 'easy livability' and the logic of its site plan."[24] The development, located in a bustling part of the Mission, near a church, hotel, and numerous businesses and apartments, attempted to uphold the ideal of public housing as decent housing for deserving working families and as an asset to the surrounding community.[25] Perhaps in response to the public debate over the Mission site, Valencia Gardens' architects took great pains to create a comfortable, livable space for residents as well as a development the Mission District would gladly call its own. This challenge fell on the shoulders of Henry A. Thomsen and William W. Wurster, notable architects from two different firms who collaborated on the design for Valencia Gardens.[26]

The SFHA's selection of Thomsen and Wurster signaled to Mission opponents a commitment to innovative, high-quality design. After opening his Berkeley office in 1924, Wurster quickly gained a name for himself in residential design with his attention to the cli-

The Contested Mission of Valencia Gardens

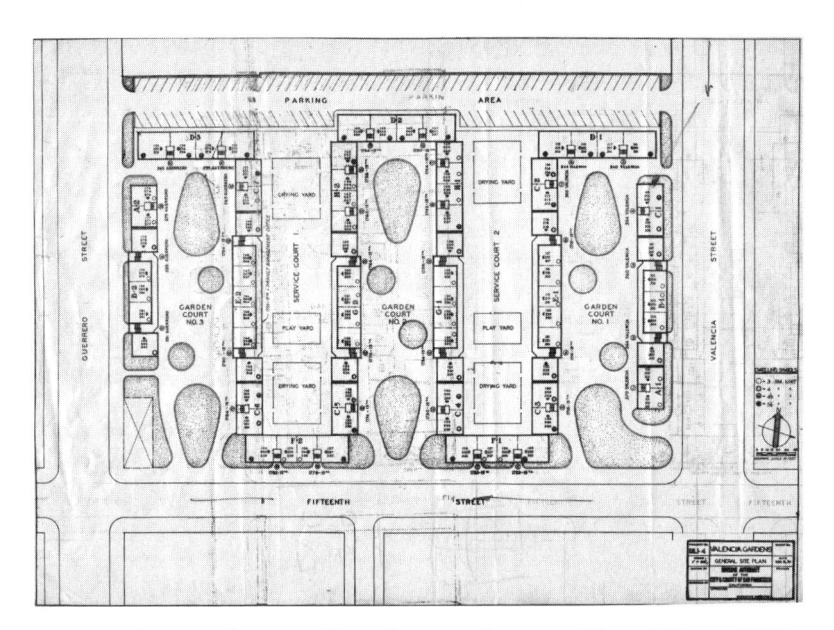

Figure 2. Valencia Gardens General Site Plan, November 1941. William W. Wurster/WBE Collection, Environmental Design Archives, University of California–Berkeley.

mate, properties of the site, technical constraints of building well, and the client's needs.[27] By the mid-1930s, he had firmly established his career, and as Marc Treib notes, "his residential designs had been lauded [and] published, . . . and he was acknowledged as one of the leading architects on the West Coast."[28] It is unclear whether Wurster had a direct interest in public housing in 1939, or if he took the contract because he needed work, or both.[29] Certainly, though, by the time he signed the "Articles of Joint Venture" with Harry Thomsen Jr. for the project in July 1940, his thinking on public housing had been influenced by Catherine Bauer. Bauer was the author of the definitive work *Modern Housing* (1934) and was the leading proponent in the United States of developing "large quantities of high quality, non-profit urban housing, while curtailing sprawl."[30] She had also worked as a city planner and as an advisor on the 1937 Housing Act, and in August of 1940, after a six-month courtship, she and Wurster wed.[31] Drawing as well on his own experiences designing understated, livable homes, Wurster, with Thomsen's and the SFHA's support, pushed the limits of the

51

Figure 3. Valencia Gardens under construction, April 1942. San Francisco History Center, San Francisco Public Library.

USHA guidelines for public housing in an effort to design buildings that would "stress the dignity of the individual."[32]

Wurster and Thomsen's plans furthered the SFHA's aim to facilitate ties between public housing residents and the surrounding neighborhood and to provide tenants with "more than shelter" by creating a high-quality design focused on individual living. Situated on five acres, the twenty-two linked three-story buildings laid out in a serpentine plan were built of fireproof reinforced concrete. The project provided eight different plan types including 114 one-bedroom units, 102 two-bedroom units, and 30 three-bedroom units. Three "garden" courtyards and two service courts provided social space, fenced-in play areas for children, storage, and clotheslines.[33] Wurster and Thomsen designed each unit with "windows on two facades to allow for cross-ventilation, light from both sides, and a view to both the formal garden and the service area."[34] The vibrant colors of the buildings—terra

Figure 4. Valencia Gardens shortly after construction was completed, December 1942. San Francisco History Center, San Francisco Public Library.

cotta, blue, and yellow—brightened the block and created a cheerful backdrop for residents.[35] Attention to small details, including a "provision for drying underclothes and stockings over the bathtub," lessened the institutional quality of the development.[36] Their efforts to emphasize "the essential humanity" of residents garnered national praise. A writer from the architectural magazine *Pencil Points* noted, "Too many times it has seemed that the designers of low-cost housing—and good housing at that—have forgotten the individual in trying to produce for the mass, to meet governmental requirements. None of this straining at restrictions is evident in the completed Valencia Gardens."[37]

The architects' own description of their work echoes these claims and demonstrates the ways in which the project space replicated the SFHA's early vision of housing "deserving" two-parent families with employed fathers and stay-at-home mothers. Reflecting the white, middle-class gender prescriptions of the day and the SFHA's view of public housing as the training ground for middle-class living, the architects celebrated their creation:

> Each apartment to be entered from a balcony has small wing walls which designate a portion of the balcony as belonging to that apartment. Each living room has a window with a low sill, and a railing for security, so that a mother may look down into the garden, or to see her children, rather than just look across at other apartments. For the same reason we painted portions of the buildings in different colors, so that the immensity might be reduced, and at the same time the whole might be lively and gay. . . . [We] pulled no punches; we always designed each idea or phase as if we, personally, were to live there; or as if it were for our most tony client. We were careful to fix the curtain rods . . . so the curtains could be pushed free of the window to make the best of light and air.[38]

The attention to details at Valencia Gardens resulted in an attractive, modern apartment complex that was intended to improve the area and showcase the possibilities of the new national public housing program.

The architects' modern, livable design also resulted in a plan that to some extent impeded tenant community formation. In their continued effort to avoid the precepts of "mass living," Wurster and Thomsen purposely avoided an emphasis "on the great axis which would only serve to show how small each family was in the sum total. There would be no emphasis on the office or community facilities as architectural motif; they would just be available when wanted."[39] As a result, the management offices and community room were located in a remote part of the project—inconspicuous to visitors and public housing residents. This design decision in some ways discouraged tenant exchange and community building within public housing. Within three years, under Executive Director John Beard's leadership, the SFHA discouraged the inclusion of community rooms within public housing projects. Nonetheless, in the community room, the laundry, and even in the manager's office, tenants at Valencia Gardens found spaces—however decentralized—to interact and forge relationships with public housing neighbors.[40]

The courtyards also aided these interactions and reflected the SFHA's early goals of fostering bonds between residents and the surrounding neighborhood as well as the architects' effort to provide some communal space. With a keen consideration of San Francisco's cold northerly wind, the architects engineered the building blocks to enclose three southern-facing courtyards and two service courts.[41] Thomas Church, a regionally known landscape architect, designed the three courtyards and planned them as social and play areas with raised planting beds supported by brick walls that functioned as seating. Eucalyptus, boxwood, and prostrate juniper were planted along with grass, creating a spacious landscaped area designed "to give the feeling of a small neighborhood."[42] Forgoing fencing or a perimeter wall, the architects allowed the courtyards to open directly onto the busy sidewalk of Valencia Street, connecting residents with people and activities of the street and surrounding community.[43] The architects suggested that the SFHA place sculptures in the garden courts to enhance the space and possibly draw in visitors.[44]

Following the architects' recommendation, the SFHA secured outdoor art to display at Valencia Gardens in 1945. Within each of the three courtyards, whimsical sculptures of animals by Beniamino Bufano, an internationally acclaimed artist, were installed. Bufano, an Italian immigrant, had adopted San Francisco as his home in 1924 and began a forty-six-year love–hate relationship with the city. His grandiose plans for creating enormous statues for the city to display, along with his eccentric lifestyle and outspokenness, provoked interest, ridicule, and even adoration from San Franciscans.[45] Bufano crafted the sculptures placed at Valencia Gardens, along with approximately twelve other pieces, during his tenure on the Works Progress Administration's Federal Art Project (FAP) between 1935 and 1942.[46] These figures, which were perhaps the most "consistently successful of his career," raised the standard for FAP sculptures by showcasing Bufano's "extraordinary ability to marry traditional subjects to modern forms without seriously violating public taste," and by introducing stainless steel, which became a Bufano trademark, to California sculpture.[47] Originally intended for placement at an aquatic theme park in the city, the sculptures were transferred from the FAP to the City of San Francisco when the FAP ended in 1942.[48]

The SFHA, looking to adorn public housing and to bring tenants and district neighbors together, requested thirteen statues from the

Figure 5. Beniamino Bufano's *Bear with Cubs*, Valencia Gardens, 1964. Photograph by Alan J. Canterbury. San Francisco History Center, San Francisco Public Library.

city for display in their developments. Valencia Gardens, SFHA Executive Director John Beard contended, was a worthy site for Bufano's pieces: "Now that the city is apparently seeking a suitable location for the exhibit of the sculpture[s] in order that the public may enjoy [them], I wish to offer Valencia Gardens for this purpose."[49] According to Beard, the statues' placement in the development would allow both the public and tenants an opportunity to enjoy the artwork. The Art Commission, demonstrating confidence in the Housing Authority and ignoring Bufano's request to place the statues in a more prominent public place, agreed to lend the agency the statues. On March 9, 1945,

Figure 6. Beniamino Bufano's *Penguins*, Valencia Gardens, 2003. Photograph by the author.

the Art Commission delivered a cat, a mouse, a cat and mouse together, a pair of seals, penguins, a bear with two cubs, a rabbit, and a frog to Valencia Gardens.[50] Over the next six decades, the Bufanos served as a critical community cohesive as well as a barometer of change at Valencia Gardens, marking later struggles and becoming emblematic of outsiders' perceptions of the public housing project.

The first residents to enjoy the architectural design features—and a few years later the sculptures at Valencia Gardens—were war

Figure 7. Beniamino Bufano's *Cat*, Valencia Gardens, 2003. Photograph by the author.

workers. The SFHA, responding to amendments in the Housing Act and to the 1940 Lanham Act, leased the apartments to some of the 150,000 war workers in the city.[51] In Resolution 306, passed by the San Francisco Housing Commission on August 18, 1942, eligible applicants for the four permanent housing projects included "those families any member of which is engaged in national defense activities," with preference given to those "most in need of housing from the standpoint of national defense: 1. Employees of Bethlehem Shipyard; 2. Civilian Employees of the Army and Navy establishments; 3. Army, Navy, Marine Corps, and Coast Guard personnel. The project will be exclusively occupied by the families and persons engaged in national defense activities."[52] The shift to house national defense workers and military families rather than low-income families arguably pleased some Mission residents who had opposed public housing: patriotic citizens earning higher wages may have seemed less threatening to public housing opponents.

The Contested Mission of Valencia Gardens

The Housing Authority housed these higher-income, noncontroversial tenants for several years after the war ended, reversing its claim to house defense workers only "for the duration of the national emergency."[53] These tenants likely stayed in public housing after the war in hopes of saving money to buy homes or rent apartments in the expensive, contracting Bay Area market. As early as 1946, the housing commissioners began discussing the return of permanent public housing projects to low-income status; they set a start date of May, with the changeover to be completed by August. Two years later, however, the Housing Authority admitted to "still [being] in the process of evicting 'high income families.'"[54] The slow progress elicited a reprimand from the federal government. On May 19, 1949, the secretary of the Housing Commission reported that the Public Housing Administration (PHA) had sent a directive "requiring stepping up removal of high income families from permanent projects so that all ineligible families will have received their 6 months notice to vacate by the end of the year."[55] A later extension by the PHA kept some higher-income tenants in public housing until August 1950. By the end of that month, low-income residents fully occupied Valencia Gardens and other permanent public housing sites.[56]

"Simpler" Days at Valencia Gardens

In the 1950s, residents of Valencia Gardens enjoyed the Bufanos and the benefits of living in an urban location near downtown with public transportation, shopping, entertainment, and hospitals nearby. Built in a bustling mixed-use district with auto repair shops, a hotel, church, mattress factory, cabinet shop, and apartments in the surrounding blocks, and close to the commercial corridor on Mission Street, Valencia Gardens provided convenient city living for low-income families.[57] During this time, residents—mainly made up of selected two-parent families screened by the SFHA—lived in a safe, well-maintained development that had the full support of the agency. An early resident, Deborah Madaris, remembers that Valencia Gardens

> seemed to be the cleanest and best kept [public housing development].... [The unit] was freshly painted, it was spanking brand new, it

> was the perfect little home for a mother.... it was so quiet after a certain time, only during daylight saving time were kids allowed to be outside, and my neighbors were really neighbors because we all watched out for one another.... Things were so simple, and I look now and say how did they get like this?[58]

The sense of nostalgia for the early years at Valencia Gardens was echoed by Gabrielle Fontanella, who lived there from 1958 to 1968 and again from 1972 to 2003:

> I grew up here and as children we were comfortable and safe ... most of the people here were just families without money raising their kids.... I had friends in the back courts as well as the front courts ... no one was suspicious of people back then ... there were just families ... small children all the way up to teenagers, they would watch out for their own brothers and sisters and watch out for the other kids too, because we all played together, it was a lot of fun and I really miss it at times—but that was a different time.[59]

During the first decade, tenants had a positive perception of their public housing project and confidence in the SFHA's ability as landlord.

Rituals and relationships contributed to a strong sense of community among residents living in Valencia Gardens during this time. Pride—in place, in family, and in the nation—was inscribed into daily rituals at Valencia Gardens, some of which were promoted by the SFHA. One lifelong resident explained the experience her mother had as a child in the early 1950s:

> Every day when the office would open up they put the flag up because they were proud because back then this was a nice family-oriented housing project. They were proud. They had joy to be there. Kids back then were not ashamed to say "Oh I live in Valencia Gardens" because you would come by on 15th Street and you would see the pride. You would see the American flag every morning they would put it up.... For a little while my mom said they had not only the American flag but also the Housing Authority flag. It didn't last long for some reason.... It was like an all-American, or what we like to think of as an all-American neighborhood, watching the flag go up each morning.[60]

Residents remembered that in the late 1950s and into the 1960s, the "lawns were impeccably kept," and at night "huge globes" of light

The Contested Mission of Valencia Gardens

would illuminate the project, securing tenants' space.[61] "Cleanliness," "safety," and "neighborliness" defined the living experience for many residents at Valencia Gardens. Diana Baez recounted that in the early years, "we used to sit outside when it was hot and drink wine and watch the kids. . . . The people who lived here were good people. . . . We used to sit down with [our] neighbors, talking, watching our kids like family."[62] Tenants nostalgically remembered the early years as an easier, simpler time.

The Bufano sculptures became an important source of communal pride and cohesion for tenants and helped shape a shared identity. Situated in the courtyards, the sculptures drew residents out, particularly children, giving them a place to meet, talk, and play. Longtime resident Francesca Soto, echoing Bufano's expressed hope that children would enjoy his creations, recollected:

> Children throughout the years have grown pretty fond of this one [the mouse] because as children growing up in the housing development, you're a real kid when you can climb on this thing, that's what separates the little kids from the older ones, when you are old enough or get enough agility to climb up on this thing, once you have made it when you are a kid—you go—Yeah, I made it! I'm not a baby anymore.[63]

Although management rules prohibited playing on the statues, many children over the years made a symbolic climb to adolescence on the Bufanos. Gabrielle Fontanella envied her brother, "who seemed to have suction feet" and could climb on the bear—a challenge with its sharp vertical design: "I was always on the kitty cats or the seals . . . the low things . . . we would pretend things. . . . We never thought of tearing them up or anything. . . . It was ours but it didn't belong to us. It belonged to everybody, so why should we mess it up?"[64] The Bufanos became a rite of passage for children in Valencia Gardens as "all the kids climb[ed] on them."[65] Bufano, who claimed to like children playing on his pieces, seemed to be pleased by the sculptures' use and importance to residents, as suggested by his appearance in a photograph with children in front of the seals at Valencia Gardens.[66]

A combination of factors contributed to the stability of the public housing project and the happiness of the tenants in the early years. Higher rents and federal dollars provided adequate funding for the

The Contested Mission of Valencia Gardens

SFHA to maintain the complex. Stable leadership at the SFHA ensured that funds were used to support the relatively new public housing program in the city. Overall stability in the Mission District also contributed to a positive living experience for residents at Valencia Gardens. As the Mission District became more economically distressed, and as federal public housing policies shifted, however, new challenges emerged for the neighborhood and for public housing tenants.

A Changing Mission

Between the late 1950s and the 1990s, the Mission District underwent major demographic and economic shifts. During this period, Valencia Gardens became increasingly isolated from the surrounding neighborhood at the same time that the public perception of public housing and its residents worsened. Residents at Valencia Gardens experienced declining rent receipts, deferred maintenance, and neighborhood scorn in response to federal policy shifts; disinvestment and management and leadership failures at the SFHA; and successive crime waves during the 1960s through the 1990s in the Mission District. Examining this period demonstrates the complexities of living in public housing, the limits of perceptions and stereotypes, and the ineffectiveness of tidy categories such as insiders-versus-outsiders and us-versus-them in understanding public housing history.

The economic and demographic changes in the Mission District and in Valencia Gardens began in the late 1950s. In the Mission District and elsewhere in the nation, middle-class American-born residents left the city for the suburbs.[67] Immigrants filled the vacancies left behind in the urban core, settling into older neighborhoods struggling with economic decline in San Francisco.[68] The Mission District's racial and socioeconomic demographics shifted with the influx of Latin and Central American immigrants in the 1950s and of Mexicans, Puerto Ricans, Cubans, South Americans, Filipinos, Samoans, and American Indians in the 1960s and 1970s, as more low-income families moved into older housing stock in the neighborhood.[69] Between 1930 and 1970, the Latino/a population in the Mission District increased markedly, rising 45 percent by 1970 even as the U.S. census showed a 17 percent decline in the city's total Latino/a population.[70] Likewise, the area "saw an influx of artisans, bohemians, students, and other counter-culture types" who also rented older buildings in the neighborhood.[71] These new Mission residents, many of whom were renters, faced challenges as absentee and low-income owners deferred maintenance and upgrades on older structures.[72]

With the neighborhood housing more Latino/as over time, the Mission District embraced a Latino cultural identification. Cafés, bars, cinemas, and grocers in the Mission provided a range of products and entertainment catering to a diverse Latino/a population. As the Chicano (Mexican American) and civil rights movements took hold in the 1960s, muralists in the Mission District, inspired by indigenous heritage and traditions of using art to address political and social issues, began collaborating on murals.[73] Many Latino/a artists "made the Mission their canvas," using art "to remake the world a beautiful place for ourselves" and deepening the district's Latino identification and pride.[74]

Dynamic, vibrant, and in flux, the Mission District was also, in sociologist Manuel Castells's words, the *Barrio* (the Latino ghetto), with family income below the city's average and public services that were inferior to those available elsewhere in San Francisco.[75] Poverty, overcrowding, crime, and drugs affected the district just as they did in other economically vulnerable neighborhoods across America. Aware of the national and local trend for cities to use federal urban renewal funds to redevelop distressed communities—and often displace poor and working class individuals in the process—Mission residents banded together to improve and protect their neighborhood. Spurring the alarm was the record of the San Francisco Redevelopment Agency (SFRA): in the late 1950s and early 1960s, more than 4,000 low-income African American and Asian American families living in the Western Addition were displaced for new development.[76] In response to growing concerns about urban renewal, in 1966 Mission-based organizations formed an "Alinsky-style community movement," the Mission Council on Redevelopment (MCOR)—which later became the Mission Coalition Organization (MCO)— to take a proactive stance on redevelopment in the district. In contrast to the long-standing narrative that this group fought against the urban renewal bulldozers, historian Ocean Howell shows that MCOR's original position was in support of the SFRA's plan that included rehabilitating buildings. Urban renewal

63

held out the hope of mitigating real estate speculation that would come with the opening of the Bay Area Rapid Transit (BART) stop in the Mission.[77] Eventually, MCOR activated its grassroots base to successfully oppose the redevelopment proposal when its demand to have full veto power over any aspect of the plan was not met. With over 12,000 members from 100 grassroots organizations participating at the peak of MCO's work in 1970, the neighborhood staved off the SFRA's urban renewal plans for the Mission, albeit reluctantly. Before it disbanded in 1973, MCO had placed hundreds of people in jobs, supported education reforms, and worked with dozens of tenant associations in the neighborhood to win improvements and rent decreases.[78]

The Latino cultural identification and grassroots community-based activism that shaped the Mission District seemed to have little impact on tenants at Valencia Gardens, where residents experienced demographic and economic shifts in a different way. At Valencia Gardens, the number of racially and ethnically diverse tenants increased over time in response to the U.S. Supreme Court's decision in the 1954 *Banks v. The Housing Authority of San Francisco* ruling to outlaw segregation in the city's public housing projects. Likewise, within a decade and a half, lower-income tenants, including single-parent families, gradually began moving into Valencia Gardens, as federal laws shifted to make public housing the domain of even poorer families. Decreased federal funding for public housing, combined with lower rental revenues from poorer tenants, resulted in deferred maintenance and fewer resources for public housing residents in the 1960s. Valencia Gardens, just as detractors in the 1940s had feared, was viewed by some district residents as causing a "decline" in the Mission. Longtime Mission residents complained about the changes in their neighborhood, expressing "fear of industrial encroachment, fear of crowded conditions, and fear that the historic neighborhood was losing its character."[79] Over time, Valencia Gardens became a target for many district residents, who blamed the changes in the neighborhood on public housing.

By 1969, Mission and Valencia Gardens residents complained about a growing shared concern about their district: gang violence. Operating along Mission Street, gangs harassed business owners and threatened customers, causing a marked decline in revenue. One prominent gang, estimated at twenty to thirty members between the ages of seventeen and twenty-two, allegedly stole from stores, hassled salespeople, and threw bottles at children walking home from school. Witnesses generally kept silent, fearing retribution. Many business owners and residents agreed that Mission Street—the main artery of the district—had "gone to hell."[80]

Gang violence continued as the Mission District's troubles increased in the 1970s. Residents of the beleaguered district, stressed by internal problems and outside criticism, looked for a scapegoat to blame. Some white critics pointed the finger first to the influx of Latino/as in the area and then to Valencia Gardens residents. Onlookers began to equate the economic difficulties of the district with demographic shifts, as Latino/as came to constitute almost half of the area's 51,000 residents by 1970. Andres Malcolm, writing for the *New York Times*, chronicled the decline of the neighborhood. He described the area's problems, noting that

> a higher unemployment rate developed among these unskilled workers. Street crime grew. Many buildings were aging. Fashionable stores gave way to thrift shops. The crowded streets were torn up for construction of a new transit system. Vandalism mounted. Sears blacked over its street level display windows. And many marginal businesses closed.[81]

One longtime Mission business owner, Tom Mayer, recalled that in the Mission District circa 1976, "there were a lot of arson fires in rundown buildings, a lot of anxiety about housing issues and displacement.... The problem was alcohol and certain kinds of drugs . . . a feeling that it was a very run down, very cheap, very bohemian place."[82]

The status of Valencia Gardens as a public housing project contributed to its emergence in the 1970s as what I term an "anti–public space." These spaces, as I define them, are ones Americans of all races, ethnicities, and socioeconomic circumstances fear as dangerous and avoid if at all possible. Unlike public spaces that function to bring people together and forge a sense of connection with a place and/or community, such as well-planned parks, anti–public spaces are isolated, ignored, and avoided. Amid the challenges facing the distressed urban neighborhood, Valencia Gardens became a symbol for the Mission's pressing problems and, over time, a repository of the surrounding community's blame for the district's problems. The national decline in public housing, along with media coverage depicting deteriorating conditions, criminal activity, and violence, shaped perceptions of Valencia Gardens and led many San Franciscans to view it as an anti–public space. Increasingly, the physical decay of the space as well as negative assumptions about public housing tenants contributed to the cognitive mapping of Valencia Gardens as a place to avoid.[83] Rather than welcoming nonresidents in to admire the Bufanos, Valencia Gardens as an anti–public space, repelled neighbors and visitors to the Mission. For residents, specific parts of Valencia Gardens became anti-public space, once criminals began repurposing stairwells and common spaces for illicit business. As nonresidents went out of their way to avoid the area in and around Valencia Gardens, criminals further seized on the public housing project for their own ends, fueling stigmatization from outsiders and tenants' fear.

The location and design contributed to the growing problems at Valencia Gardens. The development abutted Valencia Street, a busy thoroughfare where a large proportion of crime, gang violence, and drug dealing took place. Furthermore, the design of the project worked against the Housing Authority and architects' initial intent of promoting good ties between residents and the surrounding neighborhood, instead aiding criminals who used the open courtyard construction as a cut-through, its hallways and stairwells as hiding places and dealing locations, and service courts as escape routes from the police. For undercover officers, the project's layout made their job more difficult; as one remarked, "It's like chasing rats into Swiss cheese."[84] Mission business owner Tom Mayer explained that the "relationship with Valencia Gardens was uneasy because there was a perception that people dealing drugs or creating problems in the neighborhood . . . were pulling things and disappearing into Valencia Gardens." This caused the neighborhood's attitude to sour in the 1970s; neighbors began to "feel no recourse or hope for [Valencia Gardens] except to raze it or rehabilitate it."[85] With an unknown number of drug dealers inside the project and many working out of houses around the development and on the streets nearby, Valencia Gardens was marked as an anti–public space where tenants were left to cope with an intensely unpredictable living environment.

The Contested Mission of Valencia Gardens

The tensions between perceptions of public housing and the realities of tenants' lived experiences were amplified in the 1980s and 1990s. Valencia Gardens became increasingly unsafe and rundown as the SFHA dealt with decreased federal funding and, increasingly, leadership and staffing troubles. At the same time, many tenants there continued to invest time in the relationships and the public housing community, directing blame at neighbors and visitors for perpetuating criminal activity there. In reality, troublemakers lived both inside and outside Valencia Gardens; blanket stereotyping of all tenants elides the messy and fluid lines between insiders and outsiders, public housing tenants and non–public housing tenants, individual actions and community concerns. By the 1980s, the police, city officials, and some Mission District residents labeled Valencia Gardens as a dangerous den overrun by drug dealers. The popularity and increase in sales of crack cocaine expanded the drug trade in San Francisco and other cities. Journalist Susan Ward described drug trafficking in housing projects across the city as "occurring so openly and freely that police and the Housing Authority officials admit they do not have a handle on it."[86] Valencia Gardens, along with Bernal Dwellings, Hayes Valley, and Sunnydale, had severe problems. With drug dealers visible at Valencia Gardens "in the autumn sunshine—offering Angel Dust for sale" and threatening to kill tenants who refused to let dealers work out of their apartments, many families "cower[ed] in fear in their apartments, fearing for their safety."[87] Other residents, fed up with the dealing and related shootings, vandalism, and burglaries, complained to the Housing Authority and police—but they did so anonymously, fearing reprisals. At a meeting with housing officials in October 1985, over thirty tenants from Valencia Gardens, refusing to give their names, told stories of "junkies shooting up in the hallways and basements, around the clock drug dealing and too few police to stop it."[88] They acknowledged the crime and deterioration of Valencia Gardens while at the same time asking for help to improve their community.

The police and the Housing Authority, ignoring tenants' concern about retaliation, responded by asking them to become the cops' "eyes and ears" at Valencia Gardens. Even as residents sought help from the city, they expressed skepticism that the city would make "any difference in their lives in the crime-ridden project."[89] Over the next four years, the police arrested a drug ring operating out of Bernal Heights that had caused trouble at several public housing projects in the city, including Valencia Gardens. While drug trafficking began to decrease slightly in public housing and in the city, Valencia Gardens residents continued to experience gang violence and to confront gang members, some of whom lived in the city's other public housing projects.[90] Reports of drug dealing, gang fighting, and robberies in and around Valencia Gardens contributed to city and district officials' negative perceptions of the development.

Valencia Gardens' reputation as an anti–public space, the national image of public housing as a federal failure, and the publicized failures of the SFHA led San Franciscans, including some public housing applicants, to stereotype residents and their apartments as unsavory and unsafe. Building on this growing national stigma of public housing, spurred by press coverage of the problems at the Robert Taylor Homes and Cabrini Green in Chicago as well as in some San Francisco developments, a number of San Franciscans assumed the worst about Valencia Gardens and its inhabitants. Longtime San Franciscan Merna Escobar remembered fearing the project because of bad press:

> I avoided to come live in the projects because of the condition they were in and what I read about in the papers. I don't care how pretty they were in terms of painting . . . it didn't matter. There was always something very bad on the news about them and I avoided them and then the day came when I had to eat my words. Financially I could not afford the rate of a one bedroom apartment.[91]

With San Francisco's continual high rents, low-income families had few choices but to try to get an apartment in public housing.

For some Valencia Gardens tenants, the gap between perception and reality demonstrated both the real need for affordable housing options and the insistence by some residents to persevere in forging a life for themselves within public housing. Kim James, who moved to Valencia Gardens in the late 1970s, explained the difference, for her, between the public perception and lived reality of life in public housing:

> I was scared to death with no legitimate reason. After a while it got more comfortable. After all these years I don't care, I walk through anywhere, walk around anywhere. But at first it was scary. I grew up

The Contested Mission of Valencia Gardens

> thinking that the projects was a really bad place where people died of overdoses or were murdered so it was kind of a scary thought to move in here. But after a year it was fine. . . . It is not what people think. People think everybody that lives here is on welfare or drugs or an alcoholic. They stereotype people from the projects and you find after you live here for a while that none of it is true. There are a lot of people that work, that live here and a lot of people who don't work but aren't on drugs or on alcohol and are trying to make it the best they can. It is really hard—you go through years of embarrassment because "Oh, I live in the projects."[92]

Stereotypes contributed to negative perceptions of Valencia Gardens residents and also pointed to a troubling and complicated reality: some tenants were committing crimes and hastening the decline of the development, but many others were law-abiding citizens trying to build a life in a challenging environment.

The image of the project as a dangerous and run-down place, and of the residents there as fully responsible for the problems they faced, did not take into account tenants' own concerns about drugs, violence, and the physical decay of the buildings, nor did it highlight the SFHA's failure as the landlord of Valencia Gardens or the educational and economic structural disparities of the nation. The project's problems were compounded by the Housing Authority's missed maintenance schedules, insufficient federal funds to update the buildings, and inconsistencies in policies and procedures because of rapid turnover of executive directors. As crime and drug trafficking increased in the 1980s at the SFHA's "Big Four" (Sunnydale, Alice Griffith, Potrero, and Hunters Point), the agency seemed to turn its attention and limited resources to providing damage control at these public housing projects. Residents at Valencia Gardens felt neglected.

In 1985, residents' claims of being the "stepchild of public housing in San Francisco" rang true when they went without heat for several hours during the day for over three months during the winter.[93] Expressing frustration at the "steady deterioration" of Valencia Gardens, tenant Marion Maxie blamed the Housing Authority: "They don't care how many times you call because they are not doing anything about it. . . . I went to get in the shower one day last week and I had to jump out because the water was so cold."[94] Executive Director

Carl Williams refuted Maxie's accusations, claiming that the SFHA had informed residents that solar panel installations at the project would require hot water and radiators to be turned off for several hours each day. Unfortunately for residents, the Housing Authority failed to respond to their complaints that the hot water and heat did not come back on at the end of the day. Vernell Guthrie, head of the Tenants' Organization at the time and a resident since 1966, described the decline of Valencia Gardens' environment: "They used to keep the place beautiful. But it seems the Housing Authority has given up on this place. They quit caring."[95] Against the backdrop of neglect by the Housing Authority, internal problems at Valencia Gardens, and tense relations with the surrounding neighborhood, residents contended with their own worries and outsiders' loathing in their contested community.

As the Mission District declined and the media deemed Valencia Gardens "one of the city's most dangerous and dirty housing complexes," project residents experienced even more scorn and blame for the area's woes.[96] Although residents freely admitted that Valencia Gardens housed some "bad apples," overall, residents, like their neighbors in the district, feared for their safety, and wanted the drug dealers behind bars. They also wanted to stop shouldering the blame for the district's criminals, who many residents believed were "outsiders," not residents. Resident Anita Ortiz explained, "It is true we have a lot of trespassers that aren't tenants . . . gangs . . . I know almost everybody in the whole development. We have lots of outsiders. . . . They see the cops and they run in . . . and they deal. . . . But we always get the blame here. It is not the group. We might have a bad apple or two. . . . Everywhere in the world you find that."[97]

With the project becoming a repository for drugs, prostitution conducted in the hallways, and gang crime, tenants watched in frustration as the police cracked down on crime in the Mission while "ignoring" the problems at Valencia Gardens perpetuated by nonresidents.[98] Resident Maria Calderon recalled her stairwell, where people "used to have a lot of sex and drugs" and go to the bathroom. She felt "ashamed to go up there when the steps were smelly."[99] Many Valencia Gardens residents held fast to their belief that other public housing projects

The Contested Mission of Valencia Gardens

housed criminals that preyed on public housing tenants by conducting their business in project spaces across the city. Whether true or not, this framework enabled tenants to shift the blame off themselves, to feel some pride in their community for housing law-abiding tenants, and to posit a solution to their problems: keeping outsiders out.

The unrelenting problems frustrated tenants, ossified stereotypes of public housing residents, and sparked criticism of a continued source of communal pride: the Bufanos. In 1997, a researcher, Christine Bryant, wrote the Art Commission complaining about the Bufanos' location in Valencia Gardens:

> Many of the sculptures are in a very bad section of the city of San Francisco. The apartment complex on Valencia and 15th Street is in a very bad section of town; definitely not a place where many people will go to view his works. I felt frightened walking through the complex with a camera photographing the animal sculptures.[100]

Bryant further asserted that the sculptures belonged in a "safe" space frequented by middle-class visitors.[101] Rather than keeping the Bufanos at Valencia Gardens, she argued, the statues would serve the public more fully if placed "in a park like the sculpture gardens in Holland and Europe."[102] Public housing, with its low-income residents, was no place for critically acclaimed art.

Even as critics complained of the sculptures' location over the years, the Bufanos seemed to recede from public view. A series on urban hikes in the *San Francisco Examiner* reminded San Franciscans of the Bufano sculptures at Valencia Gardens and the problem with their location. By describing the public housing project's reputation as a center "for drug dealing, high crime rates, and fourth-generation welfare dependency," the writer sent an explicit warning to readers about the dangers of going into Valencia Gardens, while also challenging them to venture in to see the Bufanos: "Urban hikers may prefer the opposite side of the street, but the courtyards of Valencia Gardens include . . . forgotten sculptures by the late Beniamino Bufano."[103] While the general public was unaware of Bufano's pieces in Valencia Gardens, residents continued to view them as a positive feature of their beleaguered housing development. Gabrielle Fontanella, who

71

grew up at Valencia Gardens, recalled the importance of the Bufanos: "They were always there for me. I talked to them. They were constant companions."[104] Residents who knew of Bufano's fame and those who did not could nevertheless share an appreciation of the art work adorning their increasingly neglected public housing environment. The Bufanos served as a critical community cohesive.

Affective Activism and Community Impact

Even as Valencia Gardens residents experienced crime and deteriorating conditions over time, they contested stereotypes and tried to address project problems by forming a community within their housing project. Through informal and formal networks, many tenants looked for ways to make the place home, building relationships with public housing neighbors, finding common ground in the racially and ethnically diverse project, and taking pride in Valencia Gardens. The formal organization of the Tenants' Organization occurred later at Valencia Gardens than at many other projects in San Francisco. Arguably, the entrenchment of crime, as well as maintenance issues, contributed to the sluggish start for formal tenant activism. Nonetheless, relationship building and interpersonal connections—at times across lines of racial and ethnic difference—formed the basis for affective activism, an important form of community engagement that supported and sustained many residents. Valencia Gardens tenants struggled to form communal bonds and forge ownership of their project; in doing so they reconfigured the SFHA's early vision of public housing to fit their own circumstances and needs.

    Residents' frustration and concern with "outsiders" who damaged the project's reputation spurred community building. Stereotyped and blamed for the area's problems, tenants formed an us-against-them mentality. The use of the word "outsider" by residents to describe non-residents illuminates the difference between the Valencia Gardens community and the surrounding neighborhood while reflecting the ways in which tenants felt cut off from their Mission neighbors. Enduring and combating the chafing stereotypes of Valencia Gardens and its occupants as "lazy," "on drugs," "alcoholics," or lacking ambition also brought many residents together.[105] The stigma worked to sepa-

The Contested Mission of Valencia Gardens

rate residents from the surrounding community while drawing them together as a marginalized group living in an oppositional space.

The racial and ethnic diversity of the project separated it from the Mission community and facilitated both pride and difficulties for Valencia Gardens residents. While the Mission District was increasingly labeled as a Latino/a district, Valencia Gardens, in contrast, grew more racially and ethnically diverse over the years. After the 1954 *Banks vs. The Housing Authority* ruling, the project began housing Asian immigrants, Asian Americans, African Americans, Latino/as, and Euro-Americans.[106] Although integration was slow and spotty at some public housing projects, such as Ping Yuen and Hunters Point, Valencia Gardens increasingly housed racially and ethnically diverse tenants. Some new residents felt a sense of belonging after a period of "initiation." Tenants complained of initial fear and, for some, harassment by other residents upon first moving into Valencia Gardens. At times, racial differences created barriers for residents during their first year of trying to adjust to living in Valencia Gardens. Vietnamese tenant Hoang Kim Nguyen and her Chinese husband had problems after relocating to Valencia Gardens. She recalled, "When I first moved in kids would knock on the door and window and at holiday time, Independence Day, they throw firecrackers inside the house. . . . We didn't speak English and we didn't know how to speak to them to stop, we would say please don't, but the more we said it the more they did."[107] Another Vietnamese resident claimed that Valencia Gardens was "okay" but that she was afraid of those she saw selling drugs in the courtyard, who were African American.[108] Other Vietnamese immigrants and one Latina recounted their harassment by some African Americans when they moved in. Yet after a period of a year or so, the harassment ended, as these tenants became known to others and vice versa. Hoang Nguyen, like many others who experienced "hazing" on their arrival, recalled that the trouble lasted "for the first year after we moved in," and after that "everything [was] OK."[109] Many residents claimed that their assimilation process into the diverse public housing community was eased by a shared understanding that might best be summarized as "I don't bother no one and no one bothers me," a sentiment that was articulated repeatedly by many residents.[110] As new tenants transitioned into being "insiders," many residents, over time, came to believe

The Contested Mission of Valencia Gardens

that most people in the community were "good people" and that it was "outsiders" who brought danger to the streets around Valencia Gardens and into the courtyards.

While racial differences served as a source of tension for some residents, many Valencia Gardens tenants embraced the diversity of the project, forming connections across racial and ethnic lines. They also understood that the project's demographics resulted in scrutiny. Anita Ortiz explained, "Everybody focuses more on the development because we have got a mixture, a combination of nationalities.... If you got all the white out you'd be better, if you got all the Asians out you would be better. I don't think so. I think the more we get together, the more we try to make it work, we can make a better world."[111] When asked, Anita and other residents stressed that racial and ethnic differences were not the source of tensions among tenants: interpersonal problems stemmed from individuals' failure to get along with others. For them, race and ethnicity were "no bigger a problem than outside the projects."[112] Measuring the full impact of racial and ethnic differences on tenants over the years is not possible. However, understanding the ways tenants talked about racial diversity as a source of pride and an impetus for community building underscores the tolerance shaped by a multiracial, multiethnic group living together—a rare formation in U.S. urban and suburban spaces in the second half of the twentieth century.

A number of Valencia Gardens residents worked to overcome ethnic and racial differences and to foster an inclusive community dynamic that was a key ingredient of affective activism (in contrast to the tenants of North Beach Place, who relied on intraethnic and racial bonds, as chapter 4 explains). For residents such as Donald Ingram, who "like[d] this multi-cultural outfit," the diversity at Valencia Gardens made the project unique and served to solidify community ties.[113] Similarly, some parents described the multicultural environment as educational and said they appreciated the opportunity to raise their children in such an environment. Tenant Charla Molina suggested drawing on the diversity to promote cultural awareness, arguing that diversity classes for children in Valencia Gardens would further promote tolerance and appreciation of different cultures. It might also cut down on teasing, which at times, she said, was race based.[114]

The impetus to bridge racial, ethnic, and language barriers promoted intercultural community bonds for many residents and served as a consistent goal for others. When neighborliness occurred across race and ethnic lines, residents proudly pointed it out. Anita Ortiz's description of her neighbors demonstrated pride in improved safety and accord among her multiracial community:

> I leave my door unlocked. I can leave my windows open. I don't have bars. Nobody breaks in. The only problems I have are the pigeons! I have Asians to my left side and right. To my corner an African American. . . . I am surrounded. I know them. I need anything I know where to run. . . . My granddaughter knows who she should trust . . . and she knows where to go to get help. She is only five.[115]

Cooperation rather than racial division aided a number of residents in their daily lives. From lending money and buying presents for neighbors' children, to taking care of another tenant's children and "protecting each other," many Valencia Gardens residents benefited from forming relationships with others in the public housing project.[116] In a matrix of cooperation and reciprocity that for residents in need of child care was critical, racial differences seemed to dissolve under the shared benefits of neighborliness. While neighbor relations ebbed and flowed over time depending on the individuals living at Valencia Gardens and their attitudes and relationships, some residents throughout the history of the project enjoyed the advantages not only of neighborliness but also of friendship. These ties, along with the benefits of living in a development situated in the sunniest area of the city and conveniently located near public transportation, stores, and a hospital, fostered a strong commitment to Valencia Gardens as home.

Residents who experienced the positive potential of community cooperation also realized the tensions inherent in public housing living and looked for ways to overcome them. Both informally and formally, through the Tenants' Organization, tenants worked to facilitate community ties and overcome problems between tenants—whatever their cause. When asked how to strengthen the Valencia Gardens community, tenants offered a resounding solution: relationship building. According to Anita Ortiz, the key to community building was bringing people together:

> You get together. Make it a small potluck . . . we have been doing it and we have been seeing a great change. Thanksgiving we did. We'll do it for Christmas. We want the parents to join us. . . . This way we get to know hey you aren't as bad as we thought you were. . . . My mother used to say, you have to stretch out your hands and reach. You have to try to make the community. If you don't make the community, the community will make itself.[117]

Other residents echoed Ortiz, contending that face time dispelled negative perceptions and garnered understanding—particularly of the range of cultures represented at Valencia Gardens. One longtime resident active in the Tenants' Organization recalled how the group sponsored potlucks "where you have such a mixture it isn't even funny. I have done them in the senior room and we get Chinese food, we'll get Mexican food, Puerto Rican, Southern and Soul food and everybody chips in and helps. . . . We all try to respect each other and we try to share."[118] When discussing ways to promote community, many female residents mentioned "potlucks," "a community day," and coffee on Saturday mornings. These events, for many female residents who planned and participated in them, served as a critical component in building a stronger community. Although some residents acknowledged their role in a "Vietnamese group" or a "Latino group," participation in these subgroups did not prevent Valencia Gardens residents from advocating for and taking part in activities that brought these groups together. Resident Susie Barrara explained, "Once in a while we have a meeting with Vietnamese, Latino, and Americans all together. We get more communication and we understand each other. We try to take care of this housing together. That is what I am thinking about."[119] Through relationship building and an ethic of care, many Valencia Gardens tenants supported each other, which during times of distress in the public housing project fostered affective activism as residents worked together to strengthen their community.

In the context of continual negotiation of space, place, ethnicity, and race set against a strained relationship with the surrounding neighborhood, many residents actively participated in the formal network of the Tenants' Organization as another act of community engagement. As thousands of Mission District residents joined the Mission Coalition Organization between 1967 and 1973 to stave off urban renewal and to lobby for directing federal Model Cities funds in their neighborhood, tenants at Valencia Gardens began to organize themselves. Started in 1971 by a group of residents as the citywide Public Housing Tenants Association (PHTA) was forming, the Valencia Gardens Tenants' Organization, governed by a president, vice president, treasurer, and secretary, held monthly meetings to discuss project business and plan events. Tenants elected officers for two-year terms and officeholders were eligible for reelection.[120] The Valencia Gardens Tenants' Organization started later than tenants' groups such as the Ping Yuen Residents Improvement Association and the North Beach Place Tenants Association. Begun during a large-scale neighborhood mobilization against the city and federal government's encroachment into the Mission, the organization veered in a different direction over time, taking a nonconfrontational approach with the SFHA rather than carrying out rent strikes, writing petitions, and staging protests as residents at Ping Yuen and North Beach Place did. The organization's efforts through the years focused on relationship building within Valencia Gardens. The Tenants' Organization planned large project events, such as annual holiday parties for which they drew on funding from the Housing Authority. Over the years, the organization planned and hosted annual Halloween, Christmas, and Easter parties. Even when the Housing Authority had limited funds, the Tenants' Organization worked to continue these community-building events. Jeri Maxwell, president in 1990, recalled that the Housing Authority sent her a letter saying they would not be able to give toys to children that year: "I cried. I got mad. But then I saw the phone book and I got $3,000 that year on short notice. It is out there. All we got to do is ask."[121] Over the years, the Tenants' Organization has also lobbied for a day care center, computers, and job training in an attempt to improve the public housing community for both children and adults.

By the 1990s, the organization's efforts to increase social services for project residents became secondary to the quest for safety. In the mid-1990s, the group's complaints that outsiders were causing problems in the project prompted the Housing Authority to take action by hiring security guards to work at Valencia Gardens and other public housing sites. While the crime rate declined somewhat in the early

1990s, between March 1995 and March 1996 crime in Valencia Gardens increased 23 percent.[122] Some residents were relieved when the SFHA posted private security guards inside the project in 1996; others felt the guards violated their privacy. The president of the Tenants' Organization pushed for an additional security measure: a gate.[123] Tenants debated the need for and effectiveness of fencing and failed to reach a conclusive decision on the issue. Meanwhile, a few members of the Tenants' Organization went ahead and convinced the Housing Authority to install a perimeter gate in 1998. Their belief that the gate would keep out the criminals and other outsiders who used the hallways as a toilet led them to a unilateral decision, frustrating many members of the organization. In making Valencia Gardens a "gated community," proponents aimed to increase safety and to challenge the popular perception that residents perpetrated crime in the project. Using the same rationale as homeowner associations in suburban gated communities, tenant proponents argued that the gates would keep the bad element out. Overall, the fencing failed to solve the project's problems. The magnets on the gates were weak, and the gates were regularly propped open in response to malfunctioning keypads, leaving outsiders with easy access to the development.[124] Aesthetically, though, the large metal gates stood as a visual symbol of the chasm between residents at Valencia Gardens and the Mission neighborhood.

For many residents, the Tenants' Organization promoted community building and was a vehicle to improve Valencia Gardens, but others intentionally avoided participating. The reasons for not attending meetings varied: some residents considered their stay at Valencia Gardens short term and did not want to spend their time in meetings. Others found the bureaucracy tedious. Ethel Williams, a resident on and off from the 1970s through the 1990s, explained, "I know a lot of us don't go to the meetings. There is a certain group that goes. It is a mess when you go. So most of us don't go."[125]

Other residents who participated at one time left in response to new leadership. Married to the president of the organization in the late 1980s, Ethel Williams argued that in those days, "people came out for picnics, went to games together, etc." Her frustration at residents' lack of participation affected her own by the late 1990s. "You don't want to get into everything that is happening. I used to help my husband with

The Contested Mission of Valencia Gardens

Figure 8. View of Valencia Gardens, 2003, through the gates that were installed in 1998; Bufano's *Bear with Cubs* is visible in the background. Photograph by the author.

the Tenants' Association. I used to be in all that and now I don't do any of that any more because it is such a bother."[126] Arguments between participants and the failure of the organization to present more programs for children turned her away from the group. Bickering and fighting kept others away as well. Willie Eldridge quit the organization because he suspected that the leaders owed the Housing Authority money and believed that the group did not produce results.[127] For those who once participated and then quit, as well as for those who had never participated, the choice to disengage from the Tenants' Organization, regardless of the reason, created tension among some residents. The friction between tenants, the bureaucracy of the Tenants' Organization, differences in opinion, and inertia kept residents from embracing an organization formed to work on their behalf.

Even as nonmembers criticized the leadership at different times, the responsibility of governance and participation nurtured self-esteem and a positive view of community for many Tenants' Organization members and officers—and in particular women. Through their participation, a number of female residents, like their peers at Ping Yuen and North Beach Place, actively sought to improve their living environment for themselves and their children. These low-income women, some of whom were on welfare, had few, if any, opportunities to lead or to wield power in or outside the workplace. Participation in the Tenants' Organization empowered many female residents and gave them a chance to learn and practice management and leadership skills. Vice president from 1997 to 2000 and president from 2000 to 2003, Anita Ortiz held back tears as she described how her involvement in Valencia Gardens and the opportunity to serve in a leadership position in the Tenants' Organization changed her life:

> [Residents] have encouraged me in many things I haven't been able to succeed in outside. They have encouraged me in school volunteering. They let me work at [a Pre-kindergarten program]. Nobody will give me the chance outside. I am sorry I am choking but Valencia has changed me too much. I feel I have a lot . . . I feel like I have the world now. Outside I never had it. Here they call. Here they give me a chance. I feel like I'm in cloud 10. . . . They gave me my dignity back. I lost it when I was homeless. I feel I have more advantage out of life now than when I was a private citizen because they trust me more than when I was a private citizen. For me Valencia Gardens has done so much and I will keep doing as much as I can.[128]

The opportunity to serve in a leadership role within the Tenants' Organization was important to other tenants as well. Jeri Maxwell began assisting the president in 1989 and slowly became more involved until she won the vice presidency in 1992. Her office opened doors to a position on the Mayor's Task Force on the Mission and the Sixteenth Street Safety Force. Because she "had the time" and saw there was a need, she became involved. The opportunity to shape Valencia Gardens, especially through children's programs, increased her confidence and pride in the project. As she noted, "So much can be done here. So much. And I just want to see it done. . . . [In coming together] Valencia will become a model for the whole United States."[129]

A positive self-image from contributing to the Valencia Gardens community was not limited to tenant organization officers. College student, professional clown, and mother Omaira Correa found that her successes vis-à-vis her location living in public housing bolstered her confidence and sense of self:

> Struggling right now as a student is really good for me. I go to school and I am a professional clown. Everyone in the community loves me. . . . I have also been an example for the teenage girls here because of all the things [I do] which they admire me because of the things I have been able to accomplish. I am a certified massage therapist. . . . It is not the image people on the outside have. There is a lot of positive. . . . Being a 4.0 student is really great in the community. People look up to you. Kids look up to you.[130]

Despite the crime, tenant tensions, neighborhood disdain, and the burden of the stigma related to living in Valencia Gardens, these women found purpose and self-confidence through their interactions with and leadership positions for the community. The opportunities and responsibilities afforded to Anita, Jeri, and other leaders, and the communal praise received by Omaira were made possible through living in public housing. In contrast to negative images of public housing, the experiences of these residents and others in Valencia Gardens proved important for personal growth and confidence, as well as the development of the community.

Whether active in community affairs or not, several residents over the years established "psychological ownership" of Valencia Gardens, developing public housing into their home. For Anita Ortiz, her participation in the Tenants' Organization and subsequent interactions with residents as vice president and later president shaped her connection to Valencia Gardens. As the caregiver of three children living in a small apartment, she refused the Housing Authority's offer to transfer her to a larger unit in another project, claiming that her home was at Valencia Gardens: "I don't want to leave my location. I love my home. I'm dealing with my people. They are like family to me."[131] Although arguably the project's prime location and the sunny weather in the Mission factored into Anita's decision to stay, her clear and vocal attachment to the Valencia Gardens community revealed nonmaterial incentives for remaining—relationships, responsibility to community, and a connection to the project.

Other residents demonstrated their attachment through their use of space. Painting, decorating, putting on new doors, and tending plants were some of the ways tenants made public housing apartments, assigned by the state, home. In a translated interview, Eva Platero expressed her connection to her apartment, stating that she "feels proud to be here" and to "put so much love into it" by fixing up the kitchen and painting. Putting her "heart" and "love" into Valencia Gardens made Platero "very happy."[132] Similarly, eschewing the institutional white paint provided by the Housing Authority, Ron Dunn claimed and personalized his apartment by painting it his colors. Choosing yellow for the bathroom, red for the kitchen cabinets, along with a lavender ceiling and gray walls in another room, he created the look he wanted for his home, rather than the one imposed by the Housing Authority.[133]

By adding personal touches such as paint, photographs, curtains, and knickknacks, residents participated in the process of psychological ownership. For residents who stayed at Valencia Gardens over several decades, a strong sense of attachment occurred. The opportunity to construct a clean and safe space in and around one's apartment enabled residents to remove themselves partially from the problems and stereotypes associated with living in Valencia Gardens. In a few cases, individual steps taken to improve a resident's living environment extended to the community, forming a bridge. A resident since 1969, Ruth Hamilton brightened her apartment area by decorating, baking, and gardening:

> I tried to do a couple of things to make me feel better. A few years ago I planted a little tangerine tree. Each year it bears fruit. . . . I didn't just do it for me . . . you know the neighborhood, therefore everybody watches over the tree. Any kid touches the tree that is a no-no. Any kid sees another kid touching the trees they say that is a no-no. It is gorgeous when it blossoms.[134]

Residents living in the project for two years, like Ron Dunn, or over three decades, like Ruth Hamilton, created homes for themselves—places of comfort, places they considered their own, places that resisted the policy goal of making public housing only temporary housing for Americans.

The Contested Mission of Valencia Gardens

Residents who claimed Valencia Gardens as home and made efforts to carve out a tidy, peaceful space within their apartments at times resented tenants who did not share their standards. Longtime residents Gabrielle Fontanella and Louette Fabio complained about tenants who had "a project mentality." In contrast to tenants who "took care of their areas," these residents had "an attitude that this is a project, you don't have to pick up, you throw things on the ground, and they do it all the time. It is a project, why are you cleaning up. . . . It is like they feel they are living in a project so they don't care. It is not home to them."[135] Other tenants, claiming the rights of psychological ownership over their rented apartments, worked to better their living environment through informal and formal networks and looked to redevelopment as a possible solution for altering the image of and problems at Valencia Gardens.

"Hope" for the Future?

In 1997, Valencia Gardens came under scrutiny again, this time by the SFHA, which was seeking another public housing project that would qualify for federal HOPE VI funds. Launched in 1992 by HUD, the HOPE VI program "combined grants for physical revitalization with funding for management improvements and supportive services to promote resident self-sufficiency," aiming to replace severely distressed public housing, occupied by poor families, with redesigned mixed-income housing.[136] The HOPE VI division of the SFHA had to decide which distressed public housing project warranted redevelopment funds as they prepared to apply for a third federal grant. Valencia Garden residents—through their stories of community building and affective activism, their desire for a better environment, and their demands for social services—swayed the Housing Authority to select their project for its HOPE VI grant application. Redevelopment held out the possibility of resolving the design problems that offered criminals a place to work and hide and of providing improved amenities and social services for tenants.

The federal program also promised to reinvent public housing in the rapidly gentrifying Mission District. The dot-com boom and increasing job growth in Silicon Valley in the early 1990s accelerated change in the district that continued for years: industrial buildings were converted into high-priced lofts and trendy boutiques, and restaurants opened to serve the influx of high-income individuals into the Mission.[137] Echoing the activism of MCO in the late 1960s, the Mission Anti-Displacement Coalition formed to "incorporate the voices of the people in the Mission into development plans," while the Mission Yuppie Eradication Project called for class warfare and vandalism of residences belonging to higher-income residents.[138] Despite the outcry from activists throughout the decade, eviction rates soared, and more than 1,000 Latino families were displaced by the late 1990s. As a neighborhood with a wealth of amenities, including sunshine, two Bay Area Rapid Transit (BART) stations, and its location near downtown, the Mission attracted artists, college students, and gays and lesbians, following a "classic pattern" in gentrifying areas that was aided by changes in city ordinances and state law that favored economic growth.[139]

The tension between new investment and economic stimulation and the displacement of low-income residents inherent in gentrification was reflected in the next decade of change at Valencia Gardens. Tenants' interest in the HOPE VI funding was sparked by their participation in a 1997 oral history project. Their aim was to dispel negative images of themselves and of Valencia Gardens, including those of "Drug dealers lurking in every hallway. Drive-by shootings so frequent children hardly dare go outside. Lazy, alcoholic bums loitering under trees."[140] The Legacy Oral History Project began as a design contest in 1996. Roberta Swan of the San Francisco branch of the American Institute of Architects (SFAIA) received permission from the Housing Authority to host an architectural design competition on Valencia Gardens for exhibition at the 1998 AIA national convention in San Francisco. Swan recounted, "The original plan was to create a resident participation plan, do a design competition and continue to work together for the implementation of the plan."[141] After attending a Tenants' Organization meeting where a resident complained "people just think we are garbage if we live here," Swan widened the scope of the project to include oral interviews.[142]

Responding to tenants' statements about life in Valencia Gardens, Swan initiated the Legacy Project of the SFAIA "in an effort to

The Contested Mission of Valencia Gardens

prevent [tenants'] individual voices and stories from being drowned out by the crush of attention given to gangs and crime."[143] Swan first completed a pilot project, interviewing twelve residents and compiling a seven-minute tape from the interviews. After the tape received the enthusiastic approval of Valencia Gardens residents at a Tenants' Organization meeting, Swan presented it to the SFHA and the SFAIA. Both groups agreed to fund a full-scale oral history project. The project lasted a year, and Swan interviewed seventy-five residents. The final product of the "Legacy Oral History Project" consisted of seventy banners with interview quotes and photographs of tenants displayed at the AIA annual convention and later in the community room at Valencia Gardens. Many residents, encouraged by the community participation in the Legacy Project and the ideas put forth by architects during the design competition, hoped the SFHA would select Valencia Gardens for renovation.[144] The interest in their lives as public housing residents and the act of telling their own stories strengthened community bonds and ignited a spark for radical changes in the long neglected public housing project.

Residents' participation in the Legacy Project was a critical factor in the SFHA selecting Valencia Gardens as a HOPE VI site and likely played a role in HUD's award of HOPE VI funds to redevelop the site. According to HUD HOPE VI guidelines, "resident and community participation are key ingredients to a successful HOPE VI application. Involving residents and the community in the planning process and in shaping the HOPE VI application should start well before the application is submitted."[145] Swan's early discussions with residents about their design wish list, along with the twelve initial interviews she conducted, provided the SFHA with important evidence of resident participation. Members of the HOPE VI division of the SFHA, believing that the oral histories would clinch the grant, applied for HOPE VI money to redevelop Valencia Gardens in 1997, using residents' interviews, photographs, and letters to support their application to renovate the project. In October 1997, Mayor Willie Brown announced that the SFHA had received a $23.6 million grant to redevelop Valencia Gardens, described as "a crime-ridden eyesore in the Mission."[146] Residents' stories revealing that "the block-style apartment buildings house only their lives but their community" helped secure funds that would both refurbish Valencia Gardens and replace the community living there.[147]

With $23.6 million in HOPE VI funds and $30.8 million in leveraged public and private funds, the SFHA moved forward with design drafts for a development of mixed-income, garden-style apartments based on principles of defensible space.[148] Following HOPE VI regulations, the Housing Authority allocated up to 15 percent of the $54 million budget for social and community service programs, including child care and recreational facilities and a computer center. At first, the SFHA followed the plan outlined in the grant application—and supported by tenants—to renovate the existing apartments. This plan allowed residents to stay on-site as the buildings were gradually remodeled. However, in a move repeated at North Beach Place, the SFHA, like many housing authorities issued federal HOPE VI funds, carried out redevelopment activities that differed "dramatically from what . . . [they] originally propose[d] in their applications and describe[d] in their training and public information sessions."[149] Despite an assessment by architectural consulting firm Carey and Company Incorporated demonstrating that Valencia Gardens "appears to be eligible for the National Register of Historic Places" and should be preserved, and despite promises to Valencia Gardens residents, the SFHA decided to use HOPE VI funds to demolish and rebuild the project.[150]

The threat of relocation and the demolition of their apartments alarmed and frustrated a number of residents who had believed the SFHA would follow through on its original plan to renovate Valencia Gardens. While the lure of new buildings and better social and community services assuaged some tenants' anger, others expressed deep distrust of the SFHA. Vernell Gutherie, a long-term resident, was suspicious of the Housing Authority's plans for relocation: "what is going to happen to these people is that they aren't going to have a place to stay. Mission Housing [the nonprofit partner contracted by the SFHA to manage the property] will come in and there wouldn't be a place for them. They aren't going to put them back in here." Ms. Gutherie went on to claim that a HOPE VI award for Valencia Gardens was a tool "to get people out!"[151] Other residents worried that rebuilding would decrease the structural integrity of the project. With a nod to Wurster

The Contested Mission of Valencia Gardens

and Thomsen's design, resident Susie Barrara argued that redevelopment could yield cheap, shoddy construction: "I think even though Valencia Garden is old, I love to stay because they built it very safely. The housing they build up [now] is not safe. But here is very safe. It is all cement. It is very safe.... I said no way when I heard Valencia Gardens [might] be torn down."[152] Gabrielle Fontanella agreed, recounting that dynamite once went off at Valencia Gardens with little damage to the buildings: "We're like hey, if this place can stand up to dynamite why are we getting rid of it?"[153] The SFHA responded that demolition was cheaper and would deliver better apartments for residents.

Seeking to influence the future of Valencia Gardens, tenants continued their involvement beyond the Legacy Project, attending HOPE VI meetings and assigning leaders from the Tenants' Organization to the Valencia Gardens Task Force, a committee made up of tenant, district, and SFHA representatives. The Tenants' Organization officers invested their time in monthly and sometimes bimonthly planning meetings. From the early meetings in 1998 to discuss design drafts, to the more detailed Task Force planning meetings in 2001, many tenants united around the same, seemingly simple goal: a decent place to live. Louette Fabio, Gabrielle's mother, recalls, "People had the same issues about what they want.... They want a decent place to live and they want their kids to live in a place where you aren't looked down on. You mention where you live, oh Valencia Gardens, and people pull away or get in fights over it."[154] Tenants hoped the new development would erase the stigma long associated with their residence.

Participation by tenants at HOPE VI meetings resulted in a few important concessions. Through negotiations with the Housing Authority, the Tenants' Organization successfully secured a phased demolition plan allowing some residents to stay on-site longer. Participants also weighed in on the project design. Although residents did not agree on all the proposed features, they seemed pleased with the sketches showing defensible space elements intended to improve safety: private backyards and decks, separate walk-up entrances, secured trash access areas, and fenced-in play areas. As the plans shifted over time, tenants united around the necessity of one design element: the return of the Bufanos to Valencia Gardens. The Art Commission initially expressed ambivalence about extending the loan of the Bufanos at Valencia Gardens. However, after hearing about the Bufanos' importance to residents, and seeing the selected design, which situated the pieces out in the open near the sidewalks for public viewing, the Art Commission's worries waned.[155] Perhaps recognizing that the residents' use and appreciation of the sculptures over six decades had fulfilled the Works Progress Administration's goal to "redefine the relationship between artists and the community, so that art no longer would be consumed only by the elite who could afford to pay," the Commission supported residents' request to keep the Bufanos as part of the Valencia Gardens community.[156] The Commission agreed to clean the animals, repair their bases, and return them for display when the development reopened.

As residents looked forward to new apartments and amenities, including the Bufanos, they also had to face the reality that their community, like the Mission District, was changing. The HOPE VI program held out the promise of a lower crime rate, a cleaner project, and improved social and community services. Yet these improvements would not be available to all tenants displaced by the demolition of Valencia Gardens. As in many other HOPE VI projects across the country, the stipulation to create mixed-income housing decreased the number of low-income units available in redeveloped projects. If all tenants opted to return—and were eligible—there would not be enough units to house them. The new 260-unit development plan included 148 public housing units, 60 Section 8 units, and 52 tax-credit units for families earning substantially above the poverty line but still considered low-income in San Francisco.[157] Forty-two of the 260 units would go to seniors.[158] Following the national trend at HOPE VI sites, the SFHA has contributed to the reduction of the supply of public housing, "some of the only housing guaranteed to be affordable to families with the lowest incomes."[159] This move, coupled with San Francisco's high rental rates, inevitably pushed some low-income families out of the city to find affordable housing. Early relocation figures for Valencia Gardens confirmed the trend: of forty-six relocated households, fourteen used Section 8 vouchers, seven in San Francisco and seven outside the city; seventeen moved into other public housing projects; and fifteen were either evicted or deceased.[160] Under HOPE VI regulations, tenants who took Section 8 vouchers used to rent in the private market or who moved into other HOPE VI projects were ineligible to live at Valencia Gardens when it reopened. These restrictions, along with stricter regulations for residents, have dispersed existing low-income communities, making it difficult for neighbors to reconnect or to reform their community in the future. Although the opportunities for nicer, safer residences and a wider range of social services and amenities offered to low-income residents by HOPE VI are critical, the dismantling of the community at Valencia Gardens was a loss for a number of residents.

Tenants who wanted to return to Valencia Gardens had no guarantee that the SFHA would accept them even though they technically topped the agency's priority list for housing. Because HUD failed to issue specific regulations for the HOPE VI program, public housing authorities had the power to decide which tenants could return. The federal government's sole requirement is that housing authorities allow tenants "in good standing" the option of returning to HOPE VI sites. While this standard might appear reasonable, HUD has no official definition of "good standing." As a result, local authorities can choose what they want the term to mean and in doing so can dictate which tenants can return.[161] According to HUD, "most PHAs apply admissions criteria for HOPE VI sites that are much more stringent than those they normally use."[162] A SFHA employee, Stephen Haines, and Valencia Gardens Task Force member Gabrielle Fontanella stated in 2003 that the Task Force had not yet determined all the standards of eligibility, though they both confirmed that tenants with a police record could not move back in to Valencia Gardens.[163] National figures in 2008 showed that only 24 percent of original residents returned to HOPE VI developments.[164] Locally, Valencia Gardens residents were understandably apprehensive about the possibilities of returning after seeing scores of families relocated away from Hayes Valley, Bernal Dwellings, and Plaza East. Nonetheless, the SFHA continued to claim that approximately 60 percent of residents would return to Valencia Gardens.[165] Ultimately, many fewer residents returned, with estimates ranging between 17 percent and 52 percent.[166]

The last tenants to relocate in 2003 had trouble saying good-bye to their friends and to a location they knew as home. A resident for thirty-three years, Ruth Hamilton viewed her departure as bittersweet: "I am a little bit sad . . . you think about the children growing up here but if this is what it took to get me out of here then hey I am ready. . . . It was home and I am very thankful." Turning to resident Gabrielle Fontanella, who exclaimed, "I am going to miss you guys," Ruth responded, "We are all going to miss each other. Let's not start all this or I will start feeling really low."[167] In August 2003, bulldozers demolished the sixty-one-year-old project. The new Valencia Gardens project would house many new tenants and some returners in a reconfigured development and, increasingly, a changing neighborhood.

The New Valencia Gardens

In 2006, Valencia Gardens opened its doors to mixed-income tenants. The modern, award-winning design by Van Meter Williams Pollack for Mission Housing Development Corporation features a 300,000-square-foot complex with 260 units, a community room, day care, a learning center, a play area for children, and a small sculpture garden featuring several Bufanos. The complex includes four-story buildings that "line the primary public access streets and three-story buildings [that] flank the interior blocks," which include parking spaces and car access. The units offer separate entryways, walkways, and stoops to restore "a sense of security" and encourage "a sense of ownership and community interaction."[168] Other amenities include washer and dryer hookups in each unit, a welcoming lobby with cat and mouse Bufanos that have been "domesticated" by their placement indoors, photographs of the Mission by local artists, and a large panel display of Valencia Gardens' history that includes some of the tenants' quotations from the Legacy Project. The emphasis on history as well as education continues outside in a small courtyard off the community room. Grouped closely together in a circle, the remaining Bufanos sit, while a plaque on a wall nearby commemorates the life and work of Beniamino Bufano.

Across the street from the sleek entrance to the new Valencia Gardens is the Four Barrel Coffeehouse, a symbol of change in the

The Contested Mission of Valencia Gardens

Figure 9. Entrance to the redeveloped Valencia Gardens, 2013. Photograph courtesy of Todd Miller.

Mission District. Opened in 2008 and known for high-quality beans and roasting, a "hipster" clientele, and a focus on fostering conversation by intentionally not providing Wi-fi access, Four Barrel serves coffee to long lines of neighborhood residents and visitors in a gentrified Mission District. While maintaining pockets that echo its "gritty" working-class roots, the Mission is home to pricey housing, expensive restaurants, and loft condos and is on the shuttle route for Google employees. The new Valencia Gardens, designed with the neighborhood

The Contested Mission of Valencia Gardens

Figure 10. Interior courtyard of the redeveloped Valencia Gardens, 2008. Photograph by the author.

context in mind, mirrors the look of the twenty-first century Mission even as its public housing past is highlighted inside.

While middle-class patrons enjoy $4 lattes across the street in a space designed to "forge community," low-income residents returning to Valencia Gardens have struggled to recalibrate relationships in their new environment.[169] As key leaders in the redevelopment efforts, both Gabrielle Fontanella and Anita Ortiz seemed likely candidates to return to the new apartments. Both women returned after what they described as a multiyear "battle" with the SFHA to move back to Valencia Gardens. Thirty-nine other families returned as well. The "old-timers" continue to seek the guidance of Gabrielle and Anita even though neither of them is a Tenants' Organization officer: many residents have asked Anita to seek election since she returned. The improvements to the development are tangible to returning residents, but there is disappointment nonetheless. The SFHA promised a designated play area for children. A gated-off play area was built, but resi-

Figure 11. Street view inside the redeveloped Valencia Gardens, 2008. Interior parking is one of the features newly available to residents. Photograph by the author.

dents say it is available only to participants in the Head Start Program. Classes that the SFHA promised for low-income residents to learn about the features of their apartments and how to use the appliances and thermostat did not take place. Residents are civil to one another, but according to Anita, the Tenants' Organization lacks strong leadership to work for change. The Bufanos continue to welcome new and returning residents and to grace the lobby and courtyard. However, their care seems imperiled by kids who skateboard in the courtyard and use the base and sculptures as ramps. Residents note that more green space and play areas for youth could help alleviate this problem.[170] The construction of the units, as feared, is seen as shoddy compared with the solid, cinderblock design of the "old VG." Even so, the stigma of public housing seems to have been eliminated through demolition. The grandson of a tenant who used to live in Valencia Gardens summed up the change, saying that the new Valencia Gardens "is establishing that people aren't afraid of the neighborhood anymore.

The Contested Mission of Valencia Gardens

Figure 12. Interior courtyard of the redeveloped Valencia Gardens with Bufanos (and Bufano plaque in the background on the wall at left center), 2008. Photograph by the author.

Sad to know that you have to tear down a place to make it clear to move forward."[171]

The effect of redevelopment on tenants who return to the project and on those who do not will emerge in years to come. Reflecting on what she learned through the experience, Anita Ortiz, sitting in her new Valencia Gardens apartment, ruminated, "Community to me means working together with everyone whether it is a resident or it is a historic neighborhood because they are all one. When you look at them they are all one and you need them all. Whether it is you or your neighbor or the guy across the street—you think you don't know him but he lives there and he may be the best person to give you a hand. The community for me is togetherness."[172] Prior to redevelopment, tenants' affective activism contributed to their personal growth and in some ways shaped the redevelopment process. Although Valencia Gardens provides 260 units of affordable housing in the tight San Francis-

Figure 13. Beniamino Bufano's *Cat*, lobby area, Valencia Gardens, 2008. Photograph by the author.

co housing market, the community that was once there is gone, as is the affective activism that reinforced it.

Between 1942 and 2003, thousands of residents lived at Valencia Gardens—a place that each resident experienced differently depending on who they were, when they lived there, and even where they lived.[173] From nostalgic childhood memories of playing on the Bufanos to grim adult recollections of the smell of urine and the sight of drug dealing and gang violence, public housing living was a complex, if often harsh, experience, worsened by widespread stereotypes associated with public housing and its residents. Despite the problems and crime that were sporadically evident over the past sixty years and difficulties with the Housing Authority, district neighbors, and other tenants, many residents have forged relationships and community bonds in their multicultural project that were in and of themselves an important act of community engagement.[174] This affective activism sustained many residents during difficult times and contributed to efforts

The Contested Mission of Valencia Gardens

for change. Built under protest in 1942, Valencia Gardens has been a continually contested space where residents formed bonds of community and created a home for themselves, thus challenging the purposes and stereotypes of public housing in the United States and laying claim to the right to define its meaning for themselves and the broader community.

THREE

"Peace and Prosperity Dwell among Virtuous Neighbors"
Chinatown's Public Housing

ON OCTOBER 21, 1951, HENRY K. WONG, A CHINESE AMERICAN World War II veteran, his wife Alice, and their two children joined San Francisco mayor Elmer Robinson and his wife for a "housewarming tea." The couples sat together in a new model apartment decorated with modern furniture and Chinese accessories.[1] In accordance with Chinese tradition, the Wongs shared watermelon seeds, candied ginger, and coconut strips with the Robinsons, who in turn left a fifty-cent piece in a red paper talisman to celebrate the Wongs' impending move into their new home: a two-bedroom apartment in Ping Yuen, the first federally subsidized housing project for low-income families in Chinatown. Selected as the "first family" of the public housing project by the San Francisco Housing Authority, the Wongs, as representatives of the new public housing tenants in Chinatown, participated in the housewarming ritual before joining the mayor in front of 5,000 San Franciscans gathered to celebrate the long-awaited opening of Ping Yuen.[2]

The jubilant crowd attending the dedication ceremony witnessed a fusion of traditional Chinese and Western elements, also evident in the building design, that reflected the underlying cooperation between Chinatown activists and the SFHA. Participants saw firecrackers lit to scare devils away and performers doing the lion dance for good luck, listened to melodies of "Chinatown, My Chinatown," and at one point joined together in singing the U.S. national anthem.[3] Serving as the master of ceremonies, Housing Commissioner Charles Jung welcomed Chairman of the Housing Authority E. N. Ayer, Chinatown Housing Committee Chairman Dr. Theodore C. Lee, and Mayor Robinson to speak.[4] In his keynote address, Robinson praised Chinese Americans' contributions to the city: "it is fitting that this most distinctive of Projects

"*Peace and Prosperity Dwell among Virtuous Neighbors*"

Figure 14. The Wong family in the model Ping Yuen apartment, October 19, 1951. The SFHA selected Henry Wong, a World War II veteran, along with his wife and two children, as the "first family" of Ping Yuen for a photo op in which they celebrated Ping Yuen's dedication with San Francisco mayor Elmer Robinson. San Francisco History Center, San Francisco Public Library.

should be dedicated here in San Francisco. The Chinese are among the earliest settlers to our City. They have contributed to our City's life, culture, commerce and spiritual life for over 100 years."[5] After dedicating three buildings—Tung Ping Yuen (the eastern building), Sai Ping Yuen (the western building), and Chung Ping Yuen (the central building)— to "the little boys and girls who will be born here, who will grow up here in an atmosphere of health and happiness and the good will of all the citizens of San Francisco," the mayor presented a golden key to the Wong family.[6] Tenants, representatives from the Housing Authority, district neighbors, and members of Chinatown social service organizations came together to celebrate the realization of public housing in the overcrowded district. During the next five decades, the complex web of cooperation—and at times contestation—among these groups resulted

98

"Peace and Prosperity Dwell among Virtuous Neighbors"

Figure 15. Ping Yuen dedication, October 21, 1951. Over 5,000 people came out to celebrate the opening of public housing in Chinatown. San Francisco History Center, San Francisco Public Library.

in Ping Yuen's ongoing success as a stable and engaged public housing community.

The festivities surrounding the opening of Ping Yuen highlight the uniqueness of the development: over 5,000 people showed up to celebrate the completion of 234 public housing units with Chinese-inspired architectural details. In contrast to the uproar over the construction of Valencia Gardens by Mission District residents, Ping Yuen had the support of residents in the Chinatown district, local housing officials, and the federal government, and received resounding praise in the local, national, and international press. The *San Francisco Chronicle* lauded the $3.5 million project as "America's most distinctive set of low-cost apartments."[7] Before the dedication, the *Journal of Housing* hailed Ping Yuen as "the only public housing project in the country

99

with discernable Oriental architectural design" and "one of the few projects to receive the unanimous endorsement of all city groups, however divergent their politics."[8] SFHA officials boasted about the national and international acclaim garnered by Ping Yuen: "Newsreel cameras [and] television and radio programs recorded the event and newspapers and periodicals as far away as China and Europe devoted space to the dedication."[9] The federal government, through the State Department–run international radio broadcasting operation, the Voice of America, transmitted the story of the new housing project for Chinese Americans "to far points of the World" and most assuredly throughout communist China.[10]

While touting the consensus around the development and the critical need for housing in the crowded Chinatown district, reporters repeatedly returned to the project's distinctive architectural style. The combination of a modern, functional design with Chinese architectural motifs and a bright color scheme differentiated Ping Yuen from all other public housing projects in the city, state, and nation. The *California Housing Reporter* captured the collective awe over the project's blend of modern and Chinese elements, pointing out the juxtaposition of automatic elevators and "picturesque yellow tile roofs and multicolored dragon decorations."[11] Noticeably absent from the media's wide coverage and the SFHA's promotion of the project was an acknowledgment of the decades of segregation and governmental neglect that resulted in the historically deplorable housing conditions in Chinatown. The Chinatown press took a more nuanced stance, however, hailing Ping Yuen both as much-needed housing and as a symbol of reparation for the century of suffering the Chinese had faced in San Francisco. An article in the *Chinese Press* exulted that "Ping Yuen is a strong, handsome, living memorial to a dream and its happy realization after more than fifteen years of 'blood, sweat, and tears'—and is America's pledge that a century-old wrong is being righted."[12] Backed by local, state, and federal government officials, the Ping Yuen buildings served as a physical marker of shifting attitudes toward Chinese Americans in the United States.[13]

Coalition building in the long-neglected ethnic ghetto was a critical ingredient to the realization and continuation of public housing in Chinatown. Over time, networks and collaboration among tenants

"Peace and Prosperity Dwell among Virtuous Neighbors"

and between tenant leaders and social service organizations sustained Ping Yuen in the face of the SFHA's intermittent leadership failures, mismanagement, and financial woes, as well as increased gang activity in the district. In 1938, through the activities of Chinese American advocates and Chinatown social service organizations, and again in 1966, with the creation of the Ping Yuen Residents Improvement Association (PYRIA), Chinatown leaders used the federal housing program to improve Ping Yuen and the larger Chinatown community. The historic segregation of the Chinese in San Francisco that prompted the need for public housing in Chinatown fostered alliances and coalitions between the tenants' association and nonprofit organizations and district businesses that proved mutually beneficial.[14]

Claiming full rights of citizenship, over the years low-income Chinese American tenants organized and used petitions, letter-writing campaigns, and rent strikes to pressure the SFHA into improving their living environment. As a result, Ping Yuen has been, by the estimate of its residents and district neighbors, a successful public housing project; through an active tenants' association and the cooperation of social service organizations, residents have fought for and won improvements for their project while striving for economic development and an unprecedented amount of control over their state-run living environment.

Another critical factor that provided a strong foundation for Ping Yuen was a consideration of regionalism and local conditions. The Housing Authority's collaboration with district leaders in the 1940s and 1950s demonstrates the significance of what scholar Gwendolyn Wright identified as a key component to successful public housing—an attention to "regionalism" that goes beyond design by showing "a concern for local traditions—social and architectural—with a determination to push the federal standards and fiscal limits" and "to insist upon trying new ideas."[15] While the Housing Authority's sensitivity to and cooperation with the Chinatown community in the design phase demonstrated the agency's early goal of strengthening communities and broke with the city's pattern of ignoring Chinatown, the Authority failed as a landlord over time. In the late 1960s, Ping Yuen tenants stepped in to fill the gaps left by the Housing Authority's erratic care. Employing strategies that in some respects mirrored the coalition-building efforts of

"Peace and Prosperity Dwell among Virtuous Neighbors"

Chinatown housing activists in the 1930s and 1940s, Ping Yuen tenant leaders effectively forged partnerships with nonprofits and used community organizing within public housing to effect change in their living environment. Working together over the past five decades, Chinatown nonprofit organizations and Ping Yuen tenants have fashioned public housing to fit community needs, demonstrating the possibilities of local input and tenant leadership and the importance of coalition building as an activist strategy in public housing. A high-density public housing success story in an era when critics, scholars, and tenants deemed similar designs unworkable, Ping Yuen—Chinatown's American project—stands as a vibrant counterpoint to the failure of public housing nationally.

Constructing Community: Ping Yuen from Concept to Reality

The opening of Ping Yuen marked over a decade of careful negotiation between Chinese American activists in Chinatown, the SFHA, and the federal government. However, it was Chinese American advocates who initiated and led the call for federal public housing in their district. When the Housing Authority opened in 1938, Chinatown faced a severe housing crisis. Newspapers cited an unpublished study on Chinatown living conditions and described the district as a "slum largely unfit for human habitation, comparable with the worst in the world and where a majority of the residents live in worse squalor than in any city in China."[16] Alternative housing options were not available. The Alien Land Law prohibited Chinese immigrants from owning property, and restrictive covenants written into deeds by white homeowners barred American-born Chinese from property ownership.[17] Beyond Grant Avenue and Powell Street, the boundaries of Chinatown were imposed with "a barbed wire barrier in the form of a . . . 'we do not rent to Orientals sign,'" keeping district residents from moving outside the crowded district. The *Chinese Digest*, a magazine published by Chinese American intellectuals, explained the problem: "Until such a time when prejudiced landowners see the light, housing conditions will remain an inevitable problem in Chinatown."[18] Bounded in place,

Chinese Americans searched for ways to improve conditions in the district.

Moving outside traditional reliance on family, district, and regional associations in Chinatown to provide welfare for members and to solve local issues, Chinese American housing activists turned to state and federal assistance.[19] In June 1937, just prior to the passage of the legislation establishing public housing in the United States, housing advocate Lim P. Lee noted the importance of the bill for the district. Lee explained, "San Francisco Chinatown can request the proper housing authorities to set up housing in this community for the families of low income. In view of our congested conditions, this is one of the urgent needs."[20] Recognizing the dual bind of residential segregation and the "disincentives for landlords to renovate tenements," Chinese American activists looked to the new federal public housing program as an alternative to the discriminatory private housing market.[21]

Shortly after the San Francisco Housing Authority formed in 1938, the newly selected housing commissioners received a number of letters from Chinatown housing advocates. The Chinese Young Women's Christian Association urged the SFHA to "make every effort to remedy the social situation of overcrowded homes in the Chinese section of city."[22] Commissioner Alice Griffith, supporting the sentiment of the letter, explained, "the Chinese are very anxious to have us do something for them the same as we are doing for other sections of the city."[23] In response to the activists' pleas and the results of the 1939 Real Property Survey that confirmed the deplorable housing conditions in the district, the Housing Authority moved forward with CAL 1-5, the Chinatown housing project. The exorbitant land prices in Chinatown, however, exceeded federal limits for purchase, thwarting the agency's plans to "relieve conditions in Chinatown, which is notorious for its poor housing."[24]

Despite this setback, the leaders of the Chinatown coalition refused to abandon their shared goal of bringing public housing to the area. Working together, they formed the Chinatown Housing Project Committee in 1939 to "take up the fight to have money appropriated from the Housing Authority funds for the erection of a housing unit in Chinatown."[25] The committee's organizational members included the Chinese Chamber of Commerce, the Chinese American Citizens

Alliance, the Chinese Young Men's Christian Association, the Chinese Catholic Center, Cathay Post American Legion, and members of the Chinese Six Companies; Dr. Theodore Lee served as chair. Lee, working with the San Francisco Junior Chamber of Commerce and the Chinese Junior Chamber of Commerce, tried to convince the city that improved housing conditions in Chinatown would benefit all of San Francisco.[26] Facing the reality of high costs for public housing construction in the district, committee members used creative strategies to meet the funding goal.

Dr. Theodore Lee remembers making a direct appeal to the First Lady during her visit to Chinatown in 1939. At the time, Lee worked in the restaurant business and often hosted famous visitors free of charge as part of their tour of Chinatown. When he learned that Eleanor Roosevelt might come to his restaurant, he contacted the Chinese Junior Chamber of Commerce and asked to participate in the First Lady's tour of the district. Serving as one of the chaperones, Lee guided Eleanor Roosevelt through the district, highlighting the sites and commenting on the housing crisis. Lee recalls,

> I told her Chinatown is very unique, it is self-contained and has its own culture, but there is an ugly side that we don't like to talk about. There is the highest infant mortality rate in the city. There is inadequate housing from the days of the single men society with everyone sleeping in one big room. As a result, we have the highest tuberculosis rate in the country. The only way to help the community is to change the law.[27]

Before the tour ended, the two discussed public housing and Lee explained that land prices in Chinatown exceeded federal limits. He explained frankly that the "only way to help the community is to change the law. 'I'll talk to my husband,' she said."[28] On October 30, 1939, President Roosevelt signed the Chinatown Housing Bill, designating $1,365,000 to go toward a housing project in the district.

Having won necessary gains from the federal government, Chinatown housing activists turned their focus to garnering local support and resources. The United States Housing Authority stipulated that the remaining one-third of the funding had to come from local sources.[29] Working together, the Chinatown Housing Project Committee, the

"Peace and Prosperity Dwell among Virtuous Neighbors"

Chinese Advisory Committee, the Junior Chamber of Commerce, and representatives from other organizations lobbied for the funds, combating some San Franciscans' concerns that public housing would decrease property values. While various organizations and individuals in Chinatown supported public housing, some residents of neighboring districts resisted its development. Fearful of decreased property values in and around Chinatown, members of the tony white neighborhood Nob Hill Association fought against Ping Yuen. Dr. Theodore Lee explained,

> They knew that Chinatown was in a very high tax area, that the property was valuable. Also, to them, Chinatown was a stigma lying right there between the high-class Nob Hill residential section and Montgomery Street, the financial district. They never liked Chinatown because it was in the way. And they could never get used to Chinese New Years. All that noise during the whole week of celebration was a nuisance. So every time I would go out to speak, they would send their lawyer out to speak for the opposing side.[30]

The Chinatown Housing Project Committee employed multiple tactics to overcome opposition and secure local funding. The coalition's key strategy entailed educating the public about the health and economic benefits of public housing. Knitting together the need for safe, affordable housing with the health and prosperity of all city residents, Lee and other members of the Chinatown Housing Project Committee made hundreds of speeches to civic and community groups across San Francisco about the overcrowded housing conditions in Chinatown. The alliance of organizations for public housing in Chinatown spent months publicizing their cause, with a platform focused primarily on improving health conditions in the district and secondarily on assisting the city's economy through tourism. As part of their strategy, they also encouraged San Francisco civic clubs to lobby federal and local housing authorities.[31] The public education program coalesced around the San Francisco Junior Chamber of Commerce's poster campaign "Chinatown Housing: How Shall It Be?" As described by historian Nayan Shah, the poster displayed the district's housing options side by side. On one side of the poster, under the heading "Poor Housing breeds filth, disease, crime, and fire hazard," were photos of dirty toilets, worn-out sinks, and peeling walls found in Chinatown housing. On the other side, under the promising headline "Good Housing breeds health, safety, and good citizenship," were drawings of new buildings with pagoda-style roofs and balconies along with a rendering of a spacious interior.[32] The poster and speaking campaigns espoused the power of proper housing to "reduce the danger of plague, aid health as well as business and, at the same time, retain the lure of San Francisco's famed Chinatown."[33] The Chinese-inspired designs on the poster, rendered by architect Mark Daniels, and the committee's arguments in support of public housing in Chinatown, reached a select national audience through the magazine *Architect and Engineer*.[34] Daniels, who designed the Chinese Pavilion at the 1939 Golden Gate Exposition, issued a plea in the magazine that supported the committee's position: public housing "will form not only a beautiful background but a monument to San Francisco's romantic and historic Chinatown, the largest Chinese settlement outside of Asia. It will bring business to both the Chinese and white merchants of San Francisco. There are benefits in addition to those of health and living standards."[35] Emphasizing health and wealth creation (through tourism), the Chinatown Housing Project Committee's campaign suggested that public housing would benefit all San Franciscans.

On March 4, 1940, the committee's efforts paid off when the San Francisco Board of Supervisors unanimously passed Resolution Number 852, pledging $75,000 for the development of public housing in Chinatown.[36] In 1941, the Housing Authority began soliciting bids for the demolition of existing buildings and put out a request for proposals for architectural plans. A year later, the SFHA purchased 2.6 acres of land and commissioned architects Mark Daniels and Henry Howard with their six-story modern "American-Oriental designs" to replace existing buildings with new, much-needed housing.[37]

As the SFHA moved through the planning process for public housing in Chinatown in the early 1940s, area residents remained confined in an urban ghetto with substandard housing that resulted in significant health problems. Within the nine-block district, 15,000 residents crammed together in 3,860 dwellings, 3,000 of which had no heat. The overcrowded conditions caused a tuberculosis (TB) rate three times higher than that in the rest of the city.[38] The housing and health problems in the district stemmed from a century of legal and extralegal discrimination against Chinese immigrants and their American-born children.[39] De jure and de facto segregation sent a clear message: Chinese were not welcome. Residential segregation, upheld by the Alien Land Law and practiced by landlords outside Chinatown, forced residents of Chinese descent to live in a crowded ethnic ghetto.[40] Conditions further deteriorated between the 1920s and 1940s as more families crowded into district housing designed for single occupancy, owing in part to the new federal regulations that allowed wives of Chinese immigrants to emigrate and Chinatown's resulting shift from being a bachelor society to being a family-centered one.[41] District residents continued to suffer from the effects of this severe overcrowding when the SFHA's construction plan was delayed by World War II.

The plight of Chinatown residents began to receive widespread attention as attitudes and policies toward the Chinese began to soften during the war. China's alliance with the United States during the war and the participation of Chinese Americans in the military influenced changing perceptions of Chinese Americans.[42] In San Francisco, over 2,500 Chinese Americans joined the military in District 76, Chinatown.[43] Chinese American men enlisted to serve the U.S. military, as the *Chinese Press* noted, "to prove that they want to be men of war with Uncle Sam's 'men-o' war."[44] Their contributions, the *Chinese Press* continued, signaled that their "social and political ideals are those of American democracy."[45] Likewise, as the perceived "deviant bachelor society" gave way to a growing number of families, the increase in the adult female population transformed negative racialized images of the Chinese in America into "an assimilatable population of heterosexual nuclear families."[46] The early Cold War strategy of promoting the image of racial equality and the domestic ideal emerged in response to the federal government's growing concern about the impact the "status and treatment of Chinese Americans as a racial minority in American society had on perceptions of the United States in the Asian Pacific" after China became communist in 1949.[47] As the white nuclear family living in suburban homes and exercising unprecedented purchasing power materialized as a symbol of American national identity and supremacy over communism during the Cold War, the city of San

"Peace and Prosperity Dwell among Virtuous Neighbors"

Francisco turned its attention to improving the long-ignored housing problems in Chinatown.[48]

China's turn to communism, and the later passage of the 1949 Housing Act, provided the means to move forward with needed housing reform. Pressing the advantage of the nation's anti-communist fervor, Chinese American activists in San Francisco highlighted Chinatown residents' adaptation "to middle-class norms in consumer taste . . . and respectable domesticity" to demonstrate the potential for cultivating normative heterosexual families through better housing.[49] At the same time, white San Franciscans' long history of discrimination against Chinese Americans began to abate in response to the wartime service of Chinese Americans and the economic growth offered by tourism in Chinatown. Chinese American activists and the SFHA united to bring public housing to Chinatown, showcasing the nation's goodness and demonstrating Chinese Americans' claim to the benefits of full citizenship by offering modern apartments in state-run housing. The *San Francisco News* captured the excitement about the possibilities offered by public housing:

> For the first time in the history of Chinatown there will be real homes. Families that have endured the shocking housing of Chinatown never planned for family living will have "a real living room" where they can gather and visit, where the children can invite their friends. Each home will have its own kitchen and bath, and enough bedroom space for all the family.[50]

The author of the article noted—and prospective tenants rejoiced—that in contrast to the small, dark spaces inhabited by many residents in the district, each new apartment was designed "to receive plenty of fresh air and its windows will invite the sunshine."[51] Decent housing for some Chinese Americans in Chinatown promised to showcase democracy to the nation, communist China, and the world.

Against the backdrop of the mounting Cold War and an intense postwar housing crisis in the city, the SFHA faced two hurdles to building urgently needed public housing in Chinatown: additional funding to cover land and construction costs after the war and voter approval.[52] Hamstrung by soaring land and construction costs, the Housing Authority could move ahead on the project only after the pas-

"Peace and Prosperity Dwell among Virtuous Neighbors"

sage of the federal Housing Act of 1949 increased funds for loans and subsidies. In the wake of new federal housing legislation and the explosion of the private housing market, California voters narrowly passed ballot initiative Proposition 10 in November 1950. A victory for the anti–public housing lobby, the measure required local referenda on any proposed public housing in a city or county.[53] The law, luckily, did little to slow down the Chinatown public housing project. Housing advocates, health officials, and a number of Chinese and white business leaders continued to push the city government to uphold its "civic responsibility" by investing in public housing and social welfare. The project held out the promise of decreasing the high TB rate in Chinatown, a public health danger that threatened to spread to nearby areas.[54] This argument worked: San Francisco voters approved Ping Yuen.[55] Even the Nob Hill Protective Association endorsed Ping Yuen in hopes that the project "would keep the Chinese in Chinatown."[56] With the backing of various groups, the SFHA demolished tenements and stores, evicting forty-one families and 158 single men, to construct the new, modern Ping Yuen.[57]

The collaboration between the SFHA and the Chinatown community that made public housing a reality in Chinatown permeated the design decisions for Ping Yuen. The advocacy of the Chinatown Housing Project Committee and other district supporters resulted in the Housing Authority commissioning plans that incorporated what architectural historian Gwendolyn Wright has termed "Chinese regionalism superimposed over a functionalist design."[58] The resulting buildings blended with the neighborhood and bolstered tourism. Originally designed by Mark Daniels and Henry Howard, who turned the project over to J. Francis Ward and John Bolles after the war, the housing complex consists of three concrete six-story buildings with courtyards in the rear; the complex offered forty-six one-bedroom units, ninety-two two-bedroom units, seventy-five three-bedroom units, and twenty-one four-bedroom units. With eighty-nine units per acre, the project reportedly had the highest density of any "Bay Area family housing."[59] A modern structure with elevators, the project showcased Chinese design, including "a side-gabled terra cotta tile roof and exterior hallways accented with inset panels and colored, diamond-shaped ceramic tiles" and vertical supports with "rectangular posts with incised

"*Peace and Prosperity Dwell among Virtuous Neighbors*"

Figure 16. Ping Yuen under construction, September 27, 1951. San Francisco History Center, San Francisco Public Library.

Chinese characters indicating 'Ping Yuen.'"[60] Signaling their recognition of the importance of community buy in, the Housing Authority commissioners asked the Chinese Advisory Committee early in the process to select a name for the Chinatown project.[61] After several months, the committee chose "Ping Yuen," meaning "Tranquil Gardens," and identified the three project buildings with the Chinese words for "east" (tung), "central" (chung), and "west" (sai). The commission not only voted unanimously to use the names but also insisted "that the Chinese characters for these names be used in decorating the project."[62] With bright yellow and red paint that blended seamlessly into the neighborhood, the project fit in with the faux Chinese architectural style already used in the area. Chinese American entrepre-

110

"Peace and Prosperity Dwell among Virtuous Neighbors"

Figure 17. Ping Yuen, June 1964. Photograph by Alan J. Canterbury. San Francisco History Center, San Francisco Public Library.

neurs had hoped this style would lure tourists to the area after Chinatown was rebuilt following the 1906 earthquake and fire.[63]

Throughout the long development process, the SFHA and the Chinatown Housing Project Committee focused on public housing's role in improving health conditions in the district. When the Housing Authority first requested federal funding for Ping Yuen, Dr. Jacob Geiger of the city health department sent a letter to the Housing Commission asking for space in the public housing development for the Chinatown Health Center. Geiger, an early proponent of public housing, broke with other health officials in the 1930s by blaming poor housing conditions—rather than residents themselves—for health problems in Chinatown.[64] The causal link between housing and health as well as the central location of Ping Yuen made the relocation of the neighborhood health center appealing.[65] Demonstrating a clear un-

"*Peace and Prosperity Dwell among Virtuous Neighbors*"

Figure 18. Ping Yuen, June 1964. Photograph by Alan J. Canterbury. San Francisco History Center, San Francisco Public Library.

derstanding of the important role the health center played in the TB-stricken district, the housing commissioners approved the request in 1940 and again in 1949, with a unanimous vote to open the Chinatown Health Center in Ping Yuen.[66] Open to all residents of the district, the health center drew people living outside of Ping Yuen into the space, fostering a feeling of familiarity and ease with the public housing project.

Along with promoting public health, the SFHA targeted resources to invest in Ping Yuen as a tourist attraction. The promotion of Ping Yuen's unique public housing design billed the project as much-needed housing that would contribute to the tourist trade, the economic lifeline of the district and the city. A 1946 bulletin released by the Downtown Association and sent to the Housing Authority stressed the

"Peace and Prosperity Dwell among Virtuous Neighbors"

Figure 19. Entry gate, Ping Yuen, 1956. San Francisco History Center, San Francisco Public Library.

importance "from a trade standpoint of maintaining the Chinese character of Chinatown."[67] Responding to the need to boost tourism, the housing commissioners approved an additional structure that did more than merely echo the aesthetic of the district. Ping Yuen boasted its own tourist attraction: a reproduction of the Paliou Gate copied from the Marble Pagoda in Beijing, with an inscription over it by China's famed philosopher, Lao Tse, reading "Peace and Prosperity Prevail among Virtuous Neighbors"—an adage the Housing Authority surely supported.[68] The gate, as well as the project's design, pleased both the city and the district, mutual beneficiaries of the tourist revenue. The city even went so far as to promote the project as a tourist site, listing Ping Yuen on the Chamber of Commerce's tourist map of Chinatown.[69]

The coalition building among Chinatown housing advocates and cooperation with the SFHA resulted in public housing in the district that in many ways pushed federal limits. Collaboration, neighborhood support, and cross-sector alliances, along with the SFHA's attention to

"Peace and Prosperity Dwell among Virtuous Neighbors"

the district's assets and needs created a strong foundation for Ping Yuen. At the same time, the approval of the health center and Paliou Gate by the Housing Commission reflected long-held assumptions about residents in Chinatown. Containing Chinese Americans—and TB—in Chinatown, and marketing both faux and traditional Chinese cultural elements there, in some ways reinforced rather than alleviated Chinatown's status as a circumscribed ethnic ghetto. The tensions between ethnic segregation, exclusion, and access to affordable housing began to mount in the years after Ping Yuen opened.

Early Activism: Ethnicity and Community in Ping Yuen

The demand for apartments in Ping Yuen demonstrated Chinatown's need for public housing. When the rental offices for the project opened in the Chinese Citizens Alliance building on August 1, 1951, applicants lined up around the block. For days people queued outside the office in hopes of living in Ping Yuen; veterans and people displaced by slum clearance at the building site had priority on the list of over 600 applicants.[70] Chinese American nuclear families, "mostly veterans," became the first tenants at the project.[71] After the buildings were complete and the SFHA opened Ping Yuen—to great fanfare—selected tenants wasted little time moving into the new apartments. Veteran Watson Low summed up the transformation in his living environment: "The difference from where I lived before and here is like heaven and hell. . . . The place where I was living had a public kitchen and a public toilet and still cost too much."[72] Chang Jok Lee and her husband, George Lee, also a World War II veteran, moved out of a small hotel room on Bush Street into their apartment, which was "really new" and "very good."[73] Federally subsidized Ping Yuen provided more space, light, and amenities for an affordable rent for Low, the Lees, and other Chinese American families moving into the development. Living in public housing over the years also galvanized tenants, including Low and the Lees, to become activists for the Ping Yuen community they called home.

New public housing tenants and their neighbors in the district could view a version of the Chinese American immigration story on the wall of the Chinatown Health Center inside Ping Yuen. In the waiting room, patients saw a mural commissioned by the SFHA that celebrated the contributions of Chinese in the United States. The mural, entitled "One Hundred Years of Progress of the Chinese in the U.S." and created by James Leong, a local Chinese American artist, contained eight sequences "from Chinese [rice fields] to the departure for America and the gold rush and railroad building period ending with the role of the Chinese in World War II and Ping Yuen, a better life for the Chinese."[74] The Housing Authority carefully excluded depictions of the discrimination the Chinese had endured in San Francisco, eliminating a section depicting "the Dennis Kearny episode" proposed in the original sketches. Kearny organized the Workingman's Party in 1877—with the slogan "The Chinese Must Go"—and incited many whites to burn Chinese businesses. Paying for the $1,000 mural out of its own budget, the Housing Authority reinforced a skewed representation of the Chinese in the United States through the selection of "positive" artistic representations.[75] By sponsoring a "whitewashed" depiction of the "happy Chinese" in San Francisco, the SFHA revealed the limits of its advocacy for Chinatown as well as its own promotional agenda.

The mural sparked controversy in the district. According to Leong, "Chinatown rejected the mural. The community agreed that though some elements were historically correct, the depiction of the Chinese was not favorable." Critics lambasted Leong's inclusion of traditional Chinese folkways, including a Chinese man with a queue and Chinese women drying fish and sorting shrimp. Manifesting the tensions between American and Chinese culture and the push and pull of modernization and assimilation, other Chinese Americans criticized the Americanized depictions of a Chinese American boy with a baseball. The final panel demonstrated yet another growing reality for many Chinese Americans: high-quality affordable housing finally existed— in limited quantities—in Chinatown, but there were few other housing options in the city.[76]

While Ping Yuen offered new, modern apartments in Chinatown for eligible families, many Chinese Americans sought to move outside the district. In the wake of World War II, Chinese Americans saw racial hostilities ease and legalized discrimination end. With racially

Figure 20. Artist James Leong pointing to his mural *One Hundred Years of Progress of the Chinese in the U.S.* with residents at Ping Yuen, 1952. The mural went on to spark controversy in Chinatown, both for its representations of Chinese folkways and for Americanizing the Chinese in the United States (as illustrated by the boy with the baseball visible in this image). San Francisco History Center, San Francisco Public Library.

"Peace and Prosperity Dwell among Virtuous Neighbors"

restrictive covenants outlawed, Chinese Americans with higher incomes started buying houses outside Chinatown. As a result, class lines emerged among Chinese Americans: "living outside the ghetto connoted higher socioeconomic status."[77] Yet even as the federal government dismantled sanctioned racial segregation in housing, Chinese Americans, like African Americans, faced reinforced racial barriers.[78]

As the Lees and the Lows settled into their new low-rent apartments in 1952, Chinese immigrant Sing Sheng and his pregnant wife Grace decided to move to the suburbs of South San Francisco with their two-and-a-half-year-old son. After answering an ad in the *San Francisco Chronicle*, Seng put down a $2,950 deposit for a house in the Southwood suburb, located in the working-class residential district known as "Industrial City." Once Southwood neighbors learned of the pending sale, the owners received angry calls, letters, and threats accusing them of breaking the racially restrictive covenants of the subdivision. Southwood residents lashed out at the Shengs as well, instructing them to stay away, fearing that their presence in the neighborhood would decrease property values and increase local disturbances.[79] Rather than take the family's case to court, Sheng put his trust in democracy and asked for the entire neighborhood to vote on whether his family could live there. In a letter sent prior to the vote, Sheng echoed the local and national media's framing of the vote as either a triumph or failure of democracy: "We think so highly of Democracy because it offers freedom and equality. . . . We have forsaken our beloved in China and have come to this country seeking the same basic rights. Do not make us the victims of false democracy. Please vote for us."[80] Asserting what they viewed as their own democratic rights against the backdrop of the Cold War, neighbors voted: 174 against, 28 in favor, and 14 no-votes.[81] With their votes, neighbors prohibited the Shengs from moving into the neighborhood. Opponents echoed a common theme, calling for Sheng "to live with his own people in a Chinese track."[82] De facto segregation persisted even as Chinese Americans accessed new, legally sanctioned opportunities to live where they wanted.

As the Cold War escalated, housing immigrant and second-generation Chinese American families in Chinatown took on greater significance. With a population of Chinatown reaching 31,000 by 1960, the demand for affordable housing in Chinatown persisted.[83] In 1958, the SFHA began to appeal to the Public Housing Administration (PHA) for additional funds to build more public housing units in Chinatown. The Housing Authority placed Chinatown public housing directly into the Cold War framework by highlighting Ping Yuen's significance as a political tool and a way station for immigrants from communist China who sought a better life in the United States.[84] The commissioners reminded the PHA that Ping Yuen was "'a must see' on the itinerary of all groups referred to the Authority by the State Department and has been one of the best arguments against Communism in the Far East."[85] The housing commissioners argued that building another project with "Oriental motifs" would be worth the extra expense of the decorative elements, appeasing Chinatown residents and strengthening the fight against communism by housing more Chinese American families. The Housing Authority, promoting itself through Ping Yuen, went so far as to present visiting government officials both from the United States and abroad with miniature replicas of the Paliou Gate, symbolizing the success of Ping Yuen.[86] The PHA, unconvinced of the necessity for another "Chinese project," rejected the Housing Authority's initial request for additional monies for Chinese design elements at the Ping Yuen annex. Ironically, as the PHA turned the SFHA away, the federal Immigration Department looked to the SFHA for help, asking for photographs of Ping Yuen. Immigration officials wanted to show Chinese immigrants the high-quality facilities available to them in the United States.[87]

After battling high costs and federal regulations for four years, the Housing Authority, with the backing of the Chinatown community, finally secured federal approval in 1959 for additional funding to purchase land and the go-ahead to raise money for Chinese motifs at the new project.[88] The project was completed in 1961, and on October 29, a crowd gathered to celebrate the dedication of Ping Yuen North. At a cost of $3 million, the twelve-story building, on a Z-shaped piece of land bounded by Stockton and Powell Streets and Broadway and Pacific Avenues, provided apartments for 150 families and 44 singles (used to house elderly tenants), with total unit space for approximately 560 people.[89] The reinforced concrete building echoed the Chinese decorative motifs of the first three Ping Yuen buildings, including Chi-

"Peace and Prosperity Dwell among Virtuous Neighbors"

Figure 21. People pausing to look at Ping Yuen North, May 1962. The monumental pillar was designed to connect the project with the architecture of Chinatown. San Francisco History Center, San Francisco Public Library.

nese designs on the lower balcony and "a monumental pillar" in the garden.[90] Pitched to the federal government as a demonstration of the superiority of American values over communism, and marketed to the city as an important addition to the local economy and an "Oriental" attraction promising "to out-rival its companion project as a tourism attraction," Ping Yuen North opened "in the tradition of Chinatown" with a celebration similar to the festivities in 1951.[91]

Like Ping Yuen, Ping Yuen North's design and location was designed to appeal specifically to Chinese Americans living in Chinatown;

119

"Peace and Prosperity Dwell among Virtuous Neighbors"

Figure 22. Ping Yuen North, 2003. The design combined modern lines with Chinese-inspired details, such as the decorative element at the bottom right. Photograph by the author.

neighbors, the city, and the Housing Authority all advocated for a segregated project. As the civil rights movement was gaining national attention and many Americans began advocating for integration in housing and schools nationwide, the Chinatown neighborhood applauded the opening of another segregated federally subsidized housing project in the district. When Ping Yuen opened in 1951, the Housing Authority allocated tenant occupancy through its 1942 neighborhood pattern policy, which established an occupancy ratio for racial and ethnic groups in proportion to their population in a given neighborhood. Three years later, a week before the 1954 *Brown v. Board of Education* decision, the U.S. Supreme Court issued a mandate to the SFHA to integrate public housing in the city, upholding a California Supreme Court ruling.[92] Nevertheless, the Housing Authority continued to house Chinese Americans in Ping Yuen, and later in Ping Yuen North, despite the court ruling and President Kennedy's executive order in 1962 outlawing discrimination in public housing.

The consistent placement of Chinese Americans in the Ping Yuen projects after the high court ruling on segregation came under attack starting in the 1950s. Black activists protested the segregation at Ping Yuen, while many Chinese Americans spoke out against integration at community meetings. Historian Charlotte Brooks notes that some Chinatown residents, in pushing to protect the homogeneity of Ping Yuen, imagined integration as a "black phenomenon and at times used ugly stereotypes to describe the African American population."[93] In 1962, NAACP president Terry Francois raised the issue of segregation at Ping Yuen to housing commissioners who promised—and then failed—to study the issue. In 1963, Solomon Johnson, an African American attorney and vice chairman of the SFHA, challenged the "racial solidarity" of all Chinese families living in Ping Yuen.[94] Backed by the NAACP and drawing on the national struggle for racial integration, Johnson urged the Housing Authority to take some Chinese residents out of Ping Yuen and move blacks into the project. Integration was not only necessary, Johnson argued; it was the law. Ignoring other commissioners' claims that the "Chinese people are happy at Ping Yuen," Johnson attacked what he saw as special treatment and segregation: "Those people have no right to be in an all-Chinese project. They're discriminating against whites and Negroes. We should start moving Chinese out of there."[95] Situating his argument within the context of the racial tensions exploding in the South, Johnson pressed his point at a Housing Commission meeting: "We're sitting here talking just like the people in Birmingham—I can't believe we're really here in San Francisco." His chief opponent on the issue of moving Chinese residents out of Ping Yuen, Commissioner Mazzola, fired back, "Now you just keep Birmingham out of this room."[96]

Johnson's call for the integration of Ping Yuen received little traction, and his comments were rebuked by public officials. Mayor George Christopher criticized Johnson for putting forth a proposal that "sets a group of Chinese against a group of Negroes." Johnson responded that he had been misunderstood; his intent was to suggest that an "inter group relations officer be appointed to encourage qualified applicants for public housing to move into areas where there are existing vacancies."[97] Built for Chinese Americans in Chinatown, as demonstrated by its name, location, and architectural design, the project—while technically "open to all races"—continued to house primarily Chinese Americans who "have regularly dominated the application list." A *San Francisco Chronicle* editorial summed up the prevailing attitude of the district, the Housing Authority, and the racially and ethnically diverse applicants waiting for space in San Francisco public housing: "like Chinatown, Ping Yuen is a special case and may well remain so with offense to no one."[98]

A cartoon next to the *Chronicle* editorial illuminated the precarious racial, ethnic, cultural, and spatial politics intertwined in the proposal to integrate Ping Yuen.[99] In the foreground, an African American man in a suit stands across the street from Ping Yuen, looking on with an expression of surprise. A Chinese American man wearing traditional Chinese clothes stands in front of the project, leaning with his right arm on a concrete block labeled Ping Yuen and holding a leash in his left hand. At the end of the leash stands a dragon—mouth open, teeth showing—akin to the statues that decorate the project.[100] Chinese characters on the building further highlight the cultural gulf between the two men.[101] The Chinese American man frowns at the African American. His expression, along with the dragon's menacing look, alerts the "intruder" that African Americans are not welcome at the project. Chinatown and Ping Yuen residents, as well as the SFHA, seemed to uphold the message of the editorial and cartoon by continually promoting segregation in the district's public housing. While Ping Yuen's demographics shifted over time, starting with non-Chinese Asian residents moving into Ping Yuen North when it opened, the project continued to house only Chinese Americans, and later other Asian Americans, fueling local and national criticism of the SFHA's sustained segregation.

The bonds between the Housing Authority, residents, and community organizations shifted over time as tenants and social service agencies in Chinatown mobilized in the wake of the African American civil rights movement and as the Housing Authority struggled to maintain its projects after the federal government changed regulations and cut funding. During the 1950s and 1960s, the Housing Authority continued to recognize, celebrate, and promote Ping Yuen for its design, dedicated managers, and perfect rent record. The project stood in stark contrast to the Housing Authority's "big four" public housing developments, which were becoming riddled with safety and maintenance problems.[102] Tenants who lived in Hunters Point, located in the predominantly African American district of the same name and long suffering neglect by the city, demanded change in 1966. The Hunters Point Tenants Union pushed the SFHA to fund backlogged maintenance, threatening a rent strike and pooling tenant rent monies to fund painting and renovation projects. Within six months, the collective power of the tenants resulted in a $350,000 pledge by the city to the SFHA to refurbish the project.[103] As the Housing Authority increasingly focused attention and resources on projects with pressing problems, Ping Yuen residents, like tenants at Hunters Point, organized to help themselves, forming the Ping Yuen Residents Improvement Association (PYRIA) in 1966 with guidance from the local Economic Opportunity Council (EOC), an outgrowth of the War on Poverty program.

The tenants' organization at Ping Yuen grew out of the efforts of the EOC and later garnered the support of other social services agencies in Chinatown. Building on the community-based activism led by middle-class Chinese Americans that had helped bring public housing to Chinatown, the formation of PYRIA emerged from a locally based, federally funded initiative to organize "the poor." Created and funded by the 1964 Equal Opportunity Act, and specifically by Title II, "Urban and Rural Community Action Programs," the Chinatown–North Beach EOC of San Francisco set out to organize community programs with a federal mandate to involve the poor in the development and operation

"Peace and Prosperity Dwell among Virtuous Neighbors"

of local programs. In an effort to mobilize low-income residents in Chinatown to organize and work collectively to improve the community's living conditions, the Chinatown–North Beach EOC targeted the Ping Yuen projects in 1965. The EOC viewed the over 1,830 Ping Yuen residents as representatives of Chinatown's basic problems in the areas of employment, health, education, and housing. After overcoming initial resistance from residents, EOC workers gained ground in January 1966 when they held a meeting for tenants to discuss their problems and complaints. The tenants' list was long and detailed their frustrations at the rise in rental rates, loitering, and unsanitary conditions in elevators and stairways. This first meeting led to others, generating enough interest that residents formed PYRIA, elected officers, and wrote and approved a constitution.[104]

As the support of the EOC, and later other community organizations, aided PYRIA, it was tenant leaders—many of them Chinese immigrants—who embraced their rights to participate in and challenge the political process that influenced their lives as residents in state-run housing. Like the middle-class, second-generation Chinese American activists who had advocated for public housing, playgrounds, and social services by arguing for the "entitlement" of Chinese American families in the 1930s and 1940s, the low-income residents at Ping Yuen began to utilize the rhetoric and tools of American democracy to push for change in the late 1960s.[105] As Ping Yuen began to change slowly from a "really peaceful, clean" place where "everything was maintained well and house rules were enforced" to a project plagued by deferred maintenance and, increasingly, gang traffic, tenants including George and Chang Jok Lee decided to become involved.[106] Encouraged by the EOC to seek self-help and to participate in city-level meetings, PYRIA leaders turned advice into action. Shortly after forming, PYRIA requested and received additional police patrols and, in an attempt to promote cleanliness, wrote signs for the garbage disposal area in Chinese as well as English.

Tackling the two main complaints of tenants—safety and sanitation—the organization then took on another problem: meeting space. PYRIA officers and two EOC workers attended a Housing Commission meeting in September 1966 to request the use of the laundry room on the ninth floor of Ping Yuen North for PYRIA's meeting

"Peace and Prosperity Dwell among Virtuous Neighbors"

space and for other community services such as day care, English classes, social and educational activities, and vocational training.[107] The housing commissioners, enforcing their mandate that no visitor could speak without permission granted prior to the start of the meeting, denied the group's request to address the Commission. In a show of protest, PYRIA representatives and EOC staff walked out of the meeting.[108]

During the ensuing two weeks before the next Commission meeting, PYRIA members planned their strategy of using the commissioners' own "principled" language and housing ideals to support their proposal. At the next Commission meeting, PYRIA representatives Harry Chan and Mrs. Wong (through Chan's translation) argued on behalf of 250 PYRIA members that the Housing Authority should grant the organization space because "an association without a meeting room is like a man without a home." Contending that a meeting room would "foster better relationships among residents" and that PHA guidelines stated that tenants' associations should have a meeting place, they urged the commissioners to remodel the laundry room into a meeting space. In a clear expression of Ping Yuen's importance, both as a "model" public housing project that the city showed off to visitors and as the project with "virtuous neighbors" who paid their rent on time each month, Mrs. Wong and Mr. Chan drew on the success of the project as leverage for a meeting space:

> Historically speaking, Ping Yuen has had the best record in rent paying. In the past fifteen years, Ping Yuen residents have paid more than one and a half million dollars in rent. We have never been delinquent in paying rent, as you can see from the tribute given to Ping Yuen by the Housing Commission in 1961. The Ping Yuen residents have never asked for anything. This is the first time.[109]

At the meeting, the housing commissioners unanimously agreed to "make every endeavor to provide . . . space" for residents. But then the request stalled for three years.[110]

PYRIA members redoubled their efforts during this time, submitting a petition for space and trying to raise donations to overhaul the laundry room.[111] In 1969, PYRIA requested a different location for a community room: the space occupied by the Chinatown Health

Center, which was slated to relocate in 1970. With unanimous approval, the housing commissioners finally granted PYRIA a meeting space, commending the organization's leaders "for their persistence and spirit of pursuit."[112] The determination of PYRIA praised by the Housing Commission in 1969 became a problem for the Housing Authority a decade later.

In the 1970s, PYRIA members challenged their historically cooperative bond with the Housing Authority on issues of safety and sanitation by escalating their actions from letter writing and attending Housing Commission meetings to organizing rent strikes. Alongside public housing residents across the city and the nation, Ping Yuen tenants agitated for improvements to their living environment and expressed frustration over the increase in crime near their apartments. PYRIA's actions reflected three intertwined events: rising tensions over the housing crisis in and around Chinatown that deepened in the 1960s and erupted in the 1970s, the activism of tenants' groups such as the Public Housing Tenants Association (PHTA), and the larger pattern of rent strikes occurring across the United States.[113]

By the 1970s, the persistent housing crisis in Chinatown grew as new waves of Asian immigrants settled in and around the district. At the same time, the pro-business, pro-developer contingent and its quasi-governmental arm, the San Francisco Redevelopment Agency (SFRA), continued to push for expansion of the Financial District abutting Chinatown. These tensions, and mounting activism of nonwhites seeking equality at Ping Yuen and Hunters Point, coalesced at the International Hotel (I-Hotel) site. Located in Manilatown between Chinatown and the Financial District on Kearny and Jackson Streets, the I-Hotel was home to 196 Chinese and Filipino tenants, many poor and elderly, who rented rooms for $45 a month. In 1968, the expansion of the Financial District spread to Manilatown when Milton Meyer and Company, headed by San Francisco business magnate Walter Shorenstein, bought the I-Hotel and made plans to construct a multilevel parking lot on the site. Shorenstein secured a demolition permit and ordered the eviction of all tenants. His action drew an immediate protest from I-Hotel tenants and Chinatown neighbors, politicized Asian American college students from the University of California at Berkeley and other San Francisco area colleges and universities, and housing activists in the city. Unlike the housing advocates who prioritized families in their push for public housing in the 1930s and 1940s, Chinese American activists in the 1970s "enlarged their agenda to include the single and widowed elderly who lived in Chinatown."[114] The demonstrations around the I-Hotel became the rallying point of young activists and organizers, who drew publicity to the tenants' plight.

The battle over the I-Hotel raged on for nine years as the city, investors, tenants, and tenant supporters struggled for resolution. During that time, the Four Seas Investment Corporation, headed by Thai businessman Supasit Mahaguna, bought the hotel, protestors—including Ping Yuen tenants—picketed city hall, and Mayor George Moscone attempted to broker a deal in which the city would purchase the hotel and sell it back to the tenants for $1.3 million dollars.[115] The plan failed, and in January 1977, the Four Seas Corporation, with the backing of the court system, posted eviction notices. Five thousand protestors, including members from PYRIA, picketed at the site, linking arms to form a human barricade around the hotel to prevent evictions.[116] Their efforts postponed the evictions until August 4, when riot police pushed past 3,000 people to remove the remaining fifty tenants. George and Chang Jok Lee joined the crowd that night, fighting again to stay the evictions:

> It seemed that we all stood on the sidewalk for hours. Suddenly the horses charged.... We wanted the horses to stop charging, but the tactical squad used their billy clubs to hold us back on the sidewalk. As the horses rushed and trampled, the human chain around the hotel broke. People fell down. Tears poured out of my eyes as I heard Hongisto [then chief of police] breaking down the door to the I-Hotel. We stayed in front of the I-Hotel until three in the morning—watching every tenant being either dragged out or carried out. [117]

Chang Jok Lee remembers the pain of defeat, after marching at City Hall, picketing, and staying overnight to protest in support of I-Hotel residents: "I saw what happened at the I-Hotel and I was moved and sad.... I knew how in this country you have so much freedom."[118] The fight for housing justice continued. Although supporters and activists lost the battle to maintain low-rent housing for singles at the I-Hotel, their actions motivated tenants in Chinatown to resist developers' attempts to replace affordable housing with luxury residences.[119] Echoing the struggle for the I-Hotel, tenants across Chinatown held rent strikes in 1977 and 1978 to protest rent increases and poor maintenance.[120]

Amidst rent hikes and the decline of housing stock in Chinatown, PYRIA members also endeavored to maintain Ping Yuen as high-quality, affordable housing for residents. Setting a course for self-sufficiency and community outreach, PYRIA members wrested control over their project environment. Through petitions, rent strikes, and involvement with community agencies, PYRIA worked to improve maintenance and security and to care for residents' social needs—tasks the beleaguered Housing Authority could not accomplish. Beginning in 1976, PYRIA challenged the Housing Authority to improve maintenance after tenants complained about the lack of steady hot water and heat. Disavowing responsibility and chastising the tenants for being too clean, the Housing Authority, in a gendered response, claimed that the "women in Ping Yuen wash their clothes too often, and it drains the water."[121] The actual cause of the problem was four defective boilers that had pumped lukewarm water to residents for over two years. Frustrated by the Housing Authority's failure to respond to tenants' complaints and the "intolerable living conditions" at Ping Yuen, PYRIA submitted a petition with over one hundred signatures and threatened to start a rent strike if their needs were not met.[122] Their actions netted results. By January 1977, the Housing Authority had repaired the boilers, and more residents, impressed by PYRIA's success, joined the association.

Mrs. Lee Chan, a Ping Yuen resident for over thirty-five years, recalled the impact of PYRIA's activism: "After a month I still did not have hot water. . . . I went to the office and complained and they said they had put the order in and they can not do anything more about it. So I talked to Mrs. Wong and she said why don't you go to the Association and Mr. [George] Lee and they can get the Housing Authority to fix it." Impressed by PYRIA's attention to her concerns and success with the Housing Authority, Mrs. Chan joined the tenants' association and continued as a member for the next three decades.[123]

The success of PYRIA in challenging the Housing Authority was a critically important experience for the association leadership and the

"Peace and Prosperity Dwell among Virtuous Neighbors"

tenants because it set a precedent of achieving success by aggressively dealing with project problems. Within two years, PYRIA turned brinkmanship into an onslaught against the Housing Authority, fully exercising their democratic right to protest. The catalyst for PYRIA's actions was tragedy. On August 23, 1978, nineteen-year-old Julia Wong, returning home from work at 10 p.m., was raped and murdered in Ping Yuen North on her way up the stairs to her tenth-floor apartment. Outraged tenants claimed that Ms. Wong's death might have been prevented if the elevator had worked. PYRIA immediately requested more security from the Housing Authority, including guards, fencing, and additional lighting. The Housing Authority responded by rushing through a contract for elevator repairs and posting one guard for the project buildings.[124] Noting that Ping Yuen has the "lowest rate of reported crime of any of our projects," the Housing Authority refused to "give them special treatment" by hiring multiple security guards, fearing the response of public housing tenants across San Francisco, many of whom lived in higher-crime neighborhoods.[125] Insulted by the Housing Authority's limited response, residents chained a "motorcycle to the door leading to the stairwell where Wong was attacked to prevent others from using it" and threatened to start a rent strike on October 1 if their demands for security were not met.[126] By the end of September, after multiple meetings, the two sides seemed close to reaching a compromise over security measures that called for the city to build fences around the projects and for tenants to organize their own "watchdog force." The plan failed, however, because tenants would not withdraw their demand for nighttime security guards.[127]

The tenants' refusal to concede and their continued willingness to threaten extreme actions against the Housing Authority resulted both from Wong's death and from the escalating crime rate in Chinatown caused by gang conflict. Beginning in 1965 with the upsurge in young Hong Kong immigrants moving into the area, the number of gangs battling for control of Chinatown increased. The result was violence. During the 1970s, the rivaling Joe Boys and Wah Ching (and their allies, the Hop Sing Boys) battled over the illegal firecracker trade and extorted business owners.[128] According to Bill Lee, a Joe Boy member in the 1960s and early 1970s, youths in the Ping Yuen projects sold firecrackers and beginning in the 1970s were forced to pay part of their earnings to gangs. Some refused to pay, creating conflict between dealers and increasing fighting around the projects.[129] Gang violence reached its apex in 1977. During a confrontation between gangs, Felix Huey was murdered in Ping Yuen. (It is not known whether he resided in the projects.) Two months later, five people were killed and eleven wounded at the Golden Dragon restaurant in what police called a retaliatory attack. No known gang members sustained injuries. The incident, called the Golden Dragon Massacre, provoked fear among Chinatown residents and negatively affected Chinatown's economy. Occurring just a few blocks from Ping Yuen, the massacre marked an increase in deadly crimes in the community. In this increasingly violent atmosphere, Julia Wong's murder served as the breaking point for tenants concerned about the district's rise in crime and its penetration into their housing project.

Drawing on their earlier success against the SFHA, their experiences protesting during the I-Hotel incident and in rent strikes across the district, and their anger over the murder of a community member, PYRIA acted on its threat and began a rent strike on October 1, 1978. The leaders demanded twenty-four-hour security guards and better lighting and fencing. In their quest for safety, the association ignored Chinatown merchants' opposition to the placement of fences at Ping Yuen. Business owners viewed the fences as a deterrent to an already damaged economy reeling from the Golden Dragon Massacre. Two decades later, business leader Rose Pak reflected on the massacre's impact: "It was three years before people drifted back to Chinatown after the Golden Dragon shooting. Nightlife has never recovered from it."[130] As tourism continued to decline, intercommunity conflict over the fences only rose. Housing Commissioner A. C. Ulbade Jr., who had negotiated with the tenant leadership, revealed the complex spatial politics of Ping Yuen's location in the prime San Francisco tourist spot: "Many, many tourists come through Chinatown, and these nonproject dwellers do not want it to look like a concentration camp."[131] A number of Chinatown business owners concurred with the commissioner. In the wake of the Golden Dragon Massacre, smoke-shop owner Yee Tom complained, "business is terrible. Before the shooting the streets were crowded very late. Now at 7 o'clock everyone goes."[132] Chinatown businesses trying to regroup a year later may have consid-

"Peace and Prosperity Dwell among Virtuous Neighbors"

ered the fences another impediment to reviving the district's tourist economy. Breaking off from the Chinatown business community, Ping Yuen residents drew on bonds forged in public housing to secure their living environment.

Confident in their demands and in the support of many Ping Yuen residents, PYRIA leaders disregarded the business interests of the city and Chinatown merchants. They wrote a letter to the housing commissioners announcing that the October rent payments of 200 residents would be withheld and deposited instead into an escrow account; they then submitted the letter as a group at the September 28, 1978, Housing Commission meeting. Speaking on behalf of members, George Lee, chairman of PYRIA and veteran of the 1976 protest, declared, "it is unfortunate that we tenants must resort to such extreme measures to obtain what we regard as our right to decent and safe housing. Our choice of housing is obviously very limited. However, we find the bureaucratic mentality of the Housing Authority virtually impervious."[133] The letter, demonstrating tenants' understanding of and irritation with the Housing Authority's bureaucracy, stated that the rent strike would continue until project residents were given "adequate assurance that security guards will be provided and until they see the actual completion of the fences and the lighting."[134]

The rent strike spurred Ping Yuen residents to action and strengthened the project community. PYRIA members draped a large banner across one of the projects that read in Chinese and in English "Ping Yuen Tenants on a Rent Strike." By announcing the strike to both project tenants and other residents in Chinatown, the association worked to increase participation and support for their cause.[135] Some PYRIA members tried to bolster resident participation through canvassing tenants. Chang Jok Lee, treasurer of the association, recalls "passing out leaflets door to door, talking to the tenants, attending lots of meetings and collecting rent at 838 Pacific for 15 days each month."[136] Even residents who could not help organize supported the strike effort by withholding their rent—an action whose risk of serious consequences became clear when the Housing Authority began issuing fourteen-day eviction notices in October. Watson Low, a resident since 1952, was not active in encouraging others to join the strike because he "was working a lot at the time," but he "was part of the people who withheld

131

their rent" because there "were reasons for us to strike . . . safety was the main concern."[137] Although striking tenants had to endure eviction notices and harassment by "people who pound[ed] on their doors at night and threaten[ed] to evict them if rents aren't collected," most of them continued to participate in the strike.[138]

The Housing Authority's eviction notices did little to dampen dissent as participants gained momentum by securing the backing of the San Francisco PHTA. Formed out of public housing tenants' unions across San Francisco for "all tenants—black, brown, yellow, and white" with the support from the National Tenants Organization and the San Francisco Neighborhood Legal Foundation, the PHTA received formal recognition by the SFHA in 1971 and brought together two representatives from each public housing project in the city to serve on the steering committee.[139] As the Ping Yuen strike wore on, PYRIA won a victory against the Housing Authority when they exercised their right to a grievance hearing on November 6 to explain their reasons for withholding their rent to the PHTA representatives. The tenant-run Grievance Panel voted in favor of Ping Yuen residents withholding their rent "until the Housing Authority provides security."[140]

In a show of public housing tenant solidarity that confirmed the critical need for a decent and safe living environment universal to all residents, the Grievance Panel supported PYRIA's strike on the grounds of maintenance and security needs. Prior to the hearing, PYRIA had focused its demands solely on increased security measures. In front of their public housing peers, however, they laid out evidence of the Housing Authority's failure to meet maintenance requests "for the past eight years" as well as tenant frustration that there were no bilingual Housing Authority operators for residents (primarily elderly Chinese) to contact in case of problems or an emergency. The Grievance Panel voted in favor of the Ping Yuen tenants and in doing so charged the Housing Authority to exceed PYRIA's original demands for lighting, fences, and guards by providing better maintenance as well. The housing commissioners balked at the Grievance Panel's decision and demonstrated their ultimate control over the group's procedures and the limits of sanctioned tenant governance. Invoking Section 7 of the Grievance Procedure negotiated with the PHTA and approved by

"Peace and Prosperity Dwell among Virtuous Neighbors"

HUD, the Commission exercised its power to overrule the Grievance Panel's ruling, passing Resolution Number 2215, rejecting the panel's decision on December 7, 1978.[141]

Despite the Housing Authority's veto, both sides continued to negotiate. In late November, city supervisor John Molinari mediated a session between the Housing Authority and PYRIA and their legal representative from the Asian Law Caucus, a legal and civil rights organization founded in 1972 to serve low-income Asian Pacific American communities. During the meeting, tenants asked for "new ground rules" that would prevent the SFHA from issuing eviction notices and would void previous notices. The SFHA had issued the notices because the tenants' reasons for striking failed to comply with a state law protecting residents who held rent in escrow because of "physically uninhabitable" conditions or "physical conditions that render[ed] the units unsafe."[142] According to the legal counsel for the Housing Authority, "none of the communications from the residents site [sic] physical conditions; the complaint is lack [sic] of security guards and maintenance."[143] The negotiations continued. In a show of compromise, the SFHA agreed to stop issuing eviction notices, to observe the ruling by the Grievance Panel, to meet the security and maintenance demands of Ping Yuen tenants, and to send bilingual notices informing tenants of developments in the project.[144] These efforts laid the groundwork for the rent strike agreement signed in January 1979 that brought the three-and-a-half-month protest to an end. The 187 tenant participants won improvements for all residents at Ping Yuen. Chang Jok Lee explained that those "who stayed on the strike got results for people living here: they get linoleum floor replaced, they get the fencing . . . they have a few months of twilight security."[145] The Housing Authority set approximate dates for completing elevator maintenance and physical security improvements, including fencing and window bars in all project buildings. The agreement also called for the Housing Authority to immediately respond to the tenants' chief demand: four security guards—one for each building—to work seven days a week from 7 p.m. to 3 a.m. for nine months, the length of time the Housing Authority could guarantee funding for the positions.

For their part, PYRIA agreed to end the rent strike and submit the money in escrow to the Housing Authority. Signed by Executive

"*Peace and Prosperity Dwell among Virtuous Neighbors*"

Director Carl Williams; Cleo Wallace, the tenant representative on the Housing Commission from Hunters Point; Willie Fong; Louise Yee; and George Lee and Chang Jok Lee of PYRIA on January 11, 1979, the agreement ended the strike and provided Ping Yuen residents with a major victory.[146] The effects of the rent strike resonated in the Ping Yuen community for years in tenant activism and leadership, in the growth and strength of PYRIA, and in the association's relationship with the Housing Authority and Chinatown. Although the strike resulted in improvements for residents, the tragedy of Julia Wong's death lingered. A few longtime residents claim that even today, "when it is stormy weather you can hear the girl [Wong] still crying."[147]

Although the Housing Authority acted on some terms of the rent strike agreement, they did not follow through on their promises to provide better elevator maintenance and to hire bilingual staff members to field emergency and maintenance calls. Ping Yuen tenants intended to hold the SFHA accountable. Residents marshaled their energies again, with families withholding rent from November 1979 to September 1981. Protesting, residents had learned, could yield significant results. The PYRIA leadership, made up of many reelected officers, called on residents to join their cause. PYRIA officer Chang Jok Lee recalls:

> We started with 80 households, but some tenants discontinued their strike support for fear of eviction. We held many meetings and visited people door to door. We also had membership drives and sponsored activities to keep the striking tenants together. Since I was treasurer, I collected the rent, put it in escrow and kept the books. . . . We finally got our demands met.[148]

Although some residents quit the strike early, the tenants who remained on strike for a year again earned lasting benefits for the entire Ping Yuen community. On September 18, 1981, the Housing Authority agreed to several demands—including ones that were supposed to have been met under the 1979 agreement. The agency committed to provide elevator maintenance, hire bilingual staff, complete outstanding work and repair requests for individual units, and follow through on security measures outlined in the 1979 agreement.[149]

"Peace and Prosperity Dwell among Virtuous Neighbors"

PYRIA leaders drew on their experience with the SFHA during the first rent strike—notably, the agency's failure to follow through on agreements made to end the protest—in laying out their terms during the second standoff. The tenants' association agreed to end the strike and return the monies in escrow in parts, dependent on the Housing Authority's completion of repairs and improvements. Both sides agreed that the accrued interest would go back to strike participants, with PYRIA taking responsibility for the distribution. After battling over busted boilers, broken elevators, and worn-down interiors for years, residents succeeded in securing action on their complaints. The strike strengthened the bonds of community, both within Ping Yuen and between the housing project and the surrounding neighborhood. Chang Jok Lee recounted the generosity of strike participants who at "the end of the strike were asked to donate a portion of the interest or keep it if they so desired. Most of the people donated 50 percent of the interest, which amounted to $10,000." These funds enabled PYRIA to buy a television for the community room, to support more classes and events, and to further extend their outreach to the Chinatown District through donations to community service organizations. In another show of solidarity, residents also used some of the funds to express their appreciation to George and Chang Jok Lee for their leadership and perseverance during the two rent strikes by giving the couple a trip to visit Chang Jok's family in Japan.[150] Chang Jok Lee, George Lee, and Watson Low continued to guide PYRIA after the rent strikes with the full backing of Ping Yuen tenants. These leaders and other PYRIA officers, like their counterparts at Valencia Gardens, enjoyed their work and the sense of contributing to the betterment of their community.

Tenant activism at Ping Yuen not only strengthened the community, it also offered tenants opportunities to grow as individuals and leaders. Through her leadership positions within Ping Yuen, Chang Jok Lee challenged traditional gender roles "for an immigrant woman whose Chinese tradition frowns upon public activism by women."[151] Despite her initial reservations about becoming active in the community because she "didn't speak English well and was not used to speaking in front of people," Chang Jok emerged as a prominent activist. Through her experience picketing at the I-Hotel and her work as the

"Peace and Prosperity Dwell among Virtuous Neighbors"

PYRIA treasurer, president (taking over after George died), and the resident "go-to" person in Ping Yuen, she broke with the cultural gender norms she had grown up with in her Chinese family to work for social justice. Overcoming her own doubts and Chinese cultural norms that denied women the opportunity to pursue public leadership roles, Lee became a lifelong activist, commenting, "as long as I am fighting for a just cause, then I am not scared." Mrs. Lee seemed to downplay her leadership, however, by placing her work within the context of traditional kin networks, stating that activism "was a family affair."[152] Her leadership and activism for over three decades shaped the Ping Yuen community, earned her the respect of tenants and the wider Chinatown District, and modeled female leadership to Chinese immigrants who lived in the project. Receiving an award for her dedication to and hard work for PYRIA from the Chinatown Neighborhood Improvement Resource Center in 1985, Mrs. Lee humbly accepted the honor in front of 550 people: "I don't really deserve this, but I know if we all work together, anything can be done."[153]

The continual leadership of the Lees and Watson Low provided tenants with experienced officers who were knowledgeable about the SFHA, the procedures for getting things done, and the project's history and current needs. While these PYRIA officers shared the goal of creating an improved project environment, they did not always agree on how to accomplish the organization's aims. In 1983, George Lee stepped down as president after the SFHA hired him as a resident manager. After leaving office, Lee supported Watson Low's presidential candidacy. In 1985, Low went to bat for Lee when he was laid off by the Housing Authority because of budget cuts. Using leverage gained from PYRIA's previous success against the Housing Authority, Low reminded the Board of Supervisors that the

> Ping Yuen Tenants Association is very well known for its successful rent strikes. We would like members of the Health Committee and Board of Supervisors to get the Housing Authority to reinstate those people laid off. [Executive Director Carl Williams had proposed laying off groundskeepers and resident managers to offset the loss of $5.9 million dollars.] We want Mr. Lee's layoff rescinded otherwise we will use every means at our disposal and every possible channel to get him reinstated.[154]

"Peace and Prosperity Dwell among Virtuous Neighbors"

Low served as PYRIA president until 1987, when tenants reelected Lee, who no longer worked for the SFHA.[155]

Reaching out, Reaching in: Coalition Building for Change

With more members, an increased budget due to interest from the rent strikes, and continuity in leadership under George Lee, Chang Jok Lee, and Watson Low, PYRIA played a large role in the Chinatown community and stepped up efforts for self-sufficiency, complicating the management role of the Housing Authority and pushing the boundaries of state-run housing. PYRIA's connection to the Chinatown Neighborhood Improvement Resource Center aided Ping Yuen's community outreach and economic development goals and demonstrates the importance of coalition building. The Chinatown Neighborhood Improvement Resource Center formed in 1977 as a result of community activists working to improve the social and physical conditions of Chinatown. Activists from the Chinatown Coalition for Better Housing, the Chinatown Transportation Research and Improvement Project, the Committee for Better Parks and Recreation in Chinatown, the Chinatown Coalition for Neighborhood Facilities, and PYRIA came together with mutual needs for staffing and technical assistance. These five organizations sponsored the creation of the nonprofit Chinatown Neighborhood Improvement Resource Center (now called the Chinatown Community Development Center or Chinatown CDC). In 1978, the Chinese Community Housing Corporation (CCHC) was formed as the development arm of the Chinatown CDC to create and improve affordable housing for low-income people. Striving to improve the lives of Chinatown "residents, workers, shopkeepers, and property owners," the Chinatown CDC launched initiatives with emphases "on alleyways, and open space improvements, housing, education, litter control and clean-up campaigns, land use issues, transit and transportation, and housing development for low income residents."[156]

The partnership between PYRIA and the Chinatown CDC both reflects and reframes the long history of aid associations in Chinatown assisting residents in the area. Blurring the often stark line between

137

"Peace and Prosperity Dwell among Virtuous Neighbors"

residents and nonresidents in public housing, the Chinatown CDC and PYRIA have worked together to improve not only public housing but also the larger Chinatown district. A nonprofit established to better the lives of people in Chinatown, the Chinatown CDC has worked to fill gaps in city, state, and federal funding for what remains an economically depressed district. Over four decades, the Chinatown CDC has had a major impact on Ping Yuen by helping PYRIA win grants for physical improvements, such as graffiti removal and garden and playground renovations, and by supporting Ping Yuen's economic development.[157] With a PYRIA member serving on the Chinatown CDC board and a Chinatown CDC representative attending PYRIA meetings, the organizations have established a mutually beneficial relationship. As the Chinatown CDC has aided PYRIA through workshops and training, PYRIA has reciprocated by providing space for the Chinatown CDC to hold workshops, meetings, and training courses for residents and nonresidents. PYRIA, like the Chinatown CDC, has made efforts to support other community organizations as well, offering meeting space and giving donations to area groups over the years. By engaging with the Chinatown CDC and other nonprofit organizations in the Chinatown community, PYRIA broke new ground, creating an active tenants' association that supported not only residents but also agencies in the district, expanding the boundaries of Ping Yuen to include the surrounding community.[158]

In 1983, PYRIA, with the help of the Chinatown CDC, set a course for economic development. Growing out of tenants' frustrations over problems with the laundry rooms in Ping Yuen, the residents lobbied to manage the laundries themselves, establishing the first tenant-run Laundromat in San Francisco public housing. Tenants had begun expressing their dissatisfaction with the laundry rooms earlier in the year. Because of "vandalism, the frequent breakdowns of twenty-four washers and twelve dryers serving the complex, and the dilapidated condition of the room themselves," many residents took their laundry to "increasingly expensive Laundromats offsite" or washed their clothes by hand rather than using the existing facilities. Fully aware of the SFHA's slow bureaucracy that delayed repairs and maintenance, PYRIA and the Chinatown CDC worked to support economic development by taking control of the laundries. As a Chinatown CDC employee explained, "by renovating the laundry rooms and operating the facility themselves, the tenants' association and the Resource Center saw a chance to earn some money to fund service programs for tenants, and improve laundry service."[159]

Together, PYRIA leaders and the Chinatown CDC embarked on the most ambitious course for the tenants' association to date. With the technical assistance of the Chinatown CDC, the PYRIA leadership submitted an application for the 1983 Jobs Bill Funding Program under the Mayor's Office of Housing and Community Development to renovate the laundry rooms and acquire new machines. As an economic development project, the PYRIA laundry proposal received a $100,000 grant with stipulations that required a new level of management and responsibility from the PYRIA leadership. The Jobs Bills funding mandated that PYRIA hire and manage a tenant maintenance worker, handle the money, negotiate a lease agreement with the service distributors and supplier, and oversee the major renovations of the laundry facilities.

The combination of seasoned tenant leaders, such as George and Chang Jok Lee and Watson Low, steering the laundry project and the support of the Chinatown CDC turned the Laundromat initiative into a viable economic development program for Ping Yuen. Although the program experienced problems and ran a deficit at the beginning, it eventually proved a profitable venture. At a general tenants' meeting in 1984, residents voted to abandon the original plan of buying the washers and dryers and to rent them instead. With an understanding of the disadvantages of ownership and the advantages of renting, tenants looked at the change as a positive one because "machine rental eliminates the problem of repairs." PYRIA put the funds freed up by the reduced cost of renting equipment into more renovations.[160]

Although the PYRIA leadership urged residents to use the new laundry facility—a "clean place" with "convenient hours" (three more hours per day than under the Housing Authority), "reasonable prices," and "a pleasant environment" with bright lighting and "comfortable seating"—tenants did not use the machines as much as projected, which suggests that not all tenants supported the program.[161] PYRIA reported a usage increase of 30 to 35 percent in March 1985, but the association continued to struggle with problems, including delays in

"Peace and Prosperity Dwell among Virtuous Neighbors"

opening some of the laundry rooms, tenants abusing the system by doing laundry after hours, frequent machine breakdowns, and a deficit resulting from an "over estimation of projected usage increase."[162] Reassessing the program after ten months, PYRIA worked to remedy the problems by reducing the numbers of machines in Ping Yuen North. Despite these problems in the first year of operation, the laundry program ran a net profit of $1,768.10 in March 1988, and by 1990 the Laundromat account had grown to $20,042.15.[163] Pulling in funds that were then put back into services for Ping Yuen residents as well as the larger community, the laundry program, over time, benefited both PYRIA and Ping Yuen.

The unique partnership between the Chinatown CDC and PYRIA resulted in improvements for Ping Yuen residents and the Chinatown community, but it was not without tensions. The complexities and limits of extended community bonds in the face of self-interest emerged in 1987, when Ping Yuen North residents protested actions by the Chinatown CDC's subsidiary, the Chinese Community Housing Corporation. Started in 1978 to provide safe and affordable housing, the CCHC and Chinatown CDC partnered to integrate housing into "an overall neighborhood improvement strategy."[164] The cause of the disagreement was the CCHC's proposal to construct a five-story building for low-income senior citizens on the parking lot next to Ping Yuen North. With a commitment from HUD for a $2.4 million loan, contingent on the Housing Authority agreement to lease the land, the CCHC unveiled the architectural plans to tenants at a February 24 meeting, riling Ping Yuen North residents.[165] Tenants at the project held a news conference two weeks later, contesting the project because they felt bullied into accepting it and were concerned that the new building would "block their sunlight and further crowd their neighborhood."[166] In a case of tenant solidarity and concerns overriding larger Chinatown community needs, tenants from 170 of Ping Yuen North's 194 apartments signed a petition opposing the new complex. Demonstrating a strong sense of ownership and control of their subsidized apartments, tenants criticized the CCHC for making plans to alter their living environment without consulting them throughout the planning process. On March 19, 1987, the Ping Yuen North tenants sent a letter addressed to "friends in the Chinatown Community" asking for sup-

"Peace and Prosperity Dwell among Virtuous Neighbors"

port and explaining that what they opposed was not senior housing but the CCHC's tactics. Chastising the founding Chinatown CDC director Gordon Chin, residents stated:

> As tenants, we are very disappointed by the Resource Center and the CCHC, who have always defended the rights of the tenants against all developers in Chinatown. They have always used "quality of life" to oppose buildings that will block the sun, increase traffic, displace people and parking, etc. . . . For [Chin's] own project, he now chooses to disregard *our* rights as tenants, and our quality of life at North Ping Yuen. The open space he wants to build on is OUR front yard, OUR property, OUR home. Is it just because we're poor and live in public housing that we should not enjoy any rights and any decent portion of quality of life? . . . The issue, then, dear friends, is not senior housing. The issue is open and fair process, and an understanding of the tenants who live there every day.[167]

The PYRIA leadership, voted into office by over 400 tenants, backed the protestors. George Lee explained, "if the tenants don't want the project, we will oppose it. . . . We would like to see senior housing in Chinatown, but we don't want it built in our front yard."[168]

The tenants' disapproval stalled the project and forced the CCHC to reconsider their site selection for the forty-unit senior housing development. After five months of wrangling and negotiations, Ping Yuen North residents (with the full support of PYRIA) dropped their opposition to the project in July, winning concessions from the developer that included lowering the height of the building from five stories to four, providing a security gate at the senior housing parking lot, and creating temporary parking for Ping Yuen North tenants during construction.[169] The Bayside Senior Housing Project opened in 1990 with thirty units and a large multipurpose community room used for social events and citizenship and naturalization classes.[170] Now considered a positive addition to Ping Yuen by tenants, the Bayside project challenged the Chinatown CDC–PYRIA relationship without irreparably damaging it.

Over time, the coalition between the Chinatown CDC and PYRIA resulted in a range of other initiatives that benefited public housing and broader communities. Through sponsoring graffiti removal days,

"Peace and Prosperity Dwell among Virtuous Neighbors"

creating garden plots for tenants, and securing funding for playground renovations, the Chinatown CDC has provided continual support to Ping Yuen tenants.[171] PYRIA, as a nonprofit, donated funds to district organizations and provided meeting space inside Ping Yuen for groups across Chinatown. In 1995, the collaboration between the Chinatown CDC and PYRIA resulted in a public art project celebrating Chinese Americans' contributions in the United States, including Ping Yuen. Funded by a Community Block Grant from the mayor's office and supported by the Ping Yuen Mural Task Force, the Chinatown CDC, PYRIA, and several individuals, including Angela Chu from the Chinatown CDC and Chang Jok Lee, the mural showcased the connectivity between Ping Yuen and the surrounding district. Commissioned artist Darryl Mar used an exterior wall of Ping Yuen to create a large mural visible from blocks away. Painted in bright hues, the mural blends the past and present with images of railroad workers and World War II veterans alongside depictions of smiling children. On the left side of the mural, Chang Jok Lee smiles, looking out across Chinatown. To her left is George Lee, who looks down as if he is watching over Ping Yuen. Weaving together the history of Chinese Americans in the United States with Ping Yuen, the celebratory mural dedication reads "In memory of Sing Kan Mah and those who have struggled to make America their home."[172] Signifying the importance of individual and collective action and of Chinese Americans in U.S. and San Francisco history, the mural serves as both public and promotional art for the Chinatown district. Created over fifty years after James Leong painted his controversial mural inside Ping Yuen, the representations of Chinese Americans, including activists George and Chang Jok Lee, were created through a strong coalition between Ping Yuen and the Chinatown CDC—and seemingly appreciated by the wider Chinatown community.

By assisting with grant writing and serving as a resident resource, the Chinatown CDC collaborated with PYRIA to provide a critical social services piece needed in public housing but not supplied by the Housing Authority. Together, members of PYRIA and the Chinatown CDC have shaped federal public housing to fit the needs of the Chinatown community and in doing so have made a strong case for the importance of local autonomy and coalition building. Nonetheless,

"Peace and Prosperity Dwell among Virtuous Neighbors"

Figure 23. Mural at Ping Yuen, 2003. Photograph by the author.

the Housing Authority's position as landlord should not be overlooked. Although the agency has been unable to sustain its interest in the Chinatown community's cultural and social needs and has failed to consistently provide high-quality maintenance for residents, the Housing Authority as owner of the high-priced project land has guaranteed low-income housing for 1,500-plus residents for over fifty years. With run-down single-room occupancy hotels and low-rent family units being bought up by developers, the number of affordable housing units in Chinatown continually declined at the end of the twentieth century. The Housing Authority's commitment to retaining control over the Ping Yuen properties is critical to Ping Yuen's continued existence, protecting the project from potential sale, which would be a looming threat under private ownership. Furthermore, the SFHA, for all its failures, has supported PYRIA's efforts at economic development by turning over control of the laundries and encouraging PYRIA to continue writing grants. The Housing Authority has not, however, acknowledged the important partnership between the Chinatown

"Peace and Prosperity Dwell among Virtuous Neighbors"

CDC and PYRIA, nor given credit to the Chinatown CDC for its efforts in improving the Ping Yuen environment, a failure that has frustrated Chinatown CDC workers, who in 2002 claimed that the Housing Authority was "happy to take credit for these positive changes."[173] By recognizing the efforts of both PYRIA and the Chinatown CDC, the Housing Authority could demonstrate to HUD the need for local input and cooperation between the federal government, local housing authorities, tenants, and community organizations in improving public housing in the United States.

The complex web of cooperation, contestation, and community alliances between the Housing Authority, Ping Yuen tenants, and Chinatown social service agencies has made Ping Yuen a decent place to live and a project "many people want to get in to."[174] The support of a shifting resident population as well as the project's location near jobs, shops, restaurants, and public transportation, helped make Ping Yuen San Francisco's "most popular housing project."[175] Over the years, residents have struggled with problems including vagrancy, theft, gang violence, maintenance problems, and disagreements with neighbors in the project. Yet these issues have not dampened residents' enthusiasm about their project and the emergence of Ping Yuen as some of the best housing in the district. Considered one of the better places to live in Chinatown and described by residents as "a big family," Ping Yuen complicates the stereotype of high-density public housing in the United States as a failure.

In recent years, as longtime residents adjusted to the shifting demographics of the project—which now houses African American, Caucasian, Asian, and Latino/a families, many displaced by HOPE VI redevelopment—they have continued to cultivate bonds in the project community. After living in the project for over fifty years, Watson Low argued that the demographic changes actually improved the project even as they posed problems for residents and PYRIA leaders because many Chinese American residents do not speak English. Low claimed that "all people no matter what race, they should treat others like brothers and sisters. . . . Even though we have different people from different backgrounds and nationalities we are very good to each other." PYRIA members readily agreed with Low's assessment, perhaps signaling an opening to move toward a decades-long missed

"Peace and Prosperity Dwell among Virtuous Neighbors"

opportunity: multiracial and multiethnic activism across public housing in San Francisco.[176] As a "convenient place to live" for Chinese immigrants, "a good place to raise a family," and "a safe place," Ping Yuen has been "home" to many residents for years and in some ways has contributed to many immigrants' American Dream.[177] A longtime resident and immigrant from Hong Kong, Mrs. Lee Chan claimed "my American Dream is that my kids have their Masters and PhD. . . . I still didn't get my house but I have my kids' success."[178] Turning the American Dream's obsession with homeownership on its head, Watson Low attributed his children's success to public housing: "We are low-income person and I raise my kids because I was able to save the money from paying the rent to get them into college so public housing actually contributed a lot to my kids' education, my kids' future—so public housing is good and it is not necessary that people have to own their housing."[179] Echoing modern housing reformers' vision of public housing as a viable alternative to the private housing market, Low and other tenants at Ping Yuen challenged the SFHA's narrow definition of community and public housing. By turning their apartments and their project space into "home" and building relationships with one another, these tenants claimed the benefits of "community" and "ownership" and were "good, engaged citizens" as low-income renters.

As an active player in the larger Chinatown community and a site of decent affordable housing, Ping Yuen's past is instructive. Some of the components that have made it successful could clearly be replicated and deserve attention as the number of public housing units decreases and the affordable housing crisis grows. Inverting prevalent stereotypes of high-density public housing as a failure, Ping Yuen has proved a successful project in part because of the care and cooperation put in at the design stage—combined with other factors, including attention to specific neighborhood conditions and needs, the convenient location, and the district's willingness to support the project over time with resources such as the ongoing social services provided by the Chinatown CDC. Strong coalitions provided a critical foundation for the project over time. While some may counter with model minority–generated myths and claims that this project works only because of its location in a historically segregated Chinese American community, cross-racial and cross-ethnic alliances at Valencia Gardens and North

"Peace and Prosperity Dwell among Virtuous Neighbors"

Beach Place that resulted in direct challenges to the state for improvements prove otherwise. At Ping Yuen, activism and coalition building prevailed among residents and neighbors who marshaled a variety of democratic tools to improve America's Chinatown housing project. From letter-writing campaigns to bring public housing to Chinatown, to petitions for community meeting space, rent strikes, and cross-sector coalitions for economic development and social services, individual and collective activism has shaped Ping Yuen into the "decent and safe housing" promised in the Housing Act of 1949.

FOUR

"The Best Project in Town"
North Beach Place

> North Beach is like America, in a sense, where different
> ethnic groups come together to give it a strength and vitality
> all its own.
> —Ken Wong, *San Francisco Examiner*, December 1978

> Public housing isn't public when any citizen because of the color
> of his skin is not allowed to live there.
> —M. Colton, *San Francisco Chronicle*, 1952

AS CHINESE AMERICANS CELEBRATED THE OPENING OF PING YUEN in 1952, two hopeful African Americans applied to live in the newly built North Beach Place public housing project in predominantly white North Beach. With over 51,000 African Americans living in San Francisco amid a persistent housing shortage and entrenched residential segregation, these applicants, like thousands of others, desired a decent living environment.[1] Rather than applying to live in the nine-year-old Westside Courts, where the San Francisco Housing Authority concentrated African American tenants, Mattie Banks and James Charley sought admission to the new, modern North Beach Place. Nestled between Telegraph and Russian Hills near the waterfront, the North Beach neighborhood was an eclectic and convenient area, with the Powell-Mason cable car line exiting next to the new public housing development. Banks, separated from her husband, worked as a presser and lived in a one-room rental where she shared a bed with her two daughters. Charley, a hospital orderly, lived with his wife and three children in a two-bedroom rental where they shared a kitchen and bathroom with other families.[2] Despite their demonstrated need, the SFHA rejected both applications for North Beach Place.

A decade after adopting the neighborhood pattern policy, the SFHA continued to place tenants in specific public housing developments on the racial and ethnic composition of the surrounding community. The Housing Authority claimed, however, that Banks and Charley were not turned away because they were African American. Citing the applicants' moral shortcomings as the determining factor in denying their admittance, the SFHA demonstrated both its continued paternalism—housing residents it deemed to be "upright" citizens—and institutionalized racism.[3] Long criticized by the NAACP as well as the Council for Civic Unity and other interracial coalitions, the SFHA's segregationist policy and practices came under legal attack at North Beach Place in a case that went to the U.S. Supreme Court.[4] In this seemingly hidden piece of the national civil rights story, federally subsidized low-income housing became a vehicle by which African Americans demanded equality. The individual actions of African American applicants, and the leadership of the NAACP legal team, interrupted and challenged the SFHA's segregationist policy and practices that were simultaneously lauded locally and nationally at Ping Yuen. These efforts by African Americans opened the door for North Beach Place and other San Francisco public housing projects to become racially and ethnically diverse developments. Over the second half of the twentieth century, however, integration did not always result in cohesion. Community formations have shifted over time from intraracial and ethnic ties to stronger intergroup bonds as changing demographics, shared difficulties, and collective threats of redevelopment emerged.

The North Beach neighborhood Banks and Charley were trying to live in had a long history as a diverse neighborhood. The district originated out of the mid-nineteenth century enclaves of Italian, French, Spanish, Irish, Mexican, and South American immigrants living in the area near the waterfront. By the turn of the century, Telegraph Hill and the wharf had acquired the name "the Latin Quarter" because of the proliferation of Romance languages there. Between 1850 and 1920, Italian immigrants transformed North Beach into a *colonia* or Little Italy, a spatial and cultural designation that marked the district in the mid-twentieth century.[5] Praised by many for rapidly rebuilding North Beach after the earthquake and fire of 1906, the district residents continued to strengthen the reputation of the area as an Italian neighborhood.[6] North Beach's Italian population peaked in the mid-1930s, at 27,000 Italian-born and 30,000 locally born of Italian descent.[7] The hub of Italian American life in the Bay Area, North Beach drew immigrants and tourists alike to its markets, cafés, delis, and sights such as Saints Peter and Paul Church and Coit Tower.[8] Writing in 1939, columnist Bill Simmons described North Beach as "world famed."[9]

World War II delayed the construction of North Beach Place until the 1950s, a decade of change in the district. While Italian cuisine and a lively entertainment scene drew tourists after the war, the confluence of "poet hipsters"—the Beats—in San Francisco in the mid-1950s brought additional new visitors to the area. At the City Lights Bookstore in North Beach, founded in 1953 as a literary meeting place, disaffected East Coast Beat generation writers such as Allen Ginsburg (who wrote *Howl* in his North Beach apartment) and Jack Kerouac experimented with a new writing style based on "uncensored self-expression and altered states of consciousness induced by trance and drugs" and intersected with more politically and ecologically oriented poets later known as the Bay Area branch of the Beats: Gary Snyder, Lawrence Ferlinghetti, Bob Kaufmann, and others in the short-lived literary community.[10] Generating widespread press coverage, the presence of the Beats in North Beach brought young people from across the nation to the district. Even after the Beats left the area in the late 1950s, visitors could still find elements of bohemian culture in coffee houses and galleries, at the City Lights Bookstore, and in the district's claims of openness.[11]

Integrated by 1954 in response to African Americans' activism, North Beach Place became home to racially and ethnically diverse working-class families raising children. Both North Beach and North Beach Place continued to change in the following decade. Between 1964 and 1968, North Beach witnessed the rise and relative decline of the topless industry, drawing tourists from throughout the world to see shows like Carol Doda's topless act at the Condor Club and other adult nightclubs in the district.[12] The topless entertainment phenomenon added to the popular evening offerings in North Beach that already boasted female impersonators at the Finnochio Club, Greek dancing at the Greek Taverna, and operatic singing at the Bocce Ball.[13]

"The Best Project in Town"

As the district continued to beckon tourists with a variety of entertainment, shifting demographics impacted the district and North Beach Place. New waves of immigrants moved to San Francisco after 1965 in response to softening federal immigration restrictions, and in their wake, Chinese American residents and businesses crossed the once rigidly defined border of Columbus Avenue between Chinatown and North Beach.[14] With more Chinese Americans moving into North Beach Place, tenants beginning to put together a tenants' association in the late 1960s struggled to communicate across language and cultural barriers. District residents, meanwhile, wrestled with cultural differences, fear of the loss of Italian culture, and rising rents, sparking tensions that continued for decades. Nonetheless, North Beach residents continued to take pride in their multifaceted neighborhood, as summed up by journalist Nancy Dooley: the famous neighborhood "remains one of San Francisco's diverse corners, where different cultures, the old and the new, live cheek and jowl. They may not love one another, but they are tolerant."[15]

The noted tolerance of the district, supportive of public housing in the beginning, did not persist for North Beach Place residents. As the neighborhood became an increasingly popular tourist destination and residential section with its prime location near the San Francisco Bay, North Beach Place grew increasingly isolated from the surrounding community. With Pier 45—and, after its development in 1978, Pier 39— just blocks away from North Beach Place, the boom in hotels nearby, and the city's push for economic development, the district that has welcomed European immigrants, Asian immigrants, Beat poets, bohemian artists, and topless dancers proved unable to sustain a similar hospitality toward diverse low-income families living in public housing.

North Beach Place both mirrors and upsets historical trends of urban renewal and gentrification that have displaced low-income people from desirable neighborhoods across the United States. North Beach Place tenants, the SFHA, and the surrounding neighborhood have shaped the history and future of a housing project located in an unexpected place, inhabited by a diverse group of tenants, and widely celebrated for its redevelopment in 2004. North Beach Place's history demonstrates low-income families' efforts to live in a vibrant neigh-

"The Best Project in Town"

borhood, and their willingness to form new ties with each other and to take on the state in their struggles to do so.[16] From African Americans' fight against the Housing Authority's racial discrimination policy, to residents' attempts to shape redevelopment, the diverse tenants at North Beach Place have collectively demonstrated the importance of location and community bonds in public housing by successfully fighting for the continuation of public housing units in the district. The activism of North Beach Place tenants was more vocal and demanding than the more muted affective activism evident at Valencia Gardens. The threat of redevelopment and dislocation from the vibrant North Beach neighborhood led to unprecedented collaboration between racial and ethnic groups working to protect their shared public housing community. This cross-racial and ethnic activist alliance contributed to the continued availability of low-income housing in the highly sought-after North Beach neighborhood at what residents described as the "best project in town." The history of North Beach Place, then, serves as a nexus for examining spatial and redevelopment politics, cross-racial and ethnic mobilization and community formation, and the possibilities and challenges of mixed-income redevelopment in public housing.

Public Housing Comes to North Beach

When the SFHA began looking for areas to construct public housing in 1941, North Beach seemed like a good fit. Surveys of the area depicted the "Latin Quarter" as overcrowded and overrun with substandard buildings. North Beach residents welcomed the prospect of tearing down and replacing the district's dilapidated warehouses, which would also fulfill the "slum elimination" required by the Housing Act of 1937 to construct public housing. The development offered the prospect of decent, low-rent housing for local working-class families: "fisherman, clerks, etc. that work in the vicinity."[17] Like their neighbors in Chinatown, North Beach residents worked to shape the development to fit their needs, petitioning the Housing Authority for "a nursery school, WPA art project, and minimum amount of space for parking and maximum amount of space for a playground to be included in the Project's development."[18] Over 400 area residents advocated for these amenities, aimed at creating an attractive, livable environment for working-class families to raise children.[19]

The design responded to some of these requests while emphasizing the culture of Little Italy with regionally inspired European-style architecture. When the development opened in 1952, it boasted modern lines created by prominent regional architects Henry Gutterson and Ernest Born and landscaping by renowned landscape architect Thomas Church. Gutterson was noted for his residential designs throughout the Bay Area and for the Christian Science Benevolent Society and Arden Wood in San Francisco; Born was an acclaimed architect whose commissions included several buildings for the Golden Gate International Exposition.[20] Located on 4.6 acres on Bay, Mason, and Francisco Streets and Columbus Avenue, the thirteen three-story buildings integrated U-shaped garden court playgrounds and parking areas. According to architectural historian Gwendolyn Wright, the strong geometric forms used by Gutterson and Born demonstrated "an almost literal application of the low-cost working-class housing built by enlightened city governments in England, Austria, and Holland in the late 1920s."[21] The architects played up Mediterranean-inspired details, reflecting the neighborhood's identity as "Little Italy." The modern lines, choice of exterior paint color, and selection of Italian shrubs and landscaping contributed to "the Mediterranean feeling" praised by the SFHA. Along with these features, a bocce ball court worked into the design lent the development an international flair and local flavor suited to North Beach.[22] The 229 apartments ranged in size from one to four bedrooms and promised to relieve "the overcrowded condition of this Latin quarter of the city" and to enhance the North Beach neighborhood.[23]

North Beach Place received national and local praise. The *Journal of Housing* lauded the strong design and "the much-recommended balcony" on the apartments. The complex opened shortly after Ping Yuen in Chinatown, and the SFHA promoted both developments as "outstanding examples of the best in low-rent housing."[24] Albert Conlon, one of the first tenants in North Beach Place, praised the quality of the buildings. A hotel employee who had previously lived in a two-bedroom "hotel apartment" with his family of five, Conlon hailed the development as a national model: "I have lived in 16 States, and I

"The Best Project in Town"

Figure 24. North Beach Place under construction, May 1952. San Francisco History Center, San Francisco Public Library.

haven't seen anything to compare with these apartments here. They are wonderful."[25] The new, modern apartments filled a housing need in the area—but were at first available only to white tenants.

Exclusive Public Housing

The site, attractive design, and convenient location made North Beach Place a desirable option for public housing applicants. However, the Housing Authority initially slated the development for white families. A 1952 photo of the Martin family outside North Beach Place captures

153

Figure 25. North Beach Place showing modern architectural details, 2002. Photograph courtesy of Michael Cole.

Figure 26. North Beach Place, 2002. Photograph courtesy of Michael Cole.

"The Best Project in Town"

Figure 27. North Beach Place with community gardens, 2002. Photograph courtesy of Michael Cole.

the Housing Authority's vision for selective, race-based occupancy at the public housing project situated in a burgeoning tourist district. The husband, Theodore, stands to the left and his wife, Mary, is on the right, with their son, Teddy, in the center, holding his parents' hands in front of the new European-inspired development. The hills of San Francisco rise in the background. This white nuclear family represents the majority of applicants the SFHA aimed to serve.

As demonstrated at Valencia Gardens and Ping Yuen, the SFHA continued to use the "neighborhood pattern policy" to racially segregate public housing, a common practice in the national public housing program.[26] Unanimously adopted by the Housing Commission in 1942, the two-part policy promoted residential segregation in the public housing program. As explored in chapter 1, the policy dictated that public housing, "with a view to the preservation of public peace and good order," would not "insofar as possible enforce a commingling of races."[27] In selecting residents for the project, the SFHA worked to reproduce the "same racial composition" found in the neighborhood.

"The Best Project in Town"

Figure 28. Theodore and Mary Martin with their son, Teddy, at North Beach Place, September 12, 1952. This white nuclear family represents the ideal tenants the SFHA sought for its public housing projects in the early years. San Francisco History Center, San Francisco Public Library.

As the policy went into effect, San Francisco was undergoing dramatic demographic shifts. Immigrants arrived from Nicaragua and El Salvador to work in the shipyards, Mexicans moved to the region as part of the bracero program, and thousands of Japanese Americans left the city, faced with evacuation, detainment, and internment after Pearl Harbor. Meanwhile, thousands of other Bay Area residents went to war, and as the nation mobilized industry, employment opportunities abounded in San Francisco. African American migrants from the southeast streamed into the city to work in the shipbuilding industry, increasing the black population by 600 percent and compounding San Francisco's housing shortage.[28]

While many San Franciscans tolerated the small black population before the war, attitudes shifted when African American migrants began competing for jobs and housing. Across the city, some San Franciscans objected to African Americans moving into their neighborhoods, fearing that "Negroes depreciate property values."[29] African American migrants crammed into the 2.5-square-mile Fillmore neighborhood, once home to Japanese Americans removed during the war, increasing the population there by 500 percent.[30] In response to the growing housing crisis, the NAACP pressed the Housing Authority to create housing solutions for African Americans. In a January 2, 1940, letter to the SFHA, the local NAACP branch asked what the authority proposed to do "in meeting the need presented by the adverse housing conditions of its Negro population." As a key representative of the group with "housing needs . . . more wanton" than other racial and ethnic minorities, the NAACP demanded answers.[31] Throughout a monthlong correspondence between SFHA executive director Albert Evers and NAACP Housing Committee representative Sara Jenkins, the Housing Authority pushed back, threatening to withhold progress if the NAACP took a public stance against the SFHA. Evers wrote, "Pre-emptory demands and inadvisable public agitation may do more harm than good. . . . A possible solution is now in view, but any publicity or agitation whatever will most certainly militate against it."[32] The SFHA's answer was to open the Westside Courts public housing development in 1943. The small, 136-unit development housed African Americans under the neighborhood pattern policy. While the development provided urgently needed housing, the opening of Westside Courts had a minimal impact on the housing crisis for African Americans.

By the late 1940s, local lawmakers and citizens also began to question the SFHA's neighborhood pattern policy. African American housing commissioner William McKinley Thomas challenged the formula in 1949, calling it "a very practical form of segregation and discrimination." Undeterred by his arguments and the shift toward desegregation in the private housing market after the U.S. Supreme Court's 1948 *Shelley v. Kraemer* decision, the housing commissioners voted to uphold the neighborhood pattern policy.[33] A month later, the city's Board of Supervisors tried to undermine the policy by making new public housing units open to all tenants, regardless of race or ethnicity: the Supervisors worked a nondiscrimination clause into the cooperation agreement authorizing the SFHA to seek federal funds for

"The Best Project in Town"

the construction of 3,000 new public housing units under the Housing Act of 1949.[34]

Despite the Supervisors' action, SFHA executive director John Beard and a number of housing commissioners defended the policy as a benefit to the common good. Complicating the meanings of localism and community in public housing, they argued that the SFHA used the neighborhood pattern policy to create developments that meshed with the surrounding area. John Beard explained:

> It is desired that a housing project be an integral part of the neighborhood so that people intermingle in the social, economic and political life of the community. Public housing is intended to serve not only the tenants but the community as a whole. We don't want any cultural islands scattered about the city. An effort to change the character of a neighborhood would be accompanied by social disturbances of considerable degree.[35]

Ignoring public criticism, the SFHA refused to apply for federal monies with the Supervisors' nonsegregation clause rider. In a political move, the Housing Authority opted to poll civic and community organizations for "an expression of opinion on the nonsegregation policy."[36] National housing expert Charles Abrams lambasted the SFHA, calling its actions "an act of secession" while pointing out the decreased racial tensions in New York, Philadelphia, and Pittsburgh, where segregation in public housing had been abolished.[37] Vowing to let the people decide, the SFHA polled approximately ninety community groups listed by the San Francisco Chamber of Commerce.

Ultimately, the poll results had little, if any, impact on the compromise reached between the Housing Authority and the Board of Supervisors. Twenty-two organizations agreed to take the poll, with eleven opposing the neighborhood policy plan, nine supporting it, and two, in the end, not responding.[38] With millions in federal funds hanging in the balance, the housing commissioners and Board of Supervisors reached an agreement in February 1950 whereby the neighborhood pattern policy would remain in the 1,741 existing public housing units and apply to 1,200 deferred units (including Ping Yuen and North Beach Place) ready for construction. New public housing developments that came online would be racially integrated.[39]

"The Best Project in Town"

When North Beach opened in 1952, the development's design and location, like Valencia Gardens and Ping Yuen, connected to the primary racial and ethnic makeup of the neighborhood. The SFHA continued to promote the neighborhood pattern policy on the grounds that it fostered civic unity and provided "the fairest method of distributing the limited supply of public housing units."[40] African American tenants lived in Westside Courts, Chinese Americans resided in Chinatown's new Ping Yuen buildings, and white tenants could choose to live in Holly Courts, Valencia Gardens, Potrero Terrace, Sunnydale, or the new North Beach Place. African American applicants for public housing demanded more options. In 1952, looking for better housing for their families within the tight San Francisco housing market, Mattie Banks and James Charley submitted applications to the SFHA to live in North Beach Place, only to have, as we have seen, their applications denied. Frustrated by the segregationist policy that barred them from new, modern, subsidized housing units, these applicants, with the assistance of the NAACP, sued the San Francisco Housing Authority.

North Beach Place served as the battleground for an important piece of the Western civil rights movement, which legal scholar Carolyn Luedtke explains "has gone largely unnoticed in our national history."[41] NAACP attorneys Terry Francois and Nathaniel Colley challenged the de jure and de facto segregation of the SFHA's neighborhood pattern policy, filing a petition on behalf of eligible African American applicants denied admission to North Beach Place. Francois and Colley won an early but unenforceable victory when Judge Albert C. Wollenberg ordered the Housing Authority to "give the three persons named—and all other eligible Negroes—the same consideration as other applicants, 'without regard to race or color.'"[42] After several delays by the SFHA, Superior Court Judge Melvyn I. Cronin presided over a stopgap agreement forcing the Housing Authority to hold fifteen units for African Americans at North Beach Place pending the outcome of the NAACP's legal challenge to the neighborhood pattern policy.

In the ensuing court battles between 1952 and 1954, the Housing Authority justified segregation under the "separate but equal" doctrine and revealed a bureaucratic maze used to perpetuate racial and

"The Best Project in Town"

ethnic homogeneity in public housing. The process used to determine the demographics of each neighborhood began to unravel under questioning in the Superior Court of the state of California. NAACP attorney Terry Francois pushed SFHA executive director John Beard through questioning to understand the process for determining the racial composition of a neighborhood.

> Q: You have what you call the "neighborhood pattern" policy? Is that right?
>
> A: That is correct.
>
> Q: Under that policy you determine the racial character of the neighborhood where a project is contemplated, is that correct?
>
> A: I am unable to answer your question. That is not an administrative function.
>
> Q: You have nothing whatsoever to do with the neighborhood pattern policy?
>
> A: I have nothing to do with determining it.
>
> Q: You don't know how it is determined?
>
> A: That is not determined by me or my staff. It is determined by the Housing Commission.
>
> Q: And you execute the policy after it is determined, rather, the pattern after it is determined?
>
> A: That is correct.
>
> Q: Under this neighborhood pattern policy, at least somebody determines the racial character of a neighborhood, is that right?
>
> A: It is not done by me or by my staff.
>
> Q: You get the results of it, don't you?
>
> A: I get the instructions.
>
> Q: That the racial character of this neighborhood is such and such a thing, is that correct?
>
> A: No.

> Q: You get instructions to the effect that people in certain racial groups are not to be placed in certain projects, is that right?
>
> A: I get instructions on what races are to be housed in a project, that is correct.
>
> Q: So that the reason there are no Negroes in six of seven of these projects is because you received instructions at some time or other not to place Negroes in these projects?
>
> A: I have received instructions to house these projects with white families.

Beard went on to claim that he received these instructions from the San Francisco Housing Commission, though he could not specify who did the actual work of determining the racial character of a neighborhood.

> Q: The general members [of the Housing Commission] themselves don't go out there and make a survey of the neighborhood, do they, Mr. Beard?
>
> A: I don't know.
>
> Q: You don't know who does the work, do you?
>
> A: No.[43]

During a series of heated hearings, the severity of the Housing Authority's policy abuses emerged. Executive Director Beard testified that the agency had violated the Federal Housing Act, which called for prioritizing veteran applicants. He explained that the SFHA had assigned white nonveteran applicants to apartments at North Beach Place over African American veterans.[44] Subsequent testimony further revealed that the Housing Authority had manipulated the terms of the Federal Housing Act in order to keep the project all white. The NAACP attorneys elicited statements from tenants demonstrating that the Housing Authority had moved white families with veteran status all the way from the East Bay, rather than housing nonveterans in need in the North Beach area and in San Francisco, in an attempt to fill North Beach Place with white veterans after the NAACP mounted its legal challenge. In the event the NAACP won its case, the Housing Authority

161

could reject African American applicants based on the federal mandate to prioritize housing veterans.[45] Judge Cronin sided with the plaintiffs and charged the Housing Authority to end segregation in public housing under the Fourteenth Amendment. The SFHA appealed the decision, and the legal limbo that ensued meant that African Americans still could not move into North Beach Place.

The battle over the SFHA's neighborhood pattern policy played out in the local media, eclipsing the celebration of the design and opening of North Beach Place. Members of the city's Board of Supervisors, citizens' groups, and individuals, including some North Beach neighbors, sided with the plaintiffs, urging the SFHA to end segregation in public housing. Writing to the *San Francisco Chronicle*, Rosinda Holmes, who lived across from North Beach Place, contended that "Since our country was founded on the principle that all men should have equal rights to citizenship, I see no reason why Negroes or other families of racial minorities should not be admitted to this housing project." Holmes noted that black and white construction workers had built North Beach Place, and "if Negroes are allowed to work on the building of the project, they should be allowed to live in it."[46] M. Colton, another citizen frustrated by the SFHA's neighborhood pattern policy, praised the NAACP for its efforts in the courts and reprimanded the SFHA: "Public housing isn't public when any citizen because of the color of his skin is not allowed to live there."[47]

The Housing Authority's intractability also drew scathing criticism from several organizations across San Francisco that viewed the agency's discriminatory policies as irreconcilable with the city's long-held reputation "as a liberal, cosmopolitan city full of diverse populations living in harmony."[48] James E. Stratten, a member of the San Francisco Redevelopment Agency, called for the resignation of E. N. Ayer and John Beard, the chairman and executive director, respectively, of the Housing Authority. Justifying his position, Stratten summed up the concern of San Franciscans opposed to the SFHA's admittance policy: "I take this attitude because I think the majority of San Franciscans want San Francisco to remain the leading city in the world in its attitude toward human beings."[49] Other civic groups joined together in June 1953 at a one-day conference on the problem of segregation in public housing sponsored by the NAACP, the San Francisco

"The Best Project in Town"

Urban League, the Council for Civic Unity, and the Japanese-American Citizens League. Together these groups urged the Housing Authority to abolish the neighborhood pattern policy, claiming that "it marks our city as a center of race bigotry, which it is not in fact."[50]

Defying "the official policy of the city, the State and the Superior Court" and ignoring the vocal local opposition, the Housing Authority continued enforcing the neighborhood pattern policy and fought to maintain it. In the private housing and rental markets, San Francisco residents of all races had received the legal go-ahead from U.S. and California Supreme Court rulings in 1948 and 1952 to rent or buy housing in any neighborhood in the city. Yet in public housing, the SFHA continued to distribute tenant populations based on race and ethnicity. The agency appealed Judge Cronin's ruling in the state courts. Both the California Superior Court and the California Appellate Court ruled against the Housing Authority, arguing that "the rights of individual Negroes were being abridged when they were denied admission to specific projects."[51]

The Housing Authority would not be deterred, even by these state court rulings. In the final appeal by the SFHA, *Banks v. The Housing Authority of San Francisco* reached the United States Supreme Court in 1954.[52] The court refused to hear the case, so the California ruling deeming the neighborhood pattern policy in San Francisco unconstitutional was allowed to stand. African Americans could now move into North Beach Place and other public housing projects in San Francisco. Writing for the *San Francisco Chronicle*, Richard Reinhardt summed up the breadth of the Housing Authority's resistance and the impact of the court's decision: "After fighting for its segregation policy in four courts, employing five attorneys, and spending $7500 in public money, the Housing Authority bowed to the final rule of law." The Authority's promise to "comply 100 percent with the court's ruling" and open the city's eleven low-rent public housing projects to all eligible tenants marked a monumental shift in policy and placement.[53] Yet even as the victory in the *Banks* case promised to blaze "trails in the national fight against public housing discrimination" by overturning segregation in San Francisco public housing, the U.S. government did not formally outlaw discrimination in federal public housing nationwide until the 1968 passage of the Fair Housing Act.[54]

163

"The Best Project in Town"

Public Housing versus Tourism

The tenacity of the plaintiffs in the *Banks* case, the NAACP and their legal team, and other African Americans who wanted to live in North Beach Place paved the way for African Americans, Asian Americans, Latino/as, and other groups to live in the newly built, conveniently located project. Longtime resident Alma Lark captured the appeal of living in North Beach and the increasing diversity of the project:

> Three years after [North Beach Place] opened, I moved in. I was a parent with three kids. I had checked around the other developments and I discovered this was the best for living. . . . Everybody seemed to be friendly with each other and for moving from place to place you had adequate transportation, a theater down the street, a drug store down the street, everything was convenient. And with the atmosphere up here you see I wanted my children raised here. . . . I filled out the necessary forms. . . . And after I moved in all other nationals came like the Asians, Filipinos, Koreans, you name it, after the 1950s.[55]

The racial and ethnic diversity of North Beach Place grew in tandem with the changes in the North Beach district. By the late 1950s, the project began housing a range of racial and ethnic groups, a shift that presaged the demographic changes that increased in the 1960s and 1970s. As "Little Italy" became the hangout for Beat poets and their followers in the 1950s, North Beach gained national attention. The increased tourist interest affected the neighborhood's economy, property values, and the push for redevelopment. Over time, it also influenced the lives of North Beach Place tenants, whose project location at the end of the cable car line served as many visitors' entrée into the district.

Tenants of different racial and ethnic groups moving into North Beach Place in the 1950s, like residents at Valencia Gardens and Ping Yuen, experienced a clean, safe, congenial living environment in the heart of a burgeoning tourist district. As a child growing up in North Beach Place, Janette Huffman recalled, "no one would have called them 'projects' back then[;] the neighborhood was so safe and comfortable that everyone left their doors unlocked—even at night."[56] Although integration did not foster an instant community, some tenants formed relationships across racial and ethnic lines. When asked about racial tensions in the early years of the project, Alma Lark responded, "we didn't have any here. It was just like a big family. . . . Everyone has respected each other over the years."[57] Even if other tenants did not share Lark's view of the North Beach Place community, it is likely that residents from different racial and ethnic backgrounds commingled in the development and at the playgrounds, the shops, and the bay in the North Beach District. Fifty years later, North Beach Place tenants described racial harmony among children when they reflected on the importance of the project's diversity for their kids, even as they explained that language barriers increasingly divided the adult population.[58]

The emerging tourist trade and the gradual increase of the Chinese American population in the North Beach District and in public housing there in the 1960s altered the dynamics within North Beach Place.[59] The national and international fascination with the Beats in the late 1950s and the rise of the topless clubs in the 1960s drew a wide range of new visitors to the district, including "Summer of Love" participants in 1967. Public housing residents were "ignored by the surrounding community," which was increasingly interested in earning tourist dollars and gradually becoming ashamed of North Beach Place, especially as the complex began housing poorer families and receiving fewer repairs in response to federal legislation and budget cuts in the 1960s and 1970s.[60] As the population of Chinese immigrants in San Francisco increased, more Chinese American families moved from crowded Chinatown to North Beach. These changes resulted in a larger population of Chinese families in North Beach Place, many of whom did not speak English. Language barriers and cultural differences undermined integration. Mini-communities began forming in North Beach Place, offering support for participants but also causing misunderstandings and tensions among the different groups as tenants navigated living in a neighborhood increasingly disdainful of public housing.

The ethnic and racial divide in the project manifested in the formation of two separate tenants' organizations. Perpetually discouraged from organizing by the SFHA under Executive Director John Beard's leadership, tenants at North Beach Place and across the city began to create tenants' organizations, some with the support of local

"The Best Project in Town"

Economic Opportunity Councils, which had been established to fulfill a requirement for federal funds from President Johnson's War on Poverty. The North Beach Place Neighborhood Improvement Association (later called the North Beach Place Tenants' Association, or NBTA) formed in 1964. The group's purpose was to "improve conditions in the immediate area by providing activities for young people of each age group from pre-school to young adulthood; improve general living conditions; improve relations among tenants; and improve the community at large."[61] On December 3, 1964, Marjorie Bezzone, representing the NBTA, became the first tenant organization member on record to address the Housing Commission.[62] In 1966, residents of Chinese descent created a separate organization, the North Beach Place Chinese Improvement Association (NBPCIA), to serve the needs of Chinese American tenants, many of whom could not fully participate in the NBTA because they could not speak English. By 1969, the NBPCIA had over sixty members—over 95 percent of the Chinese American residents at the project—and the SFHA deemed it "one of the most active and viable tenant organizations within the Authority."[63] The formation of the NBPCIA seemed to pose a challenge to the NBTA and initially created friction between the groups, fueled in part by language barriers. Nonetheless, by 1969 both groups had apparently resolved their differences and established a rapport, laying the foundation for a generally peaceful coexistence between the formal tenant organizations.[64]

While formal and informal networks formed along racial and ethnic lines, all tenants at North Beach Place shared the experience of living in public housing in a vibrant, mixed-use neighborhood that included public transportation, a grocery store and Cost Plus World Market across the street, and playgrounds, the bay, and Fisherman's Wharf nearby.[65] The attractions of the area were apparent to real estate developers and business leaders as well. In the 1970s, the city, through the San Francisco Redevelopment Agency, redeveloped the Financial District, located near North Beach and Chinatown. Using federal urban renewal funds, the city demolished apartments and houses in the South of Market area to construct Yerba Buena Plaza. The drawn-out renewal project displaced over 3,000 working-class families from their residences.[66] The city promoted the Plaza as a new

"The Best Project in Town"

draw for tourists and locals. The North Beach District became a target for revitalization as well, as business developers began looking for ways to shore up tourist dollars.

A flurry of projects begun in the 1970s aimed at expanding tourism, but public housing tenants were left out of the resulting boom cycle. In 1975, Hilton opened a hotel on the corner of Bay and Jones Streets across from North Beach Place, later followed by the San Francisco Marriott Fisherman's Wharf, the Hyatt, and the Travelodge. Resident Alma Lark remembers the empty promises made by community planners regarding redevelopment in the district: "Before these hotels were built, you see, we sat right in here with community groups and discussed plans where residents would have upward mobility to work in those hotels across the street." According to Lark, the developers did not follow through on their promises to provide employment opportunities for public housing residents.[67] The chance for holistic community development and job training for public housing residents was lost.

The neighborhood surrounding North Beach Place not only changed into a hotel district, it also attracted more visitors as the entry point to Fisherman's Wharf and the newly developed Pier 39. Once a run-down pier "full of old refrigerators and junked cars," Pier 39 was transformed by businessman Warren Simmons into a forty-five-acre entertainment complex with over one hundred shops, restaurants, and numerous attractions, including a carousel, arcade, and cruises around the bay. The pier launched with a grand opening on October 4, 1978.[68] The site quickly became one of the major tourist destinations in the city, increasing visitors to the area—many of whom used the Powell-Mason cable car line adjacent to North Beach Place.

But even as tourist traffic in North Beach grew in response to new lodging and attractions, North Beach Place, like other public housing developments across the city and the nation, declined in the face of decreased federal funding to the SFHA. To North Beach Place residents, it seemed that the district and the city valued tourists over public housing tenants, who saw their development becoming a run-down, unsafe island in the midst of a thriving tourist neighborhood. Deferred maintenance and cuts in federal funding, as well as the rise in crime in and around the project, frustrated and worried tenants.

Meanwhile, neighbors blamed tenants for the social and physical deterioration of North Beach Place and increasingly viewed the development as a problem. When asked about how the neighborhood perceived public housing tenants, North Beach Place residents responded that their neighbors "didn't have anything to do with us," "felt we were beneath them," and "pointed the finger of blame at us if there is a robbery at the Safeway or at the cable car station. People from the outside always blame crime on North Beach [Place] residents."[69] Thus, North Beach Place tenants, like those at Valencia Gardens, suffered under the dual burden of a declining housing environment and the contempt of the surrounding community. Once a safe complex in a dynamic neighborhood, North Beach Place in the late 1970s and early 1980s left its tenants feeling threatened by criminals, some of whom were residents, using the project grounds as a home base and hiding place.

By 1979, tenants, fearing for their safety and encouraged by the success of the Ping Yuen rent strike, demanded additional lighting and security from the SFHA. North Beach Place tenants, like residents at Ping Yuen and Valencia Gardens, had to contend with teenage gangs who preyed on tenants and tourists alike in the late 1970s. According to the deputy chief of police, North Beach Place had become "a sanctuary for the crooks who hang out there or live there." These gang members broke into project apartments, mugged people on the street, stole purses and cars, and kept North Beach Place tenants "in a state of terror."[70]

Tenants' calls to the police and the SFHA for aid were not prioritized by either group. The Housing Authority did take some notice of the problems at North Beach Place after someone burned Christmas trees in the courtyard in early January 1979, destroying equipment in the children's play area. The Housing Commission sent two members to North Beach Place to report on conditions there. Their description revealed the severity of the project's troubles: "tenants had fear of leaving their homes" and "people were being physically attacked."[71] That same month, Laura Swartz of the S.F. Neighborhood Legal Assistance Foundation also reported on conditions to the Housing Commission, noting that tenants were "concerned about physical safety in their homes" and about having "no security bars and no outside lighting."

"The Best Project in Town"

With the Ping Yuen Residents Improvement Association's successful rent strike as a subtext, Swartz implied that North Beach Place tenants could follow Ping Yuen's lead when she stated that "conditions are far graver [at North Beach Place] than Ping Yuen in terms of security."[72] Despite the commissioners' report and Swartz's claims, Executive Director Carl Williams explained the bleak facts: "the Housing Authority does not have the resources to provide comprehensive security. Public housing residents are residents of the City and County of San Francisco and the S.F. Police Department has a clear responsibility to provide security for the entire city."[73]

Nonetheless, perhaps hoping to avoid another rent strike, the SFHA promised to provide North Beach Place tenants with brighter lighting and window grates. North Beach Place tenants responded that they would "consider a rent strike" if "those promises aren't kept."[74] In a demonstration of their fear and lack of faith in the SFHA, some residents went ahead and paid for their own security improvements to their apartments. After a neighbor scared off burglars trying to break into her apartment, tenant and NBTA president Hope Halikias used her savings to start "investing in my own prison" by putting bars on her windows.[75] Other tenants took safety into their own hands as well, installing window bars, additional locks, and grating on doors.

North Beach Place tenants, living with danger at their doorsteps, claimed that the police prioritized tourists over them in terms of protection and public safety. Hope Halikias argued that the police were more concerned about protecting tourists at Fisherman's Wharf than "entire families living in fear inside the project's apartments." She went on to describe the hierarchy of police aid: "We know we are in a tourist area and the Central Station police—they do take care of the tourists but it's inside the buildings where we need help. . . . We are left stranded there, alone."[76] Even after the Housing Authority installed window bars, residents had little relief from criminal activity, which they claimed was perpetuated mostly by "outsiders."[77] During a November 1980 Housing Commission meeting, Halikias commented on the continuing problems at the project, explaining that "there has been a rash of crime and the bars installed for protection are now being used as ladders to climb to the second floor of the apartments, and tenants are being robbed."[78]

"The Best Project in Town"

As tenants dealt with crime in and around North Beach Place, the city and neighborhood looked for solutions to what they saw as the underlying cause of such problems—having public housing located in North Beach. Whether or not the criminals were insiders, outsiders, or both was not an issue to business leaders concerned with the image of North Beach and the safety and satisfaction of visitors to the area. This concern, to some extent, may have resulted in a lack of media coverage of the crimes in and around North Beach Place, including shootings and drug deals that escalated in the 1980s as the sale of crack cocaine became more widespread. Residents argued that "acts of violence are not reported because of fear that the tourist industry would be hurt."[79] With or without media coverage of its problems, however, North Beach Place was still considered one of the top public housing developments in the city. The development's location and lower crime rate—in comparison to other public housing—made it one of the better living options for public housing tenants.[80] Yet to the city's business leaders and many residents in the North Beach District, North Beach Place was an eyesore in need of drastic measures to remedy its troubles.[81]

In the early 1980s, a local real estate developer approached the Housing Authority with a proposal to "solve" the problems at North Beach Place—or, perhaps more accurately, the problems that neighbors and businesses attributed to North Beach Place—by moving public housing residents out of the district. The developer offered to buy land in another section of the city where he would build 229 units of housing that he would "trade" the Housing Authority for North Beach Place; he would then demolish the housing project, replacing it with a hotel and retail complex.[82] While merchants in the area and some leaders found the proposal appealing, North Beach Place tenants rejected the idea of relocating from the development and area they considered their home. Garnering support from the Telegraph Hill Neighborhood Association (Tel-Hi), the Chinatown Community Development Center (CDC), and the members of the Telegraph Hill Dwellers, an organization that represented community interests of residents and property owners in Telegraph Hill, North Beach Place tenants fought the plan.[83] The collaborative effort helped stop the development proposal and also resulted in a joint effort to improve the look of North

Beach Place. Some merchants and neighbors (including the above mentioned community organizations) raised funds for and participated in repainting the development's exterior.

Alone Together: Mini-Communities and the Search for Common Ground

The ties between North Beach Place and local nonprofits played an important role in supporting tenants over time while also furthering racial and ethnic affinity group dynamics. Residents at North Beach Place benefited from the services and support of Tel-Hi and the Chinatown CDC over the years. Founded in 1890 by Alice Griffith and Elizabeth Ashe to help immigrant children in the neighborhood, Tel-Hi grew into a nonprofit resource center focused on "self-help and empowerment for people who live and work in northeast San Francisco."[84] Prioritizing education, community organizing, and direct services such as day care, Tel-Hi aimed to improve the quality of life for low-income residents in the area. Over the years, North Beach Place residents took advantage of Tel-Hi day care, classes, and other services. The Chinatown CDC also played a support role for residents. Started in 1977 when five grassroots organizations joined together to better serve the Chinatown community, over time the organization expanded its mission to "build community and enhance the quality of life for San Francisco residents."[85] Based in Chinatown, the CDC's mission and work expanded to North Beach and the Tenderloin District in the past few decades. The long-standing support of Tel-Hi and the Chinatown CDC strengthened North Beach Place—but it also demonstrated the racial and ethnic divide that separated tenants, with many African American tenants drawing on the resources at Tel-Hi while Chinese Americans went to the CDC for assistance. This division reinforced fragmentation in North Beach Place and eroded the opportunity for the kind of unified coalition building seen at Ping Yuen.

Between 1974 and 1984, the numbers of Asian Americans—mostly of Chinese descent—and African Americans living in North Beach Place increased, shifting the composition and dynamics at the project. A 1989 study of North Beach Place by anthropologists Patricia Guthrie and Janis Hutchinson examined interpersonal interactions between ethnic groups at North Beach Place during 1988 and 1989, particularly focusing on African Americans and Asian Americans, the two largest populations at the time. According to the study, these two groups rarely interacted.[86] The division between the groups, the scholars argued, emerged out of African American tenants' perceptions that Asian Americans—whom they categorized as "Chinese"—were "pushy" immigrants who "are taking resources" and "come here and have immediate access to jobs, housing, and money from the government."[87] Furthermore, African American tenants expressed resentment over what they saw as Chinese Americans forming a "separately organized political unit" facilitated by "a woman from Chinatown [who] came to the housing project to organize the Chinese American residents."[88] Guthrie and Hutchinson, however, found "no evidence that any Asian Americans are 'organized'" at North Beach Place, perhaps indicating that the North Beach Place Chinese Improvement Association had disbanded or had reduced its visibility in the project.[89]

African American tenants most likely resented what they perceived as Chinese Americans' easy access to and connection with Chinatown and the social services available through organizations there, such as the Chinatown CDC. Some African American tenants felt isolated in North Beach Place because, as one former tenant noted, they did not "believe that they have any geographic turf in the wider North Beach/Chinatown community. European Americans have a portion of North Beach at large, Asian Americans have Chinatown, whereas African Americans only have the project."[90] As a result, African American tenants claimed the project grounds as their own, and they made it "known that this [was] their space."[91] With little interaction between the groups, the majority of project notices printed only in English, and ethnic and racial perceptions and stereotypes coloring residents' thoughts and actions, Guthrie and Hutchinson concluded that "African Americans and Asian Americans [at North Beach Place] formed a residential group but not a social one."[92]

Although Guthrie and Hutchinson outlined the "paucity of interethnic interaction" in North Beach Place, they did not fully consider how the increase in crime around the project, as well as residents' shared idea of the space as home, cultivated common ground across racial and ethnic lines. In the face of growing gang-related violence

"The Best Project in Town"

and the crack cocaine trade, tenants at North Beach Place, like residents at Valencia Gardens, blamed the rise in project crime on "outsiders."[93] Tenants defined "outsiders" both as public housing residents from other projects who visited North Beach Place or were relocated there by the SFHA and as nonresident criminals preying on their community. The diverse tenants at the project collectively agreed that "outsiders"—many of whom they alleged were "problem tenants" moved to North Beach Place from other public housing developments—used the space as a base of operations, dealt drugs, and inflicted violence. These "outsiders," residents claimed, made "insiders'" "quality of life go right down the river" and threatened their "home."[94] Although tenants turned inward to their own racial and ethnic groups as their fear and frustration mounted, they continued to hold a common view that the majority of North Beach Place residents, regardless of race or ethnicity, were not responsible for the development's problems.

Despite the rise in crime and the slow deterioration of the buildings, tenant "insiders" of all racial and ethnic backgrounds shared the belief that they lived in one of the best public housing projects in the city. The convenient location and relative safety of North Beach Place compared with other complexes in San Francisco prompted residents to stay put and to strive for change. The desire to remain in the area and the support of mini-communities ameliorated the tensions between the groups Guthrie and Hutchinson studied. In fact, according to some residents, the ethnic and racial tensions described in Guthrie and Hutchinson's analysis in the late 1980s did not exist. When asked in 2002 about the strain between racial and ethnic groups documented in 1988 and 1989, African American tenants who reflected back on their experiences disputed that there were problems among residents, offering instead another interpretation of community dynamics at North Beach Place. "Asians kept to themselves. They did their thing and we didn't bother them and they didn't bother us."[95] While the inconsistencies of memory and the veil of nostalgia may have shaded tenants' responses, their explanation provides a way to understand how residents balanced their desire to live in North Beach Place with their lack of understanding of their neighbors' cultures. The mini-communities formed along ethnic and racial lines in the public housing

173

complex began to shift and meld a decade later, as tenants' shared feelings of pride and desire to continue living at North Beach Place prompted them to unite in facing the threat of relocation.

As North Beach Place tenants suffered through maintenance delays and criminal activity in and around their homes in the 1980s and early 1990s, their neighborhood continued to develop into a tourist hub. Although critics of public housing acknowledged that North Beach Place residents had to cope with "drug dealers and other criminals, most of whom do not live there," they worked to make improvements in the area for tourists, not tenants.[96] With the Hyatt Hotel opening across Bay Street in 1990 and a Barnes and Noble bookstore opening next to Cost Plus World Market later in the decade, the area beckoned tourists, and an estimated 10,000 people a week used the cable car next to North Beach Place.[97] Low-income tenants living in public housing stereotyped as "ghettos," and considered the housing of last resort in the United States, did not appeal to tourists—or to San Francisco residents.

The city's proposed answer to the problem was simple: move the tourists away from the public housing. The solution, designed to protect tourists and their spending habits, was to extend the end of the cable car line so riders would exit at Fisherman's Wharf rather than next to North Beach Place. Mayor Willie Brown, expressing his support for the initiative in 1996, argued that moving the end of the cable car line to Pier 45, four blocks away from public housing, "would enable tourists to see Fisherman's Wharf without running the gauntlet of dangers associated with street walking."[98] Although the proposal did not move forward, the solution it offered again demonstrated the value of tourists' dollars over public housing residents' quality of life.

Demolition: The Politics and Process of Redevelopment

In 1996, the San Francisco Housing Authority attempted to bridge the gap between residents' needs and business and city interests in its application for a federal HOPE VI grant to revitalize North Beach Place. The program aimed to replace severely distressed public housing, occupied by poor families, with redesigned mixed-income housing (see chapter 1).[99] Receiving grant funds offered the potential to implement new designs that eliminated hiding places for criminals, to extend in-apartment amenities and social services for tenants, and to provide retail space on the site that could appeal to city dwellers and tourists alike. The proposed transformation offered the "hope" of improving residents' living environment and blending the complex's design and residential–commercial use into the neighborhood's tourist economy.

The city and many people in the North Beach District, including business owners and investors concerned with tourist revenue and the image of the area and frustrated over North Beach Place's problems, celebrated the SFHA's award of a $23 million federal HOPE VI grant in 1996 to redevelop the public housing project. These funds, along with the additional tens of millions of dollars leveraged by the Housing Authority through public–private partnerships, created an opportunity to construct housing that melded with the surrounding community and welcomed visitors with retail shops on the ground floor. This new development also promised to alter the tenant population by codifying regulations governing which low-income residents could return and by adhering to an unusual definition of the mixed-income concept that would result in all low-income units, including public housing units for very low-income residents and tax credit units for low-income residents. For tenants, the grant generated talk of better social services, washers and dryers in their apartments, a safer design, and the opportunity to live in a new apartment as opposed to an old, run-down unit. The grant also caused alarm as tenants quickly realized the problems inherent in redevelopment: specifically, relocation. With often varying agendas, the city, the neighborhood, the SFHA, and North Beach Place tenants struggled to redesign and redevelop the project into a safe, attractive place, palatable to tourists and neighbors—and home to residents.

The battle over the future of North Beach Place demonstrates the complexities of public housing redevelopment politics generally as well as the particular problems attendant to public housing located on valuable land in a popular tourist area. Undoubtedly some North Beach residents and business owners echoed the sentiments of the North Beach Chamber of Commerce, whose director Marsha Garland remarked that the Chamber would prefer to see the project disappear.

"It's the wrong place for public housing. No one wants to be around it."[100] Rather than redeveloping North Beach Place, Garland suggested that the public housing complex "could be replaced with smaller clusters of housing throughout the city." Presumably she wanted these clusters located in districts other than North Beach.[101]

A letter to the editor written by J. D. Sexton after the *San Francisco Chronicle* reported on the HOPE VI award for North Beach Place further illuminates the deep frustration some people had about the location of the project, the high cost of redevelopment, and the idea of low-income families living in federally subsidized housing in an area like North Beach.

> I was delighted when I saw the headline "Projects near the Wharf to be Razed." (Oct. 8.) My delight was short-lived, however, since the first paragraph pointed out that, incredibly, the projects would be rebuilt in the same location. The cost is projected to be $69 million for construction plus $39 million for job training and other services for the tenants. As if that were not enough, the $22 million extension of the cable car line so that it does not end in the "crime-packed" projects is still on the table.... That means we are spending $568,000 for each family currently living there.... A public housing project does not belong at Fisherman's Wharf. That land is far too valuable to be used for that purpose.[102]

For Sexton and other opponents of public housing in North Beach, property values and land use formed the basis for inclusion or exclusion from the neighborhood. Low-income families living in public housing devalued North Beach. "The projects" belonged in San Francisco's lesser neighborhoods, not in famed, economically viable North Beach. Despite opposition, redevelopment plans for North Beach Place moved forward, creating new critics, including the tenants themselves.

The initiative to improve North Beach Place stemmed partly from tenants, who in 1993 generated ideas for improving their deteriorating, crime-ridden housing by cooperating in a study sponsored by the Housing Authority. Conducted by the design team Kaplan, McLaughlin, and Diaz, the report outlined "possible long-term approaches to improving the living environment at North Beach Place" with the stated intent of serving "as a tool for residents to use in making decisions about future improvements at North Beach Place."[103] Through a series of workshops attended by tenants, along with neighborhood and Housing Authority representatives, residents created and discussed long-term goals for development, identified the causes of problems—deferred maintenance and design features that created safety hazards—and brainstormed design alternatives. During the five workshops, one issue emerged about which tenants were adamant: displacement. The Kaplan report noted tenants' concerns: "The requirement that no residents be displaced became one of the design principles for any renovation or new construction on the site."[104] The Housing Authority drew on information in the report—and input residents had offered in the workshops—for its HOPE VI application in order to meet the HUD requirement that applicants involve tenants in the redesign process.

The cooperative relationship between the SFHA and North Beach Place residents waned over time as tenants criticized the Housing Authority's manipulation of their participation, which was a key component to winning the grant. In its HOPE VI application, the SFHA proposed replacing the 229-unit complex with 355 mixed-income apartments, costing an estimated $69 million, with 20,000 square feet of commercial space, resident services including business and computer training, free child care, computer wiring in all apartments, and secured parking. The revitalization plan also called for North Beach Place to be run by a private management firm rather than the Housing Authority. The application to the federal government included the requisite evidence of residents' support of redevelopment in the form of a letter signed by sixteen residents.

Although residents wanted improvements, many claimed they did not knowingly sign a letter of support for the HOPE VI grant. A week after the Housing Authority announced its HOPE VI award, longtime North Beach Place tenant leader Alma Lark accused the Housing Authority of tricking residents into signing a petition of support. Lark explained to *Independent* reporter Barbara Nanney that someone at the Housing Authority substituted a meeting sign-in sheet with a support letter for the redevelopment plan. The Housing Authority denied any impropriety and claimed that an SFHA employee had passed around an attendance sheet and a letter at the tenants' meeting. However, resident leaders Bethola "Bee" Harper and Cynthia Wiltz, vice president of the NBTA, claimed that they thought they had signed an attendance sheet rather than a petition in favor of redevelopment. Harper explained, "When they were passing it around I was under the impression it was an attendance sheet. Later on I found out we had agreed with what they were doing. . . . I don't think I would have agreed to sign it [if I had known it was a letter of support]. They should have told us what we signed."[105] Some tenants, including the president of the NBTA, Gregory Richardson, supported the Housing Authority's version of events. Nevertheless, for the tenants who felt they had been manipulated, the HOPE VI grant amplified their distrust of the SFHA and concern for their future. Cynthia Wiltz explained the tensions between tenants and the Housing Authority over redevelopment: "We've been used and we don't know what is going on."[106] The grant also sparked debate among tenant leaders, several of whom claimed that Gregory Richardson had signed a letter urging HUD to award funds even though he did not have the full backing of North Beach Place tenants.[107]

When the initial start-up capital from the HOPE VI grant arrived, North Beach Place tenants realized that the Housing Authority would move ahead with redevelopment plans. Aware of the well-publicized problems at other HOPE VI sites in the city, tenants tried to protect themselves. The Housing Authority came under fire from tenants and community groups for its failures at these sites, including rushing tenants out of Hayes Valley and not assisting with the relocation of all tenants at Bernal Dwellings and Plaza East. In particular, many residents who opted to take Section 8 vouchers (subsidies to live in private-market rental housing) for relocation had to leave San Francisco because they could not find housing in the city's tight rental market. Redevelopment at HOPE VI sites had resulted in tenants' dislocation from their community. Eligible residents who wanted to return had to wait three to four years for the completion of the developments, and those tenants who did return found a reduction in the number of low-income units. North Beach Place residents, in an effort to avoid these problems, pressed for a two-phase redevelopment plan that would allow all residents to stay on-site during reconstruction and a one-for-one replacement of low-income units.[108] With a clear understanding of the contracted, expensive rental market in San Francisco, tenants wanted to ensure that the Housing Authority would follow through with the proposal put forth in the HOPE VI application to construct 229 low-income units and to keep residents on-site during redevelopment.

Although the Housing Authority proposed these initiatives in its HOPE VI application, and community organizations such as Tel-Hi had endorsed the proposal on the condition that the SFHA "follow through on [these] promises," tenants remained skeptical—and with good reason.[109] In an October 1996 press conference, HUD regional director Art Agnos said that there was not enough funding to reconstruct North Beach Place in phases because the HOPE VI grant was $10 million less than the Housing Authority had requested. Residents and community organizations supporting redevelopment subsequently balked. Meanwhile, the Housing Authority engaged in damage control, meeting with tenants and reassuring them that "the agency would stick to its agreement to reconstruct the development in phases, allowing most residents to remain on the site during demolition and reconstruction."[110] Many tenants who had endured the weight of the public's negative perception of North Beach Place and witnessed the growing popularity of North Beach as a tourist spot remained dubious of the SFHA's assurances about relocation and opportunities to return. Underpinning their worries were doubts about the city's intentions to rebuild public housing on such prime real estate in North Beach.[111]

For tenants who distrusted the Housing Authority, the sense that agency employees were "politicians playing games" and making empty promises caused them to preemptively mobilize "to protect their homes."[112] In November 1996, residents began holding weekly meetings to establish a tenant-based support network with links to community organizations. Gaining support from tenants' activist groups in the city, including the San Francisco–based Eviction Defense Network, an organization devoted to helping low-income tenants facing eviction, tenants worked to have more voice in relocation and redesign plans. North Beach Place tenants' concerns grew as they watched other public housing residents scatter throughout the Bay Area as a consequence of redevelopment and the SFHA evict neighbors within their own community under the One Strike policy. Implemented in

1997 by HUD, the policy allowed local authorities to evict any public housing resident if the resident, a member of the household, or a guest violated any part of the lease. In a May 1997 report for the *San Francisco Bay Guardian*, Nina Siegal stated that six tenants from North Beach Place had recently received eviction notices.[113] Three of the six tenants claimed they had been "targeted" by the One Strike policy. James Tracy of the Eviction Defense Network linked the "unwarranted" evictions to the HOPE VI program, claiming that "the housing authority is using One Strike as a way of substantially reducing the amount of relocation money they will have to pay out before demolitions come around."[114] Responding to the displacement of public housing tenants within their project and throughout the city, North Beach Place residents escalated their meetings, activities, and demands in an attempt to gain a modicum of control over the future of their housing and their community.[115]

Tenants' suspicions over relocation and the Housing Authority's promises that those "in good standing" would "be given first crack at units when the development is rebuilt" brought disparate groups within North Beach Place together and led to unprecedented tenant activism. In April 1998, a group of North Beach Place tenants reconstituted the North Beach Resident Management Corporation (NBRMC).[116] Resident Management Corporations (RMCs), established by the federal government in the 1980s to facilitate tenant management of public housing, had little success nationwide. Nonetheless, the NBRMC mounted a challenge to the SFHA's control over their project. Tenants established the corporation with the aim of purchasing and running their development, an opportunity the Housing Authority was legally required to give them before redevelopment started. North Beach Place residents maintained that they had not received the notification letter the Housing Authority claimed to have sent informing tenants of their right to submit proposals to redevelop and manage the project. Because tenants "passed" on the opportunity (which they said they did not know about), the SFHA opened the project's redevelopment to competitive bidding.[117]

A group of tenants, unwilling to miss their final chance to manage their project, set up the NBRMC, put together a proposal, and submitted it in 1998, competing with other bidders vying to redevelop

North Beach Place. The NBRMC's plan called for rejecting the HOPE VI grant in order to avoid federal restrictions and instead securing private loans to rebuild the property. The $100 million proposal outlined a tenant cooperative to manage the complex in partnership with Human Technology Partners, Inc. Alma Lark, president of the NBRMC, explained the impetus behind the group's actions, underscoring tenants' distrust of the SFHA: "It is only natural that we are not going to give control to the Housing Authority."[118] In June, a nine-member panel made up of tenants, SFHA representatives, an area merchant, community members, a local architect, a representative from the mayor's office, and a zoning administrator selected the North Beach Development Partners' (including Bridge Housing Corporation and the John Stewart Company) proposal to redevelop North Beach Place, rejecting the NBRMC's plan and dashing some tenants' hopes for running their housing development.[119]

Refusing to go quietly, North Beach Place residents picketed, petitioned, and protested relocation and their lack of participation in the HOPE VI redevelopment process. Together with the Eviction Defense Network and Fire by Night Organizing Committee, a small national organization committed to organizing students and low-income people, "many concerned residents at North Beach" sponsored a tenant speakout and rally on August 13, 1998. With a clear understanding of the importance of their public housing location, the organizing committee held the rally at noon at the bustling cable car turnaround on Bay Street. A flyer for the event depicts a white businessman holding a dollar bill with his arm around "Da Mayor," Willie Brown, who is kicking the backside of a person who has been pushed out of the edge of the picture. To the left of the mayor is a man holding a rifle, seemingly protecting the property in the background. Behind the men looms a large house. The cartoon represents the mayor and big business as bedfellows in the effort to displace low-income residents for the sake of capital gain.[120]

Historicizing their fight to "stop urban removal," North Beach Place tenants aligned themselves not only with other public housing tenants but also with the wider community of dislocated residents in the city who had lost their homes over the years. Forging a community of the dispossessed, tenants and advocates placed their struggle within the context of other groups displaced by the city over time for the purpose of redevelopment and its purported economic benefits. North Beach Place tenants tried to gain support for their cause by reminding San Franciscans of the city's transgressions against low-income tenants, from downtown urban renewal to problems at other HOPE VI sites. The flyer they created to explain their struggle read:

> Tenants at North Beach Public Housing are currently waging a battle against another wave of urban removal; the HOPE VI demolition of their homes, administered by the San Francisco Housing Authority. HOPE VI promises much needed improvements to public housing, but has resulted in eviction and loss of homes of thousands of tenants. Bernal Dwellings remains a vacant lot reminiscent of the International Hotel (the residential hotel demolished in 1977) mere blocks away from North Beach public housing. This is the same pattern which removed low-income renters from the [South of Market Area] neighborhood, and African-Americans from the Fillmore in the 1970s. This blatant effort to remove poor people and minorities from the city, is now being supported by Mayor Brown, the Board of Supervisors, and all levels of the Department of Housing and Urban Development. Join in the support of public housing residents at a rally and speakout, as we demand housing, economic upliftment to opportunities, and self determination.[121]

The NBTA and the NBRMC led the rally, articulating demands that included a legally binding "one for one relocation during the HOPE VI demolition, guaranteed reoccupancy for all current tenants," and full tenant control of the redevelopment process beginning with the acceptance of the NBRMC plan for the project.[122] Although the Housing Authority had selected another proposal, a number of tenants still pushed for the NBRMC's plan. Carrying signs reading "We Will Not Be Removed," "United the Community of Residents of North Beach will never be Defeated," "Low Income Homes Shall-B-Saved," "Eviction Defense Network and North Beach Tenants Fighting Forced Relocation and Urban Removal," and "Don't Take Our Homes," about thirty people gathered to raise their voices against the potential pitfalls of redevelopment for residents: likely relocation and the strong possibility of being unable to return.[123] Although the number of participants was a small proportion of the total number of residents at North Beach Place, the turnout, according to housing activist James Tracy, was relatively strong for a tenant protest. Participants undoubtedly represented the concerns of residents who could not or would not—out of fear of reprisals—attend. City officials, demonstrating their view of public housing tenants as troublemakers and criminals, dispatched police to the area, where officers allegedly outnumbered demonstrators two to one.[124]

The presence of the police at the peaceful rally and the increase in One Strike evictions did not slow tenants' efforts to safeguard their homes. North Beach Place residents drafted a petition to the Housing Authority in August 1998 restating their demands. In an effort to look after their public housing community, concerned residents who signed the petition asked the Housing Authority to reconfirm its commitments to tenant protections.[125] The petition also demanded that tenants have an opportunity to review and approve all plans for revitalization. Acknowledging the multiculturalism of their project and the need to work together, tenants requested that the SFHA submit their written guarantees in English, Chinese, and Spanish.[126]

The plans for redevelopment at North Beach Place caused disagreements and tensions between tenants and drew criticism from neighbors who wanted to see the project close, but they also brought tenants and community organizations together in an effort to protect tenants' interests and future housing options. Tel-Hi and the Chinatown CDC formed the backbone of an informal support network. As important community resource centers for tenants at North Beach Place, Tel-Hi and the Chinatown CDC cautiously supported redevelopment while frequently writing to the Housing Authority demanding that the agency adhere to the promises made in the HOPE VI application.[127] Because the Housing Authority decided to apply for HOPE VI money for North Beach Place in July 1996 and had to submit the paperwork by September 10, tenants had little involvement in the initial planning process beyond the workshops that had been held earlier. The coalition, while recognizing the Housing Authority's limited time frame, pushed for resident involvement and services during the application phase and after HUD awarded the grant. Echoing tenants' demands, community organizations worked to ensure that the diverse population at North Beach Place could participate in the planning process by prompting the SFHA to print notices and information in multiple languages and insisting on translation for residents. In a September 5, 1996, letter to Assistant Secretary of Public and Indian Housing Kevin Marchman, Chinatown CDC Program Director Reverend Norman Fong hinged his organization's continued support for HOPE VI at North Beach Place on inclusion and participation of residents:

> Translation (both oral and written), particularly in Chinese and Spanish, must be budgeted by the SFHA and its consultants and subcontractors (rather than an afterthought), to enable *all* tenants to *fully* participate throughout the revitalization process, and a reasonable amount of lead time must be given to allow for translation and proper notice to tenants of all upcoming meetings and site visits.[128]

The support of Tel-Hi and Chinatown CDC staff along with other organizations buttressed tenants' attempts to control the outcome of their relocation and the future of their public housing complex. Similarly, activists' and tenants' drive to overcome language barriers helped bring tenants from different races and ethnicities together in their joint fight to protect their rights and their home.

While ethnic and racially based mini-communities had emerged over the years in the public housing project described by the SFHA as "the most racially integrated" in the city, the threat of relocation and the reality of redevelopment helped foster intergroup interactions.[129] Cooperation became easier after residents and community organizations requested and received access to multilanguage translation. When tenants understood the policies and procedures, they could unite around a common cause: their home. In a 2002 interview, Alma Lark explained that the HOPE VI grant brought "all these nationalities together," creating community bonds so close "you would think we were relatives."[130] Although the Housing Authority continued to delay putting out publications in Chinese—which, according to one tenant, was deliberate, because "[the SFHA] don't want everything translated"— Chinese-speaking tenants became more active in the North Beach community.[131] According to Lark, the Chinese population "was staying to themselves but when they found out about HOPE VI they came out and embraced us. We are like a big family."[132] Demonstrating the power of culturally based assumptions and the simple ways that com-

"The Best Project in Town"

munity connections can form, an African American resident explained, "We have social events that [tenants of Chinese descent] participate in too. Like we have a social gathering and we try to have Chinese food or something. They like our food [though] because they eat [Chinese food] every day so they want spaghetti or chilidogs. When we barbeque or whatever they are here."[133] Through social events, children playing together, and second-generation children serving as translators for their parents, the contours of the North Beach public housing community changed as tenants worked harder to understand and accommodate one another. Four decades after the U.S. Supreme Court banned segregation in San Francisco public housing, tenants joined together to integrate into a strong, more united community as they faced the uncertainties of redevelopment.

The efforts to build bridges in daily life encouraged tenants to band together to lobby for an exit contract from the Housing Authority. Starting in 1996, the Fire by Night Organizing Committee, the Eviction Defense Network, and tenants began the slow process of door-to-door organizing to mobilize residents to push for an exit contract.[134] The contract called for legally binding guarantees for one-for-one unit replacement of all demolished low-income units, a two-phase demolition, and "a limited number of reasons that could disqualify one from reoccupancy."[135] The campaign for the exit contract initially became mired in racial politics at North Beach Place, with different racial and ethnic groups harboring—and having to work through—similar suspicions about one another. Although "nearly identical" rumors about Chinese American and African American tenant leaders "on the take" for their own gain initially split tenants, the participants' willingness to sit down with each other, and with translators, led to a peaceful and a stronger coalition. In a report for *Shelterforce*, James Tracy summed up the significance of tenant unification: "The final exit contract negotiating team had Black, Chinese, and White tenants working well together, thanks in part to the conscious effort to confront rumors and innuendo."[136] Tenant teamwork paid off, with over 60 percent of tenants signing a pledge during the next two years stating they would not move until they received an exit contract. Standing by their pledge, tenants refused to be relocated when the SFHA started the process of complying with HUD mandates. Fearful that a protracted battle might result in the loss of millions in HOPE VI funds, the SFHA finally relented and agreed to sign the contract. On September 22, 1999, the executive director of the SFHA, Ronnie Davis, signed the exit contract in front of the City Board of Supervisors' Finance and Labor Committee during a hearing on the Public Housing Tenant Protection Act, a direct outgrowth of North Beach Place tenants' unity and activism.[137]

Tenants' cooperation to secure an exit contract, along with problems at HOPE VI sites across San Francisco, resulted in a groundbreaking proposal for a city ordinance to ensure public housing tenant protections. In early 2000, Supervisor Tom Ammiano pushed forward a resolution, the Public Housing Tenant Protection Act, and used the North Beach Place exit contract as the model for the legislation, incorporating tenants' demands as stated in the exit contract.[138] The proposal also implicitly criticized the Housing Authority's inadequate financial planning at North Beach Place by including a clause requiring the SFHA to secure all funding for redevelopment before beginning demolition.

The SFHA started relocating residents before the agency had secured the necessary funding to rebuild the project. In 1998, the SFHA began moving tenants out from the east block of the project, but when the Tenant Protection Act was put forward in 2000, the developers still had not secured funding for all the construction costs—and the total project cost had ballooned from $69 million to $101 million. Tenant Alma Lark highlighted the absurdity of this process: "As a matter of fact this is the first time in my life that I have been around a developer who is going to do a building and doesn't have any money. They have investors from HUD, from everybody, and they still haven't been able to close the gap."[139]

Unfortunately for public housing tenants and their supporters, the Public Housing Tenant Protection Act, poised to change HOPE VI redevelopment practices in San Francisco and to put HUD on alert about the program's problems, did not make it to the Board of Supervisors meeting on February 14, 2000, for a vote. Supervisor Amos Brown sent the proposal back to committee. Brown "didn't say why he sent the resolution back," but his move came after "SFHA executive director Ronnie Davis spoke against the proposed act," calling parts of the legislation "unnecessary," "cumbersome," and difficult to enforce because of federal regulations.[140] The act did not go before the board again.

The failure of the Tenant Protection Act was not initially a problem for North Beach Place tenants, who felt victorious after Ronnie Davis signed the exit contract. Their excitement over the contract, however, was short-lived. The turnover in SFHA leadership undermined the guarantees tenants had worked hard to claim. Despite being articulated repeatedly since 1996, the SFHA's commitment to and reassurances about a two-phase development ended in 2001. Gregg Fortner, who replaced Ronnie Davis as executive director of the SFHA, announced in August 2001 that the "project had to be done in one phase to guarantee funding—and everyone had to move."[141] Voiding the exit contract and ignoring tenants' rights, the Housing Authority, under new leadership, moved ahead with demolition in one phase to cut costs on a project that still was not fully funded. An active tenant leader described her community's feelings of desperation, acknowledging that "we fought until the last day, to do it in two phases, to get everything we wanted. . . . We tried to make sure what they were saying is right. You know when they start tearing down the building we aren't going to know what is what."[142]

Just as tenants became aware of this distressing news, they also discovered the extent of the Housing Authority's broken promises. A controversial memo began circulating at North Beach Place. The letter, dated January 2000, from developer Bridge Housing Corp. to the Housing Authority, revealed that the agencies had been considering rebuilding the project all at once for over a year. Perhaps most significantly for tenants, the memo predated Executive Director Ronnie Davis signing the exit contract. Tenants angrily countered with cries of "I am not moving." For residents "who couldn't imagine a better place to live," the prospect of relocation in the tight San Francisco market was daunting—and especially after learning of the Housing Authority's misrepresentations, many residents worried that they would not be able to come back to the place hailed by city leaders "as the best location for housing anywhere in America."[143] Residents threatened but did not pursue a lawsuit. With demolition for the eastern block imminent, the remaining families seemed resigned to their fate and that of the North Beach Place community. While residents took pride that

"The Best Project in Town"

their project, which unlike the other three HOPE VI projects in town, was to have a one-for-one replacement of low-income public housing units, they wondered whether they would be allowed to return and what changes there would be in the community. In 2002, the SFHA demolished North Beach Place, which had been described by tenants as a "small community . . . a tight-knit family that looks out for one another's children."[144] The Housing Authority then began to implement plans that would radically alter the design and community of North Beach Place. A Housing Authority–Bridge Corporation billboard standing on the site of the demolished project assured passersby that North Beach Place tenants participated in and looked forward to the new development, with the tagline "Residents Rebuilding Their Communities."[145]

Despite not winning all of their demands, the residents' efforts to protect one-for-one replacement and to have input in the redevelopment process paid off for future public housing tenants at the new North Beach Place and elsewhere. Their activism helped pave the way for high-quality affordable housing on prime real estate in San Francisco and shaped the future vision of public housing in San Francisco. The impulse of urban renewal to "clean up" an area and move out the poor, which had been so thoroughly ingrained in redevelopment strategies during the second half of the twentieth century, was challenged, reshaped, and in some instances reinforced at North Beach Place. Some previous public housing residents benefited from the change to a mixed-income community—but others did not. Prior to redevelopment, Housing Authority employee Juan Monsanto, adamantly arguing that residents would be able to return, revealed the limitations inherent in a redevelopment effort based on the notion of "improving" the design and the people living in public housing. "One of the most important things the HOPE VI program has is that the residents have the first right to return. As long as the residents are in good standing on paying [their] lease, not being convicted of a felony, and following lease guidelines."[146] With some residents relocating to other cities in California, some moving to other HOPE VI sites and thus unable to return, and others barred by stricter regulations, the community dynamics at the new development promised to change dramatically.

"The Best Project in Town"

Low-income families moving into the new North Beach Place would share their housing complex with new residents and retail franchises that they might or might not be able to afford to patronize. Residents who intended to return to their home in North Beach Place and those who did not plan to come back agreed that for better or worse, "It's not going to be like it used to be. It is going to be totally different."[147]

Visitors and locals traveling to the North Beach District and Fisherman's Wharf on the Powell-Mason cable car line in 2009 exited between two blocks of four-story residential units with a mix of retail outlets on the ground floor. A blend of muted yellow, rust, tan, and green stucco facades with numerous windows and a New Urbanism design, the buildings blend in with the surrounding neighborhood. Riders exiting the cable car could grab a latte at Starbucks, rent a car at the Budget office, or shop at the specialty grocer Trader Joe's, the anchor retailer in the North Beach Place complex.[148] The mixed-income, mixed-use development, providing one-for-one replacement, includes 229 units of public housing and 112 low-income housing tax credit (LIHTC) apartments for residents with incomes below 50 percent of the city's median, for a total of 341 units, including a separate building for seniors and a parking garage for residents and shoppers.[149]

Opened on October 22, 2004, the new North Beach Place reflects North Beach Development Associates' objective "to build high-quality, well-designed and cost-efficient, affordable multifamily housing, above ground-floor parking, and retail and commercial space of benefit to the residents and the surrounding community."[150] The SFHA financed the $108-million development with $23 million in HOPE VI funds and a public–private partnership with Bridge Housing, a nonprofit developer, and the for-profit John Stewart Company and Em Johnson Interest Inc. Together, under the umbrella of the North Beach Development Associates, the development team received $38 million in federal LIHTCs and $17 million in state tax credits, at the time the largest federal and state allocations awarded.[151] The HOPE VI grant, $1 million from the city, and an unprecedented $56 million in financing from Citibank, along with tax credits and other sources, backed "one of California's largest affordable housing developments."[152] The John Stewart Company manages both the residential and commercial properties.

"The Best Project in Town"

Figure 29. North Beach Place at the cable car turnaround after redevelopment, 2008. Photograph by the author.

North Beach Place offers a wide range of amenities for residents. The new complex includes a 3,000-square-foot incubator space for resident entrepreneurs along with 17,000 square feet of commercial space, including Tower Tours, Trader Joe's, and Starbucks.[153] Apartments offer energy-efficient appliances as well as patios or balconies. The new development also provides common areas, including a study room with computers where a range of classes are held, a family recreation room with books and a television, and interior courtyards with a variety of play areas for children. The walk-up apartments, along with increased pedestrian activity on all sides of the complex, higher levels of lighting, and "a pedestrian-oriented streetscape at the cable car terminus including outdoor seating for the new retail/commercial space," were designed to enhance safety at the project.[154] Tenants, neighbors, and visitors alike benefit from a more open design based on principles of defensible space.

Figure 30. The redeveloped North Beach Place with anchor retail tenant Trader Joe's, 2008. Photograph by the author.

Five years after the Housing Authority began efforts to move tenants out of North Beach, some returning residents made their way back to a new home. Eighty-two families, 36 percent of the previous population, returned.[155] The whereabouts of all other former tenants is unknown. Twenty-year-old Anthony Vigil, who grew up living with his grandmother in North Beach Place, was excited to return after being relocated to the Sunnydale public housing project, a neglected southeast San Francisco site with a high crime rate and run-down buildings. Vigil, hired by Trader Joe's to stock shelves at night, described his relief at moving back: "My grandmother moving back to North Beach is just truly a blessing."[156] For returning and new public housing tenants at North Beach Place, the location, amenities, and even possible job opportunities at Trader Joe's provided a rich living environment. For those who did not qualify to come back, who the Housing Authority lost track of and thus was not able to communicate

"The Best Project in Town"

Figure 31. North Beach Place interior courtyard, 2008. Photograph by the author.

with about opportunities for return, or who opted to leave permanently, the benefits of living in a safe, attractive development in a thriving neighborhood are lost, as is the community that once existed there. Nevertheless, the activism of low-income tenants, along with the willingness of the SFHA and the city to support the continued availability of affordable housing in North Beach, is a success story within the national narrative of gentrification and HOPE VI redevelopment efforts, which have often resulted in permanent displacement of low-income citizens and a reduction in the number of affordable housing units available.

Praised for outstanding New Urbanism design, celebrated with local and national awards, and touted by politicians, North Beach Place demonstrates the potential of public housing in the twenty-first century. These well-designed and well-maintained residences—in a safe, welcoming environment, in a prime location with transportation, shopping, hospitals, and jobs nearby, and with access to social

"The Best Project in Town"

Figure 32. North Beach Place interior courtyard and play equipment, 2008. Photograph by the author.

services on-site—highlight the possibilities for high-quality affordable housing.[157] As the development continues to draw attention and the developers instruct others looking to replicate the model, the community bridge building and activism of low-income North Beach Place tenants must not be forgotten. Their efforts and successes in working together, across racial and ethnic lines, to secure a just and stable living environment for themselves and others represent both the legacy and the promise for the future of public housing.

Conclusion
Looking Back, Moving Forward

BY THE TIME THE SAN FRANCISCO HOUSING AUTHORITY DEDICATED the new Valencia Gardens in 2006, the public housing program in the United States had shifted dramatically. The federal HOPE VI program ushered in significant changes in public housing, introducing opportunities for private financing and ownership of developments, implementing outsourced management, and eliminating one-for-one replacement of public housing units in redeveloped sites.[1] With these changes came a renewed emphasis on the "moral standards" and selectivity that governed the early years of the public housing program nationally and locally. Touted by supporters for providing attractive buildings, housing "deserving" tenants, and creating mixed-income developments, the HOPE VI program worked to eliminate distressed public housing and to deconcentrate poverty. It also demolished more than 157,000 apartments and displaced at least a quarter of a million people nationwide.[2]

San Francisco, unlike Atlanta and Chicago, chose to define "mixed income" as very low-income and low-income. Tenant activists at North Beach Place, with their emphasis on one-for-one replacement, helped push this preservation of public housing. Ultimately, the SFHA retained affordable housing units even in sought-after areas like North Beach and the Mission. Nonetheless, the redevelopment of North Beach Place and Valencia Gardens razed buildings and destroyed communities. The bonds of affective activism at Valencia Gardens and the cross-racial and cross-ethnic ties of North Beach Place tenants, leveraged to ensure the continued survival of public housing in the district, were severed. Some tenants chose to use Housing Choice Vouchers (formerly Section 8) to live in the private housing market; others went to another HOPE VI development or traditional public housing; others were denied admittance to the new units because they did not

Conclusion

meet the eligibility standards; and still others' choices were likely constrained through the relocation process as the SFHA tried, and failed, to track and communicate with former tenants. Ultimately, about 17 percent of Valencia Gardens households and 36 percent of North Beach households returned.[3] These low numbers raise more questions than answers about the impact of relocation practices, individual choice, life circumstances, and eligibility standards and about whether the former tenants are better off economically, physically, mentally, or socially than they were before.

Those who did return reported mixed results. Returners to Valencia Gardens, while thankful for the many improvements, viewed the quality of the construction materials as inferior to those of the "Old VG." "Flimsy" construction, coupled with sewage troubles early on, prompted legitimate concerns about the maintenance and longevity of the buildings over time. Parents and grandparents at Valencia Gardens and North Beach Place shared complaints about the play areas for children; at Valencia Gardens the small playground was often locked and prioritized for the Head Start program. The lack of additional play space encouraged youth to skateboard in the small courtyard where the Bufanos sit, frustrating residents who worked hard to ensure that the sculptures were a part of the new Valencia Gardens and worried they would be damaged. At North Beach Place, the hyperdesigned playground pieces distributed throughout the interior courtyards look sleek, but the equipment seems geared toward individual children playing alone rather than toward interactive play, a factor in the design of many playgrounds.[4]

Management, a common source of complaints in rental housing, may emerge as another critical area to mine for best practices and potential pitfalls as the SFHA continues to outsource functions it once performed. At Valencia Gardens, the developer and property management functions were divided: Mission Housing Corporation served as the developer and the John Stewart Company is the property manager. The John Stewart Company was a partner in developing North Beach Place (Bridge Housing was the lead) and is now the property manager there as well. As San Francisco sets a course for redeveloping its public housing, understanding the dynamics of trust, consistency, and successful social service delivery models in managing apartments and supporting residents is critical.

Prioritizing public housing tenants' relationships with each other is also necessary. Acknowledging the importance of community bonds and social networks in low-income communities is a critical first step, but it is not enough. The history of Valencia Gardens currently displayed in the lobby includes a timeline, photos, and a few quotes from the Legacy Project in service of a narrative that redevelopment is better—for everyone.[5] The loss of relationships, social ties, and sense of community that many residents felt is largely absent from the narrative. Creating strategies for continuing to support the relationships and, when relevant, activist ties among low-income tenants will strengthen public housing redevelopment programs. This lesson is critical for San Francisco as it moves forward with an ambitious agenda to remake its public housing program.

As HOPE VI funding trickled to a halt, San Francisco, under its new, energetic mayor, Gavin Newsom, pledged to transform public housing across the city. While the SFHA had managed to leverage $118.6 million in federal HOPE VI funds and $188.2 million in public and private monies to redevelop public housing in the Western Addition, North Beach, and the Mission District—all relatively close to the central business district—the city had not invested in the long-neglected public housing sites farther afield in the southeast part of the city, and federal support had all but disappeared.[6] Mayor Newsom summed up the situation while walking around the distressed Sunnydale public housing site: "HOPE VI has been essentially gutted by the Bush administration. Rather than waiting for Air Force One to come to SFO, we are acknowledging there is a problem [in public housing] and we are taking responsibility and we are not waiting for someone else."[7]

Naming public housing revitalization as a mayoral priority, in 2006 Newsom and Supervisor Sophie Maxwell cosponsored the HOPE SF Task Force to flesh out a local HOPE VI-like program that would "replace failed public housing developments with vibrant communities."[8] These politicians were not the sole starting point for change, however; as planning scholar Jane Rongerude notes, the SFHA, the

Conclusion

Mayor's Office of Housing (MOH), the Communities of Opportunity Program, and the mayor all clamored to claim a stake in the emerging program. Following other cities' localized efforts to improve public housing through HOPE VI–inspired models, San Francisco looked to redevelop its public housing of last resort.[9] The circumstances were dire: the SFHA managed eight public housing sites that were severely distressed and neglected, and the city continued to cope with a shortage of affordable housing. Mayor Newsom's ambitious first-term aims to end homelessness, decrease poverty, create more affordable housing, and increase the economic prosperity of the city coalesced in the HOPE SF program.[10]

The goals put forth by the HOPE SF Task Force in many ways reflected both the hard-fought battles of public housing tenants at Valencia Gardens, Ping Yuen, and North Beach Place and the lessons learned from HOPE VI failures and successes locally and nationally.[11] The new vision for public housing in San Francisco was also permeated, less tangibly, by legacies of the various modes of tenant activism—affective activism, cross-sector coalition building, and multiracial and multiethnic alliances—that resulted in strong, sustaining relationships and at times improved living environments and social services, as well as the active participation of tenants in leadership and redevelopment processes. The composition of the task force itself also signaled a more inclusive coalition shaping the future of public housing. Made up of public housing residents, city commissioners, community activists, and business and community leaders, the HOPE SF Task Force delivered recommendations in March 2007 to improve the city's public housing.[12] The HOPE SF program, the task force urged, must attend to the following:

> one-for-one replacement of public housing units, job opportunities for residents, integration with neighborhood improvement plans, creation of environmentally sustainable housing, and building a strong sense of community.[13]

With these principles guiding redevelopment, the task force recommended that the city and the SFHA partner to rebuild San Francisco's eight most distressed public housing sites into "thriving, mixed-income communities, without displacing tenants."[14] The program's four stated

Conclusion

goals include building superior housing, enhancing the lives of existing residents, serving as a catalyst for improving the surrounding neighborhood, and advancing knowledge about best practices in public housing revitalization and community development nationally.[15] The program's vision, as stated on the HOPE SF website, is nothing short of a national model of community transformation:

> HOPE SF is the nation's first large-scale public housing revitalization project to prioritize current residents while also investing in high-quality, sustainable housing and broad scale community development. In sites across San Francisco, HOPE SF will create thriving, mixed-income communities that provide residents healthy, safe homes and the support they need to succeed. Green buildings, better schools, new local businesses and onsite resident services will transform these communities and provide opportunities to the residents who have struggled here for generations.[16]

In a recognition of the physical isolation of many public housing sites located outside the central core of the city, unlike where Valencia Gardens, Ping Yuen, and North Beach Place tenants reside, the program called for redeveloping entire neighborhoods "where gunshots pierce the air many nights, apartments languish in disrepair with mold and rodent problems, and there are no grocery stores or Laundromats within walking distance."[17] Rooted both in San Francisco's progressive ideals and in the HOPE VI program's premise that neighborhoods shape residents' opportunities, the HOPE SF initiative promised to transform lives and communities by pursuing a holistic approach to neighborhood revitalization.

Through a mixture of public and private financing, interagency collaboration, and administrative changes, the city of San Francisco, under Mayor Newsom's leadership, joined Atlanta, Chicago, and Seattle in creating its own local agenda for rethinking public housing and the deconcentration of poverty.[18] Undoubtedly aware of the SFHA's troubled history of mismanagement and corruption, and riding a wave of positive press praising the redevelopment of North Beach Place and Valencia Gardens, Mayor Newsom set out to overhaul public housing. He began by pushing out SFHA Executive Director Gregg Fortner (2001–2007), the longest-standing leader of the organization in decades,

Conclusion

and hiring Henry Alvarez to replace Fortner in 2008.[19] The partnership between the MOH and the SFHA proved an important collaboration and a mechanism for rebuilding trust with tenants by identifying MOH as the lead on the city's affordable housing agenda. Financing the ambitious HOPE SF program was critical. The city issued $95 million in revenue bonds that were to be paid off over several years with "city general fund money and property tax dollars generated by redevelopment of the housing projects."[20] The initial payout was slated to help finance the first redevelopment project, the rebuilding of Hunters View in Hunters Point, projected to cost $335 million, and to include 350 public-housing and low-income apartments replacing 267 public-housing units, as well as 383 market-rate and 67 below-market-rate homes for sale. Residents will have access to amenities to include a child-care center, a teen center, a computer room, and parks.[21]

Long neglected by the city and the SFHA, and shaped by urban renewal projects that pushed African Americans out of the Fillmore District to Hunters Point, Hunters View emerged not only as a testing ground for the holistic housing and human redevelopment efforts of HOPE SF but also as a vehicle for the city to acknowledge its decades-long role in depriving that area of basic social and economic opportunities. In his 2006 State of the City address, Mayor Newsom promoted the HOPE SF program as a way for the city to "create new neighborhoods," "preserve existing neighborhoods by relieving the pressure for new housing," and "create new economic opportunities. And finally—perhaps most importantly—right a wrong."[22] Echoing the words of the Chinese American press, which had deemed the construction of Ping Yuen in 1952 an essential act of restitution by the city after a century of discriminating against Chinese Americans in San Francisco, Newsom held out the hope that a revitalized Hunters View could stem the outmigration of African American families from the city, promote economic development, decrease poverty, and heal deep wounds felt by African Americans living there.

Only time will tell if the HOPE SF program can transform the housing, neighborhood, and economic success of low-income residents—not to mention heal racial wounds—through its seemingly progressive vision. Research on the impact of HOPE VI redevelopment nationally and the lived experience of tenants locally should continue to shape

Conclusion

the HOPE SF program. A wide range of studies on HOPE VI sites across the country reveals once again the importance of local implementation and context. The varying interpretations of mixed income, among other factors, as urban design and planning scholar Lawrence Vale notes, has produced mixed outcomes for residents, relocated residents, and the HOPE VI program overall.[23] Within HOPE VI communities, many low-income residents continue to experience barriers to employment, including unmet transportation and child care needs.[24] Neither relocated tenants nor returners have demonstrated gains in terms of improved schooling options, improved mental and physical health for children or adults, or improved earnings and overall income.[25] Many relocated residents and returners acknowledged feeling safer in their new environments and saw an improvement in the housing and neighborhood when compared with their former residences. Others, including public housing tenants in Seattle, argued that their former residence was a better place to live than their new one.[26] Many residents across the country, like tenants at Valencia Gardens and North Beach Place, lost their social networks through the HOPE VI process even as the program held out the promise of improving their social capital.[27] Overall, HOPE VI results are varied, and continued research will reveal the long-term impact of redevelopment on relocated and returning residents, the implications of variation within the mixed-income model, and the long-term effect of HOPE VI redevelopment on surrounding neighborhoods.

In 2012, the economic recession and new leadership in the mayor's office became critical factors in determining the future of the HOPE SF program. Work on Hunters View commenced, although the economic downturn slowed progress. Meanwhile, public housing tenants at Valencia Gardens, Ping Yuen, and North Beach Place continued their lives and struggles in both new and old public housing developments. As beneficiaries of SFHA and HUD resources not yet realized in the southeastern part of the city, these centrally located developments melded with the surrounding neighborhoods and contributed to the tourist vibe in Chinatown, the gentrification in the Mission District, and the blend of both in North Beach.[28] Returners to Valencia Gardens and North Beach adjusted to new neighbors and rhythms in their transformed apartment complexes, and tenants at Ping Yuen grappled with the age of their project buildings and strategized with the Chinatown CDC about options for renovation or redevelopment.

The legacy of public housing tenants' activism reverberated in 2011 when City Administrator Ed Lee became the first Chinese American mayor in San Francisco's history.[29] After Gavin Newsom became lieutenant governor of California in January 2011, Lee was appointed interim mayor and then went on to win a "hotly contested campaign" in November, with the strong backing of former mayor Willie Brown and support from the African American community.[30] As mayor, Lee continued to support the HOPE SF program and the revitalization of public housing—and he brought to his new role his own experience fighting alongside low-income residents for better housing. First as an activist opposing the eviction of I-Hotel tenants and then as the law clerk with the Asian Law Caucus who represented PYRIA during their rent strike, Lee had been a critical player in advancing tenants' rights. Reflecting back on the rent strike, Lee recalled, "We tried to teach [tenants] to demand their rights."[31] PYRIA's decades of activism and successful coalition building demonstrate that tenants continued to do just that.

The efforts of tenants at Valencia Gardens, Ping Yuen, and North Beach Place to push the boundaries of the federal public housing program in San Francisco reshaped their communities and the tenants themselves. The affective activism that fueled relationships and self-efficacy for Anita Ortiz, Gabriella Fontanella, and other tenants at Valencia Gardens provided a sense of security and belonging that was sustaining for them. Although their affective activism did not achieve specific, measurable gains in terms of the return rate of residents, it shaped tenants in meaningful ways and influenced important design features—such as the inclusion of the Bufanos—that benefit the current tenants living at Valencia Gardens.[32] Coalition building and consistent leadership at PYRIA by George Lee, Chang Jok Lee, and Watson Low contributed to community building and successful lobbying for project improvements at Ping Yuen. The long-term partnership with the Chinatown CDC resulted in reliable social services and support for Ping Yuen residents, which provided a strong foundation for public housing residents over time. At North Beach Place, racial and ethnic differences, at times a barrier to a shared community identity, became

Conclusion

an important factor in creating a collaborative strategy for protecting the future of public housing in the area. Exercising a range of civic engagement and democratic practices to protect, improve, and preserve public housing, low-income tenants in all three communities challenged the popular reductive stereotype of the "projects" as crime-ridden, anti-public wastelands populated by lazy freeloaders.

The successes and failures of Valencia Gardens, Ping Yuen, and North Beach Place tenants, as well as those of the SFHA between 1938 and 2006, may prove instructive as San Francisco and other cities grapple with public housing, concentrated poverty, and economic development in the aftermath of HOPE VI and a continual decline in federal funding. Although the SFHA incorporated some lessons into the vision for HOPE SF, as described above, there is much more to reflect on as San Francisco's program continues to unfold. The following history lessons, in particular, seem relevant to the future of public housing in San Francisco and the United States:

- The SFHA over time was an organizational failure in part because of leadership breakdowns caused by the political nature of its appointments and by the leaders themselves. Strong, ethical, transparent leadership and management that includes and values honest feedback from residents—without retribution—would provide a secure foundation for the success and health of the SFHA and the communities it houses.
- Tenant relationships matter and should be viewed and valued as a critical asset and in turn a major cost of redevelopment processes. Finding ways to prevent the destruction of community ties should be an explicit redevelopment priority.
- Community formation happens in multiple and complex ways, and artistic and aesthetic enhancements, such as the Bufanos at Valencia Gardens and the Paliou Gate at Ping Yuen, can build pride in place and connectivity. Parsed another way, low-income Americans should have access to art and beauty in their living environments, whether that is in mixed-income or low-income housing.
- Ping Yuen's history emphasizes the importance of consistent, effective leadership and coalition building to create change. The Chinatown CDC's long-standing reciprocal relationship with PYRIA strengthened both organizations while also providing consistent social services support for Ping Yuen residents.

Conclusion

- As public housing residents use Housing Choice Vouchers to move into the private market, return to HOPE VI developments, or continue living in traditional public housing, attention must be paid to providing holistic social services: transportation, child care, job training, and education are integral pieces to any kind of successful affordable housing strategy and essential to ensuring that the deconcentration of poverty leads not solely to the dispersal of poverty but rather to an actual decrease in poverty.
- The history of North Beach Place reminds us of the importance of inclusion in our democracy. From the successful activism of African American tenants who fought to desegregate public housing, to tenants' effective collaboration across clearly drawn racial and ethnic lines to demand that 229 units of public housing remain in the North Beach District, a clear message emerges: creating communities with racial, ethnic, and socioeconomic diversity is worth fighting for. Establishing and sustaining truly integrated neighborhoods can yield thriving communities.

As HOPE VI and similarly inspired programs replace public housing with mixed-income communities that most often favor the higher range of low-income tenants, the very poor—who have consistently lived at the "margins of empathy" in this country, as Lawrence Vale puts it—must not be ignored.[33] The movement to build, maintain, and sustain high-quality "affordable housing" in the United States must encompass citizens at all income levels in need of affordable housing. Collectively, the lived experiences of tenants at Valencia Gardens, Ping Yuen, and North Beach Place amplify the importance of civic engagement and serve as a clarion call to action: creating thriving, stable communities for all low-income Americans, including the very low-income residents served by public housing from the early 1960s to the 1990s, will require civic inquiry and action and community organization on the part of citizens from all socioeconomic backgrounds.[34]

As federal, state, and local governments, developers, and activists wrestle with the future of the public housing program in the United States, local contexts and holistic community development should be key considerations. The voices of the past, interpreted here through oral histories, serve as critical reminders to include public housing residents in the planning process and design of the spaces they will call home. The stakes are high, and the need for quality affordable housing is acute. The vision for public housing, and our collective answer to what it should look like and do and who it is for, needs to be informed not only by economic and policy studies but also by consideration of tenants' histories, lived experiences, and democratic practices, as well as the communities they created together. We must build on this knowledge as we move to develop twenty-first-century public housing that is more than shelter.

Acknowledgments

Relationships matter and community bonds can serve as a critical source of support and inspiration. I learned these truths repeatedly through my research—and my life over the past decade. During the course of researching and writing this book, I finished my doctorate, got married, moved to Richmond, Virginia, started work at the Bonner Center for Civic Engagement at the University of Richmond, and became a mother: all of these changes brought me into new communities that along with professional and scholarly networks have sustained me in countless ways. I am delighted to thank individuals in those communities here.

Along the way, a host of incredible scholars, teachers, colleagues, and friends have supported me. The best parts of this work are because of them. The failures are all mine. The following folks have graciously offered their time and wisdom to me through conversations, reading, editing, and commenting on the project at various stages, and/or sharing their own research and ideas with me: Maureen Fitzgerald, Cindy Hammovitch, Joseph Heathcott, Douglas A. Hicks, Wesley Hogan, Ocean Howell, Brad Hunt, Alison Isenberg, Arthur Knight, Nancy Kwak, Shelley Lee, Leisa D. Meyer, John Moeser, Robert K. Nelson, Annelise Orleck, Kimberley L. Phillips, Kelly Quinn, Jane Rongerude, Kristin Szylvian, Lawrence Vale, Rhonda Y. Williams, Thad Williamson, and Eric Yellin. Without the encouragement and invaluable feedback from the Works in Progress group at the University of Richmond, made up of three outstanding colleagues and friends, Elizabeth Outka, Kevin Pelletier, and Monika Siebert, this book would not have been completed. I am humbled by their incredible commitment to this project and unflagging support. Laura Holliday was a fabulous reader and editor, and Michael Bohrer-Clancy a first-rate production editor. The excellent team and wonderful colleagues at the Bonner Center for Civic Engagement, co-led by Sylvia Gale, cheered me on and kept our collective work moving forward when I was writing. Thank you

Acknowledgments

Heather Ashton, Alexandra Byrum, Kim Dean, Terry Dolson, Bryan Figura, Sylvia Gale, Jess Hofbauer, Grace Leonard, Shelby Longland, Adrienne Piazza, Cassie Price, Michael Rogers, Black Stake, and former teammates Debbie Collins, Betsy Kelly, Judy Pryor-Ramirez, Liz Riggs, and Susannah Walker. Colleagues in the American Studies Program and History Department at the University of Richmond have made my research (and teaching) better: thank you. Pieter Martin, at the University of Minnesota Press, maintained faith in this project and has been a stalwart advocate throughout the process. My participation as a Visiting Quadrant Fellow, made possible through the collaboration of the Institute of Advanced Study and the University of Minnesota Press, provided helpful feedback from the Press and esteemed colleagues at the University of Minnesota during a pivotal time.

Researching a book on San Francisco from the East Coast became manageable thanks to financial support from the American Studies Program and the Reves Center for International Education at the College of William and Mary; a generous dissertation fellowship from the American Association of University Women, and the support of University of Richmond administrators, particularly Steve Allred and Douglas A. Hicks. Undergraduate students Lauren Lambie-Hansen, Stephanie Li, Jennifer Patchen, and Christian Terlecki and graduate student Clare Robinson provided first-rate research assistance. Many wonderful librarians contributed to this project, and it is better because of them: Waverly Lowell at the Environmental Design Archives, the entire staff of the San Francisco History Center at the San Francisco Public Library, staff at the Bancroft Library and Ethnic Studies Library at the University of California–Berkeley, Lucretia McCulley at the University of Richmond, and Mildred Sink at the College of William and Mary helped in numerous ways. Angela Chu and Reverend Norman Fong at the Chinatown CDC shared their time and wisdom as well as their files. I am grateful to them. Angela also took time out of her busy schedule to translate during my interviews with Ping Yuen residents. I owe thanks to Roberta Swan for sharing her wonderful Legacy Project interviews and her passion and ideas with me. Michael Roetzer at the San Francisco Housing Authority provided me with access to the San Francisco Housing Authority Commission minutes and articles on the SFHA. Tan Chow shared his personal files with me for

Acknowledgments

which I am grateful. Keith Nitta, George (Tad) Ware, and Todd Miller generously offered me lodging for months on end and levity, year after year, in San Francisco. The public housing residents who took the time to share their stories with me cannot be thanked enough: their oral histories shaped me, and this book, in important ways. They also inspired me to think about civic engagement in new ways. I am thankful for the time we spent together.

The unwavering love and support of my family over the years and their commitment to my education is a privilege I am grateful for every day. This book is a testament to my parents, Donna and David Howard, and their constant encouragement. My wonderful siblings, Jennifer Joyce and Matt Howard, and gracious in-laws, Robert and Kathy Nelson, and Ben Nelson and Jeanne O'Brien, have also been a source of support: thank you. The family I chose whose members have not already been acknowledged—Mollie and Jonathan Barton, Karen Barzilay, Suzanne Bessenger, Jennifer Blanchard, Nicole Cloeren, Ashley Davis, Jean DeMoss, Rachel Dunifon, Katrina and Chris Dunks, Brian Geiger, Leanne Gent, Andy Gurka, Glyn Hughes, Catrina Huhyn-Weiss, Kim Hurst, Jason James, Nicole Michels, Caroline and Tyler Nichols, Sally Richmond, Gretchen Schoel, Audrey Short, Julietta Singh, Nathan Snaza, Kendra Vendetti, Kevin Vose, and Jon Weiss—have at different times, in important ways, provided support, humor, and kindness that buoyed me.

My incomparable partner, Robert K. Nelson, has walked beside me for more than a decade, and it is because of him that I truly understand integrity and compassion. Finally, to our incredible daughter, Meseret, may you grow up to become part of communities that enrich you and find your own modes of activism to improve our world.

Notes

Introduction

1. Anita Ortiz, interview with the author, tape recording, San Francisco, May 2009.

2. In *The Politics of Public Housing: Black Women's Struggles against Urban Inequality* (Oxford: Oxford University Press, 2004), Rhonda Y. Williams aptly demonstrates the politicization of black female tenants who lived in public housing in Baltimore.

3. See, for example, John Bauman, *Public Housing, Race, and Renewal: Urban Planning in Philadelphia, 1920–1974* (Philadelphia: Temple University Press, 1987); Arnold Hirsch, *Making the Second Ghetto: Race and Housing in Chicago, 1940–1960* (New York: Oxford University Press, 1983); Gail Radford, *Modern Housing for America* (Chicago: University of Chicago Press, 1996); Lawrence Vale, *From the Puritans to the Projects* (Cambridge, Mass.: Harvard University Press, 1996); Nicholas Dagen Bloom, *Public Housing That Worked: New York in the Twentieth Century* (Philadelphia: University of Pennsylvania, 2008); and D. Bradford Hunt, *Blueprint for Disaster: The Unraveling of Chicago Public Housing* (Chicago: University of Chicago Press, 2009). For an extensive overview of public housing planning and policy, see "American Public Housing at 75: Policy, Planning and the Public Good," a special issue of the *Journal of the American Planning Association* guest edited by Joseph Heathcott (78, no. 4, December 2012). A special issue of the *Journal of Urban History*, edited by Sean Purdy and Nancy Kwak, explores public housing in the United States, Canada, the Caribbean, and Argentina (33, no. 3, March 2007). Don Parson, John Baranski, and Dana Cuff have contributed to the discussion of public housing in the West; see Don Parson, *Making a Better World: Public Housing, the Red Scare, and the Direction of Modern Los Angeles* (Minneapolis: University of Minnesota Press, 2005); John Baranski, "Making Public Housing in San Francisco: Liberalism, Social Prejudice, and Social Activism, 1906–1976" (PhD diss., University of California, Santa Barbara, 2004); and Dana Cuff, *The Provisional City: Los Angeles Stories of Architecture and Urbanism* (Cambridge, Mass.: MIT Press, 2002). Charlotte Brooks's examination of Asian Americans' housing struggles in Los Angeles and San Francisco from the late nineteenth century to the 1950s highlights the complexities Asian Americans, as "perpetual

Notes to Introduction

foreigners," faced in public and private housing. Charlotte Brooks, *Alien Neighbors, Foreign Friends: Asian Americans, Housing and the Transformation of Urban California* (Chicago: University of Chicago Press, 2009).

4. See Gerald D. Suttles, *Social Order of the Slum* (Chicago: University of Chicago Press, 1968); Lee Rainwater, *Behind Ghetto Walls* (Chicago: Aldine, 1970); Lawrence Vale, *Reclaiming Public Housing: A Half Century of Struggle in Three Public Neighborhoods* (Cambridge, Mass.: Harvard University Press, 2002); Roberta M. Feldman and Susan Stall, *The Dignity of Resistance: Women Residents' Activism in Chicago Public Housing* (New York: Cambridge University Press, 2004); Rhonda Y. Williams, *The Politics of Public Housing*; John Baranski, "Something to Help Themselves: Tenant Organizing in San Francisco Public Housing, 1965–1975," *Journal of Urban History* 33, no. 3 (March 2007), 418–42; Sudhir Alladi Venkatesh, *American Project: The Rise and Fall of a Modern Ghetto* (Cambridge, Mass.: Harvard University Press, 2002); and Kelly A. Quinn, "Making Modern Homes: A History of Langston Terrace Dwellings, a New Deal Housing Program in Washington, D.C." (PhD diss., University of Maryland, 2007).

5. Future studies may explore the breadth of public housing in San Francisco, including Hunters View, an African American public housing project plagued by disinvestment, deindustrialization, deferred maintenance, and other problems well documented in other public housing studies. Jane Rongerude examines Hunters View in her dissertation on the HOPE SF program: "The Sorted City: SF, HOPE SF, and the Redevelopment of Public Housing" (PhD diss., University of California, Berkeley, 2009).

6. My identities as a scholar, an outsider who has never lived in public housing, and a white woman not only shaped tenants' individual responses to me and our interactions but also molded the oral history process even as I tried my best to be objective. As a white academic, I inspired a measure of distrust from some of my interlocutors, who were primarily people of color and who have had a history of contention with institutional representatives. My identity as a woman, in contrast, seemed to encourage connection for many female tenants I interviewed. My role as an outsider, and the fact that I have never lived in public housing, inspired interviewees to go into considerable detail in explaining the everyday texture of their lives and struggles in their public housing environments. In addition to my own interviews, and complicating matters further, I had access to eighty hours of oral interviews conducted by Roberta Swan—discussed in chapter 2—in which her own identity markers and other contextual factors shaped tenants' responses.

7. The term "psychological ownership" is from Lawrence Vale, interview by Gail Harris, "The Connection," National Public Radio, April 28, 2003.

Notes to Chapter 1

1. "To Provide Decent, Safe, and Sanitary Housing"

1. For more information on the architecture at the Exposition, and in particular Arthur Brown's work, see Jeffrey T. Tilman, *Arthur Brown, Jr.: Progressive Classicist* (New York: Norton, 2006), 194–98. The Golden Gate International Exposition, the western counterpart to the 1939 New York World's Fair, was open from February to May 1939 and again from May through September 1940. The Exposition in San Francisco took place on Treasure Island, a man-made island adjoining Yerba Buena Island, midway between San Francisco and Oakland. The Aquacade featured a young Esther Williams, who went on to become a major Hollywood star.

2. For an analysis of the Federal Housing Administration's promotion of the private housing market through the 1935 California–Pacific International Exposition, see Matthew Bokovoy, "Spectres of Social Housing, San Diego, 1935," in *Designing Tomorrow: America's World's Fairs of the 1930s*, ed. Robert W. Rydell and Laura Burd Schiavo (New Haven, Conn.: Yale University Press, 2010), 159–75.

3. Housing Authority of the City and County of San Francisco, *Third Annual Report* (San Francisco: The Housing Authority, 1941), 8; all SFHA Annual Reports cited below were accessed at the San Francisco Public Library.

4. *Housing in Our Time* (Washington, DC: U.S. Housing Authority, [193?]), film accessed online at Prelinger Archives, www.archive.org/details/housing_in_our_time.

5. Gail Radford, *Modern Housing: Policy Struggles in the New Deal Era* (Chicago: University of Chicago Press, 1996), 118. For an in-depth analysis of the 1937 legislation, see also D. Bradford Hunt, "Was the 1937 U.S. Housing Act a Pyrrhic Victory?" *Journal of Planning History* 4, no. 3 (August 2005), 195–221.

6. Housing Authority of the City and County of San Francisco, *Second Annual Report* (San Francisco: The Housing Authority, 1940), 4. The Housing Cooperation Law further sanctioned public bodies to assist housing authorities by providing parks, playgrounds, and other improvements, and the Eminent Domain and Tax Exemption Law excused housing authority properties and bonds from taxation.

7. The first housing commissioners were appointed for staggered terms of one, two, three, and four years. According to Alice Griffith's proceedings report, the commissioners drew lots to determine their terms. Alice Griffith, "A Review of the Proceedings of the Housing Authority of San Francisco, April 18, 1938–August 17, 1943," Folder 377, Box 97-19, Stewart-Flippin Papers, Moorland-Spingarn Research Center, Howard University (hereafter MSRC), p. 2. Richard DeLeon states that the "executive authority in San Francisco's

Notes to Chapter 1

city hall is divided, dispersed, and decentralized." See DeLeon, *Left Coast City: Progressive Politics in San Francisco, 1975* (Lawrence: University of Kansas Press, 1992), 21. The San Francisco City Charter of 1932 placed legislative authority in the eleven-member Board of Supervisors who serve staggered four-year terms. The Board of Supervisors has a wide range of power, including the abilities to initiate legislation, to share the authority over the budget with the mayor, to propose charter amendments on the ballot, and to confirm some mayoral appointees. DeLeon also points out that the Board of Supervisors' meetings provide a "forum for public debate during regular sessions and committee hearings" (22). In 1977, San Franciscans passed a measure to elect the Board of Supervisors by districts rather than at-large. The five new supervisors elected included Harvey Milk, an openly gay candidate, and Dan White, a native San Franciscan, Vietnam veteran, and former police officer and fireman. On November 27, 1978, after quitting and then hearing that the mayor refused to let him rejoin the Board of Supervisors when he realized he still wanted his seat, the troubled Dan White shot and killed Mayor Moscone and Harvey Milk. By 1980, the district election system was replaced with the at-large system. In 1990, voters passed a citizen-driven ballot proposition that restricted incumbent board members to a maximum of two terms. The information on the formation of the San Francisco Housing Authority is from the SFHA, *Second Annual Report*, 4–5.

8. John Baranski, "Making Public Housing in San Francisco: Liberalism, Social Prejudice, and Social Activism, 1906–1976" (PhD diss., University of California, Santa Barbara, 2004), 108.

9. Over the years, a range of predominantly white, male, middle-class business and community leaders served as commissioners. E. N. Ayer replaced Charles Page in 1939 after Page left the commission to enter private business. I do not have other information on Page. Carlton Wall replaced M. L. Giannini after he resigned in 1940. I have not been able to locate a copy of the SFHA's *First Annual Report*, which would list information on Page and Giannini. Alice Griffith is listed as "Miss Alice Griffith" in the report that describes her as "well known for her devoted and unselfish work in the community" (SFHA, *Second Annual Report*, 24). In 1960, the SFHA described the twenty-four commissioners who had served as "representing a broad cross-section of the leaders of this community. Among them have been bankers, lawyers, realtors, doctors and representatives of organized labor and minority groups." As of 1960, Katherine Gray and Alice Griffith were the only two female appointees. Dr. William McKinley Thomas, appointed in 1946, was the first African American commissioner. Charles Jung, an Asian American, and

Jefferson A. Beaver, an African American, were appointed and served in 1960. Housing Authority of the City and County of San Francisco, *The Road to the Golden Age: A Report on the First Twenty Years of Operations, 1940 to 1960* (San Francisco: The Housing Authority, 1960), 10.

10. Nicholas Dagen Bloom, *Public Housing That Worked: New York in the Twentieth Century* (Philadelphia: University of Pennsylvania Press, 2009).

11. San Francisco public housing projects Ping Yuen, Valencia Gardens, and North Beach Place received national—and in Ping Yuen's case international—praise for their architectural design. See chapters 2, 3, and 4. In 1953, during a visit to the city, Charles E. Slusser of the Public Housing Administration (PHA) stated that the SFHA was "one of the two outstanding authorities" in the nation. The other acclaimed housing authority was the New York City Housing Authority. Minutes of the San Francisco Housing Authority Board of Commissioners Meeting, September 17, 1953, housed at the San Francisco Housing Authority, San Francisco (hereafter cited as SFHA Commission Minutes).

12. SFHA, *Second Annual Report*, 5.

13. *More Than Shelter* was the title of a film commissioned by the SFHA to depict the benefits of the new public housing program in San Francisco. "'More Than Shelter' Ready for Showing," *Low Rent Housing News*, June 16, 1941, 1.

14. The HOPE VI program was passed in 1992 and implemented under Clinton, and as scholar Jane Rongerude accurately observes, it was part of a "larger framework of welfare reform within the U.S." See Rongerude, "From Public Housing to Regulated Public Environments: The Redevelopment of San Francisco Public Housing" (ISSI Fellows Working Papers, Institute for the Study of Societal Issues, University of California, Berkeley, 2007), 1. The contours of the program changed over time, which Yan Zhang has divided into phases as follows. During the first phase (1993–94), funds supported the revitalization of distressed public housing through rehabilitation or reconstruction. Congress's decision to repeal restrictions, including one-for-one replacement, shaped Phase 2, from 1995 to 1996. During this period, HOPE VI funds were targeted toward demolishing properties, building mixed-income communities, and providing housing choice. During this phase, New Urbanist design became prevalent. The linkage between welfare reform and public housing emerged in Phase 3, between 1997 and 2000, as work and self-sufficiency requirements emerged in response to the Quality Housing and Work Responsibility Act. Local housing authorities were granted even more flexibility and "discretion in income targeting and deconcentration of poor residents." The HOPE VI program during Phase 4, between 2001 and 2008,

Notes to Chapter 1

was "scaled back significantly," forcing many cities to look elsewhere for redevelopment funds. See Yan Zhang, "Wills and Ways: Policy Dynamics of HOPE VI from 1992–2002" (PhD diss., Massachusetts Institute of Technology, 2004), cited in Jane Rongerude, "Sorted City: San Francisco, Hope SF, and the Redevelopment of Public Housing" (PhD diss., University of California–Berkeley, 2009), 35.

15. Nicholas Dagen Bloom, D. Bradford Hunt, Lawrence Vale, Rhonda Y. Williams, and others have documented how the New York Housing Authority, Chicago Housing Authority, Boston Housing Authority, and Baltimore Housing Authority aligned with federal expectations of rigorous review of applicants who wanted to live in public housing in the early years of the program. See Bloom, *Public Housing That Worked*; D. Bradford Hunt, "Was the 1937 U.S. Housing Act a Pyrrhic Victory?"; Lawrence J. Vale, *From the Puritans to the Projects: Public Housing and Public Neighbors* (Cambridge, Mass.: Harvard University Press, 2007); and Rhonda Y. Williams, *The Politics of Public Housing: Black Women's Struggles against Urban Inequality* (New York: Oxford University Press, 2005). See also Gwendolyn Wright, *Building the Dream: A Social History of Housing in America* (New York: Pantheon, 1981).

16. Wright, *Building the Dream*, 230.

17. Ibid.

18. SFHA, *Second Annual Report*, 20.

19. The specific regulations of the SFHA are not available. However, many local housing authorities followed federally recommended guidelines. The regulations listed in the text were standard at other housing authorities. A tenant who grew up in Valencia Gardens a decade after it opened verified that the SFHA upheld such regulations in San Francisco public housing. Interview with Gabrielle Fontanella and Louette Fabio by the author, tape recording, May 2003, San Francisco.

20. "Two-Story Rows and Flats," *Architectural Forum*, November 1940, 4. Other press accolades about Holly Courts included a long article, "Holly Courts Has 'Em Agog," in the April 27, 1940, *San Francisco Call Bulletin*, about the first tenants at Holly Courts.

21. Brown designed the Department of Labor and Interstate Commerce Commission building in Washington, DC. For more information on Brown's architectural legacy, see Tilman, *Arthur Brown, Jr.*

22. According to Arthur Brown Jr. biographer and scholar Jeffrey T. Tilman, Brown originally planned to build Holly Courts in the French country style with tiled roofs. Federal restrictions led Brown to change to a modern design with flat roofs. Tilman, interview by author, July 2001. Brown went on to build San Francisco's domed city hall.

Notes to Chapter 1

23. According to the SFHA, fifty-five dwelling units were eliminated through "compulsory demolition, 28 through compulsory closing, 12 through compulsory repair or improvement; and 23 were demolished by private owners after action had been instituted by the department of Public Health." SFHA, *Second Annual Report*, 12.

24. Outline of Marshall Dill's speech, Marshall Dill Papers, Folder 35, North Baker Research Library, California Historical Society.

25. "Holly Courts: Special Bulletin of the San Francisco Housing Association" (San Francisco: San Francisco Housing Association, 1940), Bancroft Library, University of California–Berkeley. The second quote is from the outline of Marshall Dill's speech, Marshall Dill Papers.

26. SFHA, *Second Annual Report*, 15.

27. Else Reisner, *Homemaking and Family Adjustment Services in Public Housing: The Experiences at Holly Courts, First Western Housing Project* (San Francisco: San Francisco Housing Authority, 1942).

28. Reisner, *Home Making and Family Adjustment Services*, 14–15.

29. SFHA, *Second Annual Report*, 15.

30. Ibid.

31. SFHA, *Third Annual Report*, 8; "Movie on Housing Is Available to Clubs," *Low Rent Housing News*, April 7, 1941, 1.

32. The program, which ran for seventeen consecutive weeks and "received favorable reviews from listeners," featured actors from the Works Progress Administration. SFHA, *Second Annual Report*, 24.

33. "'More Than Shelter,' Ready for Showing," *Low Rent Housing News*, San Francisco, June 16, 1941, 1; and untitled article in *Low Rent Housing News*, August 30, 1941, 1. William Abbenseth was a photographer for the Federal Art Project who was well known for his black-and-white photographs of San Francisco architecture.

34. SFHA, *Third Annual Report*, 3.

35. Vale, *From the Puritans to the Projects*, 3. The admitted families, as Vale outlines, eventually left public housing as they earned more money and housing authorities were forced to begin housing the neediest applicants in cities. By the mid-1950s, changes in federal housing policies undermined the merit system. By the 1970s, the poorest of the poor populated public housing (3, 8).

36. SFHA Commission Minutes, 7 October 1947.

37. Albert S. Broussard, *Black San Francisco: The Struggle for Racial Equality in the West, 1900–1954* (Lawrence: University of Kansas Press, 1993), 177. In *Alien Neighbors, Foreign Friends*, Charlotte Brooks details the debates over the construction and tenant selection process at Westside Courts. The multiracial, multiethnic Western Addition Housing Council, formed in 1940, pushed

Notes to Chapter 1

for public housing in the district, which would serve Japanese Americans, African Americans, and whites. Ultimately, Japanese American support waned as potential applicants realized that the SFHA head of household requirements barred many of them from public housing. Conservative African American groups fought for a segregated project in the Western Addition while white residents in the area opposed public housing for African Americans in their area. Brooks, *Alien Neighbors, Foreign Friends: Asian Americans, Housing, and the Transformation of Urban California* (Chicago: University of Chicago Press, 2009), 108–11, 141–44.

38. Housing Authority of the City and County of San Francisco, *Fifth Annual Report* (San Francisco Housing Authority: The Housing Authority, 1943), 5, 7. SFHA Commission Minutes, 14 May 1942. As the United States mobilized for war in 1940, workers living in rural areas migrated to urban areas in search of employment in the defense industries. This migration caused drastic housing shortages in centers of defense activity, such as San Francisco. The federal government responded to the housing crisis first by authorizing the USHA to build twenty public housing developments for civilian employers of the armed forces and defense contractors with money originally slated for public housing. When the government's other efforts to stimulate private industry in home building in centers of defense activity fell through, the government focused solely on federal public housing as a solution to the housing problem. In October 1940, President Roosevelt signed the National Defense Housing Act, also called the Lanham Act, authorizing the Federal Works Agency to build housing for workers in the defense industry who faced severe housing shortages. Representative Fritz Lanham (D-Texas) blocked the potential increase of public housing units after the war with an amendment that prohibited defense public housing from being converted to public housing for low-income families without congressional approval. For more information on the federal housing program during World War II, see Kristin M. Szylvian, "The Federal Housing Program during World War II," in *From the Tenements to the Taylor Homes: In Search of an Urban Housing Policy in Twentieth Century America*, ed. John F. Bauman, Roger Biles, and Kristin M. Szylvian (University Park: Pennsylvania State University Press, 2000), 121–22. The description of where war workers lived is from Marilyn Johnson, "Urban Arsenals: War Housing and Social Change in Richmond and Oakland, California, 1941–1945," *Pacific Historical Review* 60, no. 3 (1991), 283–308, cited in Baranski, "Making Public Housing," 143–44.

39. Baranski, "Making Public Housing," 157.

40. San Francisco Housing Authority, *Seventh Annual Report* (San Francisco: Flores Press, 1945), 4–5.

Notes to Chapter 1

41. Broussard, *Black San Francisco*, 175. African American tenants in SFHA housing had a markedly different living environment than other black inmigrants housed in the city. Prior to World War II, the city had not enacted racial covenants against the small population of 5,000 African Americans living in San Francisco. The dramatic increase in the black population during World War II, however, sparked widespread discrimination in housing. As a result, a number of tenants lived in overcrowded, rat-infested buildings in the Fillmore District, where a 1944 survey found some residents living with nine to fifteen others in a single room. Many of the dwellings did not have hot water, bathroom facilities, or enough windows to provide access to natural light. Along with suffering distressing living conditions, African American migrants also paid higher rents for substandard dwellings than did black nonmigrants and nonmigrant Chinese Americans (172–75). Broussard points out that blacks also occupied a "disproportionate share of the Western Addition's substandard housing relative to the city's population" (173). For more information on housing discrimination in San Francisco, see Deirdre L. Sullivan, "Letting down the Bars: Race, Space, and Democracy in San Francisco, 1936–1964" (PhD diss., University of Pennsylvania, 2003).

42. Photograph caption, *San Francisco Housing News*, August 1944. The caption describes the children as "two patients . . . who have achieved national fame." According to the SFHA, the photograph prompted people "from all parts of the world" to write letters responding favorably to it (SFHA, *Seventh Annual Report*, 15). The SFHA's wartime activities extended beyond overseeing a massive building program for the federal government. Along with the construction and management of temporary war housing, the SFHA set up emergency accommodations for hundreds of sea-bound servicemen on the Saratoga when the ship secretly underwent repairs in San Francisco. Additionally, at the close of the war, the agency provided housing for more than 1,000 former Allied prisoners from twenty-nine nations pending return to their homes. SFHA, *Road to the Golden Age*, 4. In a final act of wartime service, the SFHA housed 1,200 Nisei, second-generation Japanese Americans, many of whom lost their homes and land during their war internment. San Francisco Housing Authority, *Twenty-Fifth Annual Report* (San Francisco: The Housing Authority, 1963), 3.

43. SFHA Commission Minutes, 14 May 1942.

44. Alice Griffith's objection to discrimination quoted in Baranski, "Making Public Housing," 124. SFHA Commission Minutes, 14 May 1942. The first part of the resolution stated that "in the development of its program and the selection of its tenants this Authority shall provide housing accommodations for all races in proportion with the numbers of low income families

219

Notes to Chapter 1

otherwise unable to obtain decent, safe, and sanitary dwellings in each racial group."

45. Wilder left his post as executive director of the SFHA to become the director of Public Works of San Francisco. According to Alice Griffith, Evers had "gained experience in governmental procedure in the Federal Housing Administration" and together with John Bakewell Jr., Frederick Meyer, and Warren Perry had surveyed slum areas in the city and developed a plan for clearing eight blocks in the Hayes Valley District and building housing for low-income families. The plan was submitted to the federal Public Works Administration and approved but did not obtain grant funds because of timing. Griffith, "A Review of the Proceedings," 3.

46. Baranski, "Making Public Housing," 175.

47. Quote from Baranski, "Making Public Housing," 176; SFHA Commission Minutes, 18 August 1943; *San Francisco Housing Chronicle*, October 19, 1943; and Griffith, "A Review of the Proceedings."

48. Baranski, "Making Public Housing," 178.

49. Ibid., 184.

50. Ibid., 185. Quote in Mourice E. Harrison, "Report of the Mayor's Committee on Civic Unity of San Francisco," March 15, 1945, Folder 377, Box 97-19, Stewart-Flippin Papers, MSRC, cited in Baranski, "Making Public Housing," 184.

51. From Civic Unity Committee, Meeting Notes, Folders 376–81, Box 97-17, Stewart-Flippin Papers, MSRC, cited in Baranski, "Making Public Housing," 186.

52. Baranski, "Making Public Housing," 186.

53. Ibid., 187.

54. Ibid., 188. Baranski is citing "Questions and Answers," January 17, 1945, Folder 377, Box 97-19, Stewart-Flippin Papers, MSRC.

55. SFHA Commission Minutes, November 15, 1945.

56. Ibid.

57. SFHA Minutes, April 18, 1946, quoted in Baranski, "Making Public Housing," 193.

58. Mary Shepardson, "Minority Groups," *San Francisco Public Housing: A Citizen's Survey* (San Francisco: San Francisco Planning and Housing Association, 1946), 21.

59. SFHA Commission Minutes, April 18, 1946; Broussard, *Black San Francisco*, 182. Dr. William McKinley Thomas migrated to San Francisco after serving as a doctor in the army and was part of the growing number of black professionals in the city actively engaged in civic life. Thomas actively opposed segregation in San Francisco public housing. In what Albert Brossard describes as a departure from "protocol that was characteristic of commissioners,"

Notes to Chapter 1

Thomas publicly criticized Chairman E. N. Ayer and went on to offer a motion opposing segregation in the SFHA's public housing developments. His motion was dropped after failing to receive a second. Broussard, *Black San Francisco*, 222–23.

60. Catherine Bauer praised Marin County's housing authority for making strides to integrate tenants. In a letter to Ed Weeks at the *Atlantic Monthly*, Bauer described Marin City's efforts as "a model of community cooperation and morale in war housing." Catherine Bauer to Edward Weeks, editor, *Atlantic Monthly*, May 13, 1945, Folder 5, Box 2, Catherine Bauer Wurster Papers, Bancroft Library, University of California–Berkeley, cited in Baranski, "Making Public Housing," 194.

61. SFHA, *Road to the Golden Age*, 12.

62. The Housing Act of 1949 marked the entry of the federal government into local city building projects. The act, supported by a unique coalition of trade unions, real estate interests, lenders, farmers, and housing advocates, set forth five titles to reach its goal, three of which drastically altered American cities. Title I financed slum clearance under urban "redevelopment," stating that a municipality could redevelop any "substandard" neighborhood and the federal government would cover two-thirds of the costs. Title II increased authorization of Federal Housing Administration (FHA) mortgages, and Title 3 promised 810,000 units of public housing by 1955. Collectively this legislation, as implemented by cities across the United States, reshaped urban centers and the suburbs. As the FHA provided mortgage insurance to middle-class Americans moving to the suburbs, cities demolished large tracts of affordable housing with federal redevelopment funds. The act stipulated that local governments awarded funds to clear "substandard dwellings" and replace them with "predominantly residential" structures. Consequently, low-income neighborhoods gave way to office buildings, shops, parking lots, and luxury apartments that city leaders hoped would reinvigorate the tax base. See Robert E. Lang and Rebecca R. Sohmer, eds. "Legacy of the Housing Act of 1949: The Past, Present, and Future of Federal Housing and Urban Policy" *Housing Policy Debate* 11, no. 2 (2000), 291–98; and Roger Biles, "Public Housing and Postwar Renaissance, 1949–1973," in *From Tenements to the Taylor Homes: In Search of an Urban Housing Policy in the Twentieth Century*, ed. John F. Bauman, Roger Biles, and Kristin M. Szylvian (University Park: Pennsylvania State University Press, 2000), 143–62.

63. Chester Hartman, with Sarah Carnochan, *City for Sale: The Transformation of San Francisco* (Berkeley: University of California Press, 2002), 15–16. *City for Sale* includes an exhaustive analysis of the redevelopment agenda and the Yerba Buena Center controversy in San Francisco.

221

Notes to Chapter 1

64. Baranski, "Making Public Housing," 231.

65. Quote from *San Francisco News*, February 14, 1950, cited in Baranski, "Making Public Housing," 233.

66. *San Francisco Chronicle*, February 21, 1950, cited in Baranski, "Making Public Housing," 234.

67. The SFHA classified Latinos as "white" in their records. I do not have information on when Latinos moved into "white" projects. The Chinese were classified as "non-white." A fire at the SFHA in the 1960s destroyed a number of documents, including perhaps some demographic information. In untangling the racial and ethnic makeup of the agency's projects, it is important to note that the SFHA classified Latino/as as "white." More recent demographics obtained by the SFHA show the following percentages for heads of household in public housing in 1999: Asians made up 26.45 percent; blacks, 46.19 percent; Hispanics, 8.70 percent; Native Americans, 0.45 percent; other, 3.07 percent; and whites, 15.09 percent; for a total of 99.95 percent. Although I was given data on 2013 demographics, I was told it might be inaccurate. E-mail from Florence Cheng, SFHA, April 2013.

68. Baranski, "Making Public Housing," 220–21. The advocates wrote letters, met with the commissioners and Beard, and researched how tenants used community rooms in other SFHA public housing projects. Their report stated that in the last half of 1949, 200,000 people had attended lectures, programs, and events.

69. "Worst in U.S." *San Francisco Chronicle*, July 1, 1949.

70. Sullivan, "Letting down the Bars," viii.

71. For broader context on the Cold War's impact on civil rights debates nationally, see Martha Biondi, *To Stand and Fight: The Struggle for Civil Rights in Postwar New York City* (Cambridge, Mass.: Harvard University Press, 2003); Thomas Borstelmann, *The Cold War and the Color Line: American Race Relations in the Global Arena* (Cambridge, Mass.: Harvard University Press, 2001); and Roger Daniels, *Guarding the Golden Door: American Immigration Policy and Immigrants since 1882* (New York: Hill and Wang, 2004).

72. *San Francisco Chronicle*, April 20, 1951, cited in Baranski, "Making Public Housing," 222. The SFHA returned its profit to the federal government and paid the city $2,631,000 in lieu of taxes.

73. Baranski, "Making Public Housing," 227. According to the SFHA Commission Minutes of June 19, 1952, the SFHA "hereby prohibited as a tenant of any project, by rental or occupancy any person other than a CITIZEN of the United States, except that such prohibition does not apply in the case of the family of any serviceman or the family of any veteran who has been discharged (other than dishonorably) or of the family of any serviceman who

dies in the armed forces of the US within 4 years prior to the date of application to such project. The term 'tenant' means the responsible member of the family who signs the dwelling lease."

74. For example, the Yerba Buena Annex, opened in 1961, had 211 units, with 43 units set aside for elderly tenants. Likewise, the Ping Yuen Annex, opened the same year, offered 44 units of senior housing.

75. C. R. Greenstone, Chairman, San Francisco Housing Authority to John C. Houlihan, Mayor of Oakland, California, May 16, 1962, copy in SFHA Commission Minutes, May 1962.

76. Ibid.

77. SFHA Commission Minutes, February 1962–March 1963.

78. Baranski, "Making Public Housing," 284.

79. For more on white conservative backlash against the civil rights movement and the impact on housing, see Matthew Countryman, *Up South: Civil Rights and Black Power in Philadelphia* (Philadelphia: University of Pennsylvania Press, 2006); Kevin M. Kruse, *White Flight: Atlanta and the Making of Modern Conservatism* (Princeton, N.J.: Princeton University Press, 2005); and Matthew D. Lassiter, *The Silent Majority: Suburban Politics in the Sunbelt South* (Princeton, N.J.: Princeton University Press, 2006).

80. Baranski, "Making Public Housing," 285–98.

81. *San Francisco Chronicle*, November 11, 1964, cited in Baranski, "Making Public Housing," 300.

82. "Housing Authority Job Bias Charged," *San Francisco Chronicle*, May 13, 1964.

83. "Picketing at Turk St. Housing Authority," *San Francisco Chronicle*, March 19, 1965. See also "Housing Chairman Swings at Critics," *San Francisco Chronicle*, February 19, 1965; and "An Orderly Protest on S.F. Housing," *San Francisco Chronicle*, February 20, 1965. NAACP leaders met with Mayor John Shelley to express their concerns over the SFHA's discriminatory hiring practices and placement of tenants in housing projects.

84. Peter Kuehl, "Getting the Picture," *San Francisco Chronicle*, April 16, 1965.

85. Jack Lind, "Housing Board's New Rights Rules," *San Francisco Chronicle*, July 2, 1965.

86. "Housing Authority Aide Named," *San Francisco Chronicle*, April 3, 1964. The Housing Authority created the position in 1964 in an early attempt to quell criticism. Nonetheless, the United Freedom Movement lambasted the agency for failing to consult their group when writing the job description. The United Freedom Movement, an African American rights organization, had lobbied the SFHA to create the post in 1963. "Flare up over Human Relations Post," *San Francisco Chronicle*, March 20, 1964.

Notes to Chapter 1

87. "John Burton Blasts S.F. Housing Boss," *San Francisco Chronicle*, October 8, 1965.

88. A survey by an outside management firm described Beard as a leader who bypassed the housing commissioners and set his own policy. "John Burton Blasts S.F. Housing Boss," *San Francisco Chronicle*, October 8, 1965.

89. John Baranski, "Something to Help Themselves: Tenant Organizing in San Francisco Public Housing, 1965–75," *Journal of Urban History* 33, no. 3 (March 2007), 424. See also Frederick Wirk, *Power in the City: Decision Making in San Francisco* (Berkeley: University of California Press, 1974); Hartman, *City for Sale*; Judy Yung, *Unbound Feet: A Social History of Chinese Women in San Francisco* (Berkeley: University of California Press, 1995); Broussard, *Black San Francisco*; and James Brook, Chris Carlsson, and Nancy Peters, *Reclaiming San Francisco: History, Politics, and Culture* (San Francisco: City Lights Books, 1998).

90. Baranski, "Something to Help Themselves," 420.

91. Ibid.

92. Ibid.

93. Ibid, 421.

94. Ibid.

95. Ibid.

96. Hartman, *City for Sale*, 25. The center opened in 1968.

97. Kelsey Finch, "Trouble in Paradise: Postwar History of San Francisco's Hunters Point Neighborhood" (Honors thesis, Stanford University, 2008), 27.

98. Ibid., 55–56, citing information from the 1950 U.S. Census (Census Population: Preliminary Reports [Washington, DC: United States Bureau of the Census, 1951]) and the *Preliminary Master Plan: Hunters Point Naval Shipyard* (San Francisco: Naval Facilities Engineering Command, Western Division, 1970).

99. Finch, "Trouble in Paradise," 36–37.

100. Baranski, "Something to Help Themselves," 423. For a brief history on automobiles and African Americans in the twentieth century and the consistent connections between race, cars, the police, and riots, see Thomas J. Sugrue, "Driving while Black: The Car and Race Relations in Modern America," Automobile in American Life and Society Project, University of Michigan, Dearborn, www.autolife.umd.umich.edu/Race/R_Casestudy/R_Casestudy3.htm.

101. Baranski, "Something to Help Themselves," 423–24.

102. On March 9, 1966, a group of angry tenants from Hunters Point put on a "wild" demonstration at a Housing Commission meeting. Together with members of the antipoverty board (part of the Economic Opportunity

Council), the protestors encircled the board's table and closed the doors when the commissioners tried to adjourn. The tenants listed demands and sang "We Shall Overcome" in protest against the SFHA's eviction policy. The housing commissioners blamed the "anti-poverty people" for fomenting the demonstration. The commissioners seemingly did not want to believe that the tenants themselves could rise up in protest against policies and procedures affecting their lives. See J. Campbell Bruce, "Angry Uproar by Crowd at Housing Session," *San Francisco Chronicle*, March 10, 1966.

103. Donald Carter, "Eviction Moratorium Ends," *San Francisco Examiner*, February 2, 1967.

104. Ibid.

105. "S.F. Poor Face Rent Increases," *San Francisco Chronicle*, October 6, 1967.

106. Vale, *From the Puritans to the Projects*, 337. Vale notes that a 1968 HUD survey revealed that half of the nation's eighty major housing authorities were operating with a deficit, and out of the ten largest authorities, seven were near bankruptcy. Congress recognized that the amendment would cause a shortfall in revenue and voted for an increase in annual federal contributions to help offset the loss. Nonetheless, the measure did not adequately cover maintenance and upkeep in many cities.

107. SFHA Commission Minutes, February 23, 1973.

108. Donald Canter, "Some Tenants Get Paid to Live in Public Housing," *San Francisco Chronicle*, May 21, 1972. In early 1972, the SFHA finally received a $2.3 million federal subsidy that it was entitled to for the fiscal year ending September 30, 1971.

109. Baranski, "Something to Help Themselves," 432.

110. Ibid., 422.

111. Ralph Craib, "Housing Tenants Get New Power," *San Francisco Chronicle*, April 23, 1971. According to that article, the Grievance Procedure also stated that in the case of disputes over rent, tenants were required to put the disputed amount of money into escrow until the issue was heard by the Grievance Panel.

112. Ralph Craib, "S.F. Rent Strike—Public Housing," *San Francisco Chronicle*, November 2, 1971.

113. Baranski, "Something to Help Themselves," 435.

114. SFHA Commission Minutes, August 8, 1974 and September 12, 1974.

115. According to the SFHA website, over 10,000 families in San Francisco have been housed through the Housing Choice Voucher program since its inception (http://www.sfha.org/Agency-Info-Ombudsman—Communication-About-Us.html).

Notes to Chapter 1

116. Vale, *From the Puritans to the Projects,* 336.

117. Pearl Stewart, "Mob at Housing Office," *San Francisco Chronicle,* February 18, 1981.

118. Marshall Kilduff, "2 Nominated to Housing Authority," *San Francisco Chronicle,* October 19, 1976. According to the article, Reverend Jones's full term was set to last until April 27, 1980. Reverend Ulbalde, filling an unexpired term, was slated to serve on the Housing Commission through May 3, 1977.

119. Congressman Ryan visited Jonestown to investigate allegations of abuse. He left the site with sixteen people who wanted to flee Jonestown. They were ambushed by People's Temple loyalists at the airfield.

120. Hartman, *City for Sale,* 371.

121. Ibid.; Reginald Smith, "Housing Chief's Unenviable Job" *San Francisco Chronicle,* February 2, 1985.

122. Hartman, *City for Sale,* 371. Walter Scott replaced Eneas Kane as executive director. See Ralph Craib, "Housing Agency's Curious Traveling," *San Francisco Chronicle,* August 5, 1978. See Reginald Smith, "Housing Authority Paying Some Bills," *San Francisco Chronicle,* April 13, 1985, and "Keep Public Housing Livable," *San Francisco Chronicle,* February 22, 1985.

123. April Lynch, "Housing Authority Spared from HUD 'Troubled List,'" *San Francisco Chronicle,* April 12, 1993.

124. Hartman, *City for Sale,* 371.

125. Lynch, "Housing Authority Spared from HUD 'Troubled List.'" As with many issues surrounding the Housing Authority, the agency's move off of HUD's troubled list was controversial. HUD claimed that Executive Director Gilmore had skewed the agency's score in his self-assessment of the city's public housing projects, giving the SFHA the number of points necessary to move its classification from "troubled" to "standard." HUD designated the SFHA as a "standard" authority, which qualified the agency to apply for more funding. At the same time, the federal agency initiated a criminal investigation of the SFHA based on claims that "the Housing Authority provided federal inspectors with unsupported and unreliable data during a recent audit." Steven A. Chin, "City Housing Agency Faces Criminal Probe," *San Francisco Examiner,* September 15, 1992.

126. According to a HUD audit, Gilmore spent thousands of dollars on meals at restaurants and on other entertainment, including a $2,200 party celebrating the SFHA's removal from the federal roster of troubled housing authorities. Mayor Jordan had friction with Gilmore and removed him from office.

127. Chin, "City Housing Agency Faces Criminal Probe."

128. Corrie M. Anders and Charles C. Hardy, "S.F. Takes a New Look to Desegregate Schools: Officials Consider Integration of Families in Housing Projects as a First Step," *San Francisco Chronicle*, September 25, 1983. The article states that a 1983 court settlement of an NAACP desegregation suit against the San Francisco Unified School District called for a "concerted effort by housing agencies to promote rather than impede school desegregation and integration." The city aimed to desegregate schools by first desegregating subsidized housing.

129. Anders and Hardy, "S.F. Takes a New Look to Desegregate Schools"; second quote from SFHA Commission Minutes, January 13, 1983. On January 13, 1983, housing commissioners passed Resolution 2503, stating that the SFHA had a waiting list of approximately 4,600 and "whereas, applicants who reject available units by their actions indicate they are not in dire need of low income housing . . . be it resolved that 1. Every attempt will be made to refer applicants to the development which is their preference or to the geographical management area which is their preference. 2. That at the time the applicant is eligible for referral to a unit and neither the geographical nor the housing development preference is available, they shall be referred to the first available unit. 3. After an applicant for housing has been referred for leasing to the geographical management area, they shall be offered a choice of up to three units of housing in that area. 4. That applicants should turn down those three offers of housing in the geographical area, that they shall be removed from the waiting list and be prevented from applying for housing for one year's period of time. 5. That applicants who lease a unit from the Housing Authority and vacate that unit within 60 days without 'good cause,' they shall not be allowed to apply for housing for a twelve month period of time from the date of their vacate" (ibid.). The resolution was passed unanimously.

130. Anders and Hardy, "S.F. Takes a New Look to Desegregate Schools."

131. Understanding where people choose to live (if they actually have a choice) is complex. Sociologists and historians have grappled with the complexity of integration by exploring people's preferences, perceptions, and fears of isolation, sticking out, and violence. The connection for families with kids between housing and public school is another critical factor. Historians are beginning to consider the importance of researching and understanding housing and schools together. Matthew Lassiter, "Schools and Housing in Metropolitan History: An Introduction," *Journal of Urban History* 38, no. 2 (March 2012), 195–204.

132. Steve Johnson, "Projects Life Is Violent for Asian Americans," *San Francisco Mercury News*, April 11, 1994.

Notes to Chapter 1

133. Johnny Brannon, "Public Housing's Struggle with Race," *The Independent*, July 1, 1993.

134. Timothy Fong, *The Contemporary Asian American Experience: Beyond the Model Minority*, 2nd ed. (Upper Saddle River, N.J.: Prentice Hall, 2002), 166.

135. Steven A. Chin, "Asians Sue City over Violence in Public Housing," *San Francisco Examiner*, March 30, 1993.

136. Fong, 166.

137. Chin, "Asians Sue City."

138. Ibid. The families also accused the Housing Authority of negligence because the agency refused to relocate residents who were attacked.

139. Steven A. Chin, "Housing Authority Settles Lawsuit by Asian Tenants," *San Francisco Examiner*, July 20, 1993.

140. Johnson, "Projects Life Is Violent for Asian Americans."

141. Ibid.

142. Brannon, "Public Housing's Struggle with Race."

143. According to San Francisco Housing Authority figures printed in the *San Jose Mercury News* in 1994, the "segregated" projects had changed between 1988 and 1994. The predominantly black projects had seen the following changes: Alice Griffith went from having an 84 percent black population to 73 percent; Hayes Valley maintained an 88 percent African American tenancy; Hunters Point's black population grew from 74 percent to 83 percent while Hunters View decreased from 78 percent to 75 percent; Potrero Annex increased its black population from 69 percent to 79 percent, and Potrero Terrace increased from 72 percent to 83 percent; Sunnydale saw a small increase from 75 percent to 76 percent in black tenants; Westbrook went from 67 percent to 77 percent; Westside Courts decreased from 92 percent to 86 percent; and Yerba Buena went from 92 percent to 91 percent. The total percentage of African Americans living at these ten projects increased from 78 percent to 80 percent between 1988 and 1994. The Asian American population living at Ping Yuen and Ping Yuen North, meanwhile, decreased from 94 percent to 91 percent. At Ping Yuen, the Asian American population decreased from 97 percent to 93 percent, while at Ping Yuen North, the percentage went from 92 percent to 88 percent. Johnson, "Projects Life Is Violent for Asian Americans."

144. Brannon, "Public Housing's Struggle with Race."

145. Johnson, "Projects Life Is Violent for Asian Americans."

146. Brannon, "Public Housing's Struggle with Race."

147. Leslie Goldberg, "Vietnamese Describe Racial Violence in Housing Project," *San Francisco Examiner*, June 12, 1997.

148. Ibid.

Notes to Chapter 1

149. John King, "New Housing Chief Says S.F. Projects Will Improve," *San Francisco Chronicle*, March 9, 1994, 5. Floresca worked on anticrime programs in housing projects in Providence and Boston and directed New York City's housing inspection program under Mayor Ed Koch. Before taking the position in San Francisco, he worked in the White House and for HUD, where he served as senior housing management officer. Tenants attending the Housing Commission meeting about the position vocally supported Paul Fletcher, an African American and former aide to HUD Secretary Jack Kemp. The commissioners voted 5–2 for Floresca. Frustrated tenant Ed Williams summed up the position of a number of tenants in attendance: "Only blacks know the needs of other blacks. We need to consider my people, the 65 percent that are in public housing." "Housing Panel Names Director," *San Francisco Examiner*, February 15, 1994.

150. Catherine Bowman and Aurelio Rojas, "When Home Is Not Sweet," *San Francisco Chronicle*, April 3, 1995.

151. Gregory Lewis, "HUD Takes Control of S.F. Housing," *San Francisco Examiner*, March 9, 1996.

152. Catherine Bowman, "S.F. Public Housing Rated among Worst in Nation," *San Francisco Chronicle*, May 21, 1996.

153. Ibid.

154. Catherine Bowman, "Housing Continues to Decay under HUD/Tenants See Little Improvement at Projects despite Federal Takeover," *San Francisco Chronicle*, November 25, 1996.

155. Gregory Lewis, "Acting Director Restores Faith in Public Housing," *San Francisco Examiner*, February 18, 1997. Ronnie Davis grew up in a housing project in New Orleans, attended Harvard, and worked for the Cleveland Housing Authority as director of planning operations. He was Mayor Brown's choice to run the agency.

156. Ibid.

157. Ilene Lelchuk, "Housing Chief's Big New Contract City Rewards Ronnie Davis," *San Francisco Examiner*, March 15, 2000.

158. Hartman, *City for Sale*, 373. See also Chuck Finnie and Lance Williams, "Two More Arrests in S.F. Bribery Probe," *San Francisco Examiner*, November 16, 1999; and Bob Egelko and Lance Williams, "Housing Exec Guilty of Bribes," *San Francisco Examiner*, September 27, 2000. Yolanda Jones's indictment heaped more embarrassment on city hall. Jones is the daughter of Charlie Walker, a trucker and "political heavy" often described as "the mayor of Hunters Point." She also was the self-described "goddaughter" of Mayor Willie Brown (Hartman, *City for Sale*, 373).

159. Hartman, *City for Sale*, 373.

Notes to Chapter 1

160. Patrick Hoge, "S.F. Housing Chief Charged with Funds Theft in Ohio," *San Francisco Chronicle*, March 22, 2001, cited in Hartman, *City for Sale*, 373. The charges against Davis were dismissed in return for a guilty plea to a "single misdemeanor." Davis's plea meant he had to repay the Cuyahoga Housing Authority in Cleveland $4,500 and "could face a short federal prison sentence." For more information, see Patrick Hoge's "Housing Chief Felony Charges Dropped in Ohio," *San Francisco Chronicle*, October 31, 2001.

161. Vale, *From the Puritans to the Projects*, 369.

162. National Housing Law Project et al., *False HOPE: A Critical Assessment of the HOPE VI Public Housing Redevelopment Program* (Oakland, Calif.: National Housing Law Project, June 2002), 2. In 1989, Congress created an independent National Commission on Severely Distressed Public Housing as part of the Department of Housing and Urban Development Reform Act. The Commission was charged "with assessing and formulating the solutions to the problem [of] severe distress in the public housing program" (Vale, *From the Puritans to the Projects*, 370). The Commission's final report noted that there were serious problems in public housing sites considered "severely distressed" but that these projects only made up 6 percent (86,000 units) of the total stock that "fit into the category." Nonetheless, HUD responded and initiated the HOPE VI program (i). For a detailed account of the development and implementation of the HOPE VI program, see Henry Cisneros and Lora Engdahl, eds., *From Despair to Hope: Hope VI and the New Promise of Public Housing in American Cities* (Washington, DC: Brookings Institution Press, 2009).

163. National Housing Law Project et al., *False HOPE*, 14. Public Housing Authorities were permitted to use up to 20 percent of the grant for social services for the residents. Under HOPE VI, HUD also allowed private entities for the first time to own public housing, which opened up private investment through Low-income Housing Tax Credits (LIHTCs). As Vale rightly notes, the opportunity to combine mixed-finance funding to build mixed-income and often mixed-use developments at lower densities for a "carefully vetted set of new residents in new neotraditional neighborhoods made HOPE VI quite appealing to developers." Lawrence Vale, *Purging the Poorest: Public Housing and the Design Politics of Twice-Cleared Communities* (Chicago: University of Chicago Press, 2013), 23.

164. National Housing Law Project et al., *False HOPE*, i.

165. Ibid., ii. According to HUD figures listed in *False HOPE*, in 1999, for every 100 very low-income renter households, there were only 70 affordable units available to them. The situation was worse for extremely low-income renter households, with only 40 affordable units for every 100 households. Under federal definitions, "very low income" refers to households making 50

percent or below the median income of households in their geographic region. Extremely low-income families are defined as making at or below 30 percent of the area median income (iii).

166. Edward G. Goetz references a range of HOPE VI studies in his article, "Better Neighborhoods, Better Outcomes? Explaining Relocation Outcomes in HOPE VI," *Cityscape: A Journal of Policy Development and Research* 12, no. 1 (2010), 5–32. Along with the following resources, this article itself provides an excellent starting point for understanding the program: Susan J. Popkin, Bruce Katz, Mary K. Cunningham, Karen Brown, Jeremy Gustafson, and Margery A. Turner, *A Decade of Hope VI: Research Findings and Policy Challenges* (Washington, DC: Urban Institute, 2004); Rachel Garshick Kleit and Lynne Manzo, "To Move or Not to Move: Relationships to Place and Relocation Choices in HOPE VI," *Housing Policy Debate* 17, no. 2 (2006), 271–308. See Cisneros and Engdahl, *From Despair to Hope*, for a range of essays and statistics on the HOPE VI program from 1993 to 2007.

167. Between 1993 and 2007, HUD awarded over $5.92 billion in competitive grants to PHAs to redevelop 240 projects in cities across the country. See G. Thomas Kingsley, "Appendix 8," in Cisneros and Engdahl, *From Despair to Hope*, 299–315. In *Purging the Poorest*, Lawrence Vale provides remarkable analysis of the "design politics" that shaped twice-cleared communities, first for public housing and later for HOPE VI redevelopment in Atlanta and Chicago.

168. Figures available on the SFHA's website, http://www.sfha.org/HOPE-VI.html.

169. David R. Baker, "Joyful Return for First Bernal Dwellers," *San Francisco Chronicle*, March 24, 2001.

170. Ibid.

171. Elizabeth Fernandez, "S.F. Families Return to Public Housing That's New from Ground Up," *San Francisco Chronicle*, February 26, 2002.

172. Hartman, *City for Sale*, 374.

173. This figure is based on information listed on the San Francisco Housing Authority's website (http://www.sfha.org). According to a document provided by former SFHA employee Juan Monsanto to planning scholar Jane Rongerude, entitled "Hope VI Housing Relocation, Choices and Return, 1999–2006," the total decrease in public housing units was 425, and the increase in bedrooms was 415. The total number of vouchers gained through HOPE VI is listed as 572. According to my April 18 and April 22, 2013, e-mail communication with Florence Cheng, manager of Vacates and HQS at the SFHA, 48 percent of families returned to Hayes Valley, 53 percent returned to Bernal Dwellings, 40 percent returned to Plaza East, 36 percent returned to North Beach Place, and 17 percent returned to Valencia Gardens.

Notes to Chapter 1

174. Rongerude, "Sorted City," 88.
175. "Bay Boom in Housing, No End in Sight," *San Francisco Examiner*, quoted in Letters to the Editor, *San Francisco Examiner*, May 3, 1998.
176. According to some tenants at Valencia Gardens, more landlords began taking Section 8 vouchers after September 11, 2001. The increase in vacancy rates in the wake of the economic downturn following September 11 allowed some tenants to stay in San Francisco. Valencia Gardens residents, interview by the author, tape recording, San Francisco, May 30, 2003.
177. Hartman, *City for Sale*, 374.
178. "Residents Blast Housing Proposal," *San Francisco Chronicle*, July 15, 2001. Johnny Brannon, "Feds Reject Plan to Fix Troubled Housing Complex," *The Independent*, August 15, 2000.
179. Baker, "Joyful Return for First Bernal Dwellers."
180. Ibid.
181. National Housing Law Project et al., *False HOPE*, 10–11.
182. Rongerude, "From Public Housing to Regulated Public Environments," 21. Rongerude makes a compelling argument that the SFHA's model of HOPE VI, with its focus on minimizing the loss of affordable housing units and leveraging public–private partnerships through the use of experienced nonprofit developers in the city, has transformed public housing in the city into a "new post-welfare institution." The HOPE VI sites are "regulated public environments"—places in which poverty is "experienced and contained" and "where private partners distribute and maintain resources supplied by the public sector"—that shape conditions and opportunities for recipients in exchange for a "set of specific behavioral expectations that reflect a larger set of public norms" (3). The privatization of public housing, which in San Francisco includes the privatization of property and tenant management, brings land use, regulation, and the spatial politics of poverty and redevelopment together—for better or worse. Although I agree with Rongerude's deft analysis overall, I do not think the SFHA Hope VI model is ultimately "progressive." My research demonstrates that the SFHA did not meaningfully center tenant voices and concerns throughout the redevelopment process but rather used tenant input when needed for applications. It was tenants themselves who demanded a greater voice and who pushed for the one-for-one replacement that the SFHA went on to provide at North Beach Place and Valencia Gardens.
183. Through the flexibility of the HOPE VI program, the SFHA decided to define "mixed income" as bringing together very low-income and low-income families. The first two HOPE VI developments, Bernal Dwellings and Plaza East, remained 100 percent dedicated to public housing. North

Notes to Chapter 2

Beach Place had 112 units subsidized by tax credits (Rongerude, "From Public Housing to Regulated Public Environments," 12), and Valencia Gardens had 52 (Mission Housing Development Corporation, "Valencia Gardens: Fact Sheet" on file with author).

2. The Contested Mission of Valencia Gardens

1. "Protest: Citizens Will Fight 'Slum' Housing Project," *San Francisco Examiner*, May 6, 1940.
2. "Housing Authority Flayed by Mission District at Hearing," *San Francisco Examiner*, May 31, 1940. During the meeting, opponents of public housing complained that the Mission "was being accused of having widespread juvenile delinquency and of having the third highest tuberculosis rate in the city." The protestors produced a letter from the health director for the city stating that the rate of TB in the Mission was average.
3. "Supervisors' Vote Opposes Mission Housing Project," *San Francisco Examiner*, May 7, 1940.
4. "Housing Authority Flayed by Mission District at Hearing."
5. I am differentiating "neighborhood" and "community" in the same way that Gabrielle Gahlia Modan does in *Turf Wars: Discourse, Diversity, Politics and Place* (Malden, Mass.: Blackwell, 2007). She defines community as "people linked through social networks" and neighborhood as linked "to the geographical space with which a community is aligned." These definitions, then, distinguish between "*residence* and *participation* in a place. Because community is defined through social networks, it is possible to be a member of a geographical community without actually living in a geographical terrain. Likewise, it is possible to live in a neighborhood without being a part of the community" (326–27).
6. The Mission District, described by many as the "heart of San Francisco," is the oldest settled area in San Francisco. The mixed-use district is centrally located between downtown and residential neighborhoods. *City within a City: Historic Context Statement for San Francisco's Mission District* (San Francisco: Department of City Planning, 2007), 1.
7. It is important to note that Mayor Rossi as well as two members of the Housing Authority Commission also argued against the placement of public housing on the Valencia site. Woodward Gardens, once the home and gardens of Robert Woodward, featured a zoo with exotic animals, Japanese acrobats, and other amusements that drew crowds for almost three decades. See Charles Lockwood, *Suddenly San Francisco: The Early Years of an Instant City* (San Francisco: The *San Francisco Examiner* Division of the

233

Notes to Chapter 2

Hearst Company, 1978), 112. A major draw for the Pacific Coast League, organized in 1903, the San Francisco Seals played to cheering crowds at Recreation Park on Eighth Street until the 1906 earthquake destroyed it. The following year, fans made their way to the new Recreation Park, also called Valencia Street Grounds, at Fourteenth and Valencia Streets in the Mission District. The 10,000-seat stadium hosted the Seals until the larger Seals Stadium opened in 1931. Bill O'Neal, *The Pacific Coast League 1903–1988* (Austin, Tex.: Eakin Press, 1990), 274–82. According to Sally Carrighar's 1943 article, Valencia Gardens was built over the "San Francisco grounds." Sally Carrighar, "Valencia Gardens—A Prelude to Mass Housing," *Architect and Engineer*, March 1943, 21.

8. Manuel Castells, *The City and the Grassroots: A Cross-Cultural Theory of Urban Social Movements* (Berkeley: University of California Press, 1983), 106.

9. Brian Godfrey, *Neighborhoods in Transition: The Making of San Francisco's Ethnic and Nonconformist Communities* (Berkeley: University of California Publications in Geography, 1988), 142.

10. The Mission is the only district in San Francisco that developed its own urban accent, Mish, which was a blend of Irish and German resembling Brooklynese. Lynn Ludlow and Mireya Navarro, "Winds of Change Sweep Polyglot Neighborhood," *San Francisco Examiner*, October 19, 1981.

11. Godfrey, *Neighborhoods in Transition*, 147.

12. "Supervisors Oppose Mission Housing Site," *San Francisco Examiner*, May 7, 1940.

13. *City within a City*, 39, 41, and 69.

14. Ibid.

15. Ibid. McCulloch first made his allegations on May 5, 1940, to the press. His charges were not followed up on. For more information, see "Mission Site Foes Charge Petition Fraud," *San Francisco Examiner*, May 6, 1940.

16. "Mission Site Foes Charge Petition Fraud," *San Francisco Examiner*, May 6, 1940. The Board of Supervisors could suggest only that the housing commissioners change their decision. The board and the mayor had no power over the commissioners, who were appointed to their posts by the mayor and acted as an independent body.

17. SFHA Commission Minutes, May 16, 1940. Other groups listed as "waiting to address the Commission in support of both projects" included Charles Schermerhorn from the Juvenile Court; James H. Mitchell from the American Institute of Architects; Mrs. Porter from the San Francisco Center; Mrs. Kara Fontaine, homeowner in the Mission District; Mary Cady, Mission YWCA; Mrs. Snow from the Visiting Nurses Association; the S.F. Housing Council; and the Emergency Committee to Save Housing.

Notes to Chapter 2

18. Ruth E. Kraucer to Marshall Dill, May 29, 1940, Marshall Dill Papers, Folder 13, North Baker Library, California Historical Society.

19. The Housing Authority commissioners had postponed scheduled meetings for two weeks because of scheduling conflicts of its members. The Mission Property Owners and Merchants Association and its leader lambasted the move by Dill. McCulloch had written Dill on May 21, asking for an open meeting with the commissioners to lay out the opposition's arguments. See "New Hearing Demanded on Housing Sites," *San Francisco Examiner*, May 21, 1940.

20. The Real Property Survey was conducted by the Works Progress Administration for the new Housing Authority of the City and County of San Francisco in 1939 to determine which areas needed public housing. It described the Mission as "a blighted district" and listed residential properties there as having the third lowest median value for homeowners in San Francisco. See *1939 Real Property Survey, San Francisco, California: A Report on Work Projects Administration* (San Francisco: City and County of San Francisco, 1940), 16 and 24. Whereas the core of the Mission was below par, the northern section of the district was labeled "substandard," with owner occupancy at less than 20 percent and monthly rents well below the city average (Godfrey, *Neighborhoods in Transition*, 147). Figures compiled from the *Real Property Survey*.

21. "Mission Housing Meeting Set," *San Francisco Examiner*, May 27, 1940, 16; "Meet Demands Ouster of Dill in Housing Row," *San Francisco Examiner*, May 30, 1940.

22. Bernal Dwellings opened in 1953 in the southern part of the Mission District, a few miles from downtown San Francisco. The project was redeveloped with HOPE VI funds. The relocation of tenants was completed by 1997, and the new development was fully occupied in 2001. For more information on the HOPE VI redevelopment process and impact, see Abt Associates, Inc., "Interim Assessment of the HOPE VI Program: Case Study of Bernal Dwellings and Plaza East in San Francisco, California," Final Report, volume 1, March 2003, www.abtassociates.com/reports/20039785103_68878.pdf.

23. The term "psychological ownership" is from Lawrence Vale, interview by Gail Harris, "The Connection," National Public Radio, April 28, 2003.

24. Elizabeth Mock, ed., *Built in the U.S.A: A Survey of Contemporary American Architecture since 1932* (New York: Museum of Modern Art, 1944), 58.

25. Sanborn Map Company Fire Insurance Map, 1950, accessed at University of California–Berkeley, and compiled by Clare Robinson. Although some

Notes to Chapter 2

of the churches and businesses may have moved, presumably a number of them continued to operate between 1940 and 1950.

26. Other notable architects designed public housing in San Francisco after the SFHA opened. Arthur Brown Jr., architect of Coit Tower, planned Holly Courts, San Francisco's first public housing project, which opened in 1940. Ernest Born and Henry Gutterson designed North Beach Place; see chapter 4.

27. Marc Treib, ed., *An Everyday Modernism: The Houses of William Wurster* (Berkeley: University of California Press, 1995), 44.

28. Ibid., 29. Wurster has been widely recognized as the foremost proponent of the Bay Area architectural style. His legacy, nonetheless, extends beyond the borders of California. Through his architectural practice at Wurster, Bernardi, and Emmons, and as head of the architecture schools at University of California–Berkeley and MIT, he "helped shape an entire generation of architects and city planners. . . . Greatly influenced by the social and economic conditions of the 1930s, Wurster set out to design small houses that offered the same livability as those of a greater scale. Later, in response to the post-World War II housing boom, he was involved in the creation of innovative—and affordable—mass-produced dwellings that were distinguished by simplicity and economy, yet incorporated diverse human needs." His work was characterized by the use of simple, unadorned materials and his use of flexible plans (Treib, *An Everyday Modernism*, cover sleeve).

29. Gwendolyn Wright, "A Partnership: William Wurster and Catherine Bauer," in Treib, *An Everyday Modernism*, 187. Wurster's office suffered little during the Depression. Nonetheless, Wright argues that he took the Valencia Gardens contract for money.

30. "Articles of Venture," W. W. Wurster Collection (1976–2), Valencia Gardens Folder, Environmental Design Archives, University of California–Berkeley. The quotation and information about Bauer and modern housing is from Gail Radford, *Modern Housing for America: Policy Struggles in the New Deal Era* (Chicago: University of Chicago Press, 1996), 83. Radford rightly notes that Bauer did not create the concept of "modern housing," which was well established in Europe. Rather, Bauer's contribution was synthesizing ideas into a "coherent whole" that was understandable to the American public (ibid.).

31. For more information on Catherine Bauer, see H. Peter Overlander and Eva Newbrun, *Houser: The Life and Work of Catherine Bauer* (Vancouver: University of British Columbia Press, 1999); and Radford, *Modern Housing for America*.

32. Wright, "A Partnership," 195; "Valencia Gardens," *Pencil Points: The Magazine of Architecture*, January 1944, 28.

33. Site plan, Valencia Gardens, San Francisco, California, Environmental Design Archives, University of California–Berkeley, accessed through the Online Archive of California, www.oac.cdlib.org/. A year and half after Valencia Gardens opened, William Wurster visited the development and conducted two interviews to determine how well the design was working. He learned that the "fenced in areas for small children playing [were] not used at all." "Mistake on our part." Management had removed one of the fenced-in play areas by the office already. Small children, Wurster noted, "play in all the courts particularly in the garden courts under mothers' supervision." William W. Wurster, Report to the Commission of the Federal Housing Authority, not dated, Environmental Design Archive, University of California–Berkeley, accessed online through the Online Archive of California, www.oac.cdlib.org/.

34. Carey and Company, Inc., "Valencia Gardens: Historic Building Assessment Report" (San Francisco, July 1997), 2.

35. "Valencia Gardens" article in *Pencil Points*, image on 26.

36. Wurster, Report to the Commission of the Federal Housing Authority. Wurster noted in his report that he and Thomsen had decided to add a feature for a clothesline in the bathroom in response to the laundry's location in the basement. They put in "wood strips on the wall at head height which would permit hooks and lines. This is a failure for NOT ONE TENANT has used them or known what they were for."

37. "Valencia Gardens," article in *Pencil Points*, 28.

38. Ibid., 28 and 32.

39. Ibid., 28. The cost of the land was $230,000 and the general contract was for $845,000, making the total cost per room around $1,000.

40. Information gleaned from my own interviews and those conducted by Roberta Swan for the SFAIA Legacy Oral History Project; see note 59.

41. Treib, *An Everyday Modernism*, 53.

42. Carrighar, "Valencia Gardens—A Prelude to Mass Housing," 22.

43. Wright, "A Partnership," 187.

44. Wurster, Report to the Commission of the Federal Housing Authority.

45. Bufano was born in San-Fele, Italy, on October 14, 1898. He immigrated with his family to New York in 1901. Between 1913 and 1915, he studied at the Arts Student League in New York, after which he traveled to San Francisco to work on a sculpture for the Panama-Pacific International Exposition. It was then, at the young age of sixteen, that Bufano began a long and tumultuous relationship with his adopted city of San Francisco. After traveling in France, Italy, India, and China, Bufano opened his studio in San Francisco in 1924, working there until his death in 1970. Praised by critics for the "freedom in his simplification of form and movement," Bufano exhibited his work

Notes to Chapter 2

in New York, Paris, and San Francisco. Quote by English art critic Robert Fry, referenced in H. Wilkening and Sonia Brown, *Bufano: An Intimate Biography* (Berkeley, Calif.: Howell-North Books, 1972), 103. An ardent pacifist and nonconformist, Bufano became the darling of the San Francisco newspapers because he was a consistent source of story lines. The papers called him "Benny" and printed hundreds of articles about his antics, including his radical break from the San Francisco Institute of Art faculty and his controversial tenure on the city's Art Commission.

46. While on the Federal Art Project, Bufano produced a granite head of St. Francis; fourteen animal statues, including a mouse, a cat, a cat and a mouse, a bear with two cubs, a horse and a bear, a seal, a frog, a rabbit, a penguin, double seals, a crab, and two fish sculptures; a bear with a human head; and stainless steel and granite representations of Sun Yat-Sen and Louis Pasteur. Steven M. Gelber, "The New Deal and Public Art in California," in *New Deal Art: California* (Santa Clara, Calif.: de Saisset Art Gallery and Museum, University of Santa Clara, 1976), 88.

47. Ibid., 74. Bufano liked shiny, smooth surfaces and recognized that steel would make a good complement to polished granite or glazed ceramic. When he contacted the steel companies, they informed him that the material could be worked only by heating it, which discolored the finish. Bufano refused to listen, and he and the artists in his studio worked the metal, cold, into shapes they desired. For more information, see Gelber, "The New Deal and Public Art in California," 74.

48. Unsure where to place the sculptures, the city kept them in storage until 1944. Under pressure from Bufano, the Board of Supervisors voted unanimously to display the statues at the Civic Center with the intention of attracting city department heads who could lobby for permission to showcase the pieces in their jurisdiction. The display provided the city with its first "open air show in history, the first art exhibit ever held in the Civic Center and the first one-man exhibition ever prompted by City Hall legislation" (Sherman Miller, "Board Orders Exhibit of Bufano Sculptures," *San Francisco Examiner*, October 10, 1944). In 1941, Bufano was fired from the FAP, but the city supported his reinstatement in hopes that he would finish the pieces. The exhibit at the Civic Center drew crowds and enabled city department heads to view the sculptures and select any they might want for location in their jurisdiction. The city zoo and Parks Department expressed initial interest in displaying some of the pieces but eventually backed out. The continual controversy that Bufano generated made the acquisition of his pieces potentially troublesome and led both agencies to create excuses for changing their plans. The Parks Department claimed that works of a living artist belonged in mu-

Notes to Chapter 2

seums and galleries rather than in parks ("Bufano's 16 Statues Won't Stand in Park," *San Francisco Chronicle*, December 23, 1944). The Art Commission, presenting a hastily crafted excuse, refused to loan statues to the zoo, because it would be an "artistic anachronism" to place animal sculptures next to live animals at the zoo ("Storage Again for Bufano's Animals: Art Board Rules that Zoo out of Bounds," *San Francisco Chronicle*, January 1, 1945). After the exhibit at the Civic Center ended in early 1945, the sculptures were slated to go back into storage, seemingly unwanted by city agencies.

49. "Display of City Owned Bufano Sculpture Urged," *San Francisco Examiner*, October 4, 1944. The quote is from a letter to the Art Commission from John Beard, San Francisco Art Commission.

50. Bufano initially protested the loan to the SFHA and threatened to sue the city ("Bufano Art to Housing Site," *San Francisco Examiner*, March 9, 1945). The Board of Supervisors countered Bufano's protests by claiming that Valencia Gardens offered a favorable spot for his pieces. Thomas A. Brooks, Chief Administrative Officer, echoing Wurster and Thomsen's design goal of connecting tenants with the Greater Mission District, assured Bufano that "the works will be on public display where they may be viewed by both residents and visitors" (ibid.). Finally, in a show of support for the new public housing development and in defense of the decision to place the sculptures there, Brooks stated, "Valencia Gardens appears to be the most appropriate place for some of Mr. Bufano's creations. The project has attracted the attention of artists and architects throughout the Nation and received special acclaim from the Museum of Modern Art in New York City" ("Display of City Owned Bufano Sculpture Urged"). Ultimately, Bufano resigned himself to the city's decision and worked with the Housing Authority "to determine the most artistic locations" for the sculptures (*San Francisco Housing News*, March 2, 1945). The Art Commission also loaned the SFHA two statues that were placed at Westside Courts and one at the administrative office at Sunnydale ("Bufano May Sue City over WPA Statues," *San Francisco Chronicle*, February 28, 1945). I have not been able to learn anything about the frog listed in the inventory at Valencia Gardens. There is a butterfly sculpture at Valencia Gardens that, according to residents, was there early on but later removed. The butterfly was returned with the other pieces in 1989 after the Art Commission took them away for cleaning and repair following an earthquake.

51. In June 1940, the federal government amended the 1937 Housing Act in response to the local housing crises arising from war mobilization. The amendment authorized loans and subsidies for housing defense workers and supported the continued construction of permanent buildings under federal standards, with occupant priority going to defense workers. Later that year,

Notes to Chapter 2

the Lanham Act was passed, which provided direct federal financing and construction for temporary housing and social services. See Gwendolyn Wright, "The Evolution of Public Housing Policy and Design in the San Francisco-Bay Area" (PhD diss., University of California–Berkeley, 1976, 23). Wurster grumbled that the residents living in Valencia Gardens were "probably only in-migrant workers at that"—referring to the large number of migrants from other areas in the United States who moved to the Bay Area for work during the war (quoted in Carrighar, "Valencia Gardens—A Prelude to Mass Housing," 22).

52. SFHA Commission Minutes, August 18, 1942. A January 3, 1943, article in the *San Francisco Examiner* stated that, according to Housing Commissioner Timothy Reardon, "some 800 persons will be accommodated at the new $2,000,000 project and the apartments will not be rented to single persons unless their dependents live with them."

53. SFHA Commission Minutes, May 14, 1942.

54. SFHA Commission Minutes, May 3, 1946 and August 15, 1946.

55. SFHA Commission Minutes, May 19, 1949. The SFHA Commission Minutes report that during the period October 1948 to March 1949, 43 percent of the 162 families vacated from permanent projects bought homes. Capitalizing on the figures for publicity, the chairman directed the secretary to release the information to the press.

56. The SFHA Commission Minutes for January 1, 1950, state that in regard to the eviction of high-income families, who were given approximately six months to vacate public housing, "the PHA has requested that this be discontinued and has suggested that those tenants having to move from our developments because of high income be allowed until July 1, 1950. After that date 30 days will be given."

57. Sanborn Fire Map, 1950. The fire department, a candy factory, a used car lot, a casket company, a private garage, and a building trades association were also nearby.

58. Deborah Madaris, interview by Roberta Swan, San Francisco, 1997, tape recording, Valencia Gardens Oral History Collection, San Francisco History Center, San Francisco Public Library. When I began this project, Roberta Swan gave me access to all the oral histories she conducted for the Valencia Gardens Legacy Project. Since then, they have entered the public domain, and recently she donated them to the San Francisco Public Library; the Valencia Gardens Oral History Collection can be accessed through the San Francisco History Center. References to these interviews are cited below as "interview by Swan."

59. Gabrielle Fontanella, interview by Swan.

Notes to Chapter 2

60. F. Soto, interview by Swan.
61. Gabrielle Fontanella, interview by Swan.
62. Diana Baez, interview by Swan.
63. F. Soto, interview by Swan. Bufano claimed that "nothing pleases me more than to see the children of God . . . humans and animals . . . play together." Wilkening and Brown, *Bufano*, 129.
64. Gabrielle Fontanella, interview by Swan.
65. Louette Fabio, interview with Louette Fabio and Gabrielle Fontanella by the author, tape recording, San Francisco, May 2003.
66. Randolph Falk, *Bufano* (Millbrae, Calif.: Celestial Arts, 1975), 25. The photo has no caption or citation.
67. Like other cities across the United States, San Francisco experienced a mass exodus of residents to the suburbs during the 1950s. Postwar economic prosperity and automobility, along with GI bill benefits, spurred suburban growth in the city's far western neighborhoods, including Richmond and Sunset. *City within a City*, 84.
68. Ibid.
69. Castells, *The City and the Grassroots*, 107.
70. Godfrey, *Neighborhoods in Transition*, 152–53. According to Godfrey, by 1980, documented Mission District residents of Latino origin reached an average of 60 percent and climbing. Godfrey also notes that the 60 percent figure given for 1980 is likely a conservative estimate given the number of undocumented residents. The steady growth of the Latino population started during the 1930s and 1940s and continued as European immigrant groups moved to the suburbs after World War II. Godfrey claims that the Mission District, which was already a solidly working-class area, appeared to be "going further down hill in social terms" because of the influx of Latino immigrants and the exodus of white residents of European ancestry. He argues that the 1930s and 1940s constituted the beginning stages of "Hispanic *penetration*" and that the 1950s were the "real stage of ethnic invasion, as the Spanish-surnamed population rose from 11 percent in 1950 to 23 percent in 1960" (150; emphasis in original).
71. *City within a City*, 84, 107.
72. Ibid., 84.
73. In 1971, muralists transformed Balmy Alley; it later became a site for a series of murals promoting peace in Central America and the end of U.S. involvement there. See the Precita Eyes Muralists, http://www.precitaeyes.org/missionhist.html.
74. A. Murguia, *The Medicine of Memory: A Mexican Clan in California* (Austin: University of Texas Press, 2002), 124, quoted in Emily Yee, "Gentrification

___n Francisco's Mission District" (Senior project, California Polytechnic State University, 2010), 25, available online at digitalcommons.calpoly.edu/cgi/viewcontent.cgi?article=1027&context=socssp.

75. Castells, *The City and the Grassroots*, 107. The mean salary distribution in 1969 in the Mission was $8,000, while in San Francisco it was $10,098, and 11 percent of Mission families were on welfare compared with 5 percent citywide. Castells cites Stanford Research Team: Mission Model Neighbourhood. The Mission housed more people who did not have a high school degree—83 percent versus 67 percent citywide—and college-educated adults in the Mission represented 7 percent of the population compared with 17 percent in San Francisco (Castells, citing data collected from the 1970 census by the San Francisco Department of City Planning).

76. Chester Hartman, *City for Sale: The Transformation of San Francisco* (Berkeley: University of California Press, 1993), 63. For a detailed account of the San Francisco Redevelopment Agency's renewal projects and impact on low-income residents in San Francisco, see Hartman's thorough book.

77. The MCO grew out of the Mission Council for Redevelopment after 1966. Ocean Howell, *City within a City: Planning and Ethnicity in San Francisco's Mission District, 1906–1973* (Chicago: University of Chicago Press, forthcoming 2015).

78. Castells, *The City and the Grassroots*, 106 and 108; and Mike Miller, "Power to the People: The Mission Coalition Organization," *Race, Poverty, and the Environment: A Journal for Social and Environmental Justice* 15, no. 1 (2008), http://urbanhabitat.org/node/1826. For a detailed analysis of the rise and fall of the MCO, see Castells's chapter "Urban Poverty, Ethnic Minorities and Community Organization: The Experience of Neighbourhood Mobilization in San Francisco's Mission," in *The City and the Grassroots*, 106–37.

79. "Mission District to Get a Going-over at Meeting," *San Francisco Chronicle*, January 16, 1961. During the 1960s and 1970s, the Mission District experienced an increase in crime, an economic downturn, and other problems. These changes affected both district residents and public housing tenants. In the early 1960s, city officials labeled the Greater Mission District as having a juvenile delinquency problem—a mark of the neighborhood's decline. A two-year, two-volume survey of the Mission District released in 1961 reported the growth of juvenile delinquency in the Mission as the highest in the city, with an 85 percent increase between 1950 and 1958. The report also documented an increase in the dropout rate in Mission schools. Mission residents were growing fearful of the changes taking place in their area. Valencia Gardens residents shared some of these concerns and had others. The rise of vandal-

ism at the project attracted the SFHA's attention, and the agency labeled Valencia Gardens a "trouble spot" in 1960. The commissioners, in response, "inaugurated a special police coverage . . . with a squad car for two policemen on the 4:00 p.m. to midnight watch . . . making themselves visible," "checking the roof and laundry areas, stairways and spot checking the floors, [and] knocking on doors and discussing with tenants problems as tenants see it" (SFHA Commission Minutes, February 18, 1960). The SFHA also designated Yerba Buena Plaza "as one of the most troublesome projects." A squad car patrolled Yerba Buena Plaza, and the SFHA requested that the officers perform the same duties there as at Valencia Gardens along with doing additional spot checks and "going up into the elevators" (ibid.)

80. Birney Jarvis, "A Gang's Terror in the Mission," *San Francisco Chronicle*, April 25, 1969.

81. Andres H. Malcolm, "Death of a Store Jolts Historic San Francisco District," *New York Times*, February 1, 1975, quoted in Cary Cordova, "San Francisco's Borderlands: Aztlan Mythologies and Urban Realities in Constructing the Mission District" (paper presented at the Western Social Science Association Annual Conference, Albuquerque, New Mexico, April 2002), 3.

82. Tom Mayer, interview by Swan.

83. In his groundbreaking book, *The Origins of the Urban Crisis* (Princeton, N.J.: Princeton University Press, 1996), Thomas Sugrue outlines the ways in which white citizens in post–World War II Detroit created a mental geography based on racial stereotypes and the physical decline and governmental neglect of African American neighborhoods. Whites' "racial geography of the city became, in part, the basis of their decisions about where to live, what areas to avoid, and what federal social policies to support and to contest." This "cognitive mapping" informed housing and school choices, creating invisible neighborhood boundaries that many working-class whites worked to defend (121).

84. Susan Sward, "Wide-open Drug Dealing in S.F. Housing Projects," *San Francisco Chronicle*, October 4, 1985.

85. Tom Mayer, interview by Sward.

86. Sward, "Wide-open Drug Dealing in S.F. Housing Projects."

87. Ibid.

88. Susan Sward, "Public Housing Tenants Report on Drug Woes," *San Francisco Chronicle*, October 8, 1985. The Housing Authority organized several meetings on the drug problem in the city's projects. In the meetings, housing officials urged tenants "to cooperate more with authorities trying to stop drug dealing" (3).

89. Ibid.

Notes to Chapter 2

90. See Robert Popp and J. L. Pimsleur, "'Family' Drug Gang Busted in S.F," *San Francisco Chronicle*, November 19, 1985; Torri Minton, "3 Arrests after Wild Gunfight by S.F. Gangs," *San Francisco Chronicle*, January 30, 1988; and Rick DelVecchio, "S.F. Police to Step up Watch on 'Drug' Gangs," *San Francisco Chronicle*, July 28, 1988.

91. Merna Escobar, interview by Swan.

92. Kim James, interview by Swan.

93. Gabrielle Fontanella and other residents I interviewed referred to Valencia Gardens as the stepchild of housing over the past three decades. These residents claimed that the Housing Authority poured its energy and resources into the "Big Four": Sunnydale, Hunters Point, Alice Griffith, and Potrero.

94. Reginald Smith, "Cold Days inside as Well as out at S.F. Housing Project," *San Francisco Chronicle*, January 25, 1985.

95. Ibid.

96. Jason B. Johnson, "Valencia Gardens Plan Unveiled; S.F. Project's Residents Receive Virtual Tour," *San Francisco Chronicle*, May 13, 1998.

97. Anita Ortiz, interview by Swan.

98. Louette Fabio and Gabrielle Fontanella, interview by the author, May 2003. Both women asserted that the gang violence in the 1970s, 1980s, and 1990s involved few residents. Some of the gangs were from the Mission, and others came from the Sunnydale and Hunters Point housing projects. Louette and Gabrielle saw the project's location near the BART station and two major highways as one of the reasons their project attracted criminals. It was an easy location to hide in and to escape from. Louette stated that "no matter what, there were people coming from around the area and across the Bay doing things here."

99. Maria Calderon, interview by Swan.

100. Christine Bryant to Debra LaHane, Civic Arts Collection Manager, April 9, 1995, Bufano File, San Francisco Arts Commission, San Francisco.

101. "Lost Gardens: No. 14," *San Francisco Examiner*, January 2, 1987. She might have felt more comfortable viewing copies of the rabbit, the cat, the cat and mouse, and the mouse located at the Hillsdale Shopping Center in San Mateo, California, a symbol of middle-class suburbia, rather than in Valencia Gardens. The display of the figures at the shopping center uses shrubbery around the animals, precluding visitors from getting close to the figures or children from playing on them. Shrouded by plants, the copies have become decorative landscape art, pieces to pass on the way to a department store. While Bufano's sculptures are arguably more accessible at the mall, they

serve no communal function there; in contrast, they continued to do so for Valencia Gardens residents during the swell of violence and crime in the 1980s and 1990s. The fully displayed animals at Valencia Gardens have functioned as a critical community cohesive for residents—a concept critics have yet to understand.

102. Ibid.

103. Ibid.

104. Patricia Yollin, "New Habitat for Love-Worn Beasts: Museum Kids Enjoy Treasured Guardians of Valencia Gardens," *San Francisco Chronicle*, April 30, 2004. One resident explained, "I have lived in Valencia Gardens on and off for most of my life . . . people don't understand the statues, people who live here (now) don't realize the value of these, of their history. . . . The only other place I have seen the Bufanos is in front of the UC Hospital." Francesca Soto [Esteves], interview by Swan.

105. Gabrielle Fontanella, interview by the author, tape recording, San Francisco, May 2003.

106. See chapter 4 for a detailed analysis of the *Banks* case. As noted previously, war workers and veterans continued living at Valencia Gardens until 1950. It is difficult to know the racial and ethnic breakdown of tenants at Valencia Gardens before 1954 with the SFHA's neighborhood policy in effect stipulating that public housing reflect the racial and ethnic makeup of the surrounding neighborhood. Census data do not help. In 1980, census definitions of racial and ethnic categories were changed; before then Latino/as were listed as "White" or "Other." For an estimate of the Latino population in San Francisco in 1980, see Castells, *The City and the Grassroots*, chapter 13, "Urban Poverty, Ethnic Minorities, and Community Organizing: The Experience of Neighbourhood Mobilization in San Francisco's Mission District," endnote 14.

107. Roberta Swan, "The Valencia Gardens Oral History Project" (booklet, Legacy Project, sponsored by the American Institute of Architects, San Francisco chapter, 1998), Valencia Gardens Collection, San Francisco History Center, San Francisco Public Library.

108. Anonymous, interview by Swan.

109. Swan, "The Valencia Gardens Oral History Project."

110. Swan, Valencia Gardens Oral History Collection, San Francisco History Center, San Francisco Public Library.

111. Anita Ortiz, interview by Swan.

112. Ibid.

113. Donald Ingram, interview by Swan.

114. Charla Molina, interview by Swan.

Notes to Chapter 2

115. Anita Ortiz, interview by Swan.

116. Merna Escobar noted that the neighbors in her building worked to protect each other. "The minute they see one of us in trouble they call the police. They don't have to ask.... There are a lot of good people here." Merna Escobar, interview by Swan.

117. Anita Ortiz, interview by Swan.

118. Jeri Maxwell, interview by Swan.

119. Susie Barrara, interview by Swan.

120. The Tenants' Organization, under the presidency of Jeri Maxwell, filed to become incorporated by the State of California as the Valencia Gardens Resident Council. The incorporation took place in July 1997. I refer to the organization as the Tenants' Organization here.

121. Jeri Maxwell, interview by Swan.

122. Gregory Lewis, "Guards Reassure Project Residents: Pilot Program with Armed Security Could Spread through the City," *San Francisco Examiner*, April 17, 1997. While the crime rate increased at Valencia Gardens, the percentage of major crimes—homicide, rape, and aggravated assault—declined.

123. According to Gabrielle Fontanella, Jeri Maxwell in her capacity as president pushed through the resolution for the gates without taking a vote (Gabrielle Fontanella, interview by the author, telephone, August 2003). In their interviews with Roberta Swan, residents revealed that the community was divided over the gate issue. Some residents felt they were unnecessary and would further stigmatize the project, while others hoped the gates would decrease crime and show the neighborhood and the city that the troublemakers were outsiders.

124. According to Gabrielle Fontanella, the Housing Authority installed inexpensive gates that did not work properly: the keypad did not work on one entrance, and the gates were usually broken, and so were left open. Gabrielle Fontanella, interview by the author, May 2003.

125. Ethel Williams, interview by Swan.

126. Ibid.

127. Willie Eldridge, interview by Swan.

128. Anita Ortiz, interview by Swan. Anita stayed on as president until the redevelopment project was completed.

129. Jeri Maxwell, interview by Swan.

130. Omaira Correa, interview by Swan.

131. Anita Ortiz, interview by Swan.

132. Eva Platero, interview by Swan.

133. Ron Dunn, interview by Swan.

Notes to Chapter 2

134. Ruth Hamilton, interview by Swan. Most likely the tree was destroyed during the demolition of Valencia Gardens for HOPE VI redevelopment.

135. Louette Fabio and Gabrielle Fontanella, interview by the author, May 2003.

136. Susan J. Popkin, Bruce Katz, Mary A. Cunningham, Karen D. Brown, Jeremy Gustafson, and Mary Austin Turner, *A Decade of HOPE VI: Research Finding and Policy Challenges* (Washington, DC: Urban Institute, 2004), www.urban.org/publications/411002.html.

137. Yee, "Gentrification in San Francisco's Mission District," 27, citing Anne M. Nyborg, *Gentrified Barrio: Gentrification and the Latino Community in San Francisco* (San Diego: University of California, 2008).

138. Yee, "Gentrification in San Francisco's Mission District," 33.

139. A 1988 city ordinance allowed for the conversion of industrial spaces into live–work lofts and areas that were zoned for industry to bypass the building codes and avoid affordable housing contracts and "a significant portion of school taxes." Developers took advantage of the ordinance, originally backed by artists, and started a major expansion of high-priced lofts (Yee, "Gentrification in San Francisco's Mission District," 28). In his study on gentrification in the Mission, Simon Velazquez Alejandrino also points to Owner Move-ins (OMIs) as a catalyst for gentrification and the subsequent displacement of Latino/as from the Mission District. OMIs "allow an owner to evict a tenant if the owner resides in the building for 36 months following the eviction. After this period, the owner can return the unit to the rental market." Alejandrino, 20–22, cited in Nancy Raquel Mirabal, "Geographies of Displacement: Latino/as, Oral History, and the Politics of Gentrification in San Francisco's Mission District," *Public Historian* 31, no. 2 (Spring 2009), 14. Following an OMI, a landlord could rerent the unit at market value. California's 1986 Ellis Act allowed "property owners to remove all of their properties from the rental market and evict all tenants. Owners must give tenants first right of refusal if the unit is returned to the rental market. Owners must also pay $4500 to low-income tenants and $3000 to elderly or disabled tenants if evicted under the act." Gentrification makes use of this act more frequent (Alejandrino, 20–22, cited in Mirabal, "Geographies of Displacement," 15).

140. Julie Chao, "Voices of Hope Rise from Projects: Oral History of Valencia Gardens Reveals Struggle for Better Life," *San Francisco Examiner*, January 22, 1998.

141. Swan, "The Valencia Gardens Legacy Oral History Project."

142. Roberta Swan, interview by the author, July 10, 2001, Mill Valley, California.

Notes to Chapter 2

143. Julie Chao, "Voices of Hope Rise from Projects."

144. The design competition ended after the SFHA was awarded a HOPE VI grant.

145. The HUD website, under "General Guidance on Community and Resident Involvement," addresses ways to engage residents in the HOPE VI process (www.hud.gov/offices/pih/programs/ph/hope6/css/guidance.cfm).

146. Philip Matier and Andrew Ross, "That's Not Just an Elevator, It's Public Sculpture, S.F. Style," *San Francisco Chronicle*, October 13, 1997.

147. Julie Chao, "Voices of Hope Rise from Projects."

148. Architect and planner Oscar Newman developed the concept of defensible space, which stresses the importance of building design and layout in enabling residents to actively engage in their own safety and security. Newman, *Defensible Space: Crime Prevention through Urban Design* (New York: Macmillan, 1973).

149. National Housing Law Project et al., *False HOPE*.

150. Carey and Company, Inc., "Valencia Gardens: Historic Building Assessment Report," 10.

151. Vernell Gutherie, interview by Swan.

152. Susie Barrara, interview by Swan.

153. Gabrielle Fontanella, interview with Louette Fabio and Gabrielle Fontanella by the author, May 2003.

154. Louette Fabio, interview with Louette Fabio and Gabrielle Fontanella by the author, May 2003.

155. The HOPE VI application showed images of the Bufanos out near the street. The plans changed, and the Bufanos now sit close together in a small, interior courtyard off the community room.

156. James A. Henretta, Rebecca Edwards, and Robert O. Self, *American History since 1865* (Chicago: Dorsey Press, 1987), 785.

157. Ron Nyren, "Living in the Mix," *Urban Land*, March 2009. The unit mix for the redeveloped project includes forty-two one-bedroom units for seniors; eighteen one-bedrooms for families; ninety-eight two-bedrooms for families; eighty-eight three-bedrooms for families; and fourteen four-bedrooms for families.

158. Mission Housing Development Corporation, "Valencia Gardens Fact Sheet," given to the author by a Mission Housing Representative in May 2009.

159. National Housing Law Project et al., *False HOPE*, ii. According to data compiled by G. Thomas Kingsley, by 2008, $5.53 billion in HOPE VI funds had been awarded for 240 developments. Kingsley, Appendix A, in *From Despair to Hope: Hope VI and the New Promise of Public Housing in American Cities*, eds. Henry G. Cisneros and Lora Engdahl (Washington, DC: Brookings Insti-

Notes to Chapter 2

tution Press, 2009), 300–302. By September 2008, the HOPE VI program had demolished 91,802 units, rehabilitated 10,651 units, constructed 61,545 units, and occupied 69,317 units. The loss of public housing units is complicated to calculate because of predevelopment vacancy rates and other factors. Kingsley claims that the loss rate of public housing in units "is somewhere between 45 percent and 19 percent, probably closer to the lower figure." Another point of contention, along with the loss of public housing units, is the low rate of returning families. While Kingsley notes that "many program operators recognized that sizable numbers of original residents had good reasons to prefer other locations and did not want to move back" and that the outcome is no longer seen as necessarily "problematic," the reduction in low-income units and the low return rate raises important questions about the program and its effect on residents and their communities.

160. San Francisco Housing Authority website, www.sfha.org.hope/valen/htm.

161. National Housing Law Project et al., *False HOPE*, 18, 25.

162. U.S. Department of Housing and Urban Development, *HOPE VI: Building Communities, Transforming Lives* (December 1999), 14, available online at www.huduser.org/portal/publications/pubasst/bldgcomm.html; quoted in National Housing Law Project et al., *False HOPE*, 25.

163. Stephen B. Haines and Gabrielle Fontanella, interview by the author, tape recording, San Francisco, May 2003.

164. G. Thomas Kingsley, Appendix A, in *From Despair to Hope*, ed. Henry G. Cisneros and Lora Engdahl, 301. Kingsley notes that housing authorities expect that around 38 percent of the total number of families relocated will return to HOPE VI developments once they are all completed.

165. National Housing Law Project et al., *False HOPE*, iii.

166. According to a document provided by former SFHA employee Juan Monsanto to scholar Jane Rongerude, entitled "HOPE VI Housing Relocation Choices and Return, 1999–2006," 52 percent of Valencia Gardens residents returned. Other figures indicate that 37 percent of residents returned to Hayes Valley; 56 percent returned to Bernal Dwellings; and 41 percent returned to Plaza East. An e-mail correspondence with SFHA employee Florence Cheng indicated that approximately 41 families—17 percent—returned to Valencia Gardens.

167. Ruth Hamilton and Gabrielle Fontanella, interview by the author, tape recording, San Francisco, May 2003.

168. Van Meter Williams Pollack, "Valencia Gardens, Hope VI" Project Sheet, www.vmwp.com/projects/valencia-gardens.php. The newly designed Valencia Gardens won the following awards: AIA National HUD Secretary's

Notes to Chapter 2

Housing Creating Community Connection Award, 2008; *San Francisco Business Times*, Affordable Housing Project of the Year, 2007; Golden Nugget Award of Merit, Best Affordable Project—30 du/Acre or more, 2007; and the AIA San Francisco Urban Design Special Commendation Award, 2007. Ibid.

169. For more information on Four Barrel, see the company's website, fourbarrelcoffee.com.

170. Anita Ortiz, interview by the author, and Louette Fabio and Gabrielle Fontanella, interview by the author, tape recording, San Francisco, May 2009.

171. Anonymous relative of former tenant at Valencia Gardens, interview by the author, San Francisco, 2009.

172. Anita Ortiz, interview by the author, May 2009.

173. Some residents claim that the Guerrero side of the project has always been much quieter than the Valencia side on busy Valencia Street. In interviews and discussions with me, tenants on both sides agreed that Guerrero was the "better" side because there has historically been less noise and fewer problems.

174. In the early 1990s, residents of the surrounding Mission made an effort to connect with Valencia Gardens residents. Local shops including Safeway contributed funds to the project to help with their Operation Heart Program. Likewise, community service organizations in the area offered services (generally geared toward Latino/as) to residents, and two volunteers from a nearby church held art classes for children in Valencia Gardens. Nonetheless, the overall perception of residents, as expressed in their interviews with me and with Roberta Swan, was that the neighborhood looked down on them.

3. "Peace and Prosperity Dwell among Virtuous Neighbors"

1. In "Ping Yuen: A Scrapbook," the Ti Sun furniture and decorating company ran photos of the mayor and his wife inside the model apartment alongside images of the living room and dining room furniture, noting "how well the Chinese decorations and accessories fit with our Modern upholstered pieces, the record cabinet, and the square cocktail table." The model apartment demonstrated to tenants and visitors the "optimal" way to live. The SFHA purchased Frigidaire refrigerators for each of the apartments. Both the Ti Sun Company and Frigidaire promoted the use of their products in Ping Yuen. Also in the scrapbook was the February 1952 issue of *The Frigidairian*, a publication for "those who sell and service Frigidaire Products." The company showcased a large image of the Frigidaire model with a small

Notes to Chapter 3

caption showing a Ping Yuen kitchen. The caption read, "In Chinatown—Each of the 234 Chinese American families to occupy apartments in a new low-rent housing project in San Francisco, have a kitchen like this, equipped with a Frigidaire refrigerator." The Ti Sun ad noted that "thousands of people visited the model apartment and liked our furniture and the treatment by the Ti Sun decorators." Copies of both ads were found in "Ping Yuen: A Scrapbook," Ethnic Studies Library, University of California–Berkeley.

2. "Ping Yuen Means 'Tranquil Gardens,'" *California Housing Reporter*, November 1951. Henry K. Wong was a Navy Sea-Bee in the Pacific during World War II and worked as a waiter in Chinatown when Ping Yuen opened. As the "first family" of Ping Yuen, the Wongs were given the opportunity to pick which two-bedroom apartment they wanted to rent in the six-story East Ping Yuen building. They selected an apartment on the top floor with a view. "The Henry Wongs—Ping Yuen's First Family," *San Francisco Chronicle*, October 18, 1951.

3. Nate Hale, "5000 See Dedication of Ping Yuen," *San Francisco Chronicle*, October 22, 1951. The dedication took place at the east building, which opened first in November. The singing of the national anthem was reported in "Ping Yuen Is Dedicated," *Journal of Housing*, November 1951, 391.

4. The invitation for the ceremony—printed on cream paper with red ink—also lists Father Donald F. Forrester, director of the St. Mary's Chinese Mission, the Reverend C. S. Chiu, president of the Chinese Christian Union, and members of the Chinese Six Companies as part of the program. Invitation in "Ping Yuen: A Scrapbook."

5. "Ping Yuen Means 'Tranquil Gardens.'"

6. "The Henry Wongs—Ping Yuen's First Family."

7. Hale, "5000 See Dedication of Ping Yuen Housing."

8. "Ping Yuen, Chinatown Project, Is First on Building List," *Journal of Housing*, August 1949, 257.

9. Housing Authority of the City and County of San Francisco, *Eleventh Annual Report* (San Francisco: The Housing Authority, 1949).

10. Ibid. For information on the federal government's concern for and attempts to promote the status and treatment of Chinese Americans through programs such as the Voice of America at the onset of the Cold War, see Ellen D. Wu's "'America's Chinese': Anti-Communism, Citizenship and Cultural Diplomacy during the Cold War," *Pacific Historical Review* 77, no. 3 (August 2008), 391–422.

11. "Ping Yuen Means 'Tranquil Gardens.'"

12. Connie Young Yu, "A History of San Francisco Chinatown Housing," *Amerasia* 8, no. 1 (1981), 105.

Notes to Chapter 3

13. The term "Chinese American," according to scholar Yong Chen, gained prevalence after World War II. It is likely that many residents moving into Ping Yuen in 1951–52 did not use this term to describe or define themselves. I am using this term to refer to Chinese immigrants who gained access to public housing through slum clearance or by serving in World War II and to second and third generations of Americans with Chinese ancestry. Although there are no extant Housing Authority records on the specific demographics of residents at Ping Yuen over the years, newspaper articles, SFHA minutes, and accounts from residents underscore that early residents were primarily World War II veterans and second-generation Chinese Americans. Immigrants moving in, per SFHA rules, had to have at least one citizen on the lease. For these reasons, I use the term "Chinese American" throughout the chapter. See Yong Chen, *Chinese San Francisco 1850–1943: A Trans-Pacific Community* (Stanford, Calif. Stanford University Press, 2000).

14. In his book on the Chinese in San Francisco, Yong Chen demonstrates how acculturation became more visible in many aspects of Chinatown social life between 1915 and 1943. During these years, many Chinese in Chinatown embraced American movies and other non-Chinese activities, such as hosting the Miss Chinatown Pageant and eating at taverns that served American food. Furthermore, he notes that Chinese Americans also increased their participation in American politics during the wars, demonstrating "keen awareness of their political rights." Yet even as some Chinese became more Americanized, the community continued to support Chinese social and cultural values through Chinese schools and celebrations that reinforced cultural identity for immigrants and their American-born children. Chen, *Chinese San Francisco*, 40.

15. Gwendolyn Wright, "The Evolution of Public Housing Policy and Design in the San Francisco-Bay Area" (part of PhD Qualifying Exam, College of Environmental Design, Department of Architecture, University of California–Berkeley, November 22, 1976), 57.

16. "Chinatown is a Squalid Slum Comparable with Worst in the World," *San Francisco News*, July 6, 1939, quoted in Nayan Shah, *Contagious Divides: Epidemics and Race in San Francisco's Chinatown* (Berkeley: University of California Press, 2001), 231. According to Shah, the Associated Press reported the findings of the unpublished study through its international wire service.

17. Ronald Takaki, *Strangers from A Different Shore: A History of Asian Americans* (Boston: Little, Brown, 1989). Restrictive covenants were outlawed by the U.S. Supreme Court in *Shelley v. Kraemer* in 1948. Many San Franciscans hoped the ruling would provide better access to the private housing market.

Nonetheless, a local realtor predicted the ultimate outcome in some neighborhoods, stating that "the code of ethics would more or less maintain the restrictive status quo." *San Francisco Chronicle*, May 4, 1948 and May 5, 1948, quoted in Deirdre L. Sullivan, "'Letting down the Bars:' Race, Space, and Democracy in San Francisco, 1936–1964" (PhD diss., University of Pennsylvania, 2003), 126. Sullivan examines segregation and discrimination in San Francisco housing between 1936 and 1964, arguing that the city was less liberal and tolerant than it projected itself to be. See Sullivan's chapter 4 for an analysis of the impact of the *Shelley* decision in private and public housing in San Francisco.

18. Yu, "A History of Chinatown Housing," 101. Yu explains that the *Chinese Digest* was a magazine published by Chinese American intellectuals who were part of a visible, college-educated, American-born generation in Chinatown that began criticizing the community's housing, health care, and lack of employment opportunities in the 1930s. Nayan Shah describes how this group of leaders worked to replace "nineteenth-century images of the Chinese as inscrutable aliens living in mysterious clan networks of single men with images of assimilating, Americanized nuclear families" (Shah, *Contagious Divides*, 229). Their efforts reaped reward when Ping Yuen opened.

19. For Chinese communities at home and abroad, the basic unit of social control was the family network. Thomas Chinn explains that when "broader social needs were required, the family associations came into being.... As the name implies, each association includes members with the same surname." Chinn, "A History of the Chinese in California: A Syllabus" (San Francisco: Chinese Historical Society of America, 1969), 65–66. Family associations exercised substantial influence over members, punishing unruly members and protecting and helping those in need. District associations provided another level of support to businesses. District associations included members originating from certain districts in Kwangtung and performed administrative duties for businesses and groups. In San Francisco's Chinatown, the district associations formed the Chinese Six Companies, which was incorporated in 1901 under its legal name, Chinese Consolidated Benevolent Association, and was empowered to speak and act for all California Chinese in "problems and affairs which affected the majority of them" (ibid.). The Chinese Six Companies settled disputes and initiated programs for the general welfare of the Chinese in California. After World War II, the influence of family and district associations and of the Chinese Six Companies was diminished by the increasing numbers of Chinese Americans assimilating into American culture.

Notes to Chapter 3

20. Lim P. Lee, "Chinatown's Housing Problem Due for Airing," *Chinese Digest*, June 1937, accessed at the Bancroft Library, University of California–Berkeley.

21. Shah, *Contagious Divides*, 230.

22. SFHA Commission Minutes, July 21, 1938. The Chinese YWCA was founded in 1916 by a group of Chinese women and "was regarded as an act of daring in Chinatown at the time" vis-à-vis Chinese-based gender norms. Thomas W. Chinn, *Bridging the Pacific: San Francisco Chinatown and Its People* (San Francisco: Chinese Historical Society of America, 1989), 110. The organization became a major resource for the community, and in 1930 members raised $25,000 to put toward a new building designed by well-known architect Julia Morgan (ibid.).

23. SFHA Commission Minutes, July 21, 1938.

24. SFHA, *Second Annual Report*, 17. The Housing Authority's willingness to aid the Chinatown community broke with the city's history of discriminating against the Chinese and ignoring Chinatown's problems. The Housing Authority's decision to act arguably demonstrates the new agency's goal of bringing better housing to the most distressed areas in the city and its concern about tuberculosis in the district. In *Contagious Divides*, Nayan Shah persuasively demonstrates how Chinese American activists, focusing on the "need" of the "deserving" Chinatown families, zeroed in on the "contribution of decrepit housing to tuberculosis infection" (227). Similarly, the SFHA's actions reveal, to some extent, the increasingly "Sinophile sentiments" of American society in the late 1930s and early 1940s that created an environment in which the Chinese exclusion acts could be abolished following China's alliance with the United States during World War II (Chen, *Chinese San Francisco*, 255.)

25. Mark Daniels Jr. "Oriental Architecture for Chinatown Housing Unit," *Architect and Engineer*, December 1939, 37.

26. Ibid., 102. Connie Young Yu argues that the Chinatown Housing Project Committee was a grassroots committee formed in the late 1930s by housing activists in Chinatown who led the fight for better housing in the district. Connie Young Yu, "From Tents to Federal Projects: Chinatown's Housing History," in *The Chinese American Experience: Papers from the Second National Conference on Chinese American Studies*, ed. Genny Lim (San Francisco: Chinese Historical Society of America, 1983). Similarly, architect Mark Daniels Jr., in a December 1939 issue of *Architect and Engineer*, described the committee as forming in 1939 to urge the Housing Authority to appropriate funds for public housing in Chinatown (Daniels, "Oriental Architecture for Chinatown Housing Unit").

Notes to Chapter 3

27. Yu, "From Tents to Federal Projects," 135. Yu references an interview with Theodore Lee in which he claims he and members of the Chamber of Commerce took the First Lady on a tour of Chinatown in 1939 after which she talked to her husband about increasing the federal limit for purchasing land for public housing. In a 1970 interview with Victor Nee and Brett de Bary Nee, Lee explained how he managed to meet Eleanor Roosevelt and to show her around through his work in the restaurant industry. According to Lee, they took the First Lady on a tour of tenements, showing her the horrible conditions where "whole families were living in one room, sleeping on the floor. We told her about the high infant mortality rate in Chinatown, and that we had a high rate of TB, too" (Victor Nee and Brett de Bary Nee, interview with Dr. Theodore Lee, tape recording, San Francisco, Summer 1970, private collection). She supported the cause of housing in Chinatown after her return to Washington (ibid.). There is competing evidence of the story of the First Lady's involvement with public housing in Chinatown. In a 1989 *AsianWeek* article, Johnny Ng reported that plans to bring public housing to Chinatown began in 1939, when city newspapers published a study called "Living Conditions in Chinatown," which detailed the horrible living conditions in the district and the health problems arising out of them. Ng claims that a copy of the report was sent to Eleanor Roosevelt, who "helped generate more public attention to the problem and called for the improvement of housing in Chinatown in her weekly newspaper column." Johnny Ng, "Ping Yuen's Construction Was a Long-Fought Battle," *AsianWeek*, December 15, 1989. Charlotte Brooks also notes the importance of Eleanor Roosevelt's July 5, 1939, "My Day" column. The First Lady wrote about the horrible conditions in Chinatown she read about in a detailed report by the School of Social Studies in San Francisco. Roosevelt's comments embarrassed San Franciscans. According to Brooks, Roosevelt also played a role in the development of public housing in Chinatown by asking Nathan Straus of the USHA to "consider an exception" to the $1.50 per square foot limit. Charlotte Brooks, *Alien Neighbors, Foreign Friends: Asian Americans, Housing, and the Transformation of Urban California* (Chicago: University of Chicago Press, 2009), 101–102. Although I have not found other accounts of Eleanor Roosevelt's visit to Chinatown, Lee's recollection falls in line with the activism of the Chinatown Housing Project Committee.
28. Yu, "From Tents to Federal Projects," 135.
29. SFHA, *Second Annual Report*, 17.
30. Theodore Lee, interview by Nee and Nee.
31. Shah, *Contagious Divides*, 236.
32. Ibid.

Notes to Chapter 3

33. Ibid.

34. Nayan Shah states that the SFHA was reluctant to provide public housing in Chinatown because the development would take funding away from housing the white working class (*Contagious Divides*, 235). The white Junior Chamber commissioned Mark Daniels Sr. to draw up plans for the Chinatown project prior to the SFHA's approval. The drawings, which appeared in *Architect and Engineer* in December 1939, match the description of the rendering on the Junior Chamber's poster. Daniels, "Oriental Architecture for Chinatown Housing Unit," 38.

35. Daniels, "Oriental Architecture for Chinatown Housing Unit," 38.

36. SFHA, *Second Annual Report*, 17. For more information on public health, race, and citizenship in Chinatown, see Nayan Shah's *Contagious Divides*. Shah demonstrates how Chinese American activists beginning in the 1930s successfully used discourses of race and health to argue that Chinese Americans deserved access to American resources.

37. "Chinatown Housing," *San Francisco Chronicle*, 1 July 1949. The article lists the land purchase price at $380,673 and the estimated total cost of the buildings at $1,360,000 in 1942.

38. Letter to Carey McWilliams from the San Francisco Housing Authority sent in 1941; quoted in Yu, "A History of San Francisco Chinatown Housing," 104.

39. From the federal Chinese Exclusion Act of 1882, which banned Chinese immigration and outlawed naturalized citizenship, to the Alien Land Law of 1913, which prevented U.S. residents ineligible for citizenship from owning property, the Chinese in San Francisco had encountered a variety of specific anti-Chinese legislation and social policy. The majority of Chinese laborers came to California during the nineteenth century by means of the credit-ticket system, by which passage was advanced to an emigrant, who was expected to repay this debt from future earnings. Realizing they could pay Chinese workers lower wages, American businessmen hired Chinese workers to do jobs often shunned by other laborers, such as the dangerous, backbreaking work of building the transcontinental railroad. Once the railroad was complete and Chinese workers flooded the labor market, competing with white workers for jobs during the recession of the late 1870s, discrimination against the Chinese mounted. The result was the Chinese Exclusion Act, passed in 1882, which suspended immigration of Chinese laborers to the United States and prohibited the naturalization of Chinese: no state could grant a Chinese person citizenship. The act was amended and renewed in 1888 as the more restrictive Scott Act went into effect, preventing any Chinese laborer who had left the United States from returning and prohibiting

reentry certificates. The act also prevented Chinese immigrants from bringing over their wives. The Scott Act broke the Burlingame Treaty of 1868, insulted Chinese government officials, and invalidated the return certificates issued to 20,000 laborers. The 1892 Geary Act extended the Exclusion Act for ten more years and required all Chinese laborers to register with the government and to purchase certificates of residence. After one year, those without certificates were liable for deportation. These acts dramatically reduced the number of Chinese in the United States and in San Francisco. Between 1890 and 1920, the Chinese population in San Francisco dropped from 25,833 to 11,000. The 1924 Immigration Act stopped immigration altogether.

40. The Supreme Court of California invalidated the Alien Land Law in 1952.

41. The Geary Act regulated Chinese immigration until the 1920s, when the government shifted to quotas and requirements based on national origins. These changes in policy and the increase in immigration after World War I had an impact on Chinatown as families and wives began crowding into housing designed for single occupancy. In the 1920s, there was a gradual proliferation of families in Chinatown as a result of three trends. First, merchants who were exempt from the exclusion acts brought their wives over or got married on their trips back to China. Second, some laundry and restaurant owners and even some hired laborers bribed merchants to add their names as partners in business so they could bring their wives over. Finally, there was a slow increase in the population of native-born Chinese women in the 1920s. It is important to note that despite this increase in the female population, between 1924 and 1930 no Chinese women were admitted to the United States because of the 1924 Exclusion Act. In 1930, the harsh act was revised to allow for the admission of Chinese wives of American citizens who were married prior to May 26, 1924. Between 1906 and 1924, an average of 150 Chinese women per year entered the United States. From 1931 to 1940, an average of 60 Chinese women entered each year. The 1945 War Brides Act eased restrictions on the entry to the United States of wives of men in the U.S. armed forces and resulted in approximately 6,000 Chinese women entering the United States. See Victor G. and Brett de Bary Nee, *Longtime Californ': A Documentary Study of an American Chinatown* (New York: Pantheon, 1972), 149; and Judy Yung, *Unbound Feet: A Social History of Chinese Women in San Francisco* (Berkeley: University of California Press, 1995).

42. For a nuanced examination of the impact of international affairs in white Californians' changing perceptions toward Asian Americans, and the impact of this shift on housing, see Brooks, *Alien Neighbors, Foreign Friends*.

43. K. Scott Wong, *Americans First: Chinese Americans and the Second World War* (Cambridge, Mass.: Harvard University Press, 2005), 43. According to Wong, approximately 15,000 Chinese Americans, or close to 20 percent of the adult Chinese male population, joined the U.S. military during World War II (58).

44. K. Scott Wong, *Americans First*, quoting from the *Chinese Press*. The *Press* editors celebrated the U.S. Navy's decision to ease restrictions on the positions Chinese Americans could hold. Initially, Chinese Americans were confined to mess hall or cabin steward duty. The navy changed course in May 1942 (ibid., 60).

45. Ibid., 32, quoting from *California Chinese Press*, November 22, 1940. According to Wong, the *California Chinese Press* (later called the *Chinese Press*) was founded in 1940 after the *Chinese Digest* folded. The *Chinese Press* became "the most professional of the English-language Chinese American newspapers" and was geared toward a national audience of second-generation Chinese Americans (31).

46. Cindy I-Fen Chang, "Out of Chinatown and into the Suburbs: Chinese Americans and the Politics of Cultural Citizenship in Early Cold War America," *American Quarterly* 58, no. 4 (2006), 1068.

47. Wu, "'America's Chinese,'" 391. Wu describes the various ways the State Department engaged in "cultural diplomacy campaigns" abroad using the Voice of America radio program and tours and lectures by prominent Chinese Americans. Although these activities legitimated Chinese Americans' claims to full citizenship, Wu deftly argues that the programs ultimately worked to reproduce Chinese Americans' "racial otherness," marking them as "non-white" and foreign and therefore compromising their actual gains.

48. For information on the ideology of containment and the American family, see Elaine Tyler May's *Homeward Bound: American Families and the Cold War Era* (New York: Basic Books, 1988). Stephanie Coontz examines the myths and realities of the American family in the twentieth century in *The Way We Never Were: American Families and the Nostalgia Trap* (New York: Basic Books, 1993). For information on the rise of consumer culture in the postwar suburbs, see Lizabeth Cohen's *A Consumer's Republic: The Politics of Mass Consumption in Postwar America* (New York: Knopf, 2003). Cindy I-Fen Chang addresses the suburbanization of Chinese Americans and the mitigating effects heterosexual normative families had on "the alterity that racial difference posed to white society." Chang, "Out of Chinatown and into the Suburbs," 1068.

49. Shah, *Contagious Divides*, 15. Shah explains that Chinese Americans making claims for citizenship depended on the "performance of normative

Notes to Chapter 3

hygiene and heterosexual family forms" (ibid.) By highlighting "normative" Chinese American families, activists made claims to the full rights of citizenship while also alienating Chinese bachelors and others outside the heteronormative standard.

50. *San Francisco News*, March 20, 1950, quoted in Yu, "From Tents to Federal Projects," 136.

51. Ibid.

52. Once again, the high cost of building in Chinatown delayed the project from moving forward as the Housing Authority had to reject bids that exceeded federal limits: funds appropriated in 1939 and 1941 had been spent on the war. It was not until the federal Housing Act of 1949 was passed that the Housing Authority could finally restart the project.

53. Don Parson notes that both the Democratic and Republican politicians opposed the measure. The measure passed narrowly to become Article 34 of the California Constitution. Don Parson, *Making a Better World: Public Housing, the Red Scare, and the Direction of Modern Los Angeles* (Minneapolis: University of Minnesota Press, 2005), 104.

54. Shah, *Contagious Divides*, 2.

55. Carey and Co., Inc., "Historic Resource Evaluation: Ping Yuen Housing Development," prepared for the San Francisco Housing Authority, July 26, 2001, 9. (Contact Carey and Co., Inc. for report content at http://careyandco.com/contact.htm.)

56. Arthur J. Dolan Jr., president of the Junior Chamber of Commerce, quoted in Shah (*Contagious Divides*, 237), was representative of an attitude shared by the Nob Hill Protective Association.

57. Shah, *Contagious Divides*, 239. According to Shah, the SFHA hired Mary Mai Chong to work with families affected by demolition. Only low-income families were offered priority housing in SFHA units and the yet-to-be-constructed Ping Yuen development. Two families requested SFHA housing and the other families opted to find housing on their own in Chinatown. The single men were "forced to fend for themselves." In positioning Chinese American nuclear families as "deserving" of federal assistance, Chinatown leaders excluded bachelors and others living in Chinatown (ibid., 240).

58. Wright, "The Evolution of Public Housing Policy and Design," 32, 34.

59. *San Francisco Examiner*, May 17, 1995, 1. Ping Yuen offered many more two-, three-, and four-bedrooms apartments than Valencia Gardens, demonstrating the "design politics" in public housing where, as Lawrence Vale convincingly argues, "social and political preferences are expressed and manipulated through the medium of design." Lawrence Vale, *Purging the*

Poorest: Public Housing and the Design Politics of Twice-Cleared Communities (Chicago: University of Chicago Press, 2013), 30.

60. Wright, "The Evolution of Public Housing Policy and Design," 32, 34. The completion of the six-story, high-density apartments aligned with current trends in public housing construction that partly resulted from provisions of the 1949 Housing Act stressing urban redevelopment to revive blighted areas in central cities.

61. SFHA Commission Minutes, April 18, 1941. Commissioner Alice Griffith worked with the Chinese Advisory Committee on the name selection process. SFHA Commission Minutes, May 8, 1941.

62. SFHA Commission Minutes, January 15, 1942.

63. With its prominent location on 2.6 acres near the center of the district, the design of Ping Yuen played a pivotal role in maintaining the "oriental" style that emerged after the earthquake and fire of 1906. As entrepreneurs in Chinatown began to rebuild, they incorporated Chinese architectural details to beckon tourists and to ward off "the constant threat of removal and annihilation of Chinatown by the Board of Supervisors and other anti-Chinese forces." Philip Choy and Christopher Yip, *A Historical and Architectural Guide to San Francisco's Chinatown* (San Francisco: Chinatown Neighborhood Improvement and Resource Center, 1981), 25. Led by Look Tin Eli, who saw the potential of appealing to the Anglo market, many business owners in the area rebuilt structures with "oriental flavor," including pagoda-like roofs, dragons for ornamentation, and other details (none of which, ironically, were found in the rural areas of southern China where most of Chinatown's immigrants came from). For more information on Look Tin Eli and his efforts to rebuild Chinatown as a tourist attraction, see Christopher L. Yip's "The Impact of the Social-Historical Context on Chinese American Settlement," in *The Chinese American Experience*, ed. Genny Lim, 140–45. Between 1920 and 1940, Chinatown emerged as a major tourist destination within the city. A year before Ping Yuen opened, George K. Jue, former president of the Chinese Chamber of Commerce, summed up the importance of tourism to the district: "Chinatown is the number one tourist attraction in San Francisco. This trade brings to the city a total of over fifty millions [sic] of dollars every year. . . . The future, as in the past and present, depends primarily on continued tourist trade; and conversely, the tourist trade depends upon Chinatown, its number one attraction in San Francisco." George K. Jue, "Chinatown—Its History, Its People, Its Importance," lecture in the series "Know Your San Francisco," offered by Marina Adult School in cooperation with the San Francisco Junior Chamber of Commerce, Bancroft Library, University of California–Berkeley.

64. Shah, *Contagious Divides*, 2.

Notes to Chapter 3

65. Ibid., 2. Chinese American activists had successfully lobbied the Public Health Department for a neighborhood health center, which opened in 1934 on Powell Street. The center provided TB tests and immunizations for district residents.

66. SFHA Commission Minutes, September 26, 1940. The issue of the health center did not come up again until 1949 (SFHA Commission Minutes, August 18, 1949). According to the SFHA Commission Minutes from October 2, 1952, the Health Department paid $80 a month to rent the space in Ping Yuen. In 1956, the SFHA leased additional space to the Health Department and raised the rent to $300 a month (SFHA Commission Minutes, September 16, 1956). For more information on the strategies employed by Chinatown social workers, activists, and journalists in the 1930s to improve the Chinatown district by claiming their right to governmental resources, see Shah, *Contagious Divides*, 227.

67. SFHA Commission Minutes, June 20, 1946.

68. Ibid.

69. *San Francisco Chinatown* (San Francisco: San Francisco Convention and Visitors Bureau, 1963). Ping Yuen is listed under "Chinatown Points of Interest," number 28, Ping Yuen Housing Projects. Gates like the replica placed in front of the Central Ping Yuen building were traditionally used in China to commemorate heroic events. According to the Housing Authority, the replica they commissioned was the first one built in the United States. "Chinatown's Ping Yuen Dedication Today," *San Francisco Chronicle*, October 21, 1951.

70. Yu, "A History of San Francisco Chinatown Housing," 105. According to Shah, only two out of the forty-one families displaced by demolition requested housing from the SFHA. Shah, *Contagious Divides*, 240.

71. Housing Authority of the City and County of San Francisco, *Fourteenth Annual Report* (San Francisco: The Housing Authority, 1952).

72. Watson Low, interview by the author, in a group interview that also included Lee Chan, Sui Ying Tsang, Nghiep Ky Mao, and other tenants involved with PYRIA, tape recording, San Francisco, May 2003; hereafter cited as interview by author with PYRIA members, May 19, 2003. All interviews with Ping Yuen tenants were conducted in English and Chinese. Angela Chu, an employee from the Chinatown Community Development Corporation (CDC), a nonprofit that works closely with PYRIA, served as a translator when needed, translating my questions and occasionally translating the tenants' answers. Angela had worked with the tenants' association for several years and had earned the trust of the tenants interviewed. As noted later in this chapter, the tenants' association had a seat on the Chinatown CDC board

and close ties to the nonprofit. All direct quotes are given in English unless otherwise noted.

73. Chang Jok Lee, interview by the author, tape recording, San Francisco, June 2008.

74. Martin Snipper, *A Survey of Art Work in the City and County of San Francisco* (San Francisco: San Francisco Art Commission, 1975), 325. The mural was made of egg tempera painted on a prepared panel that was 17½′ × 4½′. Artist James Leong was born in 1928 and studied at the California College of Arts and Crafts. He also painted murals for the Chung Mei Home for Boys in El Cerrito. According to the SFHA Commission Minutes from July 19, 1952, the commissioners agreed with Commissioner Jung's recommendation that the Dennis Kearney section be eliminated and replaced with "something of a more constructive nature with regard to the Chinese people."

75. SFHA Commission Minutes, July 19, 1952.

76. According to James Leong, the mural idea originated with prominent Chinatown businessman H. K. Wong, who was "convinced that a mural depicting the history of the Chinese in America would help educate the general public, and the Chinatown community." *James Leong: Confronting My Roots: The Artist Reflects on His Life and Art* (San Francisco: Chinese Historical Society of American Museum, 2006), 7–8. The mural was moved to the recreation room in Ping Yuen East in 1978. Leong states that it stayed there until the late 1990s, when it was moved to the Chinese Historical Society. It now has a permanent home in the Wells Fargo Learning Center of the Chinese Historical Society (ibid.).

77. Quote from Chalsa M. Loo, *Chinatown: Most Time, Hard Time* (New York: Prager, 1991), 60. China's alliance with the United States during World War II resulted in the easing of racial hostilities and the end of discriminatory laws. These changes, along with the U.S. Supreme Court's 1948 decision declaring restrictive covenants unenforceable, afforded some Chinatown residents the chance to leave the ethnic enclave. Chalsa M. Loo explains that these shifts altered the meaning of Chinese ethnic identity as class lines emerged. Chinese Americans with better incomes moved into adjoining or outlying areas, such as the Richmond District. Thus, even as Chinatown remained the "homebase for the majority of San Francisco Chinese," it was no longer the exclusive location of Chinese residency" (60). Yet as Chinatown residents began moving out, a new influx of immigrants came in, responding to the passage of the McCarran-Walter Act, which admitted 27,502 Chinese immigrants between 1951 and 1960. Ensuing legislation had a further impact on Chinatown. A decade after the McCarran Act, John F. Kennedy used a presidential directive to permit Hong Kong refugees to enter the United

States, swelling the number of immigrants to 15,000 by 1966. The 1959 repeal of the Alien Land Law and the 1965 Immigration Act (which abolished the 1943 quota that allowed in 105 Chinese per year and increased the quota to 20,000 people per year) further altered the social and economic landscape of Chinatown. As Chinese Americans began to own property in Chinatown, more Chinese Americans moved out of the district, and an influx of 20,000 immigrants from countries across Asia began immigrating to the United States, with many landing in San Francisco. As a result, the population of Chinatown increased to 31,000 in 1960. The movement of Chinese Americans out of Chinatown, with some living in adjacent areas, spurred the growth of the district from 30 city blocks in 1940 to 224 city blocks in 1970, leading the Department of City Planning to designate core, residential, and expanded areas of Chinatown in 1970 (Loo, *Chinatown*, 51).

78. The federal government dismantled segregationist housing policies starting in 1948 with the *Shelley v. Kraemer* decision and culminating in the 1968 passage of the Fair Housing Act. Nonetheless, scholars have argued that "these policies at the federal level did little to reverse the high levels of housing segregation and ghettoization established during the first half of the twentieth century." Theresa Mah, "The Limits of Democracy in the Suburbs: Constructing the Middle Class through Residential Exclusion," in *The Middling Sorts: Explorations in the History of the American Middle Class*, ed. Burton J. Bledstein and Robert D. Johnston (New York: Routledge, 2001), 260. As Arnold Hirsch and Thomas Sugrue have demonstrated, white homeowners, many barely on the cusp of the middle class, defended the racial homogeneity of their neighborhoods through neighborhood improvement associations, homeowners' associations, and in some cases organized grassroots violence. See Arnold Hirsch, *Making a Second Ghetto: Race and Housing in Chicago, 1940–1960* (Chicago: University of Chicago Press, 1983); Mah, "The Limits of Democracy in the Suburbs"; and Thomas Sugrue, *The Origins of the Urban Crisis* (Princeton, N.J.: Princeton University Press, 1996).

79. Chang, "Out of Chinatown and into the Suburbs," 1082. Information about the treatment of the white owners by their neighborhood and general information on the Sheng case come from Mah, "The Limits of Democracy in the Suburbs," 258. Both pieces discuss the Sheng case and provide insights into the rhetoric of the Cold War and the practice of exclusion.

80. "South S.F. Area Votes to Exclude a Chinese Family," *San Francisco Chronicle*, February 17, 1952, quoted in Mah, "The Limits of Democracy in the Suburbs," 259. Mah explains that the local, national, and international press covered the story.

81. Ibid.

Notes to Chapter 3

82. Robert Lee, "Christian Ethics and Race Relations: A Community Case Study" (master's thesis, Pacific School of Religion, 1952), 21, 67, 69, quoted in Mah, "The Limits of Democracy in the Suburbs," 265.

83. Loo, *Chinatown*, 51. Immigration from other Asian countries contributed to the population increase in Chinatown as well.

84. The United States Housing Authority was created in 1937 and later renamed as the Public Housing Administration (PHA). In 1965, Congress passed a Housing Act establishing the U.S. Department of Housing and Urban Development (HUD), which replaced the PHA.

85. SFHA Commission Minutes, August 21, 1958.

86. The SFHA Commission Minutes list several instances where replicas were given out to high-level visitors. For example, the September 17, 1953, minutes record the receipt of a thank-you note from the Housing and Home Finance Agency administrator Albert M. Cole for the "miniature Ping Yuen Gate" sent to him after he visited the city.

87. Ibid.

88. Housing Authority of the City and County of San Francisco, *Annual Report of 1959* (San Francisco: The Housing Authority, 1959), 1.

89. "Chinatown Apartment Dedication," *San Francisco Chronicle*, October 29, 1961. The promotion of the project started in 1960 with the ground breaking. The Queen of Chinatown, USA, and "her court of beautiful girls" along with Mayor Christopher and "representatives of every organization in Chinatown" attended the formal ground breaking for Ping Yuen North (also called the Ping Yuen Annex). Firecrackers were set off to scare away evil spirits. Housing Authority of the City and County of San Francisco, *The Road to the Golden Age: A Report on the First Twenty Years of Operations, 1940 to 1960* (San Francisco: The Housing Authority, 1960), 13. The dedication for Ping Yuen North drew a crowd of 500 for the celebration, which included the traditional Chinese firecracker dance. "A Dedication at Ping Yuen North," *San Francisco Chronicle*, October 30, 1961.

90. SFHA, *Annual Report of 1959*, 1.

91. Ibid.

92. The U.S. Supreme Court refused to hear the case. This action upheld the California Supreme Court's decision overturning the neighborhood pattern policy in *Banks v. The Housing Authority of San Francisco*. This case is fully examined in chapter 4.

93. Brooks, *Alien Neighbors, Foreign Friends*, 225.

94. Warren Hinckle, "A Negro Takes on Chinese Housing," *San Francisco Chronicle*, June 7, 1963.

95. Ibid.

96. Ibid.

97. "'Open Housing' Proposal for Chinatown Explained," *San Francisco Chronicle*, June 11, 1963.

98. "A Specious Show of Integration," *San Francisco Chronicle*, June 10, 1963.

99. The cartoon also evokes Bill Hudson's galvanizing and widely circulated photo taken a month before in Birmingham, Alabama. In the disturbing image, an African American youth protesting peacefully is attacked by a police dog on a leash. Foster Hailey, "Dogs and Hoses Repulse Negroes at Birmingham," *The New York Times*, May 4, 1963.

100. Dragons symbolize Chinese nationalism. According to Yong Chen, the dragon was a divine symbol of the Chinese nation in Chinese mythology and folklore and the paramount image of the emperor's power centuries before it appeared on the first Chinese national flag. It remained a powerful cultural symbol among Chinese Americans, he explains, who believed it protected the dead (Chen, *Chinese San Francisco*, 129).

101. Cartoon, *San Francisco Chronicle*, June 10, 1963.

102. The big four projects were Sunnydale, Hunters Point, Alice Griffith, and Potrero, three of which were located in the southeast part of San Francisco away from the jobs, transportation, and other amenities in the city center. The Housing Authority passed a resolution in 1961 celebrating Ping Yuen's "unequalled rent record" and paying tribute to Anna Lee, a beloved project manager, for her decade of contributions to the project (SFHA Commission Minutes, August 17, 1961).

103. John Baranski, "Something to Help Themselves: Tenant Organizing in San Francisco's Public Housing, 1965–1975," *Journal of Urban History* 33, no. 3 (2007), 423–24.

104. James Lee, "The Grassroot [sic] Program in San Francisco's Chinatown Public Housing Projects: 'The Ping Yuen Residents Improvement Association'" (paper for Mr. Lewin, Political Science 140, February 1967, University of California, Berkeley), Asian American Studies Collection, Ethnic Studies Library, University of California–Berkeley.

105. Nayan Shah argues that middle-class Chinese American reformers successfully pushed for public housing by demonstrating the worthiness and needs of Chinese American families; the large number of bachelors in Chinatown were left out of the push for public housing as activists focused on housing "deserving" families. See chapter 9, "Reforming Chinatown," in Shah's *Contagious Divides*.

Notes to Chapter 3

106. Chang Jok Lee, interview by the author, 2008. Mrs. Lee joined PYRIA when the organization was formed. She stopped participating for a while after her daughter, Teresa, was born, and returned to the association in 1978.

107. SFHA Commission Minutes, September 1, 1966. The minutes state that Larry Jack Wong and Father Joseph Wong, officers of the Chinatown–North Beach Area EOC office, had written letters on behalf of the Ping Yuen Residents Improvement Association. Over time the minutes clearly demonstrate that PYRIA officers relied less on EOC workers for assistance. PYRIA members stood up for themselves, attending Housing Commission meetings and asking to speak on behalf of the tenants.

108. James Lee, "The Grassroot Program in San Francisco's Chinatown Public Housing Projects," 7.

109. This speech in its entirety appears in the appendix of James Lee's paper ("The Grassroot Program in San Francisco's Chinatown Public Housing Projects"). He cites it as Henry Chan's speech. Mrs. Wong's first name is not cited.

110. SFHA Commission Minutes, November 3, 1966.

111. At the November 3, 1966, meeting, Henry Chan presented a petition in an effort to expedite the housing commissioners' decision to seek funds for renovation of the laundry into a meeting space. The Housing Authority submitted a request for renovation funds to the Housing Assistance Administration (HAA) in November 1966. In response, the HAA in January 1967 refused to authorize additional expenditures for a meeting room on the grounds that "this type of facility . . . should have been included in the original Development program" (SFHA Commission Minutes, November 3, 1966 and January 5, 1967). Working on behalf of the tenants, the Housing Authority dispatched a letter back to the HAA pointing out that "social services has changed considerably" since Ping Yuen was built and that tenants' groups did not exist in 1951 in Chinatown or elsewhere. The executive director reiterated the Housing Authority's $10,623 request for "a tenant activities space at Ping Yuen North" (SFHA Commission Minutes, January 5, 1967). The HAA denied the request for funds a second time, basing its decision on the "current local inventory of off-site meeting space in the neighborhood which is still considered adequate, and the current usage and continuing need for the laundry space by tenants" (ibid.). The Housing Authority continued trying to find funds without success. After failing to win support or funds from the HAA, the Housing Authority alerted the PYRIA leadership that it did not have the funds to provide a meeting space. Refusing to give up, and demonstrating the importance of an organizational headquarters and meeting space to the continued growth and strength of their nascent tenants' association, PYRIA and

the EOC informed the Housing Authority that "the local community would like to embark on a program of raising monies needed" for the space. Although there was seemingly no lack of support for a meeting space for PYRIA, the funds were not raised (SFHA Commission Minutes, March 2, 1967).

112. SFHA Commission Minutes, January 30, 1969.

113. Rent strikes began to occur with frequency in American cities in the 1960s and 1970s as tenants and organizers became galvanized by the civil rights movement and frustrated by the problems of urban decay, rising rents, and the decline in living spaces for low-income tenants. Tenant unions formed in cities across the nation as housing became perceived not as "just another problem" but rather as "a right denied to some and abused by others." Stephen Burghardt, ed., *Tenants and the Urban Housing Crisis* (Dexter, MI: The New Press, 1972), 16. In 1969, tenant organizers formed the NTO, the National Tenants Organization, which had forty local affiliates who played a large role in public housing projects. From the widely publicized public housing rent strike in St. Louis in 1969 and 1970, put on with the aid of the NTO, to lesser-known rent strikes led solely by public housing tenants at the East Park Manor project in Muskegon Heights, Michigan, in 1967 and 1968, public housing residents, like other low-income tenants in run-down housing in the private market, agitated for improvements in their living environment. For more information on the rise of tenant activism in public housing and in the private market see Burghardt, *Tenants and the Urban Housing Crisis*. For specific information on the East Manor tenants' rent strike, see George V. Neagu, "Tenant Power in Public Housing—The East Park Manor Rent Strike," in Burghardt's *Tenants and the Urban Housing Crisis*, 35–46.

114. Shah, *Contagious Divides*, 245.

115. Larry Solomon, *Roots of Justice: Stories of Organizing in Communities of Color* (San Francisco: Jossey-Bass, 1988), excerpted as "The Struggle to Save the I-Hotel," http://www.nhi.org/online/issues/107/organize.html. The SFHA tried to buy the property from the Four Seas Corporation. The SFHA sent its proposal to the Board of Supervisors, who rejected it. Mayor Moscone overruled the board and submitted a proposal for the city to purchase the property for $1.3 million dollars, which the tenants would have to pay back within a short period of time. The plan did not materialize. In an interview with the author in June 2008, Chang Jok Lee recalled attending rallies at City Hall when Moscone was mayor.

116. "Mrs. Chang Jok Lee, a Long Time Chinatown Housing Advocate," n.d., from Chinatown CDC miscellaneous files.

117. Chang Jok Lee, in Nancy Diao, "From Homemaker to Housing Advocate: An Interview with Mrs. Chang Jok Lee," originally published in *Making*

Waves (Asian Women United of California, 1989), reprinted in Eleanor Palo Stoller and Rose Campbell Gibson, eds., *Worlds of Difference: Inequality in the Aging Experience* (Boston: Beacon Press, 2000), 155.

118. Chang Jok Lee, interview by the author, 2008.

119. Elderly residents at a run-down hotel owned by the Chinese Six Companies and located at 857 Clay Street held a rent strike for over seven months to protest rent increases and "unlivable conditions." The activists who formed the I-Hotel Citizens Advisory Committee in 1977 continued to fight the move to develop the land for business interests. In 1979, the building was razed and the site was "an unsightly, half-hole in the ground for almost two decades until a mayor's committee worked out the details of constructing a new housing development there." The new International Hotel, developed by the Chinatown Community Development Center, opened in 2005. The sixteen-story building has one hundred affordable units for seniors, honoring the history and activism surrounding the original structure. Kantele Franko, "I-Hotel, 30 Years Later—Manilatown Legacy Honored," *San Francisco Chronicle*, August 4, 2007.

120. In June 1977, tenants at 666 Sacramento Street picketed outside their apartment building to protest a proposed 55 percent rent increase. With the support of the Workers Committee to Fight for the International Hotel, tenants formed an association and made demands ("Chinatown Tenants Launch Rent Strikes, Pickets," *San Francisco Journal*, June 8, 1977). Other landlords in Chinatown raised rents, forcing many elderly residents living on fixed incomes out of their hotel rooms and apartments. Tenants were aided by a citywide rent freeze.

121. Dennis Hayashi, "Ping Yuen Tenants Protest Conditions," *San Francisco Journal*, September 8, 1976.

122. Ibid.

123. Lee Chan, interview by author with PYRIA members, May 19, 2003.

124. The housing commissioners passed Resolution Number 2197 on September 14, 1978, waiving competitive bidding for elevator repairs because of the "serious urgency of this security problem." During the same meeting, the director of housing operations stated that the security controls for the elevators had been ordered, but because they were coming from the East Coast, delivery would take ten to twelve weeks (SFHA Commission Minutes, September 14, 1978).

125. Ibid. According to Carl Williams, the new executive director of the Housing Authority, the SFHA could not "afford to give them round the clock security. It will pose problems with the other ... public housing sites in the

Notes to Chapter 3

city." Marshall Kilduff, "Ping Yuen Rent Strike to Begin," *San Francisco Chronicle*, September 30, 1978.

126. "Ping Yuen Talks of Rent Strike," *San Francisco Chronicle*, September 16, 1978.

127. Kilduff, "Ping Yuen Rent Strike to Begin."

128. I do not have information on the ethnic or racial background of the members. I do know that the increase in immigration sparked a rise in the number of gangs vying for control and increased gang membership. Bill Lee, "Notes Underground," *AsianWeek*, January 1, 1999.

129. Bill Lee, "Notes Underground." According to Lee, kids from East and Central Ping Yuen made up most of the fireworks dealers. It is possible that some of these dealers were also gang members. Lee explains that the gangs forced dealers to pay them a cut of their earnings. Some dealers refused to pay. Lee writes, "those who held out placed the burden on others to come up with the money. Arguments and fistfights broke out among dealers who were friends. The only alternative was to drop out and let the Hock Sair Woey (Chinese Underworld) monopolize the business, but dealers from the projects had to sell off their inventory one way or another to recoup their initial investments." Lee contends that his gang, the Joe Boys, with a membership around 150 to 175, negotiated to protect the project dealers during the Fourth of July period for firework sales. "One evening, the Hock Sair Woey enforcers came to collect their final payoff. Around 8:30 p.m., the Joe Boys faced-off against the Wah Ching and their allies, the Hop Sing Boys, on Pacific Avenue in front of the projects." In a fight that must have scared project residents, "weapons were drawn and gunfire erupted, with gangsters running up and down the street, ducking behind cars and into doorways, blasting at one another" (ibid., 5).

130. In 1995, Pak, director of the Chinese Chamber of Commerce, shared her reflection on the massacre in a *San Francisco Examiner* story. Steven A. Chin, "Police on Alert in Fireworks Turf War, Fear Business Will Drop Like after '77 Chinatown Massacre," *San Francisco Examiner*, July 2, 1995.

131. "Ping Yuen Tenants Starting Rent Strike," *San Francisco Examiner*, September 28, 1978.

132. D. A. Williams, "Civil War in Chinatown," *Newsweek*, September 26, 1977, 39.

133. SFHA Commission Minutes, September 28, 1978. George Lee was elected chairman of PYRIA after his involvement with the 1976 protest.

134. "Ping Yuen Tenants Starting Rent Strike." According to SFHA Commission minutes, the housing commissioners were surprised by the tenants'

Notes to Chapter 3

decision to move ahead with the rent strike and berated the tenant leadership for their failure to continue negotiations. Commissioner Ubalde had reported to the Housing Commission that after meeting with tenants, he felt progress was being made in satisfying their demands for security. He expressed frustration because he and Commissioner Fong, along with staff, "had exceeded themselves in the time and efforts they had put into these meetings [with PYRIA] in view of other meetings cancelled and other matters not attended to." He also noted that Ping Yuen tenants had been told that the Housing Authority had ordered "elevator safety features" and that similar crimes happened throughout the city's projects. He called the letter from PYRIA "a total breach of faith with the Commission, and staff, and with the tenants' agreement" (SFHA Commission Minutes, September 28, 1978). Before PYRIA representatives left the Housing Commission meeting on September 28, Commissioner Booker lectured them on their failure to understand the Housing Authority's position. He explained that the Housing Authority "has 8000 units and 25,000 people to administer to and that the Chinese low income dwellers should meet the authority and its staff halfway" ("Ping Yuen Tenants Starting Rent Strike").

135. "Ping Yuen Tenants on Strike," *San Francisco Journal*, October 4, 1978, 1. The association's efforts likely drew support from other area residents who had picketed against their landlords.

136. "Mrs. Chang Jok Lee, a Long Time Chinatown Housing Advocate." The money collected during the rent strike, which averaged about $100 per household, was put in escrow at the Chinatown Federal Savings and Loan. "Tenants at Ping Yuen Withhold $10,000 in Rent," *San Francisco Chronicle*, October 10, 1978.

137. Watson Low, interview by author with PYRIA members, May 19, 2003.

138. Lester W. Chang, "New Ground Rules Set in Ping Yuen Rent Strike," *EastWest*, November 22, 1978.

139. John Baranski, "Making Public Housing in San Francisco: Liberalism, Social Prejudice, and Social Activism, 1906–1976" (PhD diss., University of California, Santa Barbara, 2004), 432, quoting SFHA Commission Minutes, April 22, 1971.

140. SFHA Commission Minutes, November 16, 1978.

141. SFHA Commission Minutes, December 21, 1978. The resolution stated: "1. The Commission overruled the decision of the Grievance Panel under Section VII (A)1 of the approved Grievance Procedure. 2. The present escrow account be dissolved and immediately returned to the Controller of the Housing Authority. 3. The Housing Authority staff is instructed to continue to intensify their efforts to resolve the problems of security in Ping Yuen as

well as all developments. 4. The Commission and staff are willing to do whatever is financially feasible regarding security problems at Ping Yuen to try and resolve this present disagreement. 5. This resolution become [sic] effective immediately."

142. SFHA Commission Minutes, October 26, 1978.
143. Ibid.
144. Ibid.
145. Chang Jok Lee, interviewed by the author, in a group interview with Chang Jok Lee, Watson Low, and other Ping Yuen tenants involved in PYRIA, tape recording, San Francisco, May 29, 2003.
146. SFHA Commission Minutes, January 11, 1979.
147. Lee Chan, interview by author with PYRIA members, May 19, 2003.
148. "Mrs. Chang Jok Lee, a Long Time Chinatown Housing Advocate."
149. "Compromise and Settlement Agreement," approved by Carl Williams, Executive Director, San Francisco Housing Authority and Connie M. Perry, Legal Counsel (SFHA Commission Minutes, September 18, 1981). The Housing Authority agreed to hire bilingual personnel to field calls in Cantonese during regular office hours. The agreement also stated that bilingual residents who were on call for maintenance and security when the office was closed were entitled to free rent and reimbursement of monthly basic phone charges. The Housing Authority was also charged with maintaining all the units of Ping Yuen "in good working order" and providing inspections once every three months of areas "not contained in individual dwelling units for plumbing, heat, and hot and cold water" to discover patent and latent defects. Finally, the agency committed to put up window bars and install 100-watt bulbs in all exterior lights (the lights had been promised in the first rent strike settlement).
150. "Mrs. Chang Jok Lee, a Long Time Chinatown Housing Advocate." Chang Jok's family lived in Japan.
151. Ibid.
152. Ibid.
153. Ibid.
154. Testifying before the Board of Supervisors in support of rehiring Lee, Low stated that in Ping Yuen, "George Lee has been the most effective resident manager because he knows the tenants well and they respect him. Whenever there is a problem you can rely on Mr. Lee to take care of it for you.... Laying people off in these direct service positions will seriously reduce the quality and type of services provided for tenants." "Watson Low's Testimony at the Board of Supervisor's on February 21, 1985," in the *Ping Yuen Newsletter*, March 1985, Chinatown CDC miscellaneous files, San Francisco.

Notes to Chapter 3

155. Ibid. During his tenure in office, Low had to contend with George Lee advising him on how to run the project. Friction resulted on both sides as Low worked to govern PYRIA in his own way. Despite some tensions between these leaders, Lee eventually backed off and all three residents stayed friends while working in their own ways to improve Ping Yuen. "Comment on Conflict Resolution at the PYRIA Board Meeting," July 1, 1985, Chinatown CDC miscellaneous files.

156. "A Refresher History: The Chinatown Resource Center," *Neighborhood Improvement Update* 10 (Spring 1988), 1, Chinatown CDC miscellaneous files. The CDC is a nonprofit organization concerned with social justice and formed to bring together a range of groups already working to improve Chinatown. My research shows no evidence of links between the organization and business interests.

157. The CDC has assisted PYRIA in the areas of physical improvement, resource development, and residents' services. The CDC supported the Laundromat program in 1984, assisted in securing funding for a Ping Yuen mural, sponsored a graffiti removal day, worked on garden and playground renovations in 1995, painted ten units for senior residents, and sponsored more playground renovations in 1996, among other things. "Ping Yuen Residents Improvement Association and Chinatown Resource Center" (San Francisco: Chinatown Resource Center, n.d.), Chinatown CDC miscellaneous files.

158. Over the years, PYRIA has helped alleviate the ongoing space problem for nonprofit groups by allowing many organizations and agencies to use its facilities. For example, PYRIA sublet space to the Chinatown Coalition for Better Housing, the Economic Opportunity Council, the Veterans Administration, and other groups. Pleased with its achievements and commitment to the larger Chinatown community, PYRIA claimed that its "generosity serves as a model for how encouraging leadership capacity in one organization can benefit an entire community." "Public Housing Tenants" paper describing PYRIA, n.d., Chinatown CDC miscellaneous files.

159. "Ping Yuen Laundromat," write-up from the Chinatown CDC, 1984, Chinatown CDC miscellaneous files. The Housing Authority commissioners passed Resolution Number 2554 on November 10, 1983, approving the lease of the laundry facilities at Ping Yuen to the PYRIA (SFHA Commission Minutes, November 10, 1983).

160. *Ping Yuen Newsletter,* November 1984, 15, Chinatown CDC miscellaneous files.

161. The hours for the laundry rooms were seven days a week, 8 a.m. to 5 p.m. The prices for laundry were the same as when the Housing Authority

ran the facilities: washing was fifty cents per load and drying was twenty-five cents per load. Ibid.

162. "Laundromat Project Update," *Ping Yuen Newsletter*, March 1985, 9. The newsletter reported the level of commitment made by some residents to the community as well as the individualistic impulses that at times impeded the laundry system. Touting the generosity of Mr. Wong, the PYRIA secretary, who "took the janitor job [for the laundries] in spite of low wages" because of his "commitment to public service," the newsletter reprimanded tenants who used the laundry after hours, frustrating Mr. Wong and taking advantage of his leniency. The tenants who "insist on doing laundry past the closing time" ultimately caused Mr. Wong to leave his position as janitor.

163. Minutes of the PYRIA Board, March 14, 1988 and November 8, 1990, San Francisco, Chinatown CDC miscellaneous files. Although the laundry program continued to net a profit after 1987, the PYRIA board and other tenants experienced frustration at the number of times machines broke. At the November 8, 1990, PYRIA meeting, a tenant reported another broken dryer. The machines had been replaced in 1989 with used models and residents had complained that "the machines were always out of order." The board agreed to act by asking the Macke Company for a deduction of costs because of the broken dryer and to make an appointment with the sales manager at Macke. PYRIA's success at managing the laundry may have prompted North Beach Place tenants to ask the Housing Authority for the opportunity to take over management of the laundry at North Beach Place. In October 1993, the Housing Authority signed a Memorandum of Agreement with the North Beach Resident Council "to afford the residents at North Beach the opportunity to manage the laundry facility at the development" (SFHA Commission Minutes, October 14, 1993).

164. Chinatown Community Development Center website, www.chinatowncommunitydevelopmentcenter.org/pages/main.php?pageid=8& pagecategory=2. The main website for the Chinatown CDC is http://www.chinatowncdc.org/.

165. In a *San Francisco Chronicle* article, Gordon Chin explained that the CCHC had met with the full "Ping Yuen tenants association" in November and January. Realizing the intricacies of community ties, Chin stated that "in retrospect, we should have concentrated on the North Ping Yuen tenants." L. A. Chung, "Protest Stalls Chinatown Housing Project," *San Francisco Chronicle*, March 31, 1987.

166. Elaine Herscher, "Chinatown Project/Housing Proposal Angers Neighbors," *San Francisco Chronicle*, March 13, 1987.

Notes to Chapter 3

167. Letter to the Chinatown Community from Tenants of Ping Yuen North, March 19, 1987, Chinatown CDC miscellaneous files, San Francisco.

168. Max Millard, "Senior Housing Plan Sparks Angry Debate," *EastWest*, March 19, 1987.

169. L. A. Chung, "Chinatown Group OKs Disputed Housing," *San Francisco Chronicle*, July 23, 1987. The CCHC agreed to lower the building from five to four stories in response to the tenants' concerns about sunlight reduction. This change reduced the number of units from forty to thirty-one.

170. "Program Profile: Chinatown Community Development Center, San Francisco, California," from *On the Ground with Comprehensive Community Initiatives* (Columbia, Md.: The Enterprise Foundation, 2000).

171. "Ping Yuen Residents Improvement Association and Chinatown Resource Center" (San Francisco: Chinatown Resource Center, n.d.), Chinatown CDC miscellaneous files.

172. Darren Acoba, Joyce Lu, and Tonia Chen were also contributing artists on the mural. I do not have information on Sing Kan Mah, referenced in the mural dedication. Information on the artists and backers is found on the dedication panel of the mural located at Ping Yuen (see Figure 23).

173. Reverend Norman Fong and Angela Chu, interview by author, San Francisco, August 8, 2002.

174. Watson Low, interview by author with PYRIA members, May 19, 2003.

175. Johnny Ng, "Ping Yuen's Construction Was a Long-Fought Battle," 14.

176. PYRIA members, interview by author, May 19, 2003.

177. Watson Low, interview by author with PYRIA members, May 19, 2003.

178. Lee Chan, interview by author with PYRIA members, May 19, 2003.

179. Watson Low, interview by author with PYRIA members, May 19, 2003.

4. "The Best Project in Town"

1. Albert S. Broussard, *Black San Francisco: The Struggle for Racial Equality in the West, 1900–1954* (Lawrence: University Press of Kansas, 1993), 205–6.

2. Affidavits, Mattie Banks and James Charley, 78/180c, NAACP West Coast Regional Office Records, Carton 40, Folder 2, Bancroft Library, University of California–Berkeley.

3. For more information on the ways stereotypes of African Americans have been used against them and the conflation of "moral fitness" and race, see Melissa V. Harris-Perry, *Sister Citizen: Shame, Stereotypes, and Black Women in America* (New Haven, Conn.: Yale University Press, 2011).

Notes to Chapter 4

4. See Broussard, *Black San Francisco*, chapter 11, for information on the numerous Bay Area interracial coalitions and efforts.

5. David Arnason, "'Little Italy' or 'New Chinatown'? The Shifting Boundary between the Italian and Chinese Business Communities of San Francisco's North Beach Neighborhood" (master's thesis, California State University–Hayward, 1989), 3. The settlement of North Beach by Italians occurred in two phases. Between 1850 and 1880, primarily Northern Italians lived in North Beach. After 1880, both Northern and Southern Italian immigrants settled in the area. As a result, regionalism and localism played an important role in North Beach, creating factions and even enclaves in different places. Factionalism ended, however, in 1906, when the earthquake and fire destroyed the district. Many Italians came together to rebuild the area, and as a result, provincialism was reduced to some extent (ibid., 39). The influx of Italian immigrants in North Beach stopped in 1924 because of the passage of the National Origins Act. Around this time, second- and third-generation Italian Americans slowly began moving out of North Beach to the suburbs. This trend accelerated after World War II.

6. According to Richard Dillon, both the *Examiner* and the *Call* praised the "Italian population" for rebuilding the burned Latin Quarter. Dillon, *North Beach: The Italian Heart of San Francisco* (Novato, Calif.: Presidio Press, 1985), 161.

7. Ibid., 4. Dillon notes that the population declined after the mid-1930s as a result of deaths, strict annual immigration quotas after World War II, and the dispersal of Italian Americans throughout the city and the Bay Area.

8. The current church building with its twin spires was constructed in 1924. Coit Tower was constructed in 1933. In 1955, Washington Square Park was laid out, providing another attractive addition to the North Beach neighborhood.

9. Bill Simmons, "Like San Francisco, North Beach Grew Again from the 1906 Flames," *San Francisco Chronicle*, October 12, 1939.

10. Nancy J. Peters, "The Beat Generation and San Francisco's Culture of Dissent," in *Reclaiming San Francisco: History, Politics, and Culture*, ed. James Brook, Chris Carlson, and Nancy J. Peters (San Francisco: City Lights Bookstore, 1998), 205–206. In 1950, Lawrence Ferlinghetti came from Paris to San Francisco, where he met Peter D. Martin. Together they founded City Lights Bookstore in 1953. Allen Ginsburg arrived in North Beach in 1954, where he wrote *Howl*, which City Lights had printed in England because of the content. The poem describes the destruction of the human spirit by America's military–industrial machine "and calls for redemption through the reconciliation of mind and body, affirming human wholeness and holiness" (ibid., 206). *Howl and Other Poems* garnered public attention when a copy was seized

Notes to Chapter 4

by U.S. Customs in March 1957, setting off a court battle involving the American Civil Liberties Union; for more details, see ibid., 205–208. The Beats produced writings, held readings, and put together multimedia events in collaboration with assemblage artists. The work of these writers and their challenge to the status quo, the literary establishment, and postwar mass society and consumption, coupled with their "bohemian" lifestyles, sparked national intrigue and, for some, outrage, as Jack Kerouac's definition of Beat—"poor, down and out, dead-beat, on the bum, sad, and sleeping in subways"—was appropriated as a label for a disaffected, rebellious generation, a counter to American culture. Jack Kerouac, "The Origins of the Beat Generation," in *Marginal Manners: The Variants of Bohemia,* ed. Fredrick J. Hoffman, 1962, reprinted in *Heritage of American Literature: Civil War to the Present,* ed. James E. Miller Jr. (New York: Harcourt Bruce Jovanovich, 1991), 2054.

11. Peters, "The Beat Generation and San Francisco's Culture of Dissent," 205–6.

12. Bonnie Parker and Gary Smart, "Whatever Happened to Topless," *San Francisco Business,* July 1968, 42. Parker and Smart argue that the "death of topless" was a result of market overexposure and customers' demand for something new. They also reported that some clubs tried to revive the business by offering customers "bottomless" and "all nude scene" shows.

13. Brochure, "San Francisco's North Beach" (San Francisco: San Francisco Convention and Visitors Bureau, 1968), 2.

14. The 1965 Immigration and Naturalization Act replaced the restrictive national origins system in place since 1924 with a quota and preference system for immigrants. Each country in the Eastern Hemisphere received a quota of 20,000. Children under 21, spouses, and parents of U.S. citizens were exempt from the quotas. This new immigration policy increased the number of Asian immigrants in the United States.

15. Nancy Dooley, "A Second Look: Italian Renaissance in North Beach," *San Francisco Examiner,* July 16, 1984. For more on the changes in North Beach related to increased rents, see Richard DeLeon, "North Beach in Transition: A Study of Business Survival and Neighborhood Preservation" (San Francisco: Public Research Institute, San Francisco State University, June 1986). For changes in the business community resulting from demographic shifts, see Arnason, "'Little Italy' or 'New Chinatown'?"

16. Alma Lark, Bee Harper, Paula Clark, Ken Nim, and another active North Beach Place resident who asked for anonymity, interview by author, tape recording, San Francisco, August 2002; hereafter cited as North Beach Place tenants interview, 2002.

Notes to Chapter 4

17. SFHA Commission Minutes, September 22, 1938. Describing the site, a 1949 *San Francisco Chronicle* article noted that "razing of the present buildings—warehouses for the most part," would get under way shortly ("North Beach Place to Be Built by 1952," *San Francisco Chronicle*, October 16, 1949). Three photographs taken in 1950 of the site between Columbus, Bay, and Mason prior to demolition depict several run-down warehouses. Site of North Beach Place Housing Project Prior to Construction (photo AAD-6089), April 10, 1950 (photo AAD-6090), and ca. 1950 (photo AAD-6091), S.F. Housing Projects—North Beach file, San Francisco Historical Photograph Collection, San Francisco Public Library, http://sflib1.sfpl.org.

18. SFHA Commission Minutes, June 19, 1941. There is no mention in the SFHA Commission minutes or the *San Francisco Chronicle* and *San Francisco Examiner* of opposition to the development of North Beach Place.

19. Ibid.

20. See San Francisco Planning Department, "North Beach HOPE VI Housing Redevelopment: Final Environmental Impact Report," May 17, 2001, 36, San Francisco Public Library. Henry Gutterson, noted for his extensive residential designs throughout the Bay Area, was part of the design team for the Panama Pacific Exposition and served as staff architect for the city of Oakland early in his career. In 1916, he opened his own architectural firm in San Francisco. He designed several Christian Science churches, the Salem Lutheran Home in Oakland, and the Vedanta Society Meeting Hall in Berkeley. He also served in many urban planning and development organizations, including the Berkeley Planning Commission, the design committee for the San Francisco Civic Center, and others. Ernest Born worked under Bay Area architect John Galen Howard and for the firm Gehron and Ross in New York City before settling in the Bay Area in the 1930s. Born's other commissions included the renovation of the Greek Theatre at the University of California–Berkeley, two Stanford University campus buildings, and the design standards for thirty-three BART stations. He became a full-time professor at UC Berkeley's School of Architecture in 1952. He also served on the San Francisco Art Commission in the 1940s and 1960s and was the director of the San Francisco Art Association between 1947 and 1951. See the profiles of Born and Gutterson at the Environmental Design Archives, University of California–Berkeley, http://www.ced.berkeley.edu/cedarchives/profiles/born.htm and http://www.ced.berkeley.edu/cedarchives/profiles/gutterson.htm. Thomas Church was a landscape architect and garden designer known as the "author and pioneer of 'California Style,' using asymmetrical plans, raised planting beds, sitting walls and timber decks." Church designed the El Novillero garden at Sonoma (1947–49) and wrote *Gardens for People* in 1955. Born in

Notes to Chapter 4

Boston and educated at Harvard and Berkeley, Church did most of his work in private gardens. His other work included campus plans for the Universities of California (at Berkeley) and Stanford and the headquarters of *Sunset* magazine. See "Thomas Church: A Biography from the Garden and Landscape Guide," http://www.gardenvisit.com/biography/thomas_church#ixzz 0dYVa80Eh.

21. Gwendolyn Wright, "The Evolution of Public Housing Policy and Design in the San Francisco-Bay Area" (part of PhD Qualifying Exam, College of Environmental Design, Department of Architecture, University of California–Berkeley, November 22, 1976), 34.

22. From the design calling for bocce ball courts—a European game brought to the United States by Italian immigrants—to the selection of Italian shrubs, the architects made an effort to create a space that would appeal to the surrounding community. These choices, however, reflected a view of the district that quickly proved static as Italian Americans moved to the suburbs in droves following World War II. Likewise, these regional additions reflected the Housing Authority's "neighborhood pattern policy" in the expectation that project residents would be Italian American or Italian or European immigrant families. The Housing Authority proudly described the Mediterranean and "Old World" feeling of North Beach Place in its 1951 annual report. According to a 1945 article in *Architect and Engineer*, "the architects have adapted the project to the North Beach area by including a Bocci court." John S. Bolles, "North Beach Place Housing Project—San Francisco," *Architect and Engineer*, July 1945, 16. I have not been able to establish whether the courts were put in when the project was constructed. Nonetheless, the architects' choice to include a bocce ball court demonstrates an attention to the neighborhood's culture.

23. Housing Authority of the City and County of San Francisco, *Fourteenth Annual Report* (San Francisco: The Housing Authority, 1952), 2.

24. Ibid., 1.

25. "New Housing Project Opens," *San Francisco Chronicle*, September 14, 1952. The maximum income for tenants ranged from $180 to $249, depending on the number of people in a family. "North Beach Place to Be Built by 1952," *San Francisco Chronicle*, October 16, 1949.

26. As Jordan Luttrell explains, the public housing program placed the primary responsibility of administering low-rent housing in the hands of local housing authorities. Local housing authorities, including the SFHA, "tended to repeat the segregated living patterns of communities in which they were constructed, since site selection involved placing one project in the Negro neighborhood and one in the white neighborhood." Jordan D. Luttrell,

"The Public Housing Administration and Discrimination in Federally Assisted Low-Rent Housing," *Michigan Law Review* 64, no. 5 (1966), 875. Luttrell criticized the federal agency for failing to actively ban segregation in public housing in the wake of Executive Order 11063 in 1962, which stated that federal assistance to segregated housing was "unfair, unjust, and inconsistent with the public policy of the US" (quoted in ibid., 878). Two years later, in 1964, Title VI of the Civil Rights Act banned discrimination in any program receiving federal financial assistance.

27. SFHA Commission Minutes, May 14, 1942.

28. Deirdre L. Sullivan, "'Letting down the Bars': Race, Space, and Democracy in San Francisco, 1936–1964" (PhD diss., University of Pennsylvania, 2003), 14–15. According to Albert Broussard's *Black San Francisco*, World War II was a "demographic watershed"; the black population increased by 600 percent between 1940 and 1945 (4, 133). Information on the bracero program and immigration from El Salvador and Nicaragua cited from Charles Wollengberg, *Golden Gate Metropolis: Perspectives on Bay Area History* (Berkeley: Institute of Governmental Studies, University of California, 1985).

29. Carolyn Hoecker Luedtke, "On the Frontier of Change: A Legal History of the San Francisco Civil Rights Movement, 1944–1970," *Temple Political and Civil Rights Law Review* 10, no. 1 (2000), 29. Banks' redlining practices as well as real estate agents' blockbusting strategies contributed to deepening residential segregation as many white homeowners feared a decrease in property values if nonwhites moved into the neighborhood. See, for example, Douglas Massey and Nancy Denton, *American Apartheid: Segregation and the Making of the Underclass* (Cambridge, Mass.: Harvard University Press, 1993); and Antero Pietila, *Not in My Neighborhood: How Bigotry Shaped a Great American City* (Chicago: Ivan R. Dee, 2010).

30. Sullivan, "'Letting down the Bars,'" 15. As over 5,000 Japanese Americans, many living in the Fillmore District, "were lifted from the city's midst" in 1941, African Americans moved into the available space "for housing and living" and extended the area of settlement another six blocks downtown. A June 1943 survey of the Fillmore District by the San Francisco Department of Health and Sanitation showed that there were 27,379 whites, 9,319 African Americans, and 342 "persons of other racial extraction" in the area. Charles Johnson, "The Negro War Worker in San Francisco" (San Francisco: San Francisco Department of Health and Sanitation, 1944), 3.

31. Sara Jenkins to Albert Evers, January 2, 1940, and Albert Evers to Sara Jenkins, January 3, 1940, NAACP Papers, Library of Congress, Part II, C 19, cited in Sullivan, "'Letting down the Bars,'" 43.

32. Ibid.

Notes to Chapter 4

33. "S.F. Housing Board Keeps Racial Policy," *San Francisco Chronicle*, October 28, 1949.

34. Federal law required both the city (in San Francisco represented by the Board of Supervisors) and the Housing Authority to sign and submit a "Cooperation Agreement" in order to receive funds for new pubic housing units ("Segregation Ban in New S.F. Housing," *San Francisco Chronicle*, November 9, 1949). The amendment was suggested by Edward Howden, the executive director of the Council for Civic Unity, and drafted by Supervisor Christopher George. For more details, see "Segregation and S.F. Housing," *San Francisco Chronicle*, January 15, 1950.

35. "Segregation and S.F. Housing." Beard, in further defense of the Housing Authority's policy, stated that the SFHA borrowed the plan from Philadelphia.

36. "Housing Policy Attack," *San Francisco Chronicle*, January 11, 1950.

37. Ibid.

38. "Housing Segregation," *San Francisco Chronicle*, February 17, 1950.

39. "Housing Officials Agree to Nonsegregation in Projects," *San Francisco Chronicle*, February 21, 1950.

40. "S.F. Segregation Loses Again," *San Francisco Chronicle*, October 23, 1953.

41. Luedtke, "On the Frontier of Change," 1. The struggle for civil rights in San Francisco, as seen through the lens of public housing, demonstrates the importance of understanding local struggles across the country and their impact on national ones. As Jeanne F. Theoharis and Komozi Woodard demonstrate in their important collection, *Freedom North: Black Freedom Struggles outside the South, 1940–1980* (New York: Palgrave MacMillan, 2003), understanding the contours of the movement in different regions across the country reshapes our collective understanding and chronology of the struggle for civil rights in the United States.

42. "Court Acts on Housing Race Issue," *San Francisco Chronicle*, September 4, 1952. The three applicants listed on the petition were Mattie Banks, Tobbie Cain, and James Charley. The NAACP attorneys argued that these applicants had higher qualifications for North Beach Place than "many persons or ethnic groups whom the Housing Authority has certified for occupancy." They claimed that Mrs. Banks was the second person in line on the first day applications were taken. (Her husband was in the navy, but as Mrs. Banks's affidavit later showed, they were separated.) Cain was a World War II army veteran. I do not have other information on Tobbie Cain.

43. "The Housing Authority Testifies: Excerpts from Reporter's Transcript on Appeal from a Judgment of Superior Court of the State of California, in

280

Notes to Chapter 4

and for the City and County of San Francisco, Hon. Melyn Cronin, Judge. Mattie Banks and James Charley, Jr. on Behalf of Themselves and Other Similarly Situated, Respondents, vs Housing Authority of the City and County of San Francisco," Bancroft Library, University of California–Berkeley.

44. For an analysis of racial inequality in federal programs, see Ira Katznelson, *When Affirmative Action Was White: An Untold History of Racial Inequality in Twentieth-Century America* (New York: Norton, 2005).

45. "Hearing on Jim Crow Housing Issue," *San Francisco Chronicle*, October 9, 1952. The order of priority for tenants, according to the *Banks v. The Housing Authority of San Francisco* report, was as follows: first preference to families displaced by the project; next, families of disabled veterans, followed by veterans and servicemen; and then low-income families not displaced by the project. The record states that when "other factors are equal, families of the lowest income and in greatest need of better housing are preferred." All tenants accepted to live in public housing had to be residents of San Francisco. *Banks v. The Housing Authority of San Francisco, Pacific Reporter*, 2nd series, 120 Cal. App., 2dI, p. 671.

46. Letter to the editor from Rosinda Holmes, *San Francisco Chronicle*, September 10, 1952.

47. Letter to the editor from M. Colton, *San Francisco Chronicle*, September 18, 1952.

48. Luedtke, "On the Frontier of Change," 2.

49. "Bias Charged to S.F. Housing Chiefs," *San Francisco Chronicle*, November 9, 1952.

50. Bernard Taper, "Housing Agency Urged to Give up Segregation," *San Francisco Chronicle*, June 7, 1953.

51. "Court Voids S.F. Policy on Housing," *San Francisco Chronicle*, August 27, 1953.

52. Luedtke, "On the Frontier of Change," 7.

53. Richard Reinhardt, "S.F. Segregation in Housing to End," *San Francisco Chronicle*, May 25, 1954. On May 27, 1954, the San Francisco Housing Authority Commission passed Resolution Number 978, repealing the neighborhood pattern policy plan established under Resolution 287.

54. Luedtke, "On the Frontier of Change," 7. Title VIII of the Civil Rights Act of 1968, the Fair Housing Act, "prohibits discrimination in the sale, rental, and financing of dwellings, and in other housing-related transactions, based on race, color, national origin, religion, sex, familial status (including children under the age of 18 living with parents or legal custodians, pregnant women, and people securing custody of children under the age of 18),

Notes to Chapter 4

and handicap [disability]." See www.hud.gov/offices/fheo/FHLaws/index.cfm.

55. Alma Lark, interview by the author, tape recording, San Francisco, 2002. In the interview, Lark said she had to sue the Housing Authority to get into North Beach Place. Lark was not listed in the suit against the Housing Authority. Nonetheless, she did retain Terry Francois, one of the NAACP lead attorneys in the suit, as her lawyer. Whether she was directly involved in the case against the Housing Authority or not, it is clear that she wanted to live at North Beach Place and was able to do so because of the NAACP's victory over the Housing Authority.

56. Nina Siegal, "Rebuilding Trust: As S.F. 'Revitalizes' the North Beach Public-Housing Project Tenants Prepare to Fight," *San Francisco Bay Guardian*, November 27, 1996.

57. Alma Lark, interview by the author, 2002.

58. North Beach Place tenants interview, 2002.

59. There were other Asians moving into North Beach in the 1960s, but the majority of newcomers to North Beach were Americans of Chinese descent.

60. North Beach Place tenants interview, 2002. The Brooke Amendment, enacted in 1969, required public housing residents to pay 25 percent of their income for rent (this figure was later raised to 30 percent). For the working class, this policy resulted in a rent hike with each pay increase they received. This policy was followed by others in the 1970s and 1980s that mandated that local public housing authorities give admission preference to the poorest of the poor.

61. SFHA Commission Minutes, December 3, 1964.

62. Ibid. The observation that this was the first time on record that a tenant organization member addressed the Housing Commission is from John Baranski, "Making Public Housing in San Francisco: Liberalism, Social Prejudice, and Social Activism, 1906–1976" (PhD diss., University of California–Santa Barbara, 2004), 308.

63. SFHA Commission Minutes, March 27, 1969. The meeting minutes noted that the organization had a membership of sixty-five of the sixty-eight Chinese families in residence "plus other non-Chinese resident families."

64. Ibid. I do not know if and when the NBPCIA disbanded. I have no evidence suggesting that the NBPCIA interacted with PYRIA. Nonetheless, it is conceivable that members of the NBPCIA supported PYRIA's rent strike.

65. The Cost Plus World Market Store opened in 1956 across from the project on Bay Street.

66. For more information on San Francisco's urban redevelopment process and the controversy surrounding the construction of Yerba Buena Plaza, see

Chester Hartman's *City for Sale: The Transformation of San Francisco* (Berkeley: University of California Press, 2002).

67. Alma Lark, interview by the author, 2002. The Marriott opened in 1984, and the Hyatt opened in 1990.

68. Information on Pier 39 can be found on the Fisherman's Wharf Merchants Association website, http://www.fishermanswharf.org/Pier39.htm.

69. North Beach Place tenants interview, 2002.

70. Birney Jarvis, "Crackdown on Teenage Crime in Housing Project," *San Francisco Chronicle*, July 18, 1978.

71. SFHA Commission Minutes, January 11, 1979.

72. Ibid. In response to the Christmas tree burning incident, Commissioner Ubalde toured North Beach Place and visited with some residents. He reported to the commission that "there was an attitude of fear and apprehension over lack of security and safety."

73. Ibid.

74. Frances D'Emilio, "Fed-up Tenants Fight City Hall," *San Francisco Chronicle*, February 22, 1979.

75. Ibid.

76. Paul Ramirez, "Trouble Brewing at Other Project as Ping Yuen Tenant Rent Strike Ends," *San Francisco Examiner*, January 12, 1979.

77. North Beach Place tenants interview, 2002.

78. SFHA Commission Minutes, November 13, 1980.

79. Ramirez, "Trouble Brewing at Other Project as Ping Yuen Tenant Rent Strike Ends."

80. For more information on other public housing developments in San Francisco, see chapter 1.

81. Patricia Guthrie and Janis Hutchinson, "The Impact of Perceptions on Interpersonal Interactions in an African American/Asian American Housing Project," *Journal of Black Studies* 25 (1995), 382. San Francisco newspapers did run a few reports on the gang violence in and around North Beach Place in the late 1970s.

82. Kaplan/McLaughlin/Diaz, "San Francisco Housing Authority, North Beach Tenants Association, Planning and Process Design Alternatives for North Beach Place," 6. (Contact Kaplan/McLaughlin/Diaz for report content at http://www.kmdarchitects.com/contact.php.) Kaplan, McLaughlin, and Diaz report that the proposal was rejected for two reasons. First, the cost of buying land in another section of the city was too high; and second, the tenants of North Beach Place "organized early on to oppose the proposal."

83. The Telegraph Hill Dwellers formed in 1954 "to perpetuate the historic traditions of San Francisco's Telegraph Hill and to represent the community

interests and its residents and property owners" (Telegraph Hill Dwellers website, www.thd.org). Over the past forty years, the organization has addressed development in Telegraph Hill and North Beach.

84. In 1890, Alice Griffith, who later became one of the first Housing Authority commissioners, and Elizabeth Ashe incorporated the Telegraph Hill Neighborhood Center, Tel-Hi, for "the improvement of social and hygienic conditions of Telegraph Hill and its neighborhoods" (Telegraph Hill Neighborhood Center website, www.tel-hi.org/abouthistoryandmission.html). Through Tel-Hi they offered a garden, nursery, library, a health clinic, and classes for parents and children in the area.

85. For more information, see the Chinatown Community Development Center website, http://www.chinatowncdc.org/, and chapter 3.

86. Guthrie and Hutchinson, "The Impact of Perceptions on Interpersonal Interactions in an African American/Asian American Housing Project," 382–83. The demographics of the diverse project included the following occupancy of the 229 units: African Americans, 35.2 percent; Asian Americans, 37.8 percent; European Americans, 15.7 percent; Latin Americans, 3.9 percent; other, 2.6 percent; and unoccupied, 4.8 percent. According to the study, "units occupied by Asian Americans [were] composed of Chinese (70 percent), Vietnamese (21 percent), Koreans (4.5 percent), Filipinos (3.4 percent) and Cambodians (1.1 percent)" (ibid.). Guthrie and Hutchinson labeled units occupied by Native Americans "and units where all residents do not fall into the same ethnic group" as "Other" (383). The Chinese American population in the project included recent immigrants as well as residents born in the United States or living in the country since 1965.

87. Ibid., 386.
88. Ibid., 387.
89. Ibid.
90. Ibid., 391.
91. Ibid.
92. Ibid., 377–95. The information in the report indicated that they had studied North Beach Place, which Patricia Guthrie confirmed in a 2003 phone conversation with the author.

93. Guthrie and Hutchinson describe the increasingly public sale and distribution of crack cocaine during 1988 and 1989, resulting in numerous shootings in the projects (ibid.). According to tenants I interviewed, the problems multiplied in the 1990s, "when gangbangers and drug dealers came in [from other projects]" (North Beach Place tenants interview, 2002).

94. North Beach Place tenants interview, 2002.
95. Ibid.
96. Catherine Bowman, "North Beach Housing Plan," *San Francisco Chronicle*, October 8, 1996.
97. Malcolm Glover, "Off-Duty Cop Hurt in Beating," *San Francisco Examiner*, November 21, 1996.
98. Ibid.
99. Susan J. Popkin, Bruce Katz, Mary A. Cunningham, Karen D. Brown, Jeremy Gustafson, and Mary Austin Turner, *A Decade of HOPE VI: Research Finding and Policy Challenges* (Washington, DC: Urban Institute, 2004), www.urban.org/publications/411002.html.
100. Paul Franson, "Pondering the Projects," *North Beach Now*, November 1996, 1.
101. Catherine Bowman, "Projects Near Wharf to Be Razed," *San Francisco Chronicle*, October 8, 1996.
102. J. D. Sexton, "New Public Housing Near Wharf to Cost $568,000 per Family," *San Francisco Chronicle*, October 9, 1996. Sexton lamented that North Beach Place had been built and urged the city to "sell the land to a developer. Part of the payment for that valuable project could include providing replacement housing in a more appropriate, less valuable spot."
103. Kaplan/McLaughlin/Diaz, "San Francisco Housing Authority, North Beach Tenants Association, Planning and Process Design Alternatives for North Beach Place," 1. The report was funded by contributions from the LEF Foundation and Wharf Associates.
104. Ibid. The other design principles drafted by participants, "intended to guide any renovation or new construction on site" and listed in the report were as follows: "1. No residents should be displaced. 2. To the extent possible, the project should be oriented outward with entrances on public streets. Units above the ground floor should have access from private stairways leading directly from the street, similar to other buildings in the neighborhood. 3. The building should *not* contain shared corridors or elevators. 4. Open space should be clearly designated, either for certain types of uses (e.g. play areas) or as "private" open space for dwelling units. Play areas for children should be an important element in any new design. 5. The project should provide for retail uses of Taylor Street to improve neighborhood safety and to encourage economic development. 6. The project design should be similar to residential buildings in the surrounding North Beach neighborhood. 7. The project should provide secured parking areas. 8. The projects should contain one large community room and smaller community facilities, such as

Notes to Chapter 4

mailrooms and smaller meeting rooms located at project entrances" (Kaplan/McLaughlin/Diaz, "San Francisco Housing Authority, North Beach Tenants Association, Planning and Process Design Alternatives for North Beach Place," 11).

105. Barbara Nanney, "Tenants Furious over Agency's Letter," *The Independent*, October 15, 1996.

106. Ibid. Although the discrepancy between the claims of the president and the vice president of the NBTA may seem problematic, one possible explanation is that Gregory Richardson was working for the Housing Authority. In a group interview with North Beach Place residents conducted in August 2002, residents stated that the Housing Authority often hired tenant leaders for part-time positions (sometimes as liaisons between tenants and the Housing Authority). Tenants argued that these jobs put the employees in an awkward position and that oftentimes the employee sided with the Housing Authority because the agency provided his or her paycheck (North Beach Place tenants interview, 2002).

107. North Beach Place tenants interview, 2002.

108. The two-phase plan called for half the residents to be relocated while their buildings were demolished and rebuilt. After the new buildings were constructed on half the site, the tenants in the old section would move into the new apartments while the remainder of the site was redeveloped.

109. Barbara Nanney, "Public Housing Relocation," *The Independent*, November 12, 1996.

110. Ibid.

111. Rachel Gordon and Sally Lehrman, "Projects Near the Wharf to Be Razed: City to Replace Troubled North Beach Housing," *San Francisco Examiner*, October 8, 1996.

112. Siegal, "Rebuilding Trust." Quote about the Housing Authority by Thomas Toy, a resident of North Beach Place, cited in the article.

113. Nina Siegal, "Strike out: North Beach Public Housing Tenants Fight Evictions," *San Francisco Bay Guardian*, May 28, 1997.

114. James Tracy, "Tenants Organizing Wins One-for-One Replacement," *Shelterforce*, January/February 2000, www.nhi.org/online/issues/109/organize.html.

115. HUD's "one strike, you're out" policy was announced in 1996 and implemented in April 1997 (Siegal, "Strike out").

116. According to a letter dated June 23, 1997, Alma Lark had started the North Beach Resident Management Corporation prior to 1998. NBTA officers Thomas Toy (acting vice president) and Cynthia Wiltz (president) criticized Lark in 1997 for not holding elections for the NBRMC, arguing that the orga-

nization was not "a legitimate organization representing the interests of all the residents" and asking Lark to hold elections within sixty days. Evidence suggests that Lark took steps to legitimize the organization, which went on to submit a proposal to buy North Beach Place in 1998. Letter to Alma Lark from Thomas Toy, June 23, 1997, from personal file of Tan Chow. (Contact author for letter content.)

117. In an October 30, 1998, reply to Alma Lark, president of the NBRMC, SFHA executive director Ronnie Davis refuted tenants' claims that the SFHA had not complied with federal regulations, arguing that the SFHA "feels it surpassed the regulations by offering the property to sale to the Resident Management Council." According to Davis, the SFHA had mailed letters to the NBTA and the NBRMC and posted information about the "conditions under which any one of these organizations may consider purchase of the property." Likewise, the Housing Authority had held sixteen resident meetings between January 31, 1996, and March 27, 1997, and had considered the NBRMC's proposal for redevelopment, which the Housing Authority described as matching "the quality of other submissions in only a few instances." Letter from Ronnie Davis to Alma Lark, dated October 30, 1998, from the personal file of Tan Chow. (Contact author for letter content.)

118. Angela Rowan, "Hope vs. HOPE VI," *San Francisco Bay Guardian*, August 5, 1998. The so-called first right of refusal law in Section 412 of the federal Department of Housing and Urban Development Code requires the local housing authority to give tenants a "reasonable opportunity" to bid on the property before putting out a request for proposal. The panel rated the NBRMC's proposal last.

119. Ibid.

120. Flyer for "Tenant Speakout and Rally," Chinatown CDC miscellaneous files, San Francisco. Over 3,000 people were displaced in the 1970s as the city redeveloped the downtown area. The flyer also announced that the rally had the endorsement of the NBTA and the NBRMC and included "solidarity statements" by Myra Wallace (Coalition for Low Income Housing, former Bernal Dwellings tenant), Eric Mar (Northern California Coalition for Immigrant and Refugee Rights), Ester Chavez (Coalition for Low Income Housing), and Connie Morgenstern (Eviction Defense Network).

121. Ibid.

122. Ibid. The president of the NBTA did not support the rally. In an interview with Johnny Brannon from the *Independent,* NBTA president Cynthia Wiltz said that she "did not support the rally and questioned whether residents who participated in it fully understood" (Johnny Brannon, "Rally Protests Agency's Plans," *The Independent,* August 15, 1998). Yet during the

Notes to Chapter 4

interview with Brannon, it became clear that Wiltz herself was not clear on the plan put forth by North Beach Development Partners and selected by the Housing Authority. Some residents stated that they did not think Wiltz had been told of the Housing Authority's plans and "said they believed the agency has compromised her leadership of the tenants association by employing her for the past year as a paid 'resident coordinator.'"

123. For more information on the rally, see the following sources: Jason B. Johnson, "Residents of Projects List Demands: Tenants Want S.F. to Let Them Run the Development," *San Francisco Chronicle*, August 14, 1998; and Angela Rowan, "Hope vs. HOPE VI."

124. Tracy, "Tenants Organizing Wins One-for-One Replacement," 3.

125. The tenants reiterated the demands put forth at the rally for one-for-one replacement of low-income units, phased demolition allowing them to stay on-site longer, and the opportunity for all tenants to return.

126. "Petition to the San Francisco Housing Authority," August 1998, unsigned draft copy, from Chinatown CDC miscellaneous files. Other tenant protections listed included "no unlawful evictions without due process and full disclosure of policies, so that North Beach Public Housing residents understood their rights."

127. Letter from the North Beach Coalition to Mr. Renell [sic] Davis, Acting Executive Director, San Francisco Housing Authority, November 14, 1996, regarding the HOPE VI Project at North Beach Place in San Francisco, Chinatown CDC miscellaneous files. Other members of the North Beach Coalition who signed the letter were Reverend Norman Fong, Chinatown Resource Center; Norman Yee, Executive Director, Wu Yee Children's Services; Anna Yee, Coordinator, South of Market Problem Solving Council Enterprise Community Board; Darwin Ow-Wing, Executive Director, Community Education Services SF; Neil Gendel, Project Director, Lead Poisoning Prevention Project; Gordon Chin, Executive Director, Chinatown Resource Center; Denise McCarthy, Executive Director, Telegraph Hill Neighborhood Center; Cynthia Wiltz, North Beach Place resident; Maricella Guerrerro, North Beach Place resident; Greta Yin, Director, Kai Ming Head Start; Maurice Miller, Executive Director, Asian Neighborhood Design; Henry Luc, North Beach Place resident; Yan Hong Hu, North Beach Place resident; Gen Fujioka, Attorney, Asian Law Caucus; and Joanne Lee, Director of Housing, Chinese Community Housing Corporation.

128. Letter from Reverend Norman Fong, Program Director, Chinatown CDC, to Mr. Kevin Marchman, Assistant Secretary, Public and Indian Housing, regarding the North Beach Place HOPE VI application, September 5,

1996, Rev. Norman Fong's miscellaneous files, Chinatown CDC, San Francisco. Reverend Fong also stipulated that the SFHA must provide a written guarantee to residents that they could return to the project, that specific details of the relocation plan be translated into Chinese and Spanish, and that supportive services for tenants include provisions "for limited and non-English speaking tenants as well as expanded senior services."

129. Quote from "General Information on North Beach Place" under conditions for redevelopment as part of information for the HOPE VI grant, from Chinatown CDC miscellaneous files. In 1996, the project demographics showed that the tenant population was 50 percent Asian Pacific Islander, 32 percent African American, 14 percent white, and 4 percent other. Agenda for "Internal Strategy Meeting Regarding Hope VI/North Beach Place," October 16, 1996, sponsored by the CDC/CCHC, Chinatown CDC miscellaneous files.

130. Alma Lark, interview by the author, 2002.

131. Bee Harper, interview by the author, tape recording, San Francisco, 2002. When asked about SFHA publications in Chinese, tenants contended that "the only time we get it we have to request it." Residents mused that the process was costly to the Housing Authority. Ms. Harper, however, argued that "there are a lot of people working at housing who can do it" but that the SFHA did not have certain documents translated in order to keep information from residents.

132. Alma Lark, interview by the author, 2002.

133. Bee Harper, interview by author, 2002.

134. The proposed exit contract was a collaborative effort between residents, the Eviction Defense Network, and the National Housing Law Project. A November 1998 *North Beach Newsletter* lists the tenets of the exit contract as follows: to ensure that all agreements between the Housing Authority, Bridge Housing, and tenants are in writing; to provide fair screening criteria when residents return to the site; to provide one-for-one replacement of the 229 public housing units; to conduct a two-phase demolition and new construction; to give residents the option of remaining on-site during the demolition and new construction or receive Section 8 vouchers; to guarantee that HOPE VI Section 8 relocatees will be provided a rent subsidy if the Section 8 program is unfunded by HUD; to hire an independent relocation monitoring body; and to guarantee no reduction in the number of low-income units.

135. *North Beach Newsletter*, November 1998, Chinatown CDC miscellaneous files.

Notes to Chapter 4

136. Tracy, "Tenant Organizing Wins One-for-One Replacement," 109.
137. Ibid.
138. The Tenant Protection Act called for the SFHA to implement multiphase construction, keeping residents on-site longer, to secure all construction funds for projects before beginning demolition, to provide the same number of low-income units, and to guarantee that all tenants "except those with serious criminal records be allowed to return to their homes" at HOPE VI projects. Angela Rowan, "Amos Brown Tables Public Housing Protections," *San Francisco Bay Guardian*, March 1, 2000.
139. Alma Lark, interview by the author, 2002.
140. Rowen, "Amos Brown Tables Public Housing Protections."
141. Cassi Feldmen, "What Exit Contract?" *San Francisco Bay Guardian*, October 10, 2001. Ronnie Davis was suspended from his position as executive director of the SFHA in March 2001, shortly after his indictment in a Cleveland federal court. Under the plea-bargain agreement, Davis pleaded guilty "to a single misdemeanor of taking excess compensation" from the Cuyahogo Metropolitan Housing Authority of Cleveland, where he had served as the chief financial officer before taking the job with the SFHA in 1996. Davis had felony charges dismissed and agreed to pay $5,467 to his former employer. In 2000, HUD auditors recommended the "strongest possible disciplinary action be taken against Davis" for his mishandling of finances in Ohio and also for wasting "hundreds of thousands of dollars with poor contracting practices and overly high administrative salaries" during his tenure at the SFHA. Patrick Hoge, "Former S.F. Housing Director's Plea Bargain in Jeopardy," *San Francisco Chronicle*, January 12, 2002.
142. Anonymous North Beach Place tenant, interview by the author, tape recording, San Francisco, 2002.
143. Ilene Lelchuk, "North Beach Project Residents Ready to Fight Eviction: Housing Authority Abandons Plan for Two Stage Rebuild," *San Francisco Chronicle*, August 9, 2001.
144. North Beach Place tenants interview, 2002.
145. The sign is depicted in a photograph by Michael Cole, San Francisco, 2002. Photograph in author's file.
146. Ethen Lieser, "Public Housing Aims to Improve Lives," *AsianWeek*, June 15, 2001.
147. Anonymous North Beach Place tenant, interview by author, 2002.
148. "Regional vice president Ken Sheppard sees the move to North Beach Place as a 'slam dunk for us. Just look at the density. There's a large part of this town we're not serving.' The customer base Sheppard and Trader Joe's

most likely aim to attract is tourists staying in the nearby hotels and middle- and upper-class residents and workers from North Beach, Russian Hill, and the Financial District. While public housing tenants could choose to shop at Trader Joe's rather than the Safeway across the street, some tenants were skeptical prior to the development reopening. Benita Grayson noted, 'It's too expensive. Some things you could buy but not others.'" See Ilene Lelchuk, "A First: San Francisco Public Housing at Wharf Gets a Trader Joe's," *San Francisco Chronicle*, October 9, 2002. According to company officials, this was the first Trader Joe's to be located in an affordable housing property. "One of California's Largest Affordable Housing Communities, North Beach Place, Opens to Residents Today in San Francisco," *Business Wire*, October 22, 2004, 1.

149. San Francisco Housing Authority website, http://www.sfha.org/hopevi/northbeach.htm.

150. San Francisco Planning Department, "North Beach HOPE VI Housing Redevelopment: Final Environmental Impact Report," 13.

151. "One of California's Largest Affordable Housing Communities, North Beach Place, Opens to Residents Today in San Francisco," 1.

152. Ibid. Financing figures from Donna Kimura, "Grand Ideas Realized at North Beach Place," *Affordable Housing Finance*, August 2005, http://www.housingfinance.com/ahf/articles/2005/august/014_AHF_12-3.htm. According to "One of California's Largest Affordable Housing Communities, North Beach Place, Opens to Residents Today in San Francisco," Citibank's interim financing of $56 million, of which $24 million converted to permanent financing at the completion of the development, was "one of the largest loans of its kind in the company's nearly two-century history."

153. "One of California's Largest Affordable Housing Communities, North Beach Place, Opens to Residents Today in San Francisco." The article lists J. R. Muggs as a coffee purveyor. In 2008, Starbucks was leasing space at the cable car turnaround.

154. San Francisco Planning Department, "North Beach HOPE VI Redevelopment: Final Environmental Impact Report," 14. The apartments on the open market would run a family of four earning $56,000, or 55 percent of the area median income, about $1,198 a month for a two-bedroom apartment (Ilene Lelchuk, "A First").

155. The figure stated in "HOPE VI Housing Relocation Choices and Return, 1999–2006," provided by Juan Monsanto, formerly of the SFHA, to scholar Jane Rongerude, is a 41 percent return rate.

156. Ilene Lelchuk, "Back Home in North Beach: Residents of Project Glad to Return After Renovation," *San Francisco Chronicle*, October 2, 2004.

Notes to Chapter 4

157. Congresswoman Nancy Pelosi cited the project as an example in blending community planning and federal support. "'It shows how the wise investment of federal dollars can work effectively in a local community setting,' said Pelosi. 'It will be an integral part of the neighborhood because everyone worked together—at the federal, state and local levels—to define what was needed and secured significant public and private funding to make the development possible'" ("One of California's Largest Affordable Housing Communities, North Beach Place, Opens to Residents Today in San Francisco," 1).

Conclusion

1. Congress approved eliminating one-for-one replacement of public housing units in 1995.

2. Lawrence Vale, *Purging the Poorest: Public Housing and the Design Politics of Twice-Cleared Communities* (Chicago: University of Chicago Press, 2013). 22. Vale notes that the HOPE VI program had two different phases: a redevelopment program that started in 1992 and a separate demolition program that ran from 1996 to 2003. The displacement figures Vale lists are originally from Edward Goetz, who estimates that 80 percent of those displaced were African American. "Gentrification in Black and White: The Racial Impact of Public Housing Demolition in American Cities," *Urban Studies* 48, no. 8 (2011), 1588.

3. E-mail communication with Florence Cheng, San Francisco Housing Authority, April 22, 2013. Cheng wrote that many Valencia Gardens residents received Section 8 vouchers.

4. Anita Ortiz, interview by the author, and Louette Fabio and Gabrielle Fontanella, interview by the author, tape recording, San Francisco, May 2009; interview by the author with North Beach Place resident (not a returner) who asked to remain anonymous, 2009.

5. For a compelling analysis that compares "twice-cleared" communities in Atlanta (Techwood and Clark Howell) and Chicago (Cabrini-Green), in which slums first were cleared to build public housing and public housing then was cleared to redevelop the property into mixed-income developments, see Vale's *Purging the Poorest*. The Legacy Project panel at Valencia Gardens supports Vale's argument that "housing officials have used the creation of improved housing as a way to serve a less-impoverished constituency, while simultaneously asserting that clearance of substandard housing and dangerous neighborhoods is, in itself, a benefit to those who are freed from having to live in such conditions" (35).

Notes to Conclusion

6. The SFHA submitted four applications for HOPE VI grants—three for Hunters View—in 1999, 2000, and 2001. All four were rejected by HUD officials. Heather Knight, "Fixing Mess at Hunters View Won't Be Quick, Easy or Cheap," *San Francisco Chronicle*, September 16, 2007.

7. Ilene Lelchuck, "New Hope for S.F. Public Housing as Federal Funding Evaporates: Mayor Pushes Private Investment to Fill Gap Left by Dwindling HOPE VI Money," *San Francisco Chronicle*, March 28, 2005. The SFHA used the federal funding to leverage an additional $183 million to redevelop six public housing projects. Cecilia M. Vega, "Newsom Says He'll Ask Voters to Shell out to Fix Public Housing," *San Francisco Chronicle*, September 23, 2006.

8. Knight, "Fixing Mess at Hunters View Won't Be Quick, Easy or Cheap."

9. For an overview of the HOPE VI program and a range of essays on implementation, see Henry Cisneros and Lora Engdahl, eds., *From Despair to Hope: Hope VI and the New Promise of Public Housing in American Cities* (Washington, DC: Brookings Institution Press, 2009). For an in-depth analysis of Atlanta and Chicago's differing HOPE VI agendas, see Vale, *Purging the Poorest*. See also Susan J. Popkin, Bruce Katz, Mary A. Cunningham, Karen D. Brown, Jeremy Gustafson, and Mary Austin Turner, *A Decade of HOPE VI: Research Finding and Policy Challenges* (Washington, DC: Urban Institute, 2004), www.urban.org/publications/411002.html.

10. Jane Rongerude, "The Sorted City: San Francisco, HOPE SF, and the Redevelopment of Public Housing" (PhD diss., University of California–Berkeley, 2009).

11. Jane Rongerude notes that HOPE SF Task Force members visited North Beach Place and Valencia Gardens, learned about redevelopment efforts in other cities and "had the opportunity to speak to a panel that included a public housing resident, developer, and civic leader involved in the redevelopment of public housing in Chicago" (ibid., 51).

12. Ibid., 50.

13. HOPE SF website, http://hope-sf.org/guiding-principles.php. Other cities that have received national attention for their HOPE VI-inspired public housing initiatives include Chicago, Atlanta, and Seattle.

14. San Francisco Housing Authority website, http://www.sfha.org. Redevelopment sites include Hunters View, Sunnydale, Potrero Terrace and Annex, Westside Courts, and Alice Griffith.

15. Ibid.

16. Ibid.

Notes to Conclusion

17. Ibid.

18. The executive director of the Center for Urban Redevelopment at the University of Pennsylvania, Valerie Piper, commented, "Newsom's Hope SF program is creative, but not unique. Chicago, Atlanta, Seattle and Pittsburgh are trying similar ways to rebuild public housing. She added that the pace of the Hunters View rebuild is pretty typical" (Knight, "Fixing Mess at Hunters View Won't Be Quick, Easy or Cheap"). In *Purging the Poorest*, Lawrence Vale offers a more nuanced view of the different ways Atlanta and Chicago approached and implemented the HOPE VI program. San Francisco, unlike these cities, did not create market-rate housing as part of the HOPE VI program.

19. Henry Alvarez served as a member of the San Diego Housing Commission, as assistant director for housing and tenant services at the Washington County Department of Housing Services in Oregon, and as president and CEO of the San Antonio Housing Authority before joining the SFHA (San Francisco Housing Authority website, http://sfha.org).

20. While Newsom at one point had proposed a $100 million bond measure that required voter approval, he ultimately decided to use revenue bonds that the city could issue without going to the ballot box (Knight, "Fixing Mess at Hunters View Won't Be Quick, Easy or Cheap").

21. Carolyn Said, "SF's Hunters View Housing Project Opens," *San Francisco Chronicle*, January 10, 2013. Unlike the SFHA's sole focus on public and affordable housing units in implementing the HOPE VI program, Hunters View—a HOPE SF project—included market-rate housing options. Jack Gardner, the CEO of the lead developer, the John Stewart Company, outlined the strategy: "Instead of moving the poor to wealthier neighborhoods, we will bring wealthier people to what had been a low-income neighborhood" (ibid.).

22. State of the City address, 2006, quoted in Rongerude, "The Sorted City," 71. Rongerude persuasively argues that in "the Hunters View imaginary, redevelopment is a way of restoring justice to long neglected African American communities in the city. It accomplishes this by righting an historic and enduring wrong, the destruction of the Fillmore neighborhood" (71).

23. Lawrence Vale, "Public Housing Myths: Mixed-Income Is the Only Way to Redevelop Public Housing" (paper presented at the Urban History Association Conference, New York, October 2012).

24. Edith J. Barrett, Paul Geisel, and Jan Johnston, "The Ramona Utti Report: Impacts of the Ripley Arnold Relocation Project, Year 3 (2004–5)" (paper

prepared for the city of Fort Worth, Texas, 2006), cited in Edward G. Goetz, "Better Neighborhoods, Better Outcomes? Explaining Relocation Outcomes in HOPE VI," *Cityscape*, April 2010, vol. 12, no. 1, 9.

25. Goetz summarizes a range of studies related to children's school and social experiences in connection with HOPE VI ("Better Neighborhoods, Better Outcomes?," 8).

26. Susan J. Popkin and Elizabeth Cove, "Safety Is the Most Important Thing: How HOPE VI Helped Families," Brief no. 2 (Washington, DC: The Urban Institute, Metropolitan Housing and Communities Center, 2007); Susan J. Popkin, "The HOPE VI Program: What Happened to the Residents?" in *Where Are Poor People to Live? Transforming Public Housing Communities*, eds. Larry Bennett, Janet L. Smith, and Patricia A. Wright (Armonk, N.Y.: M. E. Sharpe), 68–90; Lynne C. Manzo, Rachel Garshick Kleit, and Dawn M. Couch, "Social Sustainability in HOPE VI: The Immigrant Experience" (paper presented at the Urban Affairs Association 35th Annual Meeting, 2005), all cited in Goetz, "Better Neighborhoods, Better Outcomes?"

27. Susan Clampet-Lundquist, "Moving over or Moving up? Short-Term Gains and Losses for Relocated HOPE VI Families," *Journal of Policy Development and Research* 7, no. 1 (2004), 57–80, cited in Goetz, "Better Neighborhoods, Better Outcomes?"

28. Arguably, the redevelopment of public housing that included all affordable housing units staved off gentrification in North Beach and Valencia Gardens. At the same time, the redevelopment of what once were anti–public spaces into attractive sites (and, at North Beach Place, neighborhood amenities such as grocery stores) contributed to the districts' desirability and thus attracted investment and development.

29. Mayor Newsom appointed Lee as city administrator in 2005.

30. "Ed Lee Elected First Asian Mayor of San Francisco," *Sun Reporter*, November 10, 2011.

31. "Mayors Lee and Quan—2 of a Kind," *San Francisco Chronicle*, February 21, 2011.

32. Thanks to Lawrence Vale for pushing me to consider the effectiveness of affective activism at Valencia Gardens in light of HOPE VI redevelopment.

33. Vale, *Purging the Poorest*, 314.

34. Lawrence Vale usefully categorizes three stages of the public housing program. The first period, from the 1930s to the late 1950s, focused on replacing slums with modern housing populated by carefully chosen families who were usually "upwardly mobile working class" rather than the poorest

families. The second period, from the early 1960s to the late 1980s, "retenanted 'the projects' with the least advantaged and most economically desperate urban dwellers." The third period, beginning with the creation of the HOPE VI program in 1992, saw the reemergence of public housing's early goals of housing the "worthy" poor (Vale, *Purging the Poorest*, 7–24).

Index

affective activism, 198, 202, 295n32; North Beach Place organizing and, 151, 195; Valencia Gardens redevelopment and, xii–xiii, xvii, 49–50, 72, 74, 76, 83, 94–96

African Americans, xiv, xviii, 12–13, 73, 219n41, 228n143, 279n70, 284n86; black out-migration, 40–41; concentrated populations, 40, 147; discriminatory policies affecting, 20, 40–41, 45, 52, 54, 137, 167, 182, 274n3 (see also neighborhood pattern policy); organizing around problems, 15, 18–19, 168–69, 177, 179, 192; prejudicial attitudes toward, 156–57, 172–73

Agnos, Art, 179

Alice Griffith public housing project, 34, 69

Alien Land Law, 102,107

Alioto, Joseph, 28

Ammiano, Tom, 186

anti–public spaces, xvii, 65–66

Art Commission, San Francisco, 71, 87–88, 239n50

Asian Law Caucus, 33, 133, 202

Ayer, Edgar Nichol (E. N.), 3, 13, 15, 97, 162, 214n9

Banks, Mattie (resident and plaintiff), 147–48, 280n42

Banks v. The Housing Authority of San Francisco, 19, 64, 73, 163, 164, 221n59, 264n92

Baranski, John, xiv, 13–15; "Making Public Housing in San Francisco," 219n44; "Something to Help Themselves: Tenant Organizing in San Francisco Public Housing, 1965–1975," 222nn72–73

BART (Bay Area Rapid Transit), 244n98; Mission stop, 64, 84

Bauer, Catherine: *Modern Housing*, 51, 221n60

Bayside Senior Housing Project, 141

Bay Street commercialization, 174

Beard, John, 4, 13, 15, 17–18, 22–23, 54, 56, 158, 160

Beat generation writers, 149, 164

Bernal Dwellings redevelopment, 38–39, 40, 41

black out-migration, 40–41. See also African Americans; relocation of public housing residents

Board of Supervisors, San Francisco, 2, 16, 17, 28, 182, 214n7, 234n16, 238n48, 260n63; efforts toward nondiscrimination in public housing, 157–58, 162; rejecting SFHA property proposal, 267n115; Resolution Number 852, 106; voting down SFHA Mission proposals, 46–48

Born, Ernest, 152, 277n20

297

Index

Bridge Housing, 187, 189, 196
Brooke Amendment, federal, 26–27, 282n60
Brooks, Charlotte, 121, 211n3, 217n37, 255n27
Brown, Amos, 186
Brown, Willie, 35, 39, 85, 174, 181, 186, 202
Brown v. Board of Education, 121
Bryant, Christine, 71
Bufano, Beniamino, 90, 237–39nn45–48, 239n51; placement of his works as problematic, 71–72; sculptures at Valencia Gardens, 55, 56, 57, 58, 61, 79, 88, 90, 93, 94, 95, 196, 238n46, 238n48; work with the FAP (Federal Art Project), 55, 56, 57, 58, 94, 95, 238nn46–48

Cabrini Green, 68
Calderon, Maria (resident), 70
California Appellate Court: ruling against the SFHA, 163
California Housing Reporter, 100
Carey and Company Incorporated, 86
CCHC (Chinese Community Housing Corporation): coalition with PYRIA, 141–42; formation, 137, 140; proposed senior building at Ping Yuen, 140–41, 273n165, 274n169
CCU (Council for Civic Unity), 15–16, 17; creation of, 14
Chamber of Commerce, 113, 158, 255n27; of North Beach, 175
Chan, Lee (resident), 128, 145
Charley, James, 147, 148, 159
China, 108, 113, 118

Chinatown: agency and community interactions in, 123; coalition building and activism in, 100–106, 113–14; gang violence in, 124, 129–30, 269n129; housing conditions (early), 100, 102–3, 106–7; 1940 resolution for public housing at, 106; public housing in, 97; rent strikes in, 128–31, 202, 267n113, 268nn119–20, 270n134, 270n136, 271n149; segregation in public housing, 100, 101, 103, 107, 114, 117, 121–23; tourism in, 18, 105, 106, 108, 109, 112–13, 119, 201, 260n63. *See also* Ping Yuen project; PYRIA
Chinatown CDC (Community Development Center), 145, 171, 172, 202, 261–62n72, 272n156, 273n164; partnership with PYRIA, 137–42, 144; support network with Tel-Hi, 183–84
Chinatown Health Center, 111–12
Chinatown Housing Bill, 103–4
Chinatown Housing Project Committee, 103, 105, 106, 109, 111, 254n26, 255n27
Chinatown murals, 116, 272n157; Leong mural, 115, 116, 262n74, 262n76; Mar mural, 142, 143, 274n172
Chinese American press, 99, 101, 200; *Chinese Digest*, 102; *Chinese Press*, 100, 107, 258n45
Chinese Americans, 98, 108, 114–16, 142, 184–85. *See also* Chinatown CDC; PYRIA
Chinese Junior Chamber of Commerce, 103

Index

Chinese Pavilion, Golden Gate Exposition, 106–7
Chinese Young Women's Christian Association, 103
Christopher, George, 17, 122, 280n34
City Lights Bookstore, 149, 275n10
Civil Rights Act, Title VIII, 281–82n54
civil rights movement, xviii, 19, 22, 23, 63, 120, 123, 159
coalition building, xviii, 100–101, 113, 137–42. *See also* tenant activism
Coleman-Curry, Kimberly (resident), 39, 41
community bonds, xviii, 46, 96, 131; activism and, 42–43, 72–73, 85, 95, 135, 140, 184, 195; cross-racial and ethnic ties, xiii, xviii, 49, 72, 74–75, 86–88, 144–46; coalition building, 100–101, 137–42; housing designs and, 54–55; ideology vs. processes of formation, xii–xiii; importance of, 151, 197; lost or threatened by relocation, 42, 195–96; mini-communities, 171–73; between public housing tenants and neighborhood, 52; SFHA goals of fostering, 54–55; struggles to forge and reforge, 92–93, 173–74
Conlon, Albert (resident), 152–53
construction issues, 16, 87, 93, 108, 196
Correa, Omaira (resident), 80–81
court rulings, 19, 163–64; California Appellate Court, 163; California Supreme Court, 19, 20, 21, 121, 163, 264n92. *See also* legal challenges to public housing policies
CREA (California Real Estate Association), 20

Cronin, Melvyn I., 159, 162, 163
cross-racial and cross-ethnic ties, xiii, xviii, 49, 72, 74–75, 86–88, 145–46, 151; loss of, due to relocations, 42, 195–96. *See also* community bonds

"Da Mayor" cartoon, 181. *See also* Brown, Willie; North Beach Place
Daniels, Mark, 106, 109, 254n26, 256n34
Davis, Ronnie, 36–37, 186–87, 229n155, 230n160, 290n141
demographics, 20, 32, 34, 74, 122–23, 148, 222n67, 284n86; shifts in, 13, 49, 64, 144, 150, 275n5
Dill, Marshall, 3, 7, 13, 48
discriminatory practices and policies, 20, 40–41, 167, 182, 274n3; race-based, 3, 6, 12, 14, 15, 155. *See also* neighborhood pattern policy
displacement. *See* relocation of public housing residents
diversity, xiv, 18, 35, 42; at North Beach Place, 164, 165, 204; at Valencia Gardens, 49–50, 73, 75–76. *See also* racial integration
dot-com boom, 83–84, 91
drug trafficking, 31, 243n88; at North Beach Place, 149, 170, 173–74, 284n93; at Valencia Gardens, 63, 65–68, 69, 70–73, 84, 95
Dunn, Ron (resident), 82

Eldridge, Willie (resident), 79
Em Johnson Interest Inc., 189
empowerment, xiii, 21, 36, 80, 171
EOC (Economic Opportunity Council), 123–25, 266n107, 267n111

299

Index

Ergina, Amancio, 28
Escobar, Merna (resident), 68
ethnic segregation. *See* segregation in public housing
Evers, Albert, 13–14, 157
Eviction Defense Network, 179–82, 185
evictions, 133, 179–80, 183. *See also* relocation of public housing residents

Fabio, Louette (resident), 83, 87
Fair Housing Act, 163, 263n78, 281–82n54. *See also* housing acts, federal
FAP (Federal Art Project): outdoor sculptures commissioned by, 55, 56, 57, 58, 94, 95, 238n46
federal funding of public housing, 4, 28, 38, 83, 104, 118, 186–87; jeopardized, 35–36; reductions in, 4, 24, 27, 48, 64, 123, 197, 203. *See also* Hope VI
federal housing acts. *See* housing acts, federal
Federal Works Agency, 218n38
FEPC (Fair Employment Practices Commission): ruling on public housing, 22, 23
Fire by Night Organizing Committee, 181, 185
Fisherman's Wharf, 166, 167, 169, 174, 176. *See also* North Beach district
Floresca, Felipe, 35, 229n149
Fong, Norman, 184, 288–89n128
Fontanella, Gabrielle (resident), 45, 60, 61, 71–72, 83, 87, 89, 92
Fortner, Gregg, 187
Four Barrel Coffeehouse, 90–91

Four Seas Corporation, 127
Francois, Terry, 121, 159, 160

gang violence, 101, 130, 144, 244n98, 269n128; in Chinatown, 124, 129–30, 269n129; at North Beach Place, 168, 172–73, 283n81; at Ping Yuen and Chinatown, 124, 129–30, 269n129; at Valencia Gardens and the Mission, 64–65, 66, 68, 95
Garland, Marsha, 175–76
gentrification, 83–84, 91, 150, 201, 247n139, 292n2; narrative of, 192; redevelopment having mixed effects on, xviii, 295n28
Gilmore, David, 31
Goldberg, Leslie, 34–35
Golden Dragon Massacre, 130–31
Golden Gate International Exposition, 1, 6, 9, 152, 213n1; Chinese Pavilion, 106–7
Grievance Panel, SFHA and tenant run, 27–28, 132–33, 225n111, 270n141
Griffith, Alice, 13, 18, 103, 171; "A Review of the Proceedings of the Housing Authority," 213n7, 214n9, 220n45, 260n61, 284n84. *See also* Tel-Hi
Gutherie, Vernell (resident), 70, 86
Guthrie, Patricia: and Janis Hutchinson, 171–73
Gutterson, Henry, 152, 277n20

Halikias, Hope (resident), 169
Hamilton, Ruth (resident), 82, 90
Hartman, Chester, 39–40
Hayes Valley redevelopment, 38, 41, 67, 89, 178
Head Start Program, 21, 93, 196

300

Index

Helpman, Martin (SFHA commissioner and tenant), 28
HEW (Department of Health, Education, and Welfare), 26
Holmes, Rosinda, 162
HOPE SF program, 5, 197–201, 294n20
HOPE VI (Housing Opportunities for People Everywhere VI): competitive funding, 37–38, 41; federal housing program, xi, xv, xvi, 5, 144, 188, 215n14, 289n134; focus on mixed-income units, xiii, 5, 88, 230n163, 292n6; goals, 195; impacts of, 39, 40, 41, 89, 180, 182, 192, 195, 201 (*see also* morality goal of public housing programs; relocation of public housing residents); resident participation in site planning, 87
Hope VI program sites: North Beach, 175–79, 180–82, 186–88; Valencia Gardens, 38, 39, 83–87, 89, 249–50n168
housing acts, federal: Fair Housing Act, 163, 263n78, 281–82n54; National Defense Housing Act (Lanham Act), 216n5; 1937 Housing Act, 2, 51, 151, 213n5, 216n15, 239–40n51; 1949 Housing Act, 108, 109, 146, 158, 221n62, 259n52, 260n60; 1956 Housing Act, 16, 19; 1965 Housing Act, 264n84. *See also* SFHA
Housing and Community Development Act (1974), 28–29
Housing Authorities Law (California), 2–3
Housing Choice Vouchers, 195, 204, 225n115; Section 8 program, 29, 37

Housing Commission, San Francisco, 2–3, 12–13, 17–18, 22, 30, 48, 58, 59, 103, 110, 112, 113, 131, 168
Housing Corporation Law, 213n6
Howard, Henry, 106, 109
Howell, Ocean, 63–64
HPTU (Hunters Point Tenants Union): tenant activism and rent strike, 25–26, 123
HUD (Department of Housing and Urban Development), 21, 26, 30, 133, 178, 231n167, 264n84; housing survey data, 225n106, 230–31n165; management of the HOPE VI Program, 83, 85, 89, 230n162, 248n145 (*see also* HOPE VI); North Beach Place and HUD, 177, 178, 183–86; SFHA and, 4, 29–32, 34–38, 41–42, 144, 201, 226nn125–26, 290n141, 293n6
Huey, Felix, 130
Human Technology Partners, Inc., 181
Hunters Point: conditions at, 25–26, 69; racial integration at, 11–13, 25, 73; rent strikes at, 25–26, 123
Hunters View: black out-migration from, 40–41; rebuilding of, 200
Huyhn, Sally (resident), 87

I-Hotel (International Hotel), 267n115; battle over, 126–28, 135–36 (*see also* PYRIA); the new I-hotel, 268n119
I-Hotel Citizens Advisory Committee, 268n119
Immigration Department, U.S., 118
Ingram, Donald (resident), 74
Italian immigrants, 148–49

301

Index

James, Kim (resident), 68–69
Johnson, Lyndon, 21, 166
Johnson, Solomon, 121–22
John Stewart Company, 181, 189, 196
Jones, Jim, 29–30
Jones, Yolanda, 36–37
Jordan, Mayor, 35, 226n126
Journal of Housing, 99–100, 152
Jung, Charles, 97
Junior Chamber of Commerce, San Francisco, 104, 105, 256n34

Kane, Eneas, 24–26, 30
Kaplan, McLaughlin: and Diaz report, 176–77
Kearny, Dennis, 115
Kennedy, John F., 20, 21
Kraucer, Ruth (resident), 48

Lapham, Roger, 14
Lark, Alma (resident), 164, 165, 167, 177, 181, 184, 186, 282n55, 286–87n116
"Latin Quarter," 148–49, 151
Lee, Chang Jok (resident), 114, 124, 127, 131, 133, 134, 135–36, 137, 142, 267n115
Lee, Ed, City Administrator, 202
Lee, George, 114, 124, 127, 128, 131, 134, 135, 136, 137, 141, 142, 269n133, 271n154, 272n155
Lee, Lim P., 103
Lee, Theodore, 97, 104, 105, 255n27
Legacy Oral History Project, 84–85, 87, 90, 197, 240n58, 292n5. *See also* oral history
legal challenges to public housing policies: NAACP suits, 19, 148, 159–62, 164, 277n128, 280n42; Proposition 14, 21; tenant inspired, 132, 133, 164. *See also* court rulings
Leong, James: mural, 115, 116, 262n74, 262n76
Little Italy, 148, 152, 164. *See also* North Beach district
Low, Watson (resident), 114, 131–32, 135, 136–37, 144–45
Low-income Housing Tax Credits (LIHTCs), 189, 230n163

Madaris, Deborah (resident), 59–60
Malcolm, Andres, 65
management of public housing, outsourced, 196–97, 199
Mar, Darryl: mural, 142, 143
Marchman, Kevin, 36
Martin, Theodore: and Mary Martin, 153, 155, 156
Maxie, Marion (resident), 69, 70
Maxwell, Jeri (resident), 77, 80
Maxwell, Sophie, 197
Mayer, Tom, 65, 66
Mazzola, Commissioner, 122
McCulloch, I. S., 45, 46–47, 234n15, 235n19
MCO (Mission Coalition Organization), 63, 64, 84, 242nn77, 78; proactive stand on redevelopment, 63–64
mini-communities, 165, 171–73, 184
Mission Anti-Displacement Coalition, 84
Mission district: Cogswell School site, 46, 48; economic and demographic changes in, 62–63; gang violence in, 64–65, 66, 68, 95; Latin cultural identification (the *Barrio*), 63–64; murals in, 63; residents opposing public

housing plans in, 45–47; traffic issues in, 47. *See also* MCO; Valencia Gardens

Mission Housing Corporation, 196

Mission Street Property Owners and Merchants Association, 45–46

Mission Yuppie Eradication Project, 84

mixed-income units, xiii, 5, 41, 86, 88, 90, 230n163, 292n6; challenges and effects of, 151, 188–89, 203–4; deconcentrating poverty and, xiii, 195; SFHA redevelopment goals of, 174–75, 177, 198–99, 230n163

MOH (Mayor's Office of Housing), 198, 200

Molina, Charla (resident), 74

morality goal of public housing programs, 2, 8–9, 41, 83, 274n3

Moscone, George, 29, 30, 127, 267n115

murals. *See* Chinatown murals; Mission district: murals in

NAACP (National Association for the Advancement of Colored People): criticism and actions regarding discriminatory policies, 15, 21, 22, 121, 148, 157, 162–63, 223n83; legal challenges to public housing segregation, 19, 148, 159–62, 164, 227n128, 280n42

National Housing Law Project: *False Hope*, 230n162

NBRMC (North Beach Resident Management Corporation), 180–81, 182, 286–87n116, 287n117

NBTA (North Beach Place Tenants Association), 166, 182, 286–87n116, 287n120, 287n122

neighborhood pattern policy: California Supreme Court ruling on, 20, 121, 163, 264n92; as race-based, 3, 6, 12, 14, 15, 155; segregated housing and, 13, 31, 121, 147–48, 159, 162–63, 278n22; SFHA adoption and implementation of, 6, 12, 147–48, 155, 157–60; SFHA resolution repealing, 281n53; struggle to oppose or modify, 15–18, 157–59

Newsom, Gavin, 197–200, 294n18

New Urbanism design, 189, 192

New York Times, 65

Nguyen, Hoang Kim (resident), 73

Nixon, Richard, 27

North Beach Chamber of Commerce, 175–76

North Beach Development Partners, 181

North Beach district, 164; Bay Street commercialization, 174, 189 (*see also* Fisherman's Wharf); tourism in, xviii, 149–50, 155, 165, 167–68, 169, 170, 174, 175, 179, 290–91n148; tourism vs. public housing interests in, 164–71

North Beach Place, xii, xviii, 39, 147, 153, 154, 155; advocacy of and plans for, 151–52; as a battleground over integration, 147–48, 150–51, 158–59; as the best project, 151–53; cross-racial and cross-ethnic alliances, 145–46, 165; demolition of, 188–89; designs and plans for revitalization, 176–80; gang violence, 168, 172–73, 283n81; HOPE VI grant for redevelopment, 175–76, 177–78, 181, 182, 186–87; the new

303

Index

North Beach Place (cont.)
development, 189–93; playground, 196; relocation goals vs. reality, 177, 179–80; segregation, 153–56; SFHA management of, 147–61, 168, 175–80, 184–89; tenant activism in redevelopment management, 180–83, 185–86, 188–89, 195
NTO (National Tenants Association), 267n113

One Strike policy, 179–80, 183, 286n115
oral history, xv, 204, 212n6; Legacy Oral History Project, 84–85, 87, 90, 197, 240n58, 292n5
Ortiz, Anita (resident), xi–xii, xv, 70, 74–76, 80, 81, 92, 94, 202

Pak, Rose, 130
Paliou Gate, 113, 114, 118, 203. *See also* Ping Yuen project
PHA (Public Housing Administration), 15, 59, 118, 125, 215n11, 240n56, 264n84
PHTA (Public Housing Tenants Association), 27–28, 77, 126, 132–33
Ping Yuen North: the new project, 118–22; resident activities, 140–41
Ping Yuen project, xii, 97, 144–46, 200, 251n2; applicants for, 114; architectural style, 100, 109–10, 111, 112–13; Asian population of, 31, 34; city promotion of, 98, 100–101, 112, 115, 117; dedication ceremony, 97–99, 264n89; Paliou Gate, 113, 114, 118, 203; racial integration at, 73, 121–23; SFHA management of, 98, 100, 106–18, 121–23, 133, 138, 143–44. *See also* PYRIA
Piper, Valerie, 294n18
Platero, Eva (resident), 82
Plaza East redevelopment, 38, 39, 231n173, 232–33n183
Pollack, Van Meter Williams, 90
Potrero public housing, 10, 22, 32, 33, 69, 228n143, 293n14
private financing and ownership of developments, 195
Proposition 10, 109
Proposition 14, 21
"psychological ownership," 50, 81, 82, 83, 212n7
public housing: competition for access to, 41–42; declension model of, xix; management of, 196–97, 199; morality a goal of, 2, 8–9, 41, 83, 274n3; "psychological ownership" of units, 50, 81, 212n17; rental fees, 26–27; social services for residents, 24, 230n163; tenant demographics, 13, 20, 32, 34, 49, 64, 74, 122–23, 144, 148, 222n67, 275n5, 284n86. *See also* redevelopment of public housing; segregation in public housing; SFHA; *and specific project*
PYRIA (Ping Yuen Residents Improvement Association), 101, 123–26; activism over the I-Hotel, 126–28, 130, 135; battle over the I-Hotel, 127–28; challenging the SFHA, 126–30; coalition with Chinatown CDC, 137–43; formation of, 10, 77; laundry

proposal, 138–40; rent strikes, 130, 131, 133–34, 135–37, 168–69, 202; resident activism, 123–26

QHWRA (Quality Housing and Work Responsibility Act), 215n14

race-based policies, 3, 6, 12, 14, 15, 155. *See also* neighborhood pattern policy

racial integration, xviii, 121; advocacy of, 15–16, 20; at Hunters Point, 12–13. *See also* diversity; segregation in public housing

racial segregation in public housing. *See* segregation in public housing

racial tensions, 14, 15, 31, 33–35, 121–22, 171–73

Radford, Gail, 2

redevelopment, economic, 43, 84, 126

redevelopment of public housing, xiii–xix, 83, 197; construction issues, 87, 196; design of housing, 39–40, 85. *See also* relocation of public housing residents

Reinhardt, Richard, 163

Reisner, Else: "Consultant for Homemaking," 8

relocation of public housing residents, 88–90, 196, 197; demolition and, 87, 174–76, 188; as an effect of redevelopment, 37–38, 40–41, 292–93n5; evictions, 133, 179–80; loss of community ties, xi, 195–96; reduction in returning tenants, 89–90, 93–95, 191, 196; relocation goals vs. reality, 177, 179–80; "stop urban removal" movement, 181–82

rent strikes, xvii, 15, 25–26, 126; in Chinatown, 128, 130–31, 267n113, 268nn119–20, 269–70n134, 270n136, 271n149; at Hunters Point, 25–26, 123, 140; at Ping Yuen (PYRIA), 130–34, 135–37, 168–69, 202. *See also* tenant activism

Resource Center, Chinatown Neighborhood Improvement (CDC), 137–42, 145, 170, 171, 183, 202, 203

RMC (Resident Management Corporation), 180

Robert Taylor Homes, 68

Robinson, Elmer, 97–98

Rongerude, Jane, 197–98

Roosevelt, Eleanor, 104, 255n27

Roosevelt, Franklin D., 104

Rossi, Angelo, 3

Rumford, W. Bryan, 20–21

San Francisco Chronicle: articles, 31, 99, 122, 147, 163, 227n128, 230n160; letters to, 162, 176

San Francisco Examiner, 34, 71, 147

San Francisco Neighborhood Legal Foundation, 132, 168

San Francisco News, 17, 108

Scott, Walter, 30

sculptures at Valencia Gardens, 55, 56, 57, 58, 61, 71–72, 94, 196, 238n46, 238n48

segregation in public housing, xii, xiv, xvi, xvii, 4, 20–22, 33–34, 147, 148, 159–63, 185, 279n29, 280n34; in Chinatown, 100, 101, 103, 107, 114, 117, 121–23; city resolution banning, 16, 17, 158; Court decision banning, 5, 19, 64;

Index

segregation in public housing (cont.) executive order banning, 20, 121, 279n26; NAACP legal challenges to, 159–62, 280n42; neighborhood pattern policy and, 13, 14, 15, 31, 121, 147–48, 155, 157, 162–63, 278n22; *Shelley v. Kraemer* decision, 157, 252n17, 263n78
senior housing, 141
"separate but equal" doctrine, 159–60
Sexton, J. D., 176
SFAIA (San Francisco Branch of the American Institute of Architects), 84–85
SFHA (San Francisco Housing Authority), 24, 30–31, 55, 88, 101, 106, 195, 197–98, 200, 203–4; "Big Four" projects, 69; court rulings against, 163–64; early public housing implementation, 3–11; financial and staffing issues, 27–29, 30; formation of, xii, xv–xvi, 2–3; and HUD, 5, 30–32, 34–38, 41–42, 144, 201, 290n141, 293n6; mismanagement and corruption in, 4, 30–31, 36–37, 101, 199; political appointments to, 4, 13, 14, 24, 35, 203; race-based policies (*see* neighborhood pattern policy); resolution repealing neighborhood pattern policy, 281n53; *The Housing Reporter* dramatization, 9; war shift toward temporary housing, 11–12. *See also* housing acts, federal
SFHA (San Francisco Housing Authority) goals: creating mixed-income units, 198–99, 230n163; fostering community bonds, 54–55; housing for "deserving" tenants, 8–9, 41, 53–54, 195, 254n24, 259n57, 265n105. *See also* neighborhood pattern policy
SFHA (San Francisco Housing Authority) site management role and actions: North Beach Place, 147–62, 168, 173, 175–80, 184–89; Ping Yuen project, 98, 100, 106–18, 121–23, 133, 138, 143–44; Valencia Gardens, 48–58, 60–62, 67–70, 77–78, 83–87, 89–93, 196
SFRA (San Francisco Redevelopment Agency), 16–17, 25, 63, 126
Shelley, John, 24, 26
Shelley v. Kraemer decision, 157, 252n17, 263n78
Silicon Valley dot-com boom, 83–84
single-room occupancy (SRO), 143
Solomon, Larry: *Roots of Justice*, 267n115
spatial and redevelopment politics, 151
Stratten, James E., 162
Sullivan, Deirdre L., 253n17
Sunnydale public housing, 10, 32, 67, 69, 159, 191, 228n143, 239n50, 244n93, 293n14
Swan, Roberta, 84–85, 212n6, 240n58
Swartz, Laura, 168

Tel-Hi (Telegraph Hill Neighborhood Association), 170, 179, 183, 184, 284n84; resource center, 171

Index

tenant activism, xii, 195; community bonds linked to, 42–43, 72–73, 85, 95, 135, 140, 184, 195; crossing racial and ethnic ties, 49, 74–75, 86–88, 144–46; at North Beach Place, 180–82, 185–86, 188–89, 195. *See also* affective activism; rent strikes

tenant management cooperative, 180–81

Tenant Protection Act: failure of, 186–87

Thomas, William McKinley, 16, 157, 214–15n9, 220–21n59

Thomsen, Henry A., 50–51

Thomsen and Wurster architects, 50–51

tourism, xi–xii, 43; in Chinatown, 18, 105, 106, 108, 109, 112–13, 119, 201, 260n63; crime causing decline, 130–31; keeping tourists away from public housing, 174; in North Beach, xviii, 149–50, 155, 164–71, 175, 179, 291n148

Tracy, James, 180, 183, 185

tuberculosis (TB), 106, 109, 112, 114, 254n24, 255n27, 261n65

U.S. government. *See* housing acts, federal

U.S. housing policy: two-tier framework of, 2

Ulbade, A. C., Jr., 130

"upstanding tenants," 41

urban redevelopment, 16–17, 260n60, 282–83n66

USHA (United States Housing Authority), 52, 104–5, 218n38, 264n84; *Housing in Our Time* (film), 1–2

vacancy rates, 39–40

Vale, Lawrence, 29, 37, 201, 204, 212n7, 217n35, 225n106, 230n163, 231n167, 259n59, 292n5, 295–96n34

Valencia Gardens: as an anti-public space, 65–66; Bufano/FAP outdoor sculptures at, 55–57, 58, 61, 71–72, 94, 238n46, 238n48; crime and deteriorating living experience at, 62–70, 72, 84; design of first project, 50–55; diversity and community at, 49–50, 60, 73, 75–76; early history of, 48–49, 50, 52; as a gated community, 78; as a HOPE VI site, 38, 39, 83, 85–86, 249–50n168; the redeveloped project, 90–96, 195, 196; relocations of residents, 88–90, 196, 197; resident concerns and activism, 86–88; residents' positive living experiences at, 59–62; SFHA management of, 48–58, 60–62, 67–70, 77–78, 83–87, 89–93, 196–97, 199; war workers as tenants, 57–59

Valencia Gardens Task Force, 87

Valencia Gardens Tenants Organization, 72, 75, 76, 77–79, 80, 81, 87, 93; women's empowerment through participation in, 80–82

veterans, 19, 114, 142, 161–62, 222–23n73, 245n106, 252n13, 281n45

Vietnamese immigrants, 73

Vigil, Anthony (resident), 191

Wallace, Cleo (SFHA commissioner and resident), 28, 134

307

Index

Ward, J. Francis, and John Bolles (architects), 109
war workers, 57–59
Western Addition/Fillmore, 14, 25
Westside Courts, 10, 147, 157, 159, 217n125
White, Dan, 213–14n7
Wilder, A. D., 3, 13, 220n45
Williams, Carl, 30–31, 70, 134, 136, 169, 268n125
Williams, Ethel (resident), 78–79
Williams, Patricia, 36–37
Wiltz, Cynthia (resident), 178, 286n116, 287n122
Wong, Julia, 129–30, 134
Wong, Ken, 147

Wong family (Henry and Alice), 97, 98, 251n2
Woodward Gardens amusement park, 46
WPA (Works Progress Administration), 9, 55, 88, 151. *See also* FAP
Wright, Gwendolyn, 101, 109, 152
Wurster and Thomsen architects: design for Valencia Gardens, 50, 52–53, 54, 86–87
Wurster, William W., 50–52, 236n28, 237n33

Yee, Leland, 35
Yerba Buena Plaza, 166–67, 282–83n66

AMY L. HOWARD is the executive director of the Bonner Center for Civic Engagement and associated faculty in American studies at the University of Richmond.